Professional Networks in Transnational Governance

Who controls how transnational issues are defined and treated? In recent decades, professional coordination on a range of issues has been elevated to the transnational level. International organizations, NGOs, and firms, all make efforts to control these issues. This volume shifts focus away from looking at organizations and zooms in on how professional networks exert control in transnational governance. It contributes to research on professions and expertise, policy entrepreneurship, normative emergence, and change. The book provides a framework for understanding how professionals and organizations interact, and uses it to investigate a range of transnational cases. The volume also deploys a strong emphasis on methodological strategies to reveal who controls transnational issues, including network, sequence, field, and ethnographic approaches. Bringing together scholars from economic sociology, international relations, and organization studies, the book integrates insights from across fields to reveal how professionals obtain and manage control over transnational issues.

Leonard Seabrooke is Professor of International Political Economy and Economic Sociology in the Department of Business and Politics at the Copenhagen Business School.

Lasse Folke Henriksen is Assistant Professor in the Department of Business and Politics at the Copenhagen Business School.

Professional Networks in Transnational Governance

Edited by

Leonard Seabrooke
Copenhagen Business School

Lasse Folke Henriksen
Copenhagen Business School

CAMBRIDGE
UNIVERSITY PRESS

CAMBRIDGE
UNIVERSITY PRESS

University Printing House, Cambridge CB2 8BS, United Kingdom

One Liberty Plaza, 20th Floor, New York, NY 10006, USA

477 Williamstown Road, Port Melbourne, VIC 3207, Australia

4843/24, 2nd Floor, Ansari Road, Daryaganj, Delhi – 110002, India

79 Anson Road, #06–04/06, Singapore 079906

Cambridge University Press is part of the University of Cambridge.

It furthers the University's mission by disseminating knowledge in the pursuit of
education, learning, and research at the highest international levels of excellence.

www.cambridge.org
Information on this title: www.cambridge.org/9781107181878
DOI: 10.1017/9781316855508

© Cambridge University Press 2017

First published 2017

Printed in the United States of America by Sheridan Books, Inc.

A catalogue record for this publication is available from the British Library.

Library of Congress Cataloging-in-Publication Data
Names: Seabrooke, Leonard, 1974– editor. | Henriksen, Lasse Folke, editor.
Title: Professional networks in transnational governance / edited by Leonard
Seabrooke, Lasse Folke Henriksen.
Description: New York : Cambridge University Press, 2017. | Includes
bibliographical references and index.
Identifiers: LCCN 2017026505 | ISBN 9781107181878 (hardback)
Subjects: LCSH: Business networks. | Organizational behavior.
Classification: LCC HD69.S8 .P755 2017 | DDC 338.8/7–dc23
LC record available at https://lccn.loc.gov/2017026505

ISBN 978-1-107-18187-8 Hardback

Contents

Figures and Tables

For images in full color please go to: http://professionalnetworks.org/

Figures

Tables

Contributors

LEONARD SEABROOKE is Professor at the Copenhagen Business School.

LASSE FOLKE HENRIKSEN is Assistant Professor at the Copenhagen Business School.

ADAM BADEN is Head of Section at the Ministry Education and Research, Denmark.

ANDREW BAKER is Professor at the University of Sheffield.

STEVEN BERNSTEIN is Professor at the University of Toronto.

MICHELE BETSILL is Professor at Colorado State University.

MEHDI BOUSSEBAA is Professor at the University of Glasgow.

JULIA DEUTSCH is in at the Trade Law Bureau of the Canadian Government.

YVES DEZALAY is Director Emeritus of Research at the Centre National de la Recherche Scientifique.

MATTHEW EAGLETON-PIERCE is Lecturer at SOAS, University of London.

JAMES FAULCONBRIDGE is Professor at Lancaster University Management School.

BROOKE HARRINGTON is Professor MSO at the Copenhagen Business School.

MATTHEW HOFFMANN is Professor at the University of Toronto.

JOHN KARLSRUD is Senior Research Fellow at the Norwegian Institute for International Affairs.

DAVID KEMPEL is Business Controller at GEA Group.

RON LEVI is Associate Professor at the University of Toronto.

MIKAEL RASK MADSEN is Professor at the University of Copenhagen.

BESSMA MOMANI is CIGI Senior Fellow at the University of Waterloo.

DANIEL MUZIO is Professor at the University of Newcastle.

ARTHUR MÜHLEN-SCHULTE works for the Funds Management Unit, UNDP Sudan.

ADRIANA NILSSON is Lecturer at the University of Liverpool Management School.

MATTHEW PATERSON is Professor at the University of Manchester.

JAMES PERRY is a Senior Associate at the Financial Conduct Authority, UK.

OLE JACOB SENDING is Director of Research at the Norwegian Institute for International Affairs.

JASON THISTLETHWAITE is Assistant Professor at the University of Waterloo.

DUNCAN WIGAN is Associate Professor at the Copenhagen Business School.

WENDY H. WONG is Associate Professor at the University of Toronto.

Acknowledgements

This book emerged as an interdisciplinary investigation into how professionals and organizations create institutions, rules, and norms for transnational governance. Drawing on international relations, organization studies, and sociology, the contributors to this collection explore professional networks in transnational governance. Following the search for the best scholars to write on this interdisciplinary topic, and the distribution of the framing chapter, most of the contributors assembled in Milan to put their draft chapters to work. The event was noteworthy not only for what filled our plates and glasses but especially for the excellent conversations that cut across the fields noted above. Our thanks go to Emelie Rebecca Nilsson for dealing with logistics and Roberto Pedersini for the seminar room in Milan. The chapters were then commented on and revised through processes of internal and external review. Most of the chapters were also road-tested with a live audience, with contributors presenting their research to the students in the Masters of International Business and Politics program at the Copenhagen Business School. Thanks to our students for critically engaging with the ideas laid out in this book, for testing their applicability in research projects and theses, and for pushing us to further develop them. We also presented the framing piece at the Department of Sociology at Columbia University, as well as to the Global and Transnational Sociology section at the American Sociological Association in San Francisco. Our sincere thanks go to all of the contributors, who came from far and wide and thoroughly engaged with our ideas. Most members of this ragtag bunch did not know each other prior to our Milan event, and we are happy to report that a number of productive collaborations have been sparked since as the contributors navigate their own professional and organizational networks.

This book has been supported by the European Research Council (ERC) grant 'Professions in International Political Economies' (#263741-PIPES). Our thanks go to the ERC for their generous funding. Further support for methodological innovation and training has been provided by the 'Hybrid Networks in Transnational Governance' project at the Copenhagen Business School. It has been a pleasure to work with Cambridge University Press on the project. Our thanks go to John Haslam for his strong support for the book, as well as to Claire Sissen for holding our hands through the publication process. Thanks also go to Karthik Orukaimani for his editorial skill and patience. Our special thanks go to the reviewers, who provided detailed reports and suggestions, and to those who provided critical comments on the framing piece and various chapters in the book, especially Cornel Ban, Peter Katzenstein, Alex Kentikelenis, Patrick Le Galès, Simone Polillo, Woody Powell, Sigrid Quack, Jeff Sallaz, Vivien Schmidt, Ann Swidler, Eleni Tsingou, Josh Whitford, and Wes Widmaier.

LEONARD SEABROOKE & LASSE FOLKE HENRIKSEN
Copenhagen & Trekroner

List of Abbreviations

APG	Accounting-led private governance
BIS	Bank for International Settlements
CBCR	Country-by-Country Reporting
CCRF	Climate Change Reporting Framework
CDP	Carbon Disclosure Project
CDSB	Climate Disclosure Standards Board
EIB	European Investment Bank
EITI	Extractive Industries Transparency Initiative
ESG	Environmental, social, and governance reporting
EU	European Union
FAO	Food and Agriculture Organization
FSB	Financial Stability Board
GATT	General Agreement on Tariffs and Trade
GMCF	Global management consulting firm
GPSF	Global professional service firms
GSK	GlaxoSmithKline
HRW	Human Rights Watch
IASB	International Accounting Standards Board
ICRC	International Committee of the Red Cross
IETA	International Emissions Trading Association
IGCC	Australian Investors Group in Climate Change
IIGCC	Institutional Investor Group on Climate Change
IIRC	International Integrated Reporting Committee
ILO	International Labour Organisation
IMF	International Monetary Fund
INCR	Investor Network on Climate Risk
IO	International organization
MPP	Medicines Patent Pool
MSF	Médecins Sans Frontières
NGO	Non-governmental organization
OECD	Organisation for Economic Co-operation and Development
OECD	Organisation for Economic Co-operation and Development

OXFAM	Oxford Committee for Famine Relief (now simply OXFAM)
SASB	Sustainability Accounting Standards Board
TAN	Transnational advocacy network
TJN	Tax Justice Network
TRIPS	Trade-Related Aspects of Intellectual Property
TWG	Technical Working Group
UN	United Nations
UNHRC	United Nations High Commissioner for Refugees
WFP	World Food Programme
WHO	World Health Organization
WIPO	World Intellectual Property Organisation
WTO	World Trade Organization

Part I

Frames and Methods

1   Issue Control in Transnational Professional and Organizational Networks

Leonard Seabrooke and Lasse Folke Henriksen

Transnational governance is a process of coordination and competition among professionals and organizations to control issues. This book is concerned with professional networks in transnational governance, particularly how professionals navigate their peer and organizational networks to control transnational issues. Recent scholarship has focused on how transnational issues are governed, concentrating on how organizational actors arrive at governance outcomes. Standards, benchmarks, and procedures commonly attract the most attention, with explanations on what actors were able to achieve what outcomes and why (Broome et al. 2018). Recent scholarship has noted how transnational governance has an increasingly hybrid character (Andonova et al. 2009), where international organizations (IOs), non-governmental organizations (NGOs), and firms are engaged in various combinations to coordinate on issues. Work on 'orchestration' also suggests that transnational governance is characterized by institutions that work less as command centres and more as enablers among different types of organizations (Abbott and Snidal 2009a; Abbott et al. 2015; Henriksen and Ponte 2017). Recent literature also points to states increasingly delegating transnational governance issues to private actors (Büthe and Mattli 2011), and professional interaction with a variety of organizations has been the norm, including a role for firms and NGOs in transnational governance networks. Firms and NGOs create alliances with fellow organizations to obtain or retain resources and knowledge with issue control in mind.

This work on transnational governance has sought to identify how non-state actors have power compared with standard frameworks that concentrate on the power of states. Much of the emphasis here has been who has authority over transnational issues. A particular focus has been on how different 'global governors' can create different forms of authority (Avant et al. 2010) or how new global rulers are emerging from organizational entrepreneurship (Büthe and Mattli 2011). The causal logic of much work in transnational governance is that organizations have a type of authority that enables them to engage in rule making. This causal chain

3

of *organizational strategy* > *authority type* > *rules and standards making* dominates the literature, with a range of scholars seeking to identify 'private authority', 'delegated authority', 'capacity-building authority', and so forth (Avant et al. 2010). Authority can also come from mixes of organizations, as the recent scholarship on hybrid governance points out (Abbott and Snidal 2009a). Coordination between the actors occurs via the organizational form. In many way, the literature is still stuck within the 'complex interdependence' framework of the 1970s (Keohane and Nye 1977; Abbott et al. 2016), as we note below.

From this common viewpoint, issue control is an outcome of organizational strategy, from what issues are selected to work or campaign on, given the capabilities of the organization. This is true for IOs, NGOs, and firms, all who carefully choose issues to control. The World Bank, for example, has expanded its issue scope through 'mission creep' during recent decades, while similar institutions, such as the European Investment Bank (EIB), have chosen not to expand into as many issue areas and have, until the recent crisis, stayed 'under the radar'. Historically, NGOs and those organizations and movements operating in transnational advocacy networks (TANs) have chosen issues linked to bodily harm or inequality of access, since such issues can more readily garner support (Keck and Sikkink 1998). NGOs select issues according to organizational resources and the capacity to expand their networks (Wong 2012a; Stroup and Wong 2017). Oxfam provides a good example of a well-resourced NGO that covers a wide variety of issues, from arms trading to climate change and others. Tax Justice Network (TJN) provides a contrasting case of a small organization armed with specialists on taxation issues (Seabrooke and Wigan 2016), see also Chapter 9 this volume. Firms also seek issue control as this volume amply documents. Controlling governance and regulation around transnational issues can give firms significant competitive advantages and can enable the construction and expansion of niche markets, such as products that are labeled sustainable (Henriksen and Seabrooke 2016). Professional service firms (PSFs) spend a great deal of time engaging in templating activities that permit them issue control rather than simple profit generation (Suddaby et al. 2007; Faulconbridge and Muzio 2008). This is certainly the case for the Big Four accountancy firms and expert influence on accounting standards (Strange 1996; Botzem 2008, Murphy and Stausholm 2017), as well as for transnational law firms seeking to provide consistent treatment of issues across national legal boundaries (Quack 2007; Faulconbridge et al. 2012). In short, organizations carefully select what issues they seek to control and what professionals are most appropriate to work with them in doing so.

This common view of how organizations select and control issues includes an important assumption about the sources of power within the system. As stated, for this work the causal chain is typically as follows: *organizational strategy* > *authority type* > *rules and standards making*. A mandate or effective claim to authority equals control over the issue. In fact, this may overplay the importance of recognized authority coming from organizations as entities. Professional and organizational networks working on the issue may well be changing how the issue is understood at the transnational level and who has the right to work on it, while organizations mandated to authoritative treatment of the issue are out of sync with movement and struggle within these networks. Professional networks may be able to circumvent formal circuits of authority in exercising issue control, as some of the chapters in this volume attest.

A key claim in this book is that competition and cooperation in professional networks for issue control is more important than what organization has a formal mandate over an issue. While organizational forms are important, professionals often form networks to circumvent and manipulate them in their battles for issue control in transnational governance. This book provides an alternative account of how issues are controlled in transnational governance. We stress how the causal chain can often be identified as *professional strategy* > *organizational opportunities* > *issue control*. This is not to dismiss the importance of authority claims but to assert that they are not the only channels of power within systems of transnational governance.

Professional strategies include plans within professional and organizational network to disrupt, reproduce, or transform how issues are treated and who is entitled to work on them (Suddaby and Viale 2011). Professional strategies are not only located within professional networks (Galaskiewicz 1985) but also come from the observation of how peers operate across different social domains and organizational types (White 2008). *Organizational opportunities* provide positions of action and platforms from which to build and expand peer networks. They are provided by differences between organizations, such as the scope of their mandate, how they hire staff, how they find resources, how distant they are from their key principles, and how centralized their knowledge production is on their issue of concern. Canny professionals can navigate these opportunity structures from the inside-out, from within organizations, as well as from the outside-in through their peer networks. .

Issue control is recognized stability in what professionals and organizations dominate the treatment of an issue in a particular way. As such, issue control has a temporal dimension (stability is temporary and can be disrupted) and a strategic dimension within a two-level network, as professionals locate themselves within both professional and organizational networks to enhance their capacities and secure resources. Analysing issue control in transnational governance as a two-level professional and organizational network is another key contribution of this volume.

To provide a hypothetical example, a professional agronomist working on food security at the UN's Food and Agriculture Organization (FAO) has a particular initiative to treat an aspect of the issue. Her boss at the FAO is not so keen on the idea and blocks activities that damage his organizational performance objectives, including competing with other UN agencies like the World Food Programme. Still, our agronomist creates a network with professionals from other IOs, as well as NGOs like CARE and firms like DuPont, to form an alliance on how to treat the transnational issue. She creates with them a professional taskforce that attaches itself to regular meetings already funded by the organizations. This taskforce creates a new transnational professional consensus on how an aspect of food security should be treated and who is best equipped to do so. A new benchmark on what constitutes a best practice has been created, and the boss at the FAO is then asked by his superiors to introduce it as common practice within the organization. Control of the issue has changed due to outside-in professional coordination, followed by inside-out organizational changes backed by formal authority. This is a hypothetical example, but one that frequently occurs in a range of issues in transnational governance.

This book is concerned with how professionals and organizations navigate networks in attempts at issue control in transnational governance. Here the transnationality of issues matters. At the transnational level of activity, professionals and organizations exhibit high levels of distributed agency in their activities, with both incremental and strategic activities taking place from a range of actors working on an issue (Quack 2007; Whittle et al. 2011). Transnationality permits greater diversity in who seeks to control issues, as well as often fracturing control through multiple levels of formal and informal governance. While conventional theories of change in transnational governance point to key drivers, such as states engaging in the 'rational design' of IOs (Koremenos et al. 2001) or norm entrepreneurs operating through NGOs (Barnett and Finnemore 2004), transnationality muddles these images by introducing greater complexity between the range of actors in the international political economy.

We also suggest that transnationality matters for professional strategies for issue control, and while efforts have been made to understand transnational community and identity formation (Djelic and Quack 2010), transnationality can also be depicted as providing an opportunity space that looks like strategic networks of a more emergent character. Issues in transnational governance are difficult to control because they cannot be held too tightly by one organization. Organizations can become fragile if they hold too tightly to a singular conception of an issue or become host to professional activity that inverts original conceptions of how the issue should be treated (as with international whaling, see Epstein 2008).

Issues must be continuously managed through attempts at control, including stratagems to obtain knowledge and resources that enhance the capacity for control (Henriksen and Seabrooke 2016).

Issues that have transnationality may be partially decoupled from professions or organizations in national spaces. Instead, they can be opened up for contestation and cooperation at a level where professionals and organizations must continuously justify and adapt their claims to legitimacy on issue control. Attempts at justification often follow professional lines, suggesting that the issue at hand is highly technical and can only be addressed with a specific skill set or ethical comportment. Justifications can also follow organizational lines, with organizations seeking to affirm their original mandate or creeping into others' territory as they seek to expand their bureaucratic capacities and reach (Weaver 2008).

Professionals in Transnational Governance

Scholarship on professionals and organizations in transnational governance can be traced to the early 1970s, especially Robert W. Cox and Harold K. Jacobson's (1973) *The Anatomy of Influence*. Cox and Jacobson identified 'initiators, vetoers and brokers' who had influence within IOs as individuals, depending on how they were positioned in the organization. This inside-out view of professionals and organizations described why IOs differed, while others worried about how growing transnationalism would accord too much power to unaccountable professionals and experts, providing an outside-in view on how professionals affect domestic organizations (Kaiser 1971). Interest in professionals and organizations as competing entities soon gave way to Robert Keohane and Joseph Nye's (1972, 1974, 1977) work on 'complex interdependence' that provided a basic network understanding of how non-state actors achieve influence over issues. This, in turn, evolved in a microeconomics-led shift into regime theory that focused on decision-making from public organizations (Keohane 1984).

The resurgence of interest in professionals in transnational governance emerged around the work on 'epistemic communities', following the view that shared scientific expertise could lead to the diffusion of knowledge and what we would in International Relations terminology now understand as norms. The members of epistemic communities were explicitly understood as a 'network of professionals' who could make an 'authoritative claim to policy-relevant knowledge' (Haas 1992). They were brought together by shared normative frameworks and understandings of what constitutes proper science in their field (Djelic and Quack 2010: 20). Much of this literature was concerned with the marginal influence of professionals in relation to the interstate system. A cognate field of literature emerged from the 'World Polity' approach, which located professionals as theorizing change within the strictures of global cultural and normative structures, with noted reluctance to attribute them 'actorness' due to these structural constraints (Meyer and Jepperson 2000). In both streams of literature, less emphasis was placed on what we identify in this volume as professional strategies: how professionals use networks to control issues and to create new markets, and how professionals create demand for their services. We are informed by this earlier literature while adding strategic elements to professional competition and cooperation. In this regard, we follow scholars working on transnational advocacy who view networks not only as a means of community formation but also as sites of 'cultural and political negotiation' (Keck and Sikkink 1998: 211).

The highly influential work on 'pathologies' in IOs placed great emphasis on how professionals are moulded by organizational cultures, so as to produce irrational policy outcomes (Barnett and Finnemore 1999, 2004). Here 'socialized' professionals produce policies through a range of pathologies, such as the 'irrationality of rationalization', 'bureaucratic universalism', 'normalization of deviance', and 'insulation'. Insulation is linked to professionals in that training is not simply technical but also involves the shaping and orientation of one's worldview, which is then accentuated when the same type of professionals are marched in line by a bureaucracy. Here professionals insulate themselves from outside voices and conform to their own norms and values (Barnett and Finnemore 1999: 722–723). The punch-line here is that technical expertise matters for IOs to have authority, but that technical expertise often comes at a high cost from pathologies that distort the policymaking process and implementation and as a result deteriorate the responsiveness of IOs. This framework provides the 'iron cage' version of earlier, more optimistic, work on epistemic communities, highlighting how scientific consensus might mediate otherwise fierce struggles between self-interested states.

More recently, work on professionals in transnational governance has continued these themes at a greater level of magnification. Jeffrey Chwieroth's (2007, 2010, 2012) studies of how professional training is important alongside organizational socialization provides an excellent example. Chwieroth demonstrates how economists trained by elite American institutions went to the IMF and then went back to their home countries, mainly in the Americas, and changed policies on capital account liberalization to conform with their professional education and IMF socialization. Importantly, the impact of professional training and socialization determines much of what is going on here, and Chwieroth and others (Nelson 2014, 2017) identify *trajectories* from professional experience rather than how it permits strategies to change how issues are controlled. This volume provides a specific contribution to this growing literature in detailing how professional strategies interact with organizational opportunities and how professionals operate from the inside-out and also the outside-in in pursuing issue control. We also contribute to methodological advances in how professionals and professional strategies can be identified from their career patterns and network position (see, in particular, Chapters 4, 11, and 12 in this volume).

Professional Tasks and Issue Professionals

Professionals and organizations seek to control issues in transnational governance, and a capacity for control over an issue has a strong relationship to how professionals understand their tasks. Following Andrew Abbott, professional tasks are composed of objective elements, such as technological advancements, organization, natural objects and facts, and slow-changing cultural structures, as well as from subjective qualities in how professionals construct the problem to be addressed by the task (Abbott 1988: 39–40). This also includes gearing the science or knowledge involved in task allocation to support 'defensive institutional work' (Lefsrud and Meyer 2012). The subjective qualities of tasks include the modalities of action for professionals in how they classify, reason, and take action on identified problems, or how they diagnose, infer, and treat their identified problems. In areas of governance that are highly technical and narrow, professional tasks and transnational issue control may go hand in hand. The response to the SARS and bird flu crises provide an example where transnational issue control was held by doctors and health scientists who diagnosed and treated the problem. Professional tasks were closely matched to issue control. By contrast, concern over demographic change and falling fertility in the OECD has led to a range of professionals assigning tasks to problems, such as doctors working on subfertility and demographers working on delayed family formation, without any particular group exercising transnational issue control despite the obvious political salience (Seabrooke and Tsingou 2015, 2016). Differentiating professional tasks and how professionals and organizations attempt to control transnational issues directs us to the work content in issue management as well as to strategies for contestation and cooperation.

Issues of transnational governance can be contested and open up considerable space for professionals who seek to influence them by bringing together resources from their personal networks that are derived from relationships with other professionals and organizations. Both professional tasks and issues can be transformed through institutionalization, including movements to liberalize what were national tasks in the creation of a transnational profession, as with neoclassically trained economists (Fourcade 2006). Changes to tasks can also occur through processes of professionalization, including demands for conducting work in particular ways, according to codes of ethics, as well as treating professionalism as a capacity to manage and organize tasks rather than the knowledge and training that inform their execution (Muzio and Faulconbridge 2008; Evetts 2013). Professionals have a strong incentive to maintain their position within a network by excluding others who do not agree with their understanding of issues or threaten their resources. In some areas, such as financial reform, professionals behave according to prestige incentives and will be reluctant to introduce controversial ideas and topics in which they have little expertise, such as shadow banking, or political power, such as tax havens. Rather, they will control debates in a manner that confirms their affiliations and prestige networks (Seabrooke and Tsingou 2014; Ban et al. 2016). Similarly, as is well known in organization studies, professionals can network to ensure that knowledge production is under their control rather than from bureaucracies formally running the organization (Kamoche et al. 2011). Furthermore, an important and poorly understood factor here is what we can refer to as professional 'style' (White 2008). The capacity to induce deference on who can control an issue is not simply a matter of formal training and socialization but also professional presentation, manners, and behaviour. Professionals invest time in 'impression management'. Clever professionals can use style to manoeuvre within professional networks and organizational networks, heightening their control over an issue and focusing their tasks.

Still organizations are far from helpless. Tightly held professional tasks can also be challenged by organizations through 'mission creep' or 'crowding', whereby those less able to provide professional services barge in nevertheless to fulfil organizational objectives (Weaver 2008: 140). Such behaviour is common from competing IOs and NGOs who seek to demonstrate policy relevance across issues even when they do not employ the relevant professionals (Cooley and Ron 2002: 17).

Following this understanding of tasks, we define professionals as individuals with abstract higher level learning and specific skill sets to address tasks. We do not restrict *professionals* to formal *professions*, such as law, medicine, etc. Many professionals attempting issue control have mixed educational backgrounds and are not usefully conceived as 'lawyers' or 'accountants', etc. We suggest that 'issue professionals' are an emergent type of actors that come from attempts at issue control (Henriksen and Seabrooke 2016). Rather than locating in specific associations, such as the American Medical Association or the like, these professionals combine knowledge and skills to enhance their attempts at control on a specific issue in transnational governance. Issue professionals differ from issue entrepreneurs in that they do not necessarily need to campaign or invent issues, but they are involved in generating, maintaining, and defending attempts at issue control (for example, see, on accounting, Botzem 2013). Issue professionals can be involved in professionalization activities, but formal institutionalization is not a requirement to be considered relevant when it comes to issue control. We highlight how issue professionals network and engage with organizations, as well as how, in some cases, organizations and organizational networks enable issue professionals. To create a shorthand, issue professionals are the actors in this book, issue control is what they want, and a two-level professional-organizational network is their context of action.

We suggest that reflecting on how professionals use networks to navigate organizational logics is much more a reflection of these characteristics rather than the formal designation of the organization. As suggested at the beginning of this chapter, the agronomist from the FAO will select to include professionals in her network based not only on their knowledge and resources but also on what access they can provide to organizational resources they are connected to. DuPont may well be able to finance a new initiative in food security that is not possible in the FAO, with the agronomist still maintaining a high degree of knowledge centralization on the issue at hand. Such interplay between professionals and organizations is how most transnational issues are governed. We suggest that issues in transnational governance exist within *a professional-organizational nexus*.

The Professional-Organizational Nexus as a Two-Level Network

We argue that it is a *professional-organizational nexus* that is the key to explaining who controls issues at the transnational level. We provide a framework for understanding how professionals and organizations interact in transnational issue networks based on differentiating professional work roles and organizational types. Professionals in our framework draw on organizational and professional domains at the same time – building alliances from where they can draw action from both domains as they seek to control issues and how they should be treated. Our claim here is that professional battles are essential for transnational issue control and that patterns of coordination and competition of professionals and organizations are decisive for actors' capacity to interpret and influence issues in transnational governance. As such, we build on earlier work on transnational governance studying 'individual behaviors, interactions and processes, with studies of institutional and cultural forces' (Djelic and Andersson 2006: 19). This agenda has long turned its attention to professionals and how they create networks to transform organizations and carve out their own markets (i.e. Dezalay and Garth 2002b). This scholarship also complements the research agenda on 'transnational communities' that studies the formation of transnational identities, including among professionals and professions (Djelic and Quack 2010). We suggest that the professional-organizational nexus can best be understood as a *two-level network*, where professionals have relationships, organizations have relationships, and where professionals and organizations interact (for a related point on the duality of persons and groups in networks, see Breiger 1974). While others prefer to describe professionals as operating in organizational fields, we stress that both professionals and organizations have agency in forming strategies – and that neither provide a passive space for the other to operate within. Rather than seeing fields as independent spaces of activity, both professionals and organizations can act as 'fields of agents' in establishing their differences and alliances (Bigo 2011: 239; Dezalay and Garth 2016). As such, professionals will seek to extend their networks through common identification with other similarly trained professionals, though often not through formal professional associations, or by creating alliances with professionals with different but complementary sets of skills (see also Lazega et al. 2017). Those who manage to exploit opportunities to enhance their influence on an issue are likely to maximize issue control beyond their intrinsic organizational capacities. This is, in part, because organizations do not participate in issue networks with their full portfolio of activities, but with specific segments of professionals working on this or that issue within the organization.

Organizations face an apparent trade-off when seeking issue control via knowledge: to dampen issue flux, organizations may choose to increase the technicality of an issue, rendering competitors without the necessary expertise obsolete. If organizations control areas of expertise that are deemed legitimate as a solution to a given issue, or if professional and organizational logics overlap, this strategy may be successful (Broome and Seabrooke 2015). But if expertise for the governance of a highly technical issue is not controlled by a particular organization, groups of professionals may gain considerable discretion and develop strategies of issue control that differ from or oppose the organizational network. Organizations may also pursue the opposite strategy of politicizing or moralizing an issue, bringing principles and values to the fore to trump expert opinion. Both strategies require engaging other organizations and professionals. A two-level perspective enables a view of organizational actorness stemming from elements that are both internal and external to the organization at hand.

There are many examples we can draw upon to raise the question of who has the formal mandate and who has issue control in professional and organizational networks. The International Labour Organization is responsible for international labour standards, but it does not dominate how labour standards are treated, with leading firms in the international political economy often providing only lip service (cf. McCallum 2013). The International Accounting Standards Board, a private body, dominates the contemporary interpretation of international accounting standards, but this does not prevent them from receiving attacks from professionals working with NGOs that seek to wrest issue control by offering alternative reporting schemes (see Chapters 7 and 9 in this volume). The United Nations Human Rights Council and Amnesty International are seemingly dominant on human rights issues, but other organizations actively develop strategies to change the issue agenda, such as the Ford Foundation's promotion of a particular conception of human rights through its influence on the formation of Human Rights Watch and its particular issue strategy (Chapter 6 in this volume).

Understanding the professional-organizational nexus as a two-level network permits us to look at relations between two different sets of actors when it comes to processes of issue control. Our two-level network consists, first, of professional networks that are interpersonal and built throughout careers and activities linked to transnational issues. Second, organizational networks exist where alliances between organizations or their subunits endure in ways that do not hinge on specific professionals.

Figure 1.1 depicts an illustration of a simple two-level network that is involved in organizing a particular transnational issue. At the top of the diagram are organizations (the white discs) that occupy different parts of the policy space on the issue of concern. This is the increasingly common way of mapping how policies are 'orchestrated' across the policy space or 'governance triangles' (Abbott et al. 2015). Here we can see a mix of organizations in the state-, NGO-, and firm-based areas of the policy space, as well as mixes of these organizational types. This book suggests that this policy space can be viewed as two separate surfaces. On the top is the surface where organizations are represented. On the bottom is a different surface where professionals actively network in their attempts to control and influence issues and how they are treated. The professionals are represented on the lower surface by black discs. They are highly networked across their different domains, which in this case are the activist, corporate, and policy worlds (Seabrooke 2014b; cf. Padgett and McLean 2006). Dashed lines between the professionals and the organizations represent ties between the two levels by way of formal or informal

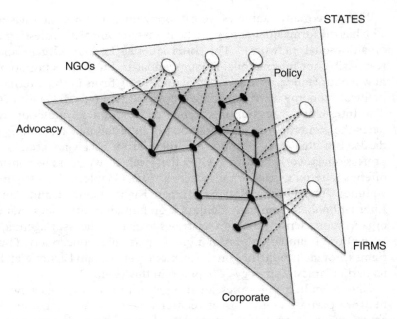

Figure 1.1 Professional and Organizational Networks across
Governance Triangles (adapted from Abbott et al. 2015)

affiliations. These are channels of information and knowledge, and of
influence over how issues are treated in transnational governance.

Describing the professional-organizational nexus as a two-level network also permits us to consider how professionals and organizations
take positions on particular issues relative to their peers (as in a field), as
well as the character of the ties between those involved on the transnational issues (as in a network). For scholars of IOs, NGOs, and TANS,
networks have been depicted as both actors and structures (Kahler 2009).
Our focus is less on the networks as coherent actors and more on professional and organizational interaction within networks. As such, professional and organizational networks must be studied through interaction
on issues of concern, through the allocation and defence of professional
tasks, and conflict and points of cooperation established by different
actors in position towards the issue.

In this sense, our understanding of networks is not at odds with
more Bourdieu-inspired works on professional fields and organizational fields (Dezalay and Garth 2010a; Madsen 2011; Delazay and
Madsen 2012), as well as what Gil Eyal has termed 'spaces between
fields' (Eyal 2011). It is also connected to recent 'linked ecologies'

work that views professionals as fluidity operating within and between institutional systems (Seabrooke and Tsingou 2009; Baker 2013a; Stone 2013a; Seabrooke 2014a; Seabrooke and Tsingou 2015). Our approach is also not at great odds with new work in international relations on 'international practices' (Adler and Pouliot 2011), which draws directly from organization studies and, in particular, Wenger's (1998) work on 'communities of practice'. 'International practices' operate from shared conceptions of 'competence' on an activity, and communities adhere this way in a fashion quite similar to the work done by Wenger and others. Our view on practices is that they are important to understand, but the literature on practices places too much stress on community building and less on competition and cooperation within overlapping networks. Once the notion of communities of practice is removed from a domestic context and placed in a transnational context, the chance of overlapping and competing notions of competence is greater. Such battles are also about issue control rather than proving a common glue for community building.

Network Theory

A network is a set of actors, or nodes, along with a set of specific relations that connect them. Relations in networks interconnect through shared points and thus form paths or pipes that indirectly link actors that would otherwise not be directly related. Much network analysis is concerned with characterizing network structures and actor positions and relating properties of structures and positions to group and actor outcomes. Network theory makes claims about mechanisms and processes that interact with a network structure to yield outcomes for actors in the network. In general, a network view of strategy pays attention to the flow of knowledge and resources and knowledge between professionals and organizations and the strategic behaviour emerging from their attempts to gain control over these flows.

The literatures on interorganizational and interpersonal networks are extensive. Interorganizational and interpersonal networks have been studied across a broad range of disciplinary traditions and empirical domains. While the literature is multifaceted, the network term is most often introduced to denote 'partnerships, strategic alliances, interorganizational relationships, coalitions, cooperative arrangements, or collaborative agreements' (Provan et al. 2007: 480), drawing attention to functions such as knowledge sharing, learning, and trust generally associated with positive outcomes. We recognize that some network ties stem from an actor's need to collaborate but draw on Harrison C. White

(1981) and Ronald S. Burt (1992) in stressing the drive towards competition in networks within and across levels of analysis.

Network theorists have produced a wide array of concepts shedding light on how strategies spring from actors embedding in network structures, or topologies, seeking to access or control resources and knowledge through these structures. They have developed a range of concepts that we quickly note here. Among important network concepts the most prominent is the view that the behaviour of individuals or organizations must be placed in the context of their social position, and the concept of 'embedded action' understands behaviour from the structure of social relations in network terms (Breiger 1974; Granovetter 1985). It is frequently opposed to an atomized understanding of action that follows a macro-micro-macro understanding of individual decision-making. A recent restatement of this view is that while 'actors create relations; in the long run, relations create actors' (Padgett and Powell 2012: 2). We stress that networks are infrequently flat and horizontal. Rather, networks contain hierarchies and power asymmetries. This includes between different types of organizations, and also among different professionals and professions. Hierarchies can be spotted by studying network topologies. Mapping the traits of professionals and organizations that are important in networks is a key aspect of the research agenda this book pursues (see also Chapter 4 in this volume).

Within two-level networks prominent professionals are often 'multiple insiders' (Vedres and Stark 2010) through shared memberships and participation in events, organizations, committees, commissions, expert groups, etc., through which they build their issue-specific personal networks, but also get access to varied organizational contexts (Lazega et al. 2008). These professionals will often inhabit similar 'thought worlds' across different organizational contexts (Baunsgaard and Clegg 2013), occasionally alerting organizations to potential conflicts with their particular objectives. Accordingly, organizations also strategize about where to send staff to participate in these events, committees etc. that give them advantages in terms of access to knowledge but also give professionals opportunities beyond their pre-defined work role.

Describing the professional-organizational nexus as a two-level network permits us to consider how professionals and organizations take positions on particular issues relative to their peers, as well as the character of the ties between those involved on the transnational issues. What we characterize as issue professionals are mobile within what Diane Stone (2013b) refers to as the 'global agora', a networked space where actors easily move between organizational forms. Our focus is not on networks as coherent actors unto themselves and more on professional and organizational interaction within networks. As such, professional and organizational networks must be studied through interaction on issues of concern, through the allocation and defence of professional tasks. We draw on network theory to assist us in doing so.

A key lesson from network analysts is that the formation of social ties in attempts to achieve control cannot be fully understood by ever more subtle categories of groups and identities, but has to take seriously the concrete patterns of interaction in which individuals and organizations are embedded (Granovetter 1985). A network is a set of actors, or nodes, along with a set of specific relations that connect them. Relations in networks interconnect through shared points and form paths or pipes that indirectly link actors that would otherwise not be directly related. This conception enables a view of a network as a connected system, where local behaviours are linked to the system as a whole. Much network analysis is concerned with characterizing network structures and actor positions and relating structural properties and positions to group and actor outcomes. Network theory makes claims about the mechanisms and processes that interact with a network structure to allow certain actors in the network to act (Borgatti and Halgin 2011).

Two-level networks also exhibit so-called 'small world' network characteristics that have implications for the strategies of issue control that professionals and organizations may pursue. The idea of a small world comes from the experience that actors in a 'big world' often experience being surprisingly close to each other (Watts 1999). In transnational governance the professional networks have large geographical distances and the number of individuals and organizations doing work may be in the thousands. This multiplies the social distances across which coordination must be performed. Forging ties to central organizations can minimize these distances, creating what have been termed 'global microstructures' (Knorr Cetina and Bruegger 2002; Henriksen 2013). Such tie formation is often facilitated by pre-established interpersonal ties that establish trust about the motivations of counterparties. Small world characteristics come into place when the formation of a few ties decreases the average social distance between actors significantly. Even if these networks are clustered inside organizations or densely concentrated around organizational alliances or professional communities, a few connections across these clusters or alliances is likely to lead to the experience of the network as a small world. Through being central nodes in a network professionals can use their skills and knowledge to shape the way organizations treat and organize issues (Kroeger 2011; Huang et al. 2013).

Understanding the character of ties between professionals is also important. We know that professionals build connections transnationally by spending otherwise valuable work time at seemingly 'fluffy' conferences or events that may actually be important in organizing how issues are treated (Lampel and Meyer 2008). This network activity can be experienced as superfluous, but 'sharing a card' may actually be enough reason to contact a potential ally. Such 'weak ties' may generate unique knowledge of activities that are at a greater social distance from an actor's immediate neighbourhood (Granovetter 1973). This is not only useful for people who are searching for new challenges in their professional lives, but also important in understanding why organizations value professionals who can demonstrate high job mobility. Professionals of high job mobility that are not linked to any particular organization or organizational type can be seen as 'weak but broad' in their embedding strategy across two-level networks. Their sources of knowledge as well as their reach for influence are likely to be more 'robust' (Padgett and Ansell 1992; Bothner et al. 2010).

Furthermore, getting a new idea often occurs with actors occupying sparse network regions (Burt 2004) abundant with 'structural holes' (Burt 1992). Structural holes are network locations where two nodes are disconnected, presenting an opportunity for a third node to bridge the gap and gain control of the flow of information between the otherwise disconnected nodes. On transnational issues, where network densities are comparatively low, exploiting disconnections can be a successful strategy for organizations and professionals working to change perceptions on particular issues (Goddard 2009). The structural properties of networks are important in understanding how agents can behave and how transnational governance occurs within two-level dynamics.

Structure of the Book

The volume places particular emphasis on the application of a range of methods and has a dedicated **Frames and Methods** section that introduces readers to methods for studying professionals and organizations. These include 'field' studies that rely on prosopography, observations of professional and organizational activity, as well as the use of sequence analysis, a method derived from genetics, to study trends and differences in career patterns, and social network analysis, particularly two-mode networks, that permits distinctions to be made between professional networks, organizational networks, and the relationship between the two.

Yves Dezalay and **Mikael Madsen** discuss a post-Bourdieusian approach to transnational professionals, focusing on the 'field' as a reflexive method. This chapter also provides a historical perspective of how the embedding of professionals in the interstitial spaces of fields has evolved, locating transnational legal professionals. An important element here, and for this volume, is the development of prosopographic methods, the tracing of individuals and groups and their characteristics for understanding changes in professional networks. Delazay and Madsen also remind us that this kind of research requires the scholar to reflect on her or his assumptions in legitimizing professionals' practices. **Brooke Harrington's** chapter continues this theme in providing an explanation of how to initiate an ethnography with elites in transnational environments. Harrington locates a series of challenges for this kind of research, including access to the elites, the researcher's presentation of self, and, importantly, ethical issues surrounding ethnographic research. She also outlines the benefits of ethnographic research in tracing how transnational professionals behave and understand their world.

Our own chapter on network and sequences provides an introduction to these methods for tracing professionals, emphasizing how they are located in professional and organizational networks, as well as the importance of career experience in explaining why particular professionals become important brokers. The chapter provides a hypothetical example of how network and sequence analyses can be combined to illuminate not only two-level network dynamics, but also to discuss propensities among actors within the network.

Following the Frames and Methods section are three sections that are organized according to organizational types, with 'Professionals and Non-Governmental Organizations', 'Professionals and International Organizations', and 'Professionals and Market Organizations'. Arranging the sections in this manner may seem to contradict one of the central points of this volume: that professionals can move across organizational networks as they seek to control issues in transnational governance, and that organizational denomination (NGO, IO, or Firm) tells us little about what organizations actually do within their own networks. However, the book is arranged around what types of organizations are dominant within the case presented, with authors frequently demonstrating overlaps and ambiguities between organizational forms as they follow professionals and their networks.

In the **Professional and Non-Governmental Organizations** section the chapters discuss competition dynamics among professionals working on humanitarian relief; the link between organizational form and the capacity to generate political salience on human rights issues;

competition between activists and accountants over transnational environmental governance networks; and professional mobilization among activists to challenge international financial reporting standards. **Ole Jacob Sending**'s chapter points to the importance of experience rather than formal educational training for professionals working in transnational humanitarian networks. Sending uses a field analysis to locate how professionals working in the field of humanitarian relief draw on their experience to challenge what they consider to be excessive professionalization from competing organizations. He highlights how claims to authority are made by professionals within their professional and organizational networks, especially where these claims are being made in a subordinate position to traditional legal authorities. In contrast to Sending, **Wendy Wong, Ron Levi**, and **Julia Deutsch** reverse the sights, focusing on how the Ford Foundation and its creation of Human Rights Watch ushered in particular forms of professionalization. Wong and colleagues explain how the organizational network for human rights is tightly controlled, with lead organizations such as the Ford Foundation funding what they consider to be legitimate projects and programs. Such dominance within the organizational network shapes how the professional network behaves, with professionals seeking to legitimate themselves within the existing order (cf. also Kim and Sharman 2014).

The chapter by **Jason Thistlethwaite** highlights how NGOs were pioneers in mobilizing accountants and accountancy tools to propagate environmental and social performance standards. The chapter shows how competition for issue control occurred between different NGO-firm partnerships, leading to the formation of a new professional logic that blends market and civil society logics. Thistlethwaite demonstrates how environmental and social disclosure professionals emerged in a move to occupy an structural hole between more purist financial performance professionals and non-purists that worked to internalize other dimensions in investors' decision-making. **Adam Baden** and **Duncan Wigan**'s chapter testifies how a small group of professionals with complementary skills and experience on financial reporting working from a garden shed, the NGO Tax Justice Network (TJN), have been able to change how the issue of tax avoidance is dealt with in transnational policy organizations such as the OECD. TJN leveraged professional resources to become a key broker in the process leading to the adoption of the new legislation on tax avoidance, providing a broader activist network with the professional knowledge necessary to push the issue of tax avoidance globally and intervene in crucial technical debates as a new reporting standard emerged.

Matthew Eagleton-Pierce moves on to discuss the role of professionals in the World Trade Organization (WTO) system with a particular focus on a new category of NGO-based 'critical technicians' who have turned out to be instrumental as agenda-setters in the policymaking process. This group stems from the 1990s anti-GATT movement but has 'professionalized' their social critique through long-term strategic investments in research on trade, trade regulation and policy. This professionalization has provided them with knowledge and professional legitimacy to enter the trade policy stage as critical technicians, repositioning traditional activist NGO voices within and across networks of trade professionals, broadly speaking, as well as more specifically in WTO negotiations. Eagleton-Pierce illustrates this development with evidence from the WTO African Cotton Initiative, an initiative spearheaded by Oxfam along with a network of other NGO players. In this case critical technicians created a strategic space of influence for Oxfam by combining solid research, strong partnerships with different organisations. The study bears a striking resemblance to Baden and Wigan's study of professional activists on extractive industries. In both cases styles of professional action draw on a combination of more traditional activist forms of policy engagement with a solid knowledge base that enhances the responsiveness of policymakers to criticism of existing regulation.

The Professionals and International Organizations section provides chapters on the role of esteem in professional networks concerned with macroprudential financial regulation and international trade agreements and policy; the evolution of different policymaking networks involved in setting up emissions trading governance systems; career trajectories and the rigidity of epistemic cultures in global health policy, and the role of crisis mapping professionals in the politics of development aid. **Andrew Baker**'s chapter stresses how esteem can be used by professionals to consolidate issue control by promoting specific regulatory changes that favour their position in the two-level network of economists and central banks. Changes in the system of esteem ascription among central bankers before and after the crisis were an important background factor in the shift to 'macroprudential' thinking at the Bank of International Settlements and related central bank networks. Baker argues that these changes refocused professional activities on tasks and techniques, data collection and research programmes, and policy instruments to render new regulatory frames operational in central banks around the world. Through inter-personal esteem games regulators who were peripherally situated in the two-level networks of central banking were able to move into the core.

Adriana Nilsson also traces the emergence of a new type of issue professional from the organizational struggles of the WTO and the WHO around issues of broadening global access to medicines. This new health 'access professional' has become central in driving debates about medical, legal and socio-economic barriers to health by drawing on a remarkably diverse set of training, skills and experiences. The inherently multi-issue character of this emergent policy field has given rise to the prominence of professionals that combine expertise in law, medicine and economics as well as experiences derived from careers that cut across IOs, NGOs and firms. Nilsson argues that this property enables them to promote global access to medicine through their skilled interactions with different networks and logics, even in a complex, multi-level issue field driven by diverse and often conflicting interests.

Matthew Paterson, Matthew Hoffmann, Michele Besttsill, and **Steven Bernstein** look at the role of professional networks in the diffusion of emissions trading schemes. They use social network analysis to assess the network structure of key venues where emissions trading instruments were designed, developed and propagated, also locating the dominant professional identities in this highly technical issue area. In doing so, they locate two distinct 'roads' to 'emissions trading', the US network with a remarkable centrality of economists and the 'EU/IGO network' with the dominant presence of policy analysts. They speculate on the consequences of the initial composition of these networks for the emergence and diffusion of venue-specific policy instruments and discuss the increased importance of emissions trading professionals who receive specialized training. **John Karlsrud** and **Arthur Mühlen-Schulte** draw attention to the role of new information and communication technologies, and the professionals mastering these technologies, in changing how humanitarian crises are dealt with, particularly within the UN system. A new group of professional known as 'crisis mappers' have specialized in rapidly providing information about hard-to-access locations. These 'mapsters' change existing pecking orders in the UN crisis system and undermine experience-based forms of expertise in ways that fundamentally alter what is considered to be legitimate professionalism in the field of humanitarian action.

The section on **Professionals and Markets** provides cases on the emergence of Global Professional Service Firms (GPSF) and how professionals within them organize to transplant firm practices and governance regimes; the rise of consultants as arbiters of knowledge on how to govern, and the role of lawyers, engineers and economists in debates on how to re-price the internet. The chapter by **James Faulconbridge** and **Daniel Muzio** advances existing work on GPSFs and the institutionalization of transnational governance regimes. It does so through a thought-provoking reconsideration of the identities, projects and effects of the firms in question. They contend that in their attempts to develop new markets, services and internal organizational models, GPSFs exercise issue control far beyond their immediate activities – as they challenge governance regimes, disrupt/create jurisdictions, and transform identities, practices and systems of regulation in the professions themselves. Three prevalent strategies that GPSFs use to exercise issue control in two-level networks are identified: one associated with the 'scope of control', one 'defining scales of knowledge resources', and lastly one engaged with 'the production of ecologies of linked interests'. **Mehdi Boussebaa**'s chapter explores a similar theme by zeroing in on how Global Management Consulting Firms' (GMCFs) exercise of issue control in neo-colonial networks, reinforcing traditional core-periphery hierarchies of power and status in the international political economy. The chapter illustrates how these hierarchies are sustained within the organization by directing the flow of knowledge from core offices to offices in the periphery across knowledge management systems, consultant peer networks, and multinational team structures. Boussebaa's chapter points to the need for further researching resistance strategies among lower status professionals located in the periphery in carrying out pre-defined work tasks for higher status professionals located in core countries.

Bessma Momani sheds light on the importance of management consultants in her study of how they control public policy transnationally by providing advice to governments around the world. Through participant observation and interviews Momani identifies four professional strategies that management consultants draw on to control public policy, including control of 'unique knowledge' and databases, claims to identify the 'big picture' through forecasting of trends and patterns, positive messaging to motivate 'feel-good' problem-solving, and the simplification of ambiguity into actionable items. Through these strategies, management consultants, like brokers, thrive on the uncertainty of their clients by offering ambiguous terms to displace this uncertainty. In **James Perry** and **David Kempel**'s chapter, organizational and professional struggles for internet regulation are analysed, drawing on a unique dataset of responses to a European Commission industry consultation. Their analysis reveals that the 'professional logics' of lawyers, engineers and economists are mobilized by different industry interests (infrastructure vs. content) to lobby emergent regulations on 'net neutrality'. These professional logics provide different frames of argumentation that industries make use of as they justify their own position in favour of or opposition to internet regulation.

The final chapter concludes by reflecting on the range of professional-organizational dynamics present in this volume. We identify particular professional trajectories that are important to dynamics within the cases and link professional strategies to network theories of change. We also provide further guidance on how we might disaggregate organizations into particular forms of organizing, locating characteristics that can be seen as opportunities structures for issue professionals. The conclusion also comments on the future methodological agenda and the integration of network-based methods with prosopographic methods, be they ethnographic, interview-based, or computational. Finally, we reaffirm that our framework views issue professionals as the actors, issue control as their key objective, and a two-level professional-organizational nexus as the key context of action. In short we present a further agenda for studying the role of professional networks as drivers of change in transnational governance.

2 In the 'Field' of Transnational Professionals
A Post-Bourdieusian Approach to Transnational Legal Entrepreneurs

Yves Dezalay and Mikael Rask Madsen

Taking a strict Bourdieusian position inevitably poses a challenge to the underlying conceptual framework of this book. In the transnational fields we have studied using Bourdieusian-inspired approaches, for example, international commercial arbitration (Dezalay and Garth 1996), international human rights (Dezalay and Garth 2006; Madsen 2010, 2011a, 2011b, 2016) or the emergence of environmental law (Dezalay and Madsen 2006; Dezalay 2007), we have continuously observed that one of the central characteristics of professional 'strategies of internationalization' is that they combine professional and organizational resources. In other words, in the actual games of internationalization and transnational domination – what Seabrooke and Henriksen refer to as 'issue-control' – the boundaries between professional and institutional logics often are blurred, and tacitly so. While it is, therefore, in itself difficult to distinguish very clearly between professional and organizational logics, it is also potentially counter-productive to the final analysis as the transnational professionals themselves, through this double game, are continuously producing both new professional and organizational categories and always with the goal of defining and controlling specific transnational issues (Kauppi and Madsen 2013; Dezalay and Garth 2016).

Seabrooke and Henriksen, the editors of this volume, are, of course, fully aware of this. But it is probably worth repeating the need to be somewhat reluctant towards – and even suspicious of – sociological analysis which endorses and thereby effectively hides the professional strategies on which it builds its analysis. This risk it entails is precisely the kind of analytical blindness which Pierre Bourdieu criticized when discussing the sociology of professions (Bourdieu and Wacquant 1992: 242–244; Madsen 2011) and called for a reflexive sociology. And since the aim of this chapter is to provide a (post-)Bourdieusian approach to understanding transnational professionalization, it is obviously fitting to start our analysis by inquiring into the construction of the problematique of this book: issue-control in transnational professional networks and organizations. If we are to take the idea of reflexive sociology seriously – in our view the best way of engaging with the work of Bourdieu (Bigo and Madsen 2011; Madsen 2011) – it consists above all of a critical interrogation of the construction of the object of inquiry and the methods devised for explaining it, what Bourdieu termed the 'double rupture' (Bourdieu et al. 1991). We will return to the notion of reflexive sociology below when discussing field studies.

With regard to the specific object of inquiry in focus in our analysis, transnational legal fields and entrepreneurs, we have repeatedly observed a set of structural relations that inevitably challenge approaches building on the more traditionalist canon of the sociology of professions which generally exclude issues related to social capital (Abbott 1988). In order to explain strategies of internationalization it is in our view key to understand the structures which prompt such practices, that is, the forms of stratification inscribed in and reproduced by the national legal fields, and how these are articulated in both internal and external battles to the legal field: the structural constraints and opportunities which help explain the different alliances between legal professionals and, for example, NGOs or other professionals, or between different factions of the legal profession. A good example is the emergence, in the beginning of the twentieth century, of international institutionalized law. This process was helped by the convergence of interests between business lawyers, seeking to reposition themselves as international statesmen and philanthropists, and professors of international law, at the time a marginalized position at law faculties, who sought to gain more diplomatic traction (Sacriste and Vauchez 2007).

Another important feature of strategies of internationalization is that they often correlate to what we have termed 'cosmopolitan capital' (Dezalay 2004). In many cases, strategies of internationalization serve to raise barriers of entrance to international markets of professional expertise, which often are often highly selective and carry a great deal of prestige and typically are linked to more traditional 'family modes' of reproduction of legal elites. Generally, there has been increased international competition in the field of law that has been spurred by an enormous growth in graduates in law over the last half century. Alongside this growth legal elites have increasingly turned towards international markets for preserving their privileges and prestige. Very often, access to key positions within the great international legal institutions is not simply a question of legal merits or administrative procedures. What can be observed, for example, in the field of international commercial arbitration is an individual co-optation between judges and lawyers which influences the role of social capital (Dezalay and Garth 1996). This differs from Seabrooke's (2014a) notion of 'epistemic arbitrage' that investigates similar knowledge interfaces but does not explore, to the same extent, what we believe is the critical sociological underpinnings of that interaction.

A third feature of our more Bourdieusian research into transnational legal professional elites, which inevitably challenge more traditional views of international professionals, is our insistence on the importance of the strategies and politics of the state in this regard. This is perhaps of particular importance with respect to law and lawyers, as the state is key to understanding the genesis, structuration and differentiation of national legal fields (Brundage 2008; Bourdieu 2012; Dezalay and Madsen 2012). This imbrication of the state and state power in the construction of the legal field can be observed strongly first during the Renaissance in Europe but continues into the many and largely parallel national constructions of law. Most important, however, in this regard, it plays a fundamental role in the structuration of transnational spaces of legal practice which very often are inscribed in longer processes of colonialism and hegemonic battles like the Cold War (Dezalay and Garth 2010b; Madsen 2010).

For these different reasons, we will in the following first discuss the genesis and transformation of legal fields before outlining a set of empirical strategies for understanding transnational legal fields, practices and elites.

The central place of law and lawyers in contemporary global governance is largely due to the ways in which they, through a long historical process, have been ingrained in national fields of power. In the following two sections, we first explore this relationship between law and power and then, secondly, how it is a resource in transnational professional battles over issue-control. In both cases, we will seek to go back to the historical genesis of the main features of law and lawyers' power in order to outline the necessary structural framework for understanding contemporary transnational practices and professional battles.

Legal Fields as Historically Connected and Interstitial Spaces

Generally speaking, two fundamental axioms structure legal fields: the embeddedness of legal fields in the fields of national power and how the production of legal knowledge and associated hierarchies of professional competences is part of the reproduction and legitimation of social elites.

(i) The embeddedness of legal fields in national fields of power is particularly visible in professional battles. Generally, the opposing strategies and alliances between different fractions of legal professionals are played out simultaneously in terms of legal capital, social capital and political or state resources that groups are able to mobilize. These important variations in capitals are made possible by the ways in which legal fields are structured as crossroads. Legal fields are basically spaces that permit, and at the same time favour, strategies of a double game played typically by an elite of the law, as counsellors to the Prince (or merchant princes) as in medieval Europe, or in modern times as, for example, legislators, politicians or high functionaries of the state. These various roles with respect to law allow for the construction of alliances beyond law and thereby a valorization of capitals that are not strictly speaking legal but nevertheless often decisive for the furthering of transnational professional projects.

(ii) Another central feature of the transnational power of legal professionals are the subtle social mechanisms related to the reproduction of legal learning and the hierarchy of professional competences as one of the components of the reproduction and legitimation of social elites. This relationship is largely due to the fact that the law is both a governmental expertise, which is homologized and guaranteed by the institutions of national states, and more than a governing knowledge by its claim of universal validity. The contradictions tied to this double logic of reproduction of legal capital – through scholarly paths that are more or less selective and meritocratic, but also through inherited capital transmitted through family lineage (including through the mechanism of the biases built into processes of apprenticeship or co-optation) – are a permanent source of tensions and internal conflicts which serve as one of the engines of the transformation of the legal field more generally.

These relative contradictions are also inherent in the legal field as a result of the double genesis of the field, which combines at the same time the rationality of the law and state justice, but also the authority of traditional leaders – communal, religious or feudal – that exercise de facto a legal justice with respect to the groups under their responsibility. As Martines shows with respect to the geneses of the legal profession in medieval Italy, the development of a state justice that is rationalized and professionalized comes at the expense of feudal justice that it helps to disqualify as archaic and biased (Martines 1968). Nevertheless, this competition is accomplished though a hybridization brought about by strategies of reconversion. Martines also explains the cost and the cultural barriers which reserved access to the new law faculties to the descendants of old feudal lines, who gained control of this new law and justice model.

This new 'noblesse de robe', in Bourdieu's terms, is able through this process to combine a capital of traditional authority with learned legitimacy and a delegation of state power. Legal capital is inscribed in the modes of reproduction of social hierarchies, which help both to renovate them and to render them more legitimate. As Berman showed, the common law is an example of this hybridization, mixing royal justice and feudal justice (Berman 1983). Taking advantage of the weakness of the royal bureaucracy, leading feudal groups profited from royal writs by imposing themselves as justices of the peace of the new common law. This process continues through the permanent tension between codification and custom, judges and mediators – notably apparent at the time of the colonial transplantation of imperial justice (Dezalay and Garth 2010b). These contradictions are further exacerbated by the fact that the faculties and schools of law are strictly connected with the reproduction of the ruling classes and modes of governance. The ruling elite, the churches, the state and multinationals have always sustained and financed faculties of government in order to be able to select and educate their collaborators and successors. This way, paradoxically, their grip on politics – or the world of business – is built in part on the learned processes upon which the autonomy of this professional field resides.

This discussion, even if in a very summary form, of the two axioms we presented above shows that a sociology of the legal field must be deployed simultaneously on a plurality of national fields and spaces, but also on interstitial spaces between these different universes. Obviously, this is perhaps particularly essential for Europe, where there long have been clear connections between the national and transnational. It is necessary also to add an historical dimension essential to an understanding of the transformation of these fields, both for the internal logic and the fact of interactions between different spaces. This analysis can be made more economical, in fact, both in terms of synchrony and diachrony, through research at a number of sites, because agents possessing a diversity of capital, which permits them to circulate and intervene in multiple spaces, are very often also the persons who occupy the dominant positions in each of the spaces. The ubiquity of this mobility of elites contradicts the facade of autonomy constructed by each of these spaces through an ensemble of institutions, of learning and of norms, even of specific habituses. It is therefore vital to be able to follow the trajectories of these influential agents, since they provide insight into how these fields continually interact while maintaining the relative autonomy essential to their internal operation and their social credibility.

The Courtiers of Law: Strategies of a Double Game in and between Fields of Power

Contrary to the depiction of international law – and the internationalization of legal practices – as developments that followed the construction of nation states with diplomatic practices evolving into principles to tame power relationships, Martines shows that the patricians of law drew on their cosmopolitan capital to gain their positions at the top of the new 'noblesse d'etat' (Martines 1968). Elite jurists positioned themselves very early as courtiers of the international in the name of universal principles of learned law valid for civil law as well as canon law. In fact, if we look deeper at the process, we see that the success of the learned capital was at the same time inseparable from investments in cosmopolitan capital. These jurists acquired their cosmopolitan capital through trips that they took at a very young age, as well as the long years spent in the prominent universities such as Bologna, where they met their counterparts from other cities. They took advantage of numerous opportunities to grow their international capital whether in legal practice or in the service of the state.

The legal field in the world Martines depicts was constructed around the circulation of individuals and learned and relational resources between state spaces – or more precisely between different levels of state institutions found inside and outside the boundaries of the city states. They included local communal, religious or feudal enclaves which maintained a certain autonomy, especially jurisdictional, up to learned and religious institutions with influence or authority in a kind of interstate market involving legal expertise with legitimacy across borders and with access reserved to the descendants of the great patrician families – those able to take full advantage of a learned capital claiming to be universal through combination with cosmopolitan relational capital.

This trans-frontier dimension seen in the early European legal history supports a clarification of the analysis developed by Kantorowicz (1997). The reliance on the multiple sites to construct cosmopolitan capital enabled legal elites to succeed in playing on two essential scales. They constructed their professional autonomy and credibility, but they also put their expertise in the service of the new holders of state power – which then allowed the acquisition of the capital of political notoriety and influence vital to continuing professional success. The descendants of aristocratic and patrician families, therefore, played a particular role in the construction of the modern state because they could rely on family resources that permitted them to connect themselves to trans-frontier power through networks situated above – but also within – the city states.

Since the role of international courtier was central to the genesis of the European legal field, it is necessary to examine its relationship to institutionalization and normalization within the group of nation states. Our hypothesis is that the role of international courtier is not just key to the genesis of states but that it continues to play a vital role that is still restricted to an influential and selective fraction of the legal elite. That role was quite evident in the story of law and the European Community (Cohen and Madsen 2007; Madsen 2010; Vauchez 2010; Cohen 2013).

Before going deeper into these examples below, we wish to emphasize the particular merit of this way of approaching the transnational legal fields and entrepreneurs. It provides a fluid conception of legal fields as multidimensional spaces with shifting relationships and positions (Bourdieu 2012: 518). It facilitates a focus on how the positions of the holders of legal capital are quite mobile, with jurists able to play between different spaces and to modify their strategies and the positions they take in relation to opportunities available – within various spaces – in different historical and political contexts.

This conception of the legal field as fluid and shifting while maintaining a kind of 'crossroads' position[1] between religious, state, community, etc. is highly adequate for making intelligible the transnational practices of lawyers and competing professionals. It introduces the possibility of analysing not only the role of jurists as courtiers and diplomats between different fields of power but also strategies in periods of transition that link together different political regimes which succeed each other in national histories. This same paradigm also takes into account the diversity of connections between law and state in different national spaces (Dezalay and Madsen 2009, 2012). More generally, this approach helps to explain and demonstrate the paradox formulated by Kantorowicz: the clerks of the law affirm their autonomy with respect to power at the same time as they put their expertise in the service of power. As shown by numerous works of history (Martines 1968; Brundage 2008; Whaley 2012) and consistent with this theoretical approach, the relative mobility of jurists – e.g., between different royal courts or principalities and the hierarchies of the church – is the best guarantee of their autonomy, in the sense that it permits them to break from holders of power who are too heavy-handed or undertake activities that threaten the clerks' credibility.

The embedding of legal fields within national fields of power is combined therefore with a relative mobility of legal professionals who not only can circulate among different national spaces on the basis of their expertise and claim to universality but can also undertake strategic reconversions in the process of political transitions while serving as providers of continuity between successive regimes.

In the Field

This deconstruction of the origins of legal power provides a framework for understanding how legal power is being constructed today at the

---

[1] This conception was developed earlier by Christophe Charle in 1989 in a short programmatic note where he observed that legal professions served as 'professional crossroads where social capital is converted more easily into other diverse forms of capital: economic, intellectual, political' (119).

transnational level (see also Dezalay and Madsen 2012). But, just as it is necessary to deconstruct power in order to reveal it at the theoretical level, the same is very much the case when we seek to empirically analyse how legal entrepreneurs construct transnational power. In Bourdieusian terms, the conceptual tool for this is what is referred to as reflexivity (and in earlier works as the 'double rupture') (Bourdieu et al. 1991). The aim was to construct a more scientifically autonomous object of research in the social sciences and one different from the 'intuitive readings and spontaneous classifications' that often have dominated this field of inquiry's identification research objects (Bourdieu et al. 1991).

This basic search for objectivization is, however, not restricted to the research object as such but also implies a critical examination of the dominant academic preconstructions of the specific subject area in question (i.e., a critical analysis of the research tradition and the application of that tradition by the researcher) (Madsen 2011a). With regard to understanding the geneses of law, lawyers and the state, deploying reflexive sociology basically implies a double historicization as we have shown: a historicization of both the object and the academic construction of that object. It entails more generally developing a genuine sociological inquiry guided by sociological systemization and questions and not by the political, legal or moral stakes of the subject in question. As we tried to show in our more theoretical and historical outline above, this opening of the black box of the object (Latour 1987: 2–3) is perhaps particularly important with regard to law because of the long and particular history of law and the legal profession and the historically different roles and positions law and lawyers have played with respect to state and society.

Generally, Bourdieusian reflexive sociology calls for a sociological engagement that is both conceptual and empirical at the very same time – that is, a reflexive engagement with theory, method and empirical data collection as not only interdependent but also mutually constitutive elements of sociological practice. So far we have deployed the approach to discuss theory and more historical empirical findings. In what follows, we resume this analysis of transnational legal fields with a particular focus on the third element, namely the actual conduct of such an empirical analysis 'in the field' of the field.

The Symbolic Power of Law as Object of Empirical Inquiry

In the previous sections we generally highlighted how transnational legal fields, regardless of their often highly institutionalized appearances, are structurally somewhat ambiguous. This relative ambiguity is the background to what we referred to as double games in terms of the agents' usage of inter- or transnational venues to advance national interests – and vice versa. And because of the strategic opportunities offered by international fields and institutions, partly the effect of their tendency towards perpetual transformation, the boundaries between law and politics tend to be less strict than what can be inferred from national fields. This is also central to developing research strategies that can help the researcher gain access to the deeper sociolegal dynamics of the globalization of law and lawyers. As the agents in question here often rely on a number of double games, as well as multiple identities, the researcher – if not very carefully tracing these multiple movements – is capable neither of going beyond the very symbolic discourses produced in these interactions nor of escaping them.

In the specific case of the sociology of law, there is moreover often an explicit interest in integrating the work of the researcher in these symbolic practices, as many of the entrepreneurs of legal globalization rely on academic and quasi-academic resources for legitimizing their practices. A very good example of these issues is found in the field of human rights. The promotion of human rights is largely based on an attempt of making human rights legitimate objects of legal and political contention. But in such social contexts in which the distinctions between political and legal practices are at best vague, the sociologist of law, when seen from the point of view of the agents, provides a perfect object for legitimizing weakly institutionalized or legalized practices. This is probably particularly exacerbated in the case of the sociology of law, as the researcher is potentially a catalyst for providing if not law then learned legal discourse on these emerging legal structures such as human rights. In many studies of the globalization of law, this risk of adapting to discourses of power and legitimacy is not seen as a problem however. Particularly, in the more activist forms of inquiry, the choice of empirical terrain is directly informed by the convergence of scientific and political agendas. Yet, in the sort of approach propounded in this chapter, such a choice poses a real problem, as it essentially conflicts with the underlying aim of establishing a more objectively defined object of inquiry.

The response to this dilemma, which can be drawn from Bourdieu's work, is for the researcher both to follow the agents and their actions in order to empirically document actual movements and to seek to impose a different and scientifically guided agenda. Basically, the researcher has to follow the agents in order to observe what is the alleged core of the game, but at the very same time he or she must also examine and reframe the issues at play by, for example, relating them to the agents' multiple national and international interests. In this reflexive engagement, the sociologist has the advantage that he or she has far greater mobility within the field than the actual agents who by definition are more trapped by their specific position in the field.

Closely connected, the sociologist also has the advantage over the agents that he or she can more objectively contrast the positions within the field. The agents' perceptions of the field and its structures are based upon subjective experiences, and they only rarely share the global, structural view of the field that is the sociologist's starting point and ultimate scientific objective. Yet, the many and different accounts being presented throughout the research process provide critical data for interrogating the agents and escaping their neutralizing and naturalizing discourses. But to do so, the sociologist necessarily must take full advantage of his or her mobility in the field. In practice, and very different from the agents' manoeuvring capabilities, the researcher can interview the opposing camps, if not at the same time then immediately after each other, following a research logic that breaks with the logic of the practices of the respective agents. In fact, it is by following such a zigzag course inside the field that the researcher can fully benefit from the information gained in previous stages of the research process, including knowledge of personal bonds and enmities. What we suggest here is basically to turn the logic of field inside out as a means for deconstructing social practices and reconstructing them in terms of fields.

We have applied this more qualitative form of field analysis in numerous inter- and transnational settings. A guiding line of inquiry in these studies of transnational fields has been to study the relational networks and personal trajectories of the agents of the fields in question. Yet, these background social structures are used not only to conduct prosopographic analysis but also to explore the underlying battles forming the structures of the field, using agents as the starting point: How are the agents situated in more fields than the ones with which they are immediately identified, and how do they mobilize different capital in each of these different social spheres? These more hidden lines, which are revealed by analysis of the agents' multiple specializations, provide guidance for moving beyond the dominant – and often naturalized – institutional and categorical structures of the field in question. Take, for example, the fabrication of new legal expertise: Notwithstanding the way in which legal expertise is by definition presented as highly differentiated knowledge, its transformation takes place in the margin of official categories or on the frontiers of disciplines.

This means that the data needed for understanding such processes of conversion are available only if one challenges the social categories – which are often uncritically applied by the agents themselves – with the goal of reconstructing the socio-professional battles that have formed them. Such an analysis is feasible only if the researcher has multiple points of departure for retracing and understanding the new social categories as the outcome of both antagonistic positions and subjective bonds. In other words, the described mobility of the researcher within the field is absolutely key to conducting an analysis that is formed both by the oppositions of positions and by their subjective links, such as alliances and networks.

The Collective Biographies of Transnational Fields

The different research strategies we have briefly outlined all come down to the basic problem of ensuring a scientific autonomy in the engagement with normative discourses – that is, avoiding the sociologist being turned into yet another double agent of globalization, playing multilevel games. These strategies are all building on the problem we discussed in the initial section of this chapter concerning what Bourdieu framed as the necessity of a 'double rupture' (Bourdieu et al. 1991). This scientific ideal, which we refer to here as reflexivity, concerns, as noted, both the subject and the researcher and is, at the end of the day, related to the scientific process of uncovering the agents' (and the researcher's) orientations and predispositions and how these shape their habits vis-à-vis other positions in the field (Champagne et al. 1999: 51). Reflexivity thus implies two very closely related actions: first, a critical reflection on the preconstructions that dominate a given subject area and, second, a self-critique as the means to considering one's own scientific and social assumptions of the subject area. This is not an operation that is done once and for all but is instead an ongoing measure for questioning findings and the way they are gathered.

In our research, we have generally used qualitative interview methods for mapping transnational fields. More specifically, we have applied a relational biographic method as a measure for comparing elements of individual trajectories with the aim of bridging them in terms of a field. The approach has enabled us to assess the various resources – forms of networks, competences and capital – that have been critical for creating positions within specific fields. Basically, by following the course by which a disputed subject area has been established as a field, these studies have attempted to identify the key points of transformation and how these changes are reflected in the practices and trajectories of the agents: the way the agents have oriented themselves vis-à-vis new opportunities, strategic challenges or simply the increased structuration of a given field. Moreover, the biographies of the players suggest which capital and resources have been brought into play at the different stages of structuration.[2]

---

[2] With the term trajectories, we underscore the difference between our approach, which highlights how individual action is greatly constrained and informed by the more objective and structural ordering of fields, and biographic methods, which tend to place more emphasis on specific actions of individuals. cf. Bourdieu 1994.

It might sound almost like a contradiction in terms, but this approach of assembling the collective relational biographies of a given field is used as a means to examine the field's structural transformations, but as documented in the agents' actual practices. Hence, the agents' practices are studied with regard to their ability to influence the general structuration process of the field. Yet, at the same time, to bridge micro and macro levels of analysis, this analysis also explores the flip side of the question – namely, how the general social structures of the field are inscribed in the agents' practices. Above all, this empirical usage of agents' trajectories offers a means of decoding the different struggles that have existed at different stages of the historical structuration of the field (Dezalay and Garth 2002a: 10).

This approach clearly implies a certain dominance of agents over institutions, as the assumption is that the agents' trajectories provide concrete empirical examples of the different battles related to the build-up of the field and its institutions. Put differently, the agents embody the development of the field: What the agents say and how they say it, to an extent, reveal their position both within and outside the field in terms of social class, political affiliations, etc. However, the method performs not by individual cases but by assembling a cumulative story that can be established by comparing a high number of trajectories within a particular field. It thereby provides the intellectual means for constructing an objectively different account of the field that is not limited by the self-representations of institutions, professions, social movements, etc. Indeed, rather than taking the legal definitions of, for example, institutions as the starting point for their understanding, this approach explores how legal institutions and practices emerged on the basis of the legitimacy of collective entities of agents and their common capital and ideas within broader constraining social structures (for an example, see Madsen 2011a).

To identify the dynamics of a field by, among other things, mapping it by the means of its collective and relational biography is, in practice, an ongoing attempt at sociological reconstruction and objectivization. Our emphasis of structures and relations, as revealed through the practices of the agents, has turned out to be particularly useful when analysing fields in which the stakes are very political but typically presented in very different ways by the agents, and perhaps notably legal agents. The more or less fixed standpoints presented by agents involved in, for example, human rights politics are often a real hindrance for a deeper understanding of the field. This is exactly where the outlined methods serve a very clear purpose in terms of addressing the agents' involvement in and around the particular subject, as well as in terms of their multiple identities.

By interviewing the agents about their personal trajectories rather than their legal or political involvement, the researcher can assess how they pursue multiple strategies, even if they often prefer presenting themselves as associated only with a particular stance. This form of analysis cannot be based on singular or individual cases but naturally requires multiple points of entrance to the field if the goal is to challenge the officialized discourses, which for the agents themselves often appear completely naturalized. Our approach basically provides for breaking up the discourse into its many overlapping and even opposing texts and for identifying its co-writers. This echoes the very definition of 'field' as these conflicting narratives reflect the stakes in the field and the agents' positions in the field. The analysis of the field is then carried out by examining the correspondence between the positions (the agents) and the position-takings (the stakes). For the same reasons, the approach is not limited to more politicized spheres of social life but applies across all fields and agents, literally ranging from 'mercenaries of imperialism' to 'missionaries of the universal' (Dezalay 2004).

Conclusion

We have in this chapter sought to combine an outline of a theoretical and historical understanding of the power of legal professionals, particularly the elite of legal professionals, with an introduction to some of the key research strategies we have developed in order to study precisely transnational legal elites. Our main point in turning the subject of this book slightly around and scrutinizing some of the structural preliminaries for professional power and the battle over issue-control is that to devise effective research strategies for understanding global professional elites one needs to first deconstruct the very form of power they bring into the global sphere. In the case of law, this above all requires understanding the complex genesis of legal power as part of the genesis of the state.

Our approach of focusing on the agents – or couriers – of globalization reveals how professional and organizational resources are linked in inter-professional battles over issue-control at the global level. The very production of new professional categories and institutions is in other words very often closely connected to attempts at gaining control at the global level over new markets, ranging from moral politics to global capitalism. Our basic contention is that these processes of professional competition are not simply battles over professional control; they are also part of more general processes of, for example, elite reproduction of national legal fields and beyond. They are, so to say, a prolongation of national battles over domination and reproduction of elites. We agree with Seabrooke that professional competition is in part an epistemic competition and resulting arbitrage (Seabrooke 2014a). But we also insist on the importance of the larger structures behind professional competition for making it sociologically intelligible.

To capture these rather complex micro–macro interrelations, we have introduced a post-Bourdieusian framework of analysis. As argued, Bourdieusian reflexive sociology offers a highly adequate tool for crafting an empirical approach which is reflexive of the ways in which the development of concepts, institutions and practices are part of the same object. To take the Bourdieusian perspective seriously, this naturally implies interrogating the construction of the object and the naturalizing tendencies of academic discourse on that very object. Deploying reflexive sociology for the purpose of understanding transnational professional competition therefore unavoidably implies challenging some of the assumptions of mainstream sociology of professions notably in the tradition of Abbott (1988). While battles over jurisdiction are evidently important also in the Bourdieusian framework, the key difference is in the broader sociological picture that is taken into account when taking the Bourdieusian route. And the key point is that this bigger picture matters fundamentally for also understanding the battles over jurisdiction.

3 Studying Elite Professionals in Transnational Settings

Brooke Harrington

How should we study hyper-mobile elites such as the transnational professionals featured in this volume? Little has been written about the methodological challenges attendant upon such research. All the usual difficulties of studying elites apply, including the physical remoteness of gated communities and private islands, the prevalence of gatekeepers, and other obstacles to data gathering (Mikecz 2012; Ostrander 1993). But when the subject of research includes work taking place across numerous sites around the globe, the difficulties of gathering data are multiplied by distance and complexity. This chapter proposes ethnography as a practical solution to many of these challenges.

Indeed, ethnography may be one of the *only* practical methods for producing knowledge about elite professionals. Quantitative data notoriously underrepresent the wealthy and powerful (Davies et al. 2008); this is a major limitation even in datasets such as the US Survey of Consumer Finances, which oversample at the top of the socioeconomic spectrum (Budría et al. 2002; Kennickell 2009). By the same token, archival material – such as public records or corporate documents – is sometimes tainted by efforts to sanitize or even deliberately distort professionals' decisions and actions (Davies 2001).

One of the privileges elites enjoy is the ability to exempt themselves from surveillance in the form of data collection efforts. This may be motivated by concerns about privacy, or the desire to avoid exposure or embarrassment (Gilding 2010). Among professionals in particular, the desire for discretion can be linked to the knowledge-control issues discussed by Seabrooke and Henriksen (editors of this volume). In addition to those problems, it can be difficult as a practical matter to persuade individuals who bill hundreds of Euros per hour to spend time answering research questions.

Given these constraints on gathering quantitative data from elites, it is surprising to find evidence that some – including busy professionals – are willing to engage face-to-face with social scientists (Gilding 2010; Thomas 1993). This may be the result of a kind of Hawthorne effect

(Roethlisberger and Dickson 1939): the attention provided by the social scientist renders implicit homage to the professionals' status and expertise. Being acknowledged publicly as someone worthy of scientific attention is a form of flattery. Thus, if research is to be conducted at all on these groups – if we are to answer anthropologist Laura Nader's (1972) call to "study up" the status ladder – then it may need to be done through the face-to-face encounters characteristic of ethnographic research.

The following sections elaborate on this claim. First, the chapter defines what is meant by the terms "professional elite" and "ethnography," since both are the subject of some scholarly disagreement. Next, the chapter details how the study of transnational professionals amplifies many of the challenges present in other research on elites, including practical matters, self-presentation, and ethics. Finally, the chapter argues for what can be gained analytically from an ethnographic approach to these professionals.

What Is a Professional Elite?

"Elite" is an undertheorized term (Harvey 2011; Richards 1996), making the notion of a "professional elite" even more difficult to define. McDowell argued that it is a "class-specific" (1998: 2135) phenomenon, involving not only a particular set of skills, knowledge, and prestige but a set of cultural practices and norms transmitted through families, networks, and exclusive educational institutions. McDowell's study, which focused on merchant bankers in the City of London, highlights a tension in the application of the term "professional elite" in an international setting: while elite status is often the product of local meanings and social structures (and can be unstable over time), the emergence of transnational fields such as finance has elevated certain status markers to the global level. The hyper-mobility (Beaverstock et al. 2004) of contemporary elites has contributed to the diffusion of a system of valuation in which being an Oxbridge graduate, or a Swiss banker, carries positive significance virtually everywhere.

As an emergent classification, the term "professional elite" casts a wide net, broad enough to include celebrities, economists, lawyers, political leaders, and even clergy (Stephens 2007). Zuckerman (1996) further subdivides the term to distinguish an "ultra-elite," composed of professionals who possess extraordinarily high levels of expertise and status not only relative to the social structure as a whole but relative to their own elite milieux. Among scientists, this could include the Nobel laureates Zuckerman studied. In other domains, this could include CEOs of major corporations or heads of state (Mikecz 2012; Useem 1984).

Professionals involved in transnational governance are elites in terms of their locations within the global political, economic, scientific, and legal structures. What Conti writes of the World Trade Organization (WTO) lawyers he studied also holds true of the professionals described in this volume: "their actions influence the daily activities of millions of people around the globe" (Conti and O'Neil 2007: 64).

The extent of these professionals' status and influence may not be accurately reflected by their formal titles (Harvey 2011). Indeed, the process of globalization has meant that some of the most influential professionals and forms of expertise are fragmented spatially and organizationally, engaging through networks that transcend the boundaries of traditional institutional forms, such as the university, the corporation, or the nation-state (Parry 1998). In the context of transnational governance, strategic positions within the cartographies of power and knowledge are more significant than positions within particular organizations or institutions (see Chapter 1, Chapter 18).

What Is Ethnography?

While there is disagreement among scholars as to what constitutes an ethnography (Sanday 1979), it is typically grounded in data gathered from observation (participant or nonparticipant), interviews, and material culture, including documents and objects of significance to those being studied (Harrington 2002, 2003). Analytically, the focus is on meaning, interpretation, and interaction. This approach is based on a distinct philosophy of science derived from the work of Max Weber, who advocated for "a science concerning itself with the interpretive understanding [*Verstehen*] of social action" (Weber 1968 [1925]: 4).

The emphasis on interpretation, which is shared by disciplines such as history and anthropology, stands in distinction to the focus on explanation (*erklaren*) found in the natural sciences, such as physics and chemistry. While explanation-oriented research seeks to define universally valid laws of causality, the objective of studies oriented to interpretive understanding is to create historically contextualized typologies of action. From these differing goals stem different approaches to research design: "the emphasis on *verstehen* encourages more inductive research designs and demands that developments at the macro-level are explained with reference to their micro-foundations" (Beckert and Streeck 2008: 19).

Thus, the anthropologist Clifford Geertz described ethnography as "a form of knowledge" (1973: 5) rather than simply a method for obtaining data. He continued:

[D]oing ethnography is establishing rapport, selecting informants, transcribing texts, taking genealogies, mapping fields, keeping a diary, and so on. But it is not these things, techniques and received procedures that define the enterprise. What defines it is the kind of intellectual effort it is (1973: 5).

That effort involves synthesis of minute observations and other data points into a coherent whole. As one of the founders of classical anthropology put it, "[t]he Ethnographer has to construct the picture of the big institution" (Malinowski 2003 [1922]: 84). The promise of insight on micro–macro linkages has driven the diffusion of ethnography from its origins in anthropology to its present position as a well-established approach among sociologists and organizational researchers.

A central tool of the ethnographic approach is a positioning that Wacquant (2004) has termed "observant participation." That is, researchers embed themselves in a setting for an extended period – Sanday (1979) defines one year as a minimum, but such projects are now almost unheard of – during which they "subject themselves to the life contingencies of our subjects ... [in] a kind of deliberate experiment of the self" (Mears 2013: 21). The objective is not only to witness what is happening in the research site but to experience it. This provides insights that cannot be reproduced through other methods.

Research embeddedness of the kind implied by ethnography is particularly useful in studying the practices of elites such as transnational professionals. This is because the sophistication of these participants and their organizations can pose a serious threat to the researcher's ability to gain insight (Richards 1996). For example, executives are often adept at rebuffing efforts to access information that might undermine the public image of themselves and their firms. Indeed, many receive training to polish these impression management skills for media appearances and testimony before government agencies.

In the same way, documents may prove a disappointing source of data, since they can be created to give an intentionally superficial, if not outright misleading, record of events (Davies 2001; Glynn and Booth 1979). Through observation and embedded experience, ethnographers can gain "privileged – however fleeting – glimpses into the private domain" of elites who are otherwise surrounded by barriers to access (Atkinson and Silverman 1997: 315). And while interviewing alone may collect only "canned" responses from professionals, ethnography can reveal how things really work: negotiations, decision-making, and discussions often unfold along lines that may differ considerably from the official version presented after the fact, whether in interviews or documents.

Thus, while ethnography may include interviews and archival research, those data sources cannot be substituted for "observant participation." Skilled professionals can mislead an interviewer, or confound an archival researcher, but it is harder to keep up the charade with an embedded ethnographer. A performance cannot be sustained indefinitely: masks slip. Furthermore, the trust and rapport established in ethnographic encounters can open doors to new and valuable data sources, from introductions to other informants to the provision of information otherwise unobtainable or previously unknown. In these ways, ethnography can access "information not ... available (if ever) for public release" (Richards 1996: 200).

Challenges: Access, Obstacles, Self-Presentation, and Ethics

Access has always been one of the major challenges facing ethnographers (Harrington 2003). While the obstacles loom particularly large in the study of elites, such as transnational professionals, they can arise anywhere that scholars seek information that could be compromising to participants. Even getting nonelites to discuss matters that would ordinarily be private, such as their personal beliefs or what they do with their money, demands a careful and time-consuming approach (Harrington 2008). With professional elites, those difficulties are amplified by the addition of highly specific challenges connected to geographical location, class, time, and the presence of gatekeepers, among others. The following sections will address these practical problems in detail, along with the implications for self-presentation and research ethics.

Practical barriers to access. As Nader put it in her seminal paper on "studying up," powerful people are "out of reach on a number of planes: they don't want to be studied" (1972: 302). Elites make themselves inaccessible in part by interposing an array of secretaries, personal assistants, bodyguards, and other service personnel between themselves and the rest of the world (Gilding 2010; Marcus 1983). These "human shields" present a considerable challenge to access, even in the age of email and mobile phones (Conti and O'Neil 2007). When the objective is to study elite professions, securing the cooperation of potential research participants requires first gaining access to their gatekeepers; this may entail engaging in the same processes of identification and rapport that will later be repeated with their employers (Harrington 2003). Cultivating these relationships requires patience and time – often on a scale not compatible with the publish-or-perish rhythm of academic careers.

For those researchers able to overcome the barriers to entry presented by gatekeepers, there are often difficulties surrounding elites' (un)willingness to be forthcoming with data. With professionals, there may be even more at stake than concerns about personal exposure or embarrassment. As Seabrooke and Henriksen (this volume) have observed, professional power and jurisdictional boundaries are maintained in part by information control. For transnational professionals in particular, those boundaries can be highly contested; disseminating expert knowledge through researchers risks losing control of some of that professional monopoly power.

Thus, Australian sociologists Smart and Higley, setting out to examine their nation's power structure from the perspective of those at the top, wrote of "doubts about whether many of the persons in the sample would grant us interviews on these subjects, or, at least, interviews of sufficient length to be worthwhile" (1977: 249). But they, like a number of other researchers (e.g., Kogan 1994), discovered that a surprisingly large number of busy professionals welcome the chance to talk with an attentive listener. In addition to the status acknowledgment provided by the research setting, Gilding (2010) surmised that elites regard the interview as a chance to unburden themselves, in a quasi-therapeutic sense, and/or to promote themselves and their agendas to an audience of scholars and policy-makers they might not ordinarily reach. The latter motive is particularly significant for transnational professionals, as Useem (1984) showed in his study of the "inner circle" of business leaders in the United States and the United Kingdom.

In transnational settings, an overlooked challenge connected with gaining access to elites is simply the high cost of making contact. Arranging and engaging in ethnography that spans several locations around the globe often require international phone calls and travel to far-flung or remote locales (Stephens 2007). Securing funding to cover these expenses, especially when the risks of being denied access remain high, imposes high costs on researchers themselves. Those who wish to study elites, particularly in transnational settings, must be prepared to spend a great deal of time on grant proposals and other fund-raising activities (Conti and O'Neil 2007: 63).

While these considerations may apply to any international research, they are accentuated in the study of transnational professionals by the necessity of *multi-sited* work (Marcus 1995). That is, an ethnography of a remote people in the South Pacific may incur considerable costs in terms of making arrangements and traveling to the site; but once the researcher arrives, she generally stays put – in classical ethnography, the researcher could be embedded for years. To study a hyper-mobile elite, however, one must follow or visit the experts in multiple sites around the world. Many of them work in urban centers such as London or Zurich (e.g., Muzio and Faulconbridge 2013), where expenses for hotels, transportation, and other basics are extremely costly. On top of that, the need to travel from one research site to the next, in order to follow the transnational movement of experts' work and influence, mounts quickly into significant expenses.

Such considerations are particularly relevant to the study of professionals, such as wealth managers (Harrington 2016, 2017b) and consultants (Momani, this volume), who travel frequently, and may be away on assignment for weeks at a time. This is more than just a matter of the professionals being "busy." The global hyper-mobility of this group is part and parcel of their work: no study of transnational professionals can fail to gather data on this mobility and its significance in the practice of expert authority.

Self-Presentation. Researchers who overcome the initial barriers to accessing professional elites encounter a new set of challenges in face-to-face ethnographic settings. To gather data effectively, they must be able to establish rapport with participants (Ostrower 1993). This entails a self-presentation strategy that some researchers find difficult to execute: claiming a position as the status equals of those they are studying, at least for the duration of an interview (Conti and O'Neil 2007; Hermanowicz 2002).

Since most academics cannot realistically claim to wield as much power, influence, or wealth as elite professionals, the field of expert knowledge is usually the only terrain in which they can hope to meet as status equals. In the context of ethnography, then, presentation management entails the projection of authority. This task can be particularly difficult for scholars who are young and/or female. Concerns about rejection and embarrassment abound, particularly around the challenges of "modifying dress and appearance, and mastering specialized forms of knowledge," including class-based manners and distinctions (Conti and O'Neil 2007: 63).

The complex, multilayered challenge this presents can make social scientists "timid" (Nader 1972: 302) about studying elites. Exceptions include a few notable scholars who were born into families of power and privilege. One of the best-known exemplars is E. Digby Baltzell, a scion of the Social Register who later became a sociology professor at the University of Pennsylvania; in this role, he coined the acronym WASP (1964) to describe the White Anglo-Saxon Protestant aristocracy which formed his milieu. Someone like Baltzell would be unlikely to feel intimidated in the presence of professional elites, many of whom might have emerged from more modest backgrounds than his own.

But unlike Baltzell, most social scientists are not trained in the *habitus* characteristic of elites (Bourdieu 1977; Harrington 2017b). They lack "the right credentials and contacts" (Odendahl and Shaw 2002: 306) necessary not only to gain access but to keep it. Without this background, it is particularly difficult to deploy "tone," "gestures," and "appropriate language" (Harvey 2011) when face-to-face with transnational professionals. The resulting uncertainty and awkwardness can be fatal to establishing the rapport necessary to collecting high-quality data; they can also be very distracting for the researcher (Thomas 1993). Indeed, ethnographers working with elite professionals often report intense anxiety and exhaustion in connection with research encounters (Gilding 2010; Conti and O'Neil 2007).

Ethical Challenges. To establish rapport with elite professionals, researchers must convey respect without appearing "too deferential" or "sycophantic" (Richards 1996: 201). The danger of the latter lies not only in losing the footing of status equality with participants but in impairing the researcher's own ability to take a critical perspective on the data (Gilding 2010). Professional elites can be charming, persuasive, and charismatic – important factors in their rise to positions of power and influence. Researchers cannot ignore these traits without doing violence to their informants' "complex personhood" (Gordon 1997). At the same time, they cannot let empathy become complicity, lest the research become an uncritical amplifier for the elites' own agendas. This is particularly important given that highly placed political, business, and scientific leaders have been known to mislead and deceive interviewers (Davies 2001).

In addition to preserving their critical perspective, disclosing that perspective poses a separate set of challenges. Marcus (1983) argues that, to a greater extent than in any other domain of social science, research on elites is shaped by the political beliefs of the researcher. These "must be acknowledged and managed such that it avoids overshadowing the empirical claims" (Conti and O'Neil 2007: 66). This does not necessarily imply disclosure of those positions to research participants; rather, in their publications, ethnographers should disclose enough biographical and reflexive material about their work in the field that readers can assess the impact of those factors on the analyses.

But what of the ethics of honest personal disclosure to the research participants themselves? Many ethnographers recommend sharing personal details about themselves with informants as a form of reciprocity (Harrington 2003). But this strategy carries some special risks in studies of elite professionals. For example, while interviewing WTO lawyers, Conti wrote that he "feared that an honest display of my politics could lead to an early ending of the interview if not provoking defensiveness in the respondent throughout" (Conti and O'Neil 2007: 75).

Sometimes, rapport can be maintained on this "don't-ask-don't-tell" basis. But professional elites linked to controversial practices – a common condition in transnational governance – often have an acute awareness of their fragile public legitimacy and their consequent vulnerability to criticism. In such cases, honesty and disclosure may be ineffectual.

I encountered this problem in my own research on wealth managers (Harrington 2016). Wealth management is a quintessentially transnational profession: practitioners specialize in creating cross-border structures to help high-net-worth individuals avoid taxation and other constraints on their fortunes. Though these practices are generally legal, the growing public antipathy toward them has brought negative reputational consequences to the wealth management profession (Harrington 2017a). This sense of being labeled the "bad guys" of the global economy is keenly felt as an injustice by many practitioners. As a result, several who participated in my ethnography of the profession sought to test my beliefs and ideological position vis-à-vis their work.

For example, one practitioner in the British Virgin Islands (a well-known tax haven central to wealth management practices) prefaced our meeting by stating that he had read two of my scholarly journal articles (Harrington 2012a, 2012b) and found them to be "left-leaning" and "disapproving of what the [wealth management] industry and wealthy people are doing." He was unmoved by my truthful response that I didn't see the profession as either good or bad, but was motivated primarily by curiosity about its workings. He concluded the meeting by suggesting that "you should be thrown off the island based on your writings" (Harrington 2016). I learned later that deportation has been used before to shut down researchers on tax havens (Goodman 2014). Given this individual's position, I decided that the ethical response in this case was to thank him for his time and treat his comments as data, rather than making any further effort to change his mind.

Analytical Benefits of an Ethnographic Approach

Despite the many challenges described above, ethnographic methods can provide unique insight into elite professions and transnational governance. This is a consequence of the kind of information ethnography excels at obtaining. Specifically, this method yields concrete, actor-centered, relational data: the kind needed to understand how the events, decisions, and actions lead up to outcomes of global significance.

These characteristics are particularly significant to the study of transnational professionals because they provide insight on the sources of institutional change at the micro-level. Detailed observation and analysis of the encounters professionals have with clients, peers, and policy-makers allow for the construction of multi-level models linking individual practices and decisions with global structures (Harrington 2015; Smets and Jarzabkowski 2013).

For the same reasons, ethnography is useful for shedding light on the shifting fields and power structures characteristic of transnational professions. As Foucault (1977) and Gramsci (1992) have shown, power is not a fixed property of individual actors, or something possessed only by elites. Rather, it flows from relationships and interactions – phenomena into which ethnography delves deeply, advancing social scientific knowledge on the dynamics of conflict and change on a global scale.

Ultimately, ethnographic studies of transnational professionals allow scholars to build models that challenge dominant perspectives on globalization, such as the "World Polity" approach (Meyer et al. 1997), or theories that privilege structural relationships among states and classes (Poulantzas 2000; Skocpol 1979). Such perspectives have overlooked the negotiated encounters that make up the bulk of professional activity on a day-to-day basis. As a result, they can tell us little about how those interactions are connected to global norms, policies, and practices in the professions (Carruthers and Halliday 2006).

Conclusion

No matter what methods they use, researchers want access to the "back stages" of professional practice – the parts that "are carefully protected from outsiders and ... only known to insiders" (Mikecz 2012: 483). Ethnography allows scholars to break through the barriers surrounding access to elites, and to dispense with the readily available (but often superficial and misleading) data about them. It provides an effective means to observe and analyze the links between professional activities and transnational institutions.

Although every method has its limitations, the downsides of using survey, experimental, and archival data to study elite professionals are particularly pronounced. The absence of elites generally from survey or experimental research has been noted (Davies et al. 2008), along with the unreliability of public records and corporate documents (Davies 2001). In any case, these data sources are by definition retrospective and provide little insight into underlying processes.

This is not to say that participants in ethnographies always provide honest and complete data. They don't (Richards 1996). But the multiple data sources involved in ethnography, along with the embeddedness of the researcher, allow for triangulation (Jick 1979), leading to more reliable inferences.

The drawbacks to conducting ethnographic research on transnational professionals include the high costs in terms of time, money, and effort put into negotiating the demands of self-presentation and interpersonal ethics. To this list can be added a final challenge for researchers: the difficulty of publishing such research in the form of journal articles, which are increasingly the currency of professional success in the social sciences. Lengthy descriptive passages, which are the usual way of presenting evidence used to build theory from ethnographic data, often run afoul of the tight word counts and forms of argumentation used in such journals. It is also difficult to do justice to theoretical innovation within the discursive norms of journal articles, which rely heavily on citation and illustrations of how one's work "builds on" or "extends" recent studies (Uzzi et al. 2013).

In spite of all this, this chapter will close with a call for more ethnographies of transnational professionals. The costs are high. But ultimately, there may be no better way to understand and analyze global governance than to embed oneself within the worlds of the professionals responsible for it.

4   Networks and Sequences in the Study of Professionals and Organizations

Lasse Folke Henriksen and Leonard Seabrooke

This chapter provides an introduction to two classes of methods that we find particularly fruitful for studying two-level networks of professionals and organizations, social network analysis (SNA) and sequence analysis (SA). The methods enable data-driven analysis of two-level networks through various kinds of measures and maps. SNA techniques are particularly useful for depicting the structure of relations within as well as between professional and organizational networks, and for locating key players and their network characteristics. SNA offers techniques for exploring the distribution and evolution of skills and experience within two-level networks, and for locating groups of professionals and emergent forms of professionalism based on the analysis of, for example, career pathways. Taken together, the methods make up a powerful analytical toolkit for exploring the micro-level structure of power and influence in two-level networks, including where specific forms of professional knowledge and expertise are located within such structure. This chapter takes a 'nuts-and-bolts' approach to methods and their use in studying professional networks in transnational governance. We provide a brief introduction to those methods and construct a hypothetical case to demonstrate how they work.

Social Network Analysis

Social networks permit relationships and connections among actors. They can contain people that know each other very well and are similar in many ways, as well as people who are diverse and may not know each other well. The point of studying social networks is to get at the types of relationships between people and organizations, and to differentiate why certain kinds of network relationships are important for the flow of information within a group, to ascertain who controls knowledge, and also to investigate who has power. Conventionally, a social network is defined as a set of social actors, or nodes, along with a set of specific relations, or edges, that connect them. Relations in networks interconnect through shared points and thus

50

form paths or pipes that indirectly link actors that would not otherwise be directly related (Borgatti and Halgin 2011). SNA is now an established area of research that has gone through substantial progress in recent decades, with models and concepts developed to conceive of increasingly subtler configurations of agency and structure.

Social networks make up structures of interactions between actors whose actions are enabled and constrained by their location in the overall network. Actors that occupy central positions, for instance, are better able to influence agendas and impose rules than actors that are located peripherally. As a method, and an approach, SNA stresses the role that actors take on in networks rather than the roles and titles they occupy within their organizations.

As an analytical category, the network concept asks us to pay attention to relations and connections of people and organizations, rather than to the stable substances or attributes of social entities (Emirbayer 1997). As Bearman puts it, "categorical models rarely partition people in a way that confirms with observed action, because individual activity in the world is organized through and motivated not by categorical affiliations but by the structure of tangible social relations in which persons are embedded" (Bearman 1993, 10). Some scholars use the network concept to refer to a specific institutional form (e.g., Powell 1990 who contrasts 'networks' with 'markets' and 'hierarchies'), whereas we reserve the term as an analytical category with no a priori assumption about the nature of the organizing principle. Networks may contain hierarchies or be more markedly horizontal, but the structure of the network will take shape from its dominant organizing principle(s). SNA therefore lends itself particularly well as a methodological strategy to uncover the kinds of social structure that we put focus on in our theoretical approach (see Chapter 1), being agnostic about formal authority and instead paying attention to professional strategy in the context of two-level professional and organizational networks.

Much network analysis is concerned with characterizing network structures and actor positions, and with relating properties of structures and positions to group and actor outcomes. It makes claims about mechanisms and processes that interact with network structures to yield outcomes for network actors (Borgatti and Halgin 2011). Theorists have produced a wide array of concepts shedding light on how actors strategically embed in network structures or topologies, and seek to access or control resources and knowledge through these structures. First, they argue that individuals must be placed in the context of their social position, and thus "embedded action" is useful to understand behavior from the structure of social relations in network terms (Granovetter 1973, 1985). While network embedding is a generic trait of actionable strategies, different positional "embeddings" yield different action spaces for the actors that populate those positions or spaces.

The broker is a case in point. Brokers are known for gaining disproportionate control over the flow of information and resources in networks by
connecting otherwise distant regions. These regions are termed "structural
holes" and they are a source of network control because they facilitate the
flow of nonredundant information (Burt 1992). The strategy of professionals
who engage in brokerage is one of "divide and conquer" at the local network
level. Control over the process of bridging structural holes has to be kept
intact. The interest of professional brokers is to create and maintain structural holes, which is what makes them non-redundant actors in a system
(Kellogg 2014). This gives them autonomy to manipulate the content of
information and thus shape the way issues are treated. It also provides them
with opportunities to get new ideas about issue treatment (Burt 2005). Since
their positions within structural holes give them insights into different bodies
of professional knowledge, they can become "epistemic arbiters" that create
new concepts to shape future issue treatment (Seabrooke 2014a).

To flesh out what brokerage might look like in our two-level network
framework, we construct stylized scenarios of professional brokerage that
work within or across organizational networks through ties with their
professional peers (the professional network level). For simplicity we

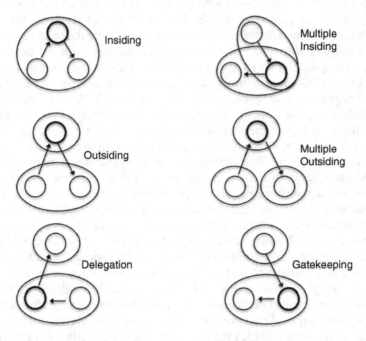

Figure 4.1 Brokerage Types (adapted from Gould and Fernandez
1989)

treat brokerage as a local directed triadic process whereby a professional task is being coordinated (Burt 1992). Our triadic process consists of a source actor, a destination actor, and a broker, where the latter is defined as an actor connecting two other actors that are not connected.[1]

We refer to insiding as a process of professional brokerage that occurs inside an organization. This scenario will be relevant for cases of issue control where competing issue treatments circulate within an organization (e.g., between departments dominated by economists and departments dominated by lawyers) and where the professional network structure inside the organization reveals structural holes occupied by professional brokers. These brokers can then use their privileged access to unconnected regions of an intra-organizational network to control how, where, and when alliances are formed between actors that promote competing issue treatment. The upside for the brokers here is that he/she can manipulate how information influences issue treatments between divergent professional groups. The downside is that autonomy is likely to erode in the longer run as social cohesion across groups expands. As an alternative strategy brokers can block the formation of alliances if he/she does not evaluate the outcomes of such alliances as beneficial for their idea about issue treatment. At times brokers are insiders in several organizations, such as when they are employed in dual positions. This is especially common with lawyers who are often employed in academia, in the market, and in policy at the same time. We refer to this particular network position as multiple insiding. Multiple insiders do not occupy structural holes in the traditional sense, even if their interorganizational ties are nonredundant. Instead, they act as "structural folds" by forming overlaps between organizational boundaries, allowing for the integration of issue treatment. Multiple insiders do not "divide and conquer" insofar as they thrive from processes of professional issue integration (Vedres and Stark 2010).

We refer to outsiding and multiple outsiding as processes of professional brokerage that occur across organizations. In the case of outsiding, a professional or a group of professionals from one organization uses a tie to a professional or group of professionals from another organization to push issues with competing professionals inside their own organization. The broker here will often rely on superior organizational authority in order to control changes in issue treatment. For instance, an economics unit in a large NGO that deals exclusively with human rights issues wants to push socioeconomic welfare issues but is met with resistance from the human rights lawyers who are keen to remain focused on civil and political rights. They are active in alerting a powerful World Bank department to the

---

[1] Our brokerage typology adapts and expands the terminology developed by Gould and Fernandez (1989).

opportunities of framing income inequality in human rights terms to attract support from other NGOs. The organizational-professional authority of the World Bank economists together with new funding opportunities convinces the human rights lawyers that there is traction in expanding their issue focus to also cover socioeconomic rights. A new issue alliance is formed. The World Bank insists on a definition of inequality and welfare that is compatible with their current projects and models which the human rights economists are forced to accept. And it can be even more complex, such as with cases of multiple outsiding where a professional from one organization seeks issue influence in a second organization through ties with a professional from a third-party organization.

Delegation occurs when brokers exert issue influence through extra-organizational ties through delegation from a colleague. Brokers in this case work from the inside and out. This configuration can come into place when brokers use ties from their professional association to get action outside their own environmental environment. A complementary process is gatekeeping when a professional from a different organization seeks influence on the colleague of a broker who in this case acts as a gatekeeper for influencing issue treatment inside his/her organization.

The different forms of brokerage can be used to draw analytical distinctions on professional strategies in two-level networks where professional activities take place within or between organizational boundaries in various constellations. A two-level network of organizations and professionals engaged in controlling issues in transnational governance can contain many or few local potential points of brokerage. According to Burt"s theory, this will tell the analyst about whether issue control is distributed or concentrated and where issue control is located. With relevant network data this typology also provides testable measures that can be verified qualitatively or quantitatively.

An Example and Some Measures

In the following hypothetical example we illustrate how data from the organizational affiliations of professionals can be used to construct a relational data matrix for SNA. We also introduce three centrality measures to characterize the network positions of various actors in our hypothetical example. In our hypothetical example we have a NGO, FoodJustice, two international organizations (IOs), the Global Food Programme (GFP) and the Transnational Health Authority (THA), and two firms engaged in the activity, OrgSpray Inc. and CropFast Inc.

FoodJustice has been very active in agenda-setting and has campaigned against spraying in the general public as well as engaging in intensive lobbying at the GFP and THA for an international Memorandum of Understanding banning the chemical spraying of crops. It has recently produced a highly influential report on the negative consequences of chemical spraying on public health around the world where CropFast was a running case. In addition, it has created an alliance with OrgSpray, which is a fast-growing corporation selling organic spraying substances. FoodJustice and OrgSpray are currently partnering up to develop a voluntary standard that will work to certify crops not yet subjected to any chemical spraying. They have also invited THA to join the standard as a public authority that may enable its implementation across a wide array of jurisdictions due to its extensive connections with national health authorities. GFP is highly skeptical of the banning of chemical spraying because the projected yield of global agricultural production is expected to drop, weakening food supply in a global market where demand is on the rise. GFP is about to publish a report on rising food prices in light of the imposition of stricter spraying regulations in Central American countries. It turns out that one of the key authors of this report used to work as an agricultural analyst for CropFast, which has large market shares in Central America.

We construct a network matrix based on the current and former affiliations of the team members working on the issue from each of the five organizations. We only count "strong" affiliations where employment has been for five years or more; that is, when a person has worked for two organizations for five years or more she ties those organizations together. This type of affiliation network is also referred to as a two-mode network, because it consists of two-actor modalities – in this case persons and organizations tie together through shared affiliations. For this analysis we use the most accessible SNA software UCINET, including its visualization package NetDraw. The two-mode network matrix in which persons are columns (coded according to their current employer) and organizations are rows where a person is coded as having an affiliation with an organization when the cell crossing the two modes is coded 1 (Table 4.1). If they do not have an affiliation the code is 0. This matrix can be imported directly into UCINET and NetDraw and analyzed.

By inspecting the visualized graph, as illustrated in Figure 4.1, we can gain an initial understanding of the issue-control dynamics involved in this case. Clearly, FoodJustice has been able to promote the issue transnationally because of close ties with various IOs and OrgSpray, which represents a competing nonchemical spraying technology. But the organizational agency of FoodJustice is closely linked to the professional network of their core anti-spraying campaign team member FJ1 who provides links to THA as well as OrgSpray.

Table 4.1 *Network Matrix Illustration*

	FoodJustice	GFP	THA	OrgSpray	CropFast
FJ1	1	0	1	1	0
FJ2	1	1	0	0	0
FJ3	1	0	0	0	0
FJ4	1	0	0	0	0
GFP1	0	1	0	0	0
GFP2	0	1	1	0	0
GFP3	1	1	0	0	0
GFP4	0	1	0	0	1
THA1	0	1	1	0	0
THA2	0	0	1	0	0
THA3	0	0	1	0	0
OS1	0	0	0	1	0
OS2	1	0	0	1	0
CF1	0	0	0	0	1
CF2	0	0	0	0	1
CF3	0	1	0	0	1

The importance of TJ1 is also reflected in his high network centrality score. In SNA, centrality analysis is perhaps the most oft-used way of establishing who has strategic advantages in a network. The most simple centrality measure is degree centrality, which is a simple count of the number of direct ties that an actor has in a network. While degree centrality is an adequate measure of local connectivity, it does not capture an actor's overall centrality in a network. To measure actors' overall centrality we use so-called geodesic measures, which take into account the number of paths that connect an actor with the overall network. Two actors who are connected directly have a geodesic path length of 1 whereas two actors connected indirectly by a third actor (brokerage) have a geodesic distance of 2. Closeness centrality is a measure of the average geodesic distance from one actor to all other actors in the network. Betweenness centrality, in contrast, counts the degree to which an actor "blocks" geodesic paths between other actors in the network, that is, whether other actors are dependent on that actor in terms of reaching others in the network (Freeman 1979). We provide the three normalized centrality scores for each of the team members in Table 4.2.

While FJ1 has been important as an issue entrepreneur, the chances of her making a difference in terms of convincing the GFP team members – and subsequently the management – that a Memorandum of Understanding on banning should be promoted are slim. Here, there is

Table 4.2 *Actor Ranking by Normalized Centrality Scores*

	Degree	Closeness	Betweenness
FJ1	0.6	0.636	0.258
GFP4	0.4	0.593	0.15
CF3	0.4	0.593	0.15
FJ2	0.4	0.686	0.143
GFP3	0.4	0.686	0.143
GFP2	0.4	0.66	0.104
THA1	0.4	0.66	0.104
OS2	0.4	0.538	0.06
FJ3	0.2	0.507	0
FJ4	0.2	0.507	0
GFP1	0.2	0.538	0
THA2	0.2	0.493	0
THA3	0.2	0.493	0
OS1	0.2	0.393	0
CF1	0.2	0.385	0
CF2	0.2	0.385	0

a fierce competitive struggle between the linkers of CropFast, THA, and FoodJustice to GFP. In this hypothetical case we do not decide on an outcome of this struggle but point to the tensions going on around GFP. Given that betweenness is the more important network characteristic, we might predict that CropFast will be the winner in terms of the high betweenness of its connectors. Yet, this betweenness is mostly generated by them being the exclusive connectors of CropFast staff to the rest of the network. By contrast, striking the big deal on banning, closeness centrality might prove more useful because it allows being the gravitational point which enables the bringing together of a diversity of actors to negotiate where the issue should be headed.

Now we have an affiliation network that shows how our various issue professionals are linked to the organizations. We have a rough idea of who may have power within the network based on their ties to different organizations. To get a better understanding of the agency involved among the various brokers in the network, it will be useful to take a closer look at the career sequences of team members. This would allow us to investigate if there is a relationship between the background of their positions and the roles that they might substantially play in terms of the issue of banning. Careers can reveal important characteristics about actors' experiential backgrounds and may illuminate important aspects of how actors ended up occupying certain network positions. They can also suggest how issue professionals navigate those positions in their own favor.

Sequence Analysis

Most quantitative analyses of historical transitions focus on explaining events as outcomes and not as processes that carry structure. In contrast, sequence analysis contributes to a more holistic approach to social processes, understanding singular states as embedded in the process of unfolding that is a sequence. In this perspective what comes after a certain temporal state may be equally important to what comes before. The present is not merely a result of the past but also inscribed in percep-tions of the future. While there is a literature in international political economy literature that deals explicitly with sequencing of events (Posner 2010), we suggest that sequences of careers are important in understand-ing two-mode professional and organizational networks. In this sense it is part of an armory of prosopographic methods (the study of groups). Prosopographic methods commonly include "field" methods inspired by Pierre Bourdieu and others, as well as those who focus on the importance of narrative structures rather than assuming causality from the static macro–micro–macro chain of logic that permeates the social sciences (Abbott 2001). While other prosopographic methods concentrate on posi-tion taking within a field (see Dezalay and Madsen, this volume), multiple corresponding social factors (Le Roux and Rouanet 2009), and ethnogra-phy (Harrington, this volume), we suggest that sequence analysis can tell us a great deal about individuals within a group and how they operate within their social system (Blanchard 2011). One form of sequence analy-sis is to trace careers. Tracing professional careers is one means of creating a narrative. When combined with network analysis we suggest that this approach is able to tell us a great deal about propensities within the system under study. In other words, it can tell us about likely outcomes rather than isolated causes. Careers are a good target for these forms of analysis because careers often follow predictable "ladders" where single moves are embedded in path-dependent systems. Deviation from "normal" careers is then also interesting, especially if those concerned are more central within a network.

We identify career structures by using an optimal matching (OM) analysis of sequences. OM algorithms have been derived from bioinfor-matics and applied in medical and biological sciences (think of DNA strands) and, more recently, sociology and political science (Abbott 2001; Abbott and Tsay 2000; Seabrooke and Nilsson 2015). In parti-cular, the OM method has been applied to a range of cases (Abbott and Hrycak 1990), including the rise of female executives in finance (Blair-Loy 1999), the transnational emergence of welfare systems (Abbott and Deviney 1992), environmental standard-setting (Henriksen 2015;

Henriksen and Seabrooke 2016), and the role of consultants in the IMF (Seabrooke and Nilsson 2015). OM assesses sequences of information to assess the degree of similarity or difference among them by using pattern search algorithms. The basic technique provided by the OM algorithm is to identify differences in sequences and then the "cost" of transforming one chain of sequences into others. This transformation is done through insertions, deletions, and substitutions. The OM algorithm works its way through all dyadic pairs of sequences in a given set, seeking to find the most efficient way of transforming one sequence into another. The output is a measure of difference between sequences, which equals the cost of the transformation (Stovel et al. 1996). Relatively similar sequences thus require less work than sequences that are relatively more different. The assignment of costs is one of the key aspects of this method and the focus of controversy is how this approach generated results (Hollister 2009), which we address below.

Let's consider the affiliation matrix generated in the previous section and then think about the location of the individuals and what their career experience may mean for how they are located in the network. This relationship between career experience and network position may be an attribute of the individual, such as being highly prestigious in one kind of job, or because they are known for their mixed career experience and broader knowledge on the issue at hand. A more central network location may also be because a particular organization has chosen to support them. So there are some important chicken-and-egg questions here that can only be unraveled with other qualitative information such as interviews, ethnographic techniques, and the use of field methods (see the other contributions in this section of the book). Still, we plough on.

If we take all the individuals noted earlier and work through their CVs, their LinkedIn accounts, and have phone calls or personal interviews with them to verify their career history, then we can code their careers into some reasonable states.

GOVgen	Generalist at a government agency
GOVspec	Specialist at a government agency
NGOgen	Generalist working for an NGO
NGOspec	Specialist working for an NGO
IOgen	Generalist working for an international organization
IOspec	Specialist working for an international organization
MNCgen	Generalist working for an MNC
MNCspec	Specialist working for an MNC

Table 4.3 *Career Sequence Illustration*

	1995	2000	2005	2010	2015
FJ1	IOspec	MNCspec	IOspec	MNCspec	NGOspec
FJ2	GOVgen	GOVgen	IOgen	GOVgen	NGOgen
FJ3	MNCspec	MNCspec	NGOspec	NGOspec	NGOspec
FJ4	NGOgen	GOVgen	NGOgen	NGOgen	NGOgen
GFP1	GOVgen	IOgen	IOgen	IOgen	IOgen
GFP2	GOVspec	IOspec	MNCspec	IOspec	IOspec
GFP3	GOVgen	GOVgen	IOgen	IOgen	IOgen
GFP4	MNCgen	MNCgen	MNCgen	MNCgen	IOgen
THA1	MNCspec	MNCspec	MNCspec	IOspec	IOspec
THA2	GOVgen	IOgen	IOgen	IOgen	IOgen
THA3	GOVgen	IOgen	GOVgen	IOgen	IOgen
OS1	MNCspec	MNCspec	MNCspec	MNCspec	MNCspec
OS2	GOVspec	GOVspec	GOVgen	NGOgen	MNCgen
CF1	MNCspec	MNCspec	MNCspec	MNCspec	MNCspec
CF2	NGOgen	NGOgen	GOVgen	GOVgen	MNCgen
CF3	GOVgen	IOgen	IOgen	MNCgen	MNCgen

The coding must be relevant to the case. For this one we have the specification of generalist or specialist in order to give us information about their kind of work role within the organization, and whether their skills are transferrable across organizational platforms or whether they follow special skills related to the issue at hand. Both scenarios are also possible. We could have also coded for formal training (agricultural economist and others, for example) or for professional association (American Association of Agronomy and others, for example). For this case we suggest that a mix of organizational types and the distinction between generalized and specialized work roles is most appropriate. Following this we have coded the actors in our hypothetical in Table 4.3 for five-year intervals, from 1995 to 2015.

The next step is to assign the cost of moving between different states in the system. The assignment of each transformation (insertion, deletion, and substitution) has a "cost," which can be determined in a deductive or inductive manner. To determine the cost deductively a matrix is developed with assigned for all dyadic pairs of states. Here, the cost should reflect the "social effort" of making the transition between two states. In OM analyses there has been much discussion about how to assign costs and the benefits of focusing on substitutions in specified time periods rather than uneven career sequences and relying on time-warping insertions and deletions (Gauthier et al. 2009; Lesnard 2010). Costs can also

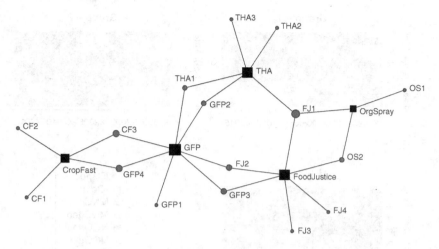

Figure 4.2 Affiliation Network Graph

be assigned inductively by calculating transition rates based on the observed sequences. Here, transitions that are less frequent will be assigned a higher cost based on the assumption that the social effort of making the transition is high. Here the logic may be that the social effort also carries a great risk. So, for example, making a move from being a specialist for a MNC to a generalist for a government agency may entail a higher social effort and risk than a transition from being a specialist for a MNC to a specialist for a NGO. In the former case the peer network involved may view the move as "one way" in that the individual concerned would lose professional prestige among her or his peers and not be able to go back to the former career position. Following this logic a move from being a MNCspec to GOVgen may cost "3" while a move from MNCspec to NGOspec may only cost "1." For this hypothetical example we have followed the default settings in the software package, which assigns transformation as a cost of "2."

Following these settings and the application of the OM algorithm the individuals and their career sequences are then matched up and placed into clusters or groups. Figure 4.2 contains the three groups generated by applying the OM algorithm to this population and their careers.

From the optimal matching we can distinguish three clear groups and the career structures they exhibit (Figure 4.3). Each line across represents an individual and their career. We can see that Group 1 is dominated by

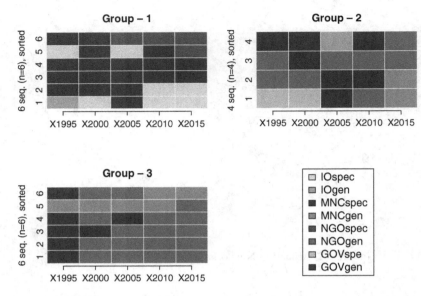

Figure 4.3 Three Career Types (For full colour images please refer to www.professionalnetworks.org)

specialists who work for MNCs, with significant transitions from being a specialist for a MNC into working as a specialist for NGOs and for IOs. The individual who is line 1 in this group, who is GFP2, has a mixed career and has been able to use her specialized skills across a range of organizational types. If we refer back to Figure 4.1, we can see that this person is a broker between GFP and THA. The other broker, THA1, is line 2 in Group 1 and has had a career of working for a MNC and then into an IO. We suggest that GFP2's mixed career experience places them in a good position for issue control and how the issue is treated by the IO community. Even more central to the network is FJ1, who is line 5 in Group 1 and is someone who exhibits "revolving doors" in moving as a specialist between IOs, MNCs, and a NGO. Again, we suggest that FJ1's mixed career history while maintaining a career as a specialist is why she is the most central person in the network and the only one linking up an IO, NGO, and MNC. Group 1 also includes some people who have had "vanilla" careers and only one transition, and these same people, such as FJ2, OS1, and CF1, are isolates in Figure 4.1 (and lines 6, 3, and 4, respectively).

Group 2 is a mixed bag of careers with a high number of transitions between different states. The individual who is in line 1 in this group, OS2, has started as a specialist in a government role and then transitioned to working as a generalist across all of the organizational types, suggesting that he is someone known for organizational capacities. Looking back at Figure 4.1, this person is a broker between FoodJustice and OrgSpray. Another interesting aspect of Group 2 is that those placed here are nearly all generalists with high mobility, suggesting that these people are the ones establishing the architecture and modalities for discussion, if not providing the key scientific content on banning particular chemicals. These issue professionals are the ones who can embed decisions made about banning into their organizational types while those in Group 1 are more likely to control the content of technical discussions.

Group 3 is a group of generalists with lesser mobility than Group 2. We can see here that there is a common career path of being a generalist for a government agency and then becoming a generalist for an IO. This group also has isolates, such as THA2 and THA3 (lines 2 and 4). The powerful brokers in the network are not in this group, but located in Group 1, in particular, and also in Group 2.

Software

Multiple SNA software packages are available to perform calculations and visualizations of network data. The packages most commonly used by beginners are UCINET and Netdraw (Borgatti et al. 2014). UCINET has a range of different functions for managing network data and calculating measures of structural properties at the network-, group- and actor levels, including various centrality measures. Netdraw has an accessible graphical user interface to do simple network visualizations. Both packages are useful for small- to medium-sized networks, but work less well for large-scale networks or time series analysis. For such purposes the SNA packages written for the R statistical software environment are more appropriate (e.g., statnet or sna), although they do require some prior familiarity with R programming language. Sequence analysis can also be performed in the R package TraMineR, which we did for our illustrative sequence analysis (Gabadinho et al. 2011). TraMineR contains functions to calculate a wide range of sequence measures and various algorithms to generate sequence measures (e.g., OM).

Conclusion

This chapter presents the basics of network analysis and sequence analysis and how their integration is important for understanding professional-organizational networks. Our hypothetical case demonstrates the power of these methods in revealing new information that we would not see if we stuck to reading organizations' behavior by their organizational type, or if we clustered professionals into standard interest group analyses. Rather, we suggest that issue professionals can use careers strategically to enhance their chances at issue control and place themselves centrally within professional and organizational networks.

Part II

Professionals and Non-Governmental Organizations

5   Contested Professionalization in a Weak
Transnational Field

Ole Jacob Sending

A key feature of humanitarianism is that relief is to be offered on the basis of needs, and not political loyalty, religion, or some other factors. It is arguably the single most important way in which humanitarian actors can claim to stand above or outside 'politics'. This makes the definition of what constitutes needs an important one, since it is the dominant operative rule for how to allocate resources to victims of humanitarian crises. Prior to the 1990s, humanitarian workers had principally relied on their practical experience and rules of thumb to make decisions about what type of needs existed and how to address them. Over time, however, scientific measures to identify and measure needs took over, in the form of 'needs assessments'. The emergence of so-called 'evidence-based humanitarian action' – of which needs assessment is a key component – is interesting because it challenges the position of those that have traditionally been dominating in debates about things humanitarian: those with extensive field experience, whose claim to authority is based not on abstract knowledge but on hard-to-codify rules of thumb of what works and what does not in humanitarian crises (cf. Sending 2017).

I analyse the emergence of and contestation over the reliance on needs assessments and on 'evidence-based action' as a conflict over what constitutes a source of professionalism in the humanitarian field. The humanitarian professional has traditionally devalued what is generally considered the hallmark of professionalism – the reliance on abstract knowledge to define and control certain issues and attendant tasks (Abbott 1988). Part of the reason for the privileging of practical experience over abstract knowledge stems from the fact that humanitarian relief is already made up of a range of highly specialized professional actors from medicine, nutrition, sanitation, logistics, etc. What unites them is the distinct attributes of a humanitarian situation in which these different professionals work, in particular the stress on working in difficult, often extreme, situations to save lives. I argue below that those with humanitarian field experience have strategically nurtured and deployed the uniqueness of the situation of humanitarian crises as a source of professional authority against the pressure to rely on standardized tools such as needs assessments. They have combined this claim about the supremacy of practical experience with another key feature of humanitarian relief: the claim to speak on behalf of and being witnesses for victims of humanitarian crises.

The move towards professionalization of the humanitarian field since the late 1990s – through such initiatives as Sphere, discussed below – indicates that the humanitarian field is being transformed and that practical experience from humanitarian crises is no longer sufficient alone to establish authority or issue control. I attribute this outcome to two primary factors highlighted by the editors in their introduction. First, these actors' source of professional authority hails from a claim to the uniqueness of humanitarian crises, including the temporal dimension of having to make decisions quickly. As such, it is hardly amenable to codification and thus abstraction, a key source of professional authority. Second, the organizational logic where these humanitarian workers are employed is fundamentally shaped by their most important constituency – their donors. The push for 'professionalization' and the use of more 'objective' methods to assess needs came in no small part from donors, telling humanitarian organizations that they had to better demonstrate efficiency, effectiveness, and accountability. This organizational logic trumps the logic of the network of humanitarian professionals: there is a structural obstacle for humanitarian professionals to network and build momentum across different organizations because of the particular relationship that humanitarian organizations have with donors. And this feature of the field of humanitarian relief tells us something important: while it is distinct and autonomous as a task and issue – controlled by humanitarian professionals – it is not so politically and financially. There were, and are, few avenues available to humanitarian professionals to mobilize *across* humanitarian organizations within their networks to challenge overall humanitarian policy. This is not so much because of a lack of strength of these professional networks, but rather because of the structurally weak position of humanitarian organizations to challenge state policies on humanitarian issues – what we can call the lack of relative autonomy of the field of humanitarian relief.

The Humanitarian System as a Field

The humanitarian system is defined by three key features. First, it is networked in that there is no discernible organizational hierarchy. This holds for most fields of global governance, but in the humanitarian system the network assumes a much more horizontal character: while the International Committee of the Red Cross (ICRC) is the guardian of the

Geneva Conventions and is arguably *primus inter pares*, the humanitarian system is divided into sub-issues over which some organizations have a greater issue control than others, but where overall authority to govern the system is lacking (Barnett 2011). The United Nations High Commissioner for Refugees (UNHCR) is central to refugee governance, as is the World Food Programme (WFP) on food aid, for example. Second, the system is characterized by strong community norms about what it means to be a humanitarian actor, with policing by humanitarian actors of those that are seen to violate these norms. Debates within the humanitarian field turn to a considerable degree on what humanitarian actors' identity is and what constitutes appropriate humanitarian action. A case in point is how other humanitarian actors reacted to what was then seen as a violation on the part of the Médecins Sans Frontières (MSF) of a constitutive norm of humanitarian action – that of neutrality – in Ethiopia in 1984 (Kennedy 2008). Feldmand (2007) notes that moral dilemmas are inherent in the humanitarian field, but these dilemmas derive their poignancy from the fact that the actors in the field commit to and share the substantive values that define humanitarian action. In other fields, there is less sharing of such substantive, identity-defining values, and debates in the humanitarian field are to a considerable degree fuelled by implicit or explicit tensions between different interpretations of these substantive values (Sending 2015b).

Third, and most importantly, the humanitarian field has limited autonomy from its political environment. With Steinmetz (2008), we may say that the humanitarian field is 'settled', being defined by a shared conception of the evaluative criteria by which to judge what constitutes proper humanitarian action. Most fields that are settled also enjoy relative autonomy. Not so with the field of humanitarian relief: its boundaries are simply not strong enough to withstand external pressure, and the very nature of the issues over which they have control is *caused* by events external to the field itself, such as war and natural disasters. Certainly, non-state actors are everywhere in the humanitarian field, and some of the most powerful ones, such as ICRC and Oxfam, are arguably more powerful than some inter-governmental organizations, set up by states for the same purpose (Sending 2015a). And yet, humanitarian organizations are everywhere dependent, often on states, for their funding and operations.

This is not to say that states are always more powerful than non-state actors. Far from it. It is an empirical question as to what types of resources (symbolic or material) count as 'power' in any given social setting. China and Russia, for example, are not active participants in the field of humanitarian relief, and are therefore not influential *participants* in the field as such. They are nonetheless important in shaping the framework conditions for humanitarian action through their membership in the UN Security Council. Moreover, states have specific power resources at their disposal that should be differentiated. States acting as donors have the power of the purse to shape NGOs' behaviour in specific ways, for example, by incentivizing them to adopt certain standards, or by demanding mechanisms for accountability for how funds are used. The upshot of this is that there are both direct and indirect forms of influence on the field of humanitarian relief. This is why it is important to capture how and when humanitarian actors can be said to have different types of autonomy from outside forces.

Because humanitarian actors operate within parameters set by other actors in this way, it becomes important to specify how network logics and organizational logics combine in distinct ways: the more autonomous the field, the more avenues exist to mobilize through professional networks across different organizations. A relative lack of autonomy privileges, I argue, organizational logics as a driver of change, since external actors – states in particular – apply their levers on organizations and interact with these. As I detail below, the professionalization of the field of humanitarian relief, with introduction of so-called evidence-based decision-making and standardized practices, occurred through a push from donors, prompting humanitarian organizations to coordinate to develop standards, leaving humanitarian professionals within these organizations to follow suit, with few avenues to explore alternative arenas for mobilizing professional networks independent of their employers. The more humanitarian actors are dependent on states for their funding and ability to operate, the more important organizational logics will be in shaping the relative influence and position of professional networks. Conversely, a humanitarian actor whose operations are funded mostly by private sources is more susceptible to changes dominated by professional networks that cut across organizations.

Practical Experience, Proximity, and Needs

In *Distant Suffering*, Boltanski (1999: 24) notes – with reference to the 'politics of pity' – that the description of suffering cannot merely be factual. Boltanski avers that

factual description exists and functions within a system of representation resting on a subject-object kind of set-up. This structure is appropriate for representations of nature, but when persons are being described it can always be criticized in the name of common humanity.

The implication is that those that observe suffering – in seeking to describe and explain it – are immediately forced to do so in a way that can serve to fuse observation with action. They are engaged in the production of a 'motivated truth' (Redfield 2006) – one that is driven by a concern with alleviating suffering. At the same time, the subject–object structure of representations means that the object – individuals in humanitarian crises – will tend to be described in such a way that the agency to relieve suffering rests primarily with the subject describing things, not the object being described.

While this subject–object structure is a generic one for all forms of governance, it has a distinct significance in the field of humanitarian relief. How is this structure implicated in how humanitarian actors engage one another and compete for positions of control over particular issues or tasks? What are the resources – material and symbolic – that are brought to bear? Humanitarian organizations seek to establish themselves as credible and authoritative through claims to them having a unique access to and proximity to those in need – they lay claim to issue control through 'knowing the victim'. The most important aspect of this type of knowledge is that which is about the victim's 'needs', since it is the operationalization of humanitarian principles. Traditionally, the subjective identification of humanitarian professionals with those in need, and their drawing upon past experience and practice of how to operate in crises, was the bedrock of humanitarian action. Seasoned humanitarians would arrive, draw on tested methods for how to assess the situation and the needs of the local population, and get on with the job. The humanitarian actor, in flak jacket, represented both the subjective and the objective dimension of needs: the commitment to identify with and speak for victims of the crisis was fused with the supposedly objective measures that came from established practice and experience. That the outside world would take humanitarian actors' statements about needs – based on their experience and judgement – at face value is an indication of high levels of trust, which is a key element of professional authority (Aboott 1988; Halvorsen 1995).

Their claim to control the content of these tasks is bound up with their authority to determine where the boundary between the humanitarian and 'political' is to be drawn. That authority is grounded in references to International Humanitarian Law and to claims about the unique experience and expertise that humanitarian actors have to operate in emergency situations (whether caused by natural disasters or by violent conflict). Hugo Slim (2005) has observed, for example, that the stress on moral purity by humanitarian actors is part and parcel of how they maintain their authority vis-à-vis others. Liisa Malkki (1996) has described how the continual construction of humanitarianism as outside of politics affects how humanitarian actors categorize, understand, and interact with refugees. Humanitarian practices of organizing and producing knowledge of refugees work to silence the refugees' own histories, privileging instead 'physical, non-narrative evidence', since the latter operates at the level of the moral and humanitarian, not historical and political. Malkki notes that

history tended to get leached out of the figure of the refugee, as imagined by their administrators. This active process of dehistoricization was inevitably also a project of depoliticization. For to speak about the past, about the historical trajectory that had led the Hutu as refugees into the western Tanzanian countryside, was to speak about politics. This could not be encouraged by the camp administrators; political activism and refugee status were mutually exclusive here, as in international refugee law more generally (1996: 385).

The tendency to engage in depoliticization is characteristic of all humanitarian organizations. The example of Medicins Sans Frontieres (MSF) is instructive in this context, as its genesis shows how professional logics fused with the particulars of humanitarian ideals to shape organizations' self-presentation and operations. The Biaffra secession is typically said to be the founding moment of the MSF: frustrated with the ICRC's complacency in not criticizing the warring parties, some humanitarian individuals established the MSF to chart a new type of humanitarianism. Govi nuances this picture by drawing attention to distinctively professional aspects of those working within humanitarian organizations:

At a time when humanitarian expertise was only starting to take shape, MSF was viewed by its founders as a tool for bolstering the role of medical experts in the aid apparatus ... MSF's members, who professed that they were not 'secular saints' but 'men and women who have chosen a profession whose principal end is to serve humanity, and which they intend to implement so as to realise this purpose (Govi 2011: 52).

The role and status of professional groups is, in this light, a key part of the story of humanitarianism. Put differently, if the claimed universalism of humanitarian ideals is what shields humanitarian actors from regarding themselves as political, the practical mechanism through which this is made possible is the insistence that their advocacy flows from their role as bearing witness and in providing qualitatively better and different knowledge about crisis situations. Because they are present in conflict areas, and because they give victims of humanitarian crises shelter, food, and medicine, they can also represent those who cannot speak for themselves by bearing witness and speaking out on their behalf. This claim to representation is fused with an epistemic claim to authority in that humanitarian actors are able, by virtue of their presence, to report on violations of international humanitarian law, on the needs of the victims, on the logistical and political challenges of delivering relief, etc. This fusion of claims to both moral and epistemic authority is most clearly expressed in the ideology of MSF, where advocacy is seen to flow

directly from ... experience in the field, through medical data and eyewitness accounts ... Conceiving of fieldwork as a filter for advocacy initiatives implies that we are obliged to report what is happening when faced with the consequences. It also implies that we confront political actors with their responsibility (DuBois 2008: 1).

A central feature of the humanitarian relief is that advocacy is not seen as political. Such advocacy is either seen to be with reference to universal principles, in which case it is a matter of holding states to account for their legal obligations, or it is reporting on or serving as a channel of communication from victims to the international community and so the individual – defined in terms of basic needs or rights (more on this below) – figures as a source of, or manifestation of, universality. Beyond the idea of witnessing as a source of advocacy, humanitarian actors' mere presence in areas where a humanitarian crisis is unfolding is, in the eyes of other actors, a central source of their authority. The identification with the victim as a source of both epistemic and moral authority vis-à-vis the outside world is intimately linked to the humanitarian identity. The following description of professionalism as being intimately linked to demonstrating passion and dedication without regard for monetary or other rewards is here important:

To be a true member of the group one had to demonstrate passion, devotion, selflessness and a rebellious spirit – all driven by a concern for others, not self-interest. A proper humanitarian likewise deferred obligations to kin to care for strangers. Such transcendent dedication was difficult for national staff to demonstrate, weighed down as they were by their local connections (Redfield 2012: 367).

The traditional image of humanitarian actors – of the seasoned field operative, in flack jacket – was called upon to manage humanitarian responses. This ideal of practical experience and lived life in crises feeds on a distinction between what Hannah Arendt called vita activa and vita contemplativa, with the former prevailing over the latter (Arendt 1958). This is a central part of the humanitarian identity: the tasks over which humanitarians seek control are all about action, speed, and operational capacity. Biographies and practitioners' accounts of professional careers as humanitarian actors often center on their efforts to save lives in difficult, often dangerous, situations (Egeland 2009).

Luc Boltanski (1999) links this aspect of humanitarianism to a 'culture of authenticity'. But it must also be understood against the backdrop of how such authenticity is produced and how the mark of authenticity may change over time. This is where the professional dynamics of humanitarian organizations become important: what used to be the hallmark of authenticity – witnessing and local knowledge – now increasingly operates alongside technically produced needs assessments and systematic analyses, based on scientific methods. And the increased importance of such tools for producing authenticity is in part a result of the structural features of the field of humanitarian relief (Krause 2014), where state actors – acting as donors or as hosts to humanitarian operations – have shaped humanitarian organizations in significant ways.

Granted, certain technical skills and competencies have always been of paramount importance – in sanitation, medicine, nutrition, logistics, etc. But this technical aspect of humanitarian relief has historically been overshadowed by the ability to put these to use effectively 'in the field' and to produce authenticity through witnessing and demonstrating proximity to those in need. The upshot of this has been that academic credentials and scholarly research are not accorded any significance as a source of learning or guidance. This extends to the culture inside humanitarian organizations also at headquarters. A former employee at a major humanitarian organization told me how, upon telling her boss that a friend had recently finalized a master's degree in humanitarian studies, he responded: 'Oh no, she's become PhD positive.'[1] Such views of academic or abstract knowledge – a hallmark of professional power, as the editors note in their introduction – are often devalued by humanitarian actors. There are frequent references to academic knowledge being of little relevance. One humanitarian actor noted flatly that 'research has a bad name'; another brought attention to the temporal dimension of humanitarian work – 'we have no time for research, we have to get the job done'; while yet others referred to 'the interests of the victims comes first, all the rest is bullshit' and that 'research is a luxury we can't afford'.[2] This privileging of experience over generic knowledge is distinct for the humanitarian field, and offers a clue to the types of professional logics that prevail within and between professional networks and humanitarian organizations.

This has changed in significant ways over the last two decades, where highly specialized techniques for assessing needs – 'needs assessments' – prevail as the source from which to determine needs and thus to operationalize the principle of impartiality. And this transformation is best understood in terms of the combined effects of professional logics internal to the field, and the structural features of humanitarian relief, where state actors have set new parameters for humanitarian action, demanding more accountability and hard evidence of efficiency in operations.

---

[1] Personal communication, Oslo, October 2011.
[2] Interviews UNHCR (#2), ICRC (#3), OCHA (#1), respectively.

The Humanitarian Self as Expert and the Emergence of 'Evidence-Based Policymaking'

According to the conventional story, two factors were critical in the emergence of highly technical and regulated 'needs assessments'. First, humanitarian organizations themselves had already in the early 1990s started to develop some standards for humanitarian relief in an effort to 'professionalize' humanitarianism (Buchanan–Smith 2003).[3] Second, humanitarian organizations did a lot of soul searching after the series of conflicts in the Great Lakes region in the mid-1990s and the Rwanda genocide in particular. They had helped genocidaires and made decisions on behalf of civilians – refugees and IDPs – that later proved disastrous. Donors grew wary of the accountability of humanitarian organizations and demanded greater oversight and more objective measures of 'needs'. These concerns motivated the Joint Evaluation of Emergency Assistance to Rwanda (JEEAR), the third study report of which (Eriksson et al. 1996) helped advance the idea of formulating standards to be used in delivering and prioritizing humanitarian relief and to produce account-ability vis-à-vis donors. That donors were inclined to push for such changes in the humanitarian sector must, in turn, be linked to the more general trend towards an 'audit culture' (Strathern 2000) and associated push to establish 'evidence-based' humanitarian decision-making. Taking their cue from debates within medicine from the late 1970s onwards about ways to move from medical practice based on the indivi-dual doctor's experience to systematic evidence on what works (Bradt 2009).

When analysed in terms of the analytical tools introduced by Henriksen and Seabrooke, however, a different interpretation can be offered, which supplements some of the pioneering work done on state–NGO relations (Cooley and Ron 2002) and on advocacy networks (Keck and Sikkink 1998). Research on state–NGO relations has demonstrated how states indirectly shape the agenda of NGOs, how pressure for accountability leads to stronger emphasis on professionalization within NGOs. And the research on the role and functioning of advocacy networks has similarly identified factors that help explain issue-emergence, particularly as regards humanitarian issues, whether in terms of attributes of the issue in question, the existence of norm-entrepreneurs, or the availability of a favourable pool of norms to support it (Carpenter 2007). While network properties have been found to be of importance (Carpenter 2011), the framework offered in this volume – with its focus on both network logics

---

[3] Interview by phone with former humanitarian official, 8 November 2012.

and organizational logics – foregrounds the importance of capturing how the structural features of any given issue-area or field impact on the available resources of specific actors both within and across different organizations to advance their objectives. The explanation for the triumph of a particular mode of demonstrating 'authenticity' in terms of technical measures of needs has to do with how donors' push to introduce standards shifted the balance within humanitarian organizations between those with extensive experience from crisis situations to those in charge of donor contact and resource mobilization. In a nutshell, humanitarian professionals with career trajectories defined by successive stints in humanitarian crises were unable to contest the move to standardize how to measure 'needs' and allocate time and resources on its basis. And they were not able to do so – I argue – because of the structural holes that existed, and exist today, barring against the formation of networks that cut across organizational boundaries. As long as donors were relatively hands off and did not demand much in the way of accountability and measurement of how funds were allocated between different groups, humanitarian professionals with extensive field experience ruled within their respective organization. Once humanitarian organizations were forced to standardize and draw up rules for the measurement of needs as a means to placate donor concerns, those responsible for resource mobilization and contact with donors at headquarters became de facto standard setters for those operating in the field. They were transformed from back-office support of the sharp end of humanitarian relief to being standard-setters for those delivering relief in crises.

The push for evidence-based humanitarian action had been long in the making. Already in the 1970s epidemiological studies made their way into debates about how to organize humanitarian relief more effectively. Studying the effects of the cyclone that hit Bangladesh in late 1970, Sommer and Mosley (1972) argued in the *Lancet* that the use of systematically collected and analysed data was missing and could have improved the humanitarian response significantly. During the 1970s and 1980s, a string of studies emerged that similarly brought epidemiological methods from public health to bear on how to collect and analyse data about humanitarian crises (Noji and Toole 1997). In that sense, Walker and Purdin (2004) are correct in stating that humanitarian actors had already started a process aimed at 'professionalization' prior to the Sphere project and the large push for such a process in the aftermath of the Rwanda evaluation.

Nonetheless, the move towards 'professionalization' and so-called evidence-based decision-making took off as part of donors' demands for stronger accountability mechanisms, who wanted clearer demonstration of effectiveness of use and impact. The resulting initiatives to establish new methods to measure needs by using scientific tools ran against the authority of humanitarian professionals, which was based on claims to proximity to those in need and experience-based judgements about proper action. The push for professionalization was resisted by humanitarian professionals, for it was a direct challenge to their very source of authority, and professionalism, within humanitarian organizations. Today, some twenty years after it was initiated, this process of professionalization is fairly well institutionalized, with significant implications for what constitutes proper humanitarian work and skills of humanitarian professionals. And yet, there is a strong ambivalence towards such methods.

Needs Assessments and Organizational Rivalry

The most significant outcome of these efforts to establish professional standards for humanitarian relief is the Sphere project, which brings together most of the major humanitarian organizations. The cornerstone of Sphere is the 'Humanitarian Charter', which describes 'the core principles that govern humanitarian action and asserts the right of populations to protection and assistance' (Sphere 2000: 1). Other important initiatives include the Active Learning Network for Accountability and Performance in Humanitarian Action (ALNAP) and efforts by the UN-led Inter-Agency Standing Committee (IASC) to establish professional standards and codes of conduct for humanitarian agencies such as UNHCR and the Office for the Coordination of Humanitarian Affairs (OCHA) (Harvey et al. 2010).

With 'needs' being the operationalization of the core principle of impartiality, the stakes in the field revolve very much around *how* needs are to be assessed and what type of *role* or agency that the humanitarian actor gets from it. That is, the proximity to and identification with suffering individuals is the prevailing criterion of evaluation for receiving and giving recognition. What constituted 'needs' and how they should be prioritized and balanced were primarily for humanitarian actors to determine, based on their practical experience and attendant judgement. Here, the use of judgement on the part of humanitarian actors was central. With needs assessments becoming central to how organizations were organized and could secure funding, judgements are transported from the seasoned relief worker's agency in emergencies and to those that perform and use needs assessments. In accordance with Seabrooke (2014a), we can say that those responsible for donor contact and resource mobilization become something akin to 'epistemic arbiters' in that they assemble and communicate to others technically produced measures of 'need'.

While needs assessments are very much determined by practical challenges and the availability of data, there is considerable ideological debate about what constitutes proper and good standards for relief work. Note that needs assessments are meant to transcend the gap between relief workers and victims of humanitarian crises by bringing the affected populations into humanitarian decision-making. There is a doxic flair to statements by humanitarian organizations that needs assessments are absolutely necessary for humanitarian relief to be delivered at all. Introducing a study of efforts to establish joint needs assessments across the humanitarian field, the authors note, for example, that '[w]ithout accurate and timely information about humanitarian needs, it is not possible to provide effective and efficient responses that meet those needs' (Currion and Willits-King 2012: 1). Another study brings out the extent to which the introduction of technical needs assessments is tempered by the previously dominant category of humanitarian actors' experience-based judgement:

The humanitarian enterprise, more than many areas of human endeavour, takes place in operating environments that fall far short of ideal, . . . [R]isk analysis and needs assessment in these environments is not an exact science. Good approximations, based on sound judgement, experience and analysis, are the basis of appropriate responses (Darcy and Hofman 2003: 9).

Needs assessments are tailored to get 'as close as possible to the individual in need of help' – but they are simultaneously tailored to the mandate and expertise of each humanitarian actor. One study finds that '[a]ssessment typically is subsumed within a process of resource mobilisation, with assessments being conducted by agencies in order to substantiate funding proposals to donors' (Darcy and Hofman 2003: 5). Another review notes, seeking to explain why system-wide or joint needs assessments are few and far between, that needs assessments are both a technical exercise and a political asset (Ramalingam and Mitchell 2008). As one respondent put it: 'The World Food Program, given their mandate and expertise, will never conclude from a needs assessment that there is no need for food aid.'[4] This feature of the humanitarian field, that there is a communitarian feel to humanitarian organizations yet fierce competition for funding, suggests that this is not so much a story of 'turf battles' between humanitarian actors, since the positions and strategies that different actors take cannot be reduced to the size of the budgets sought.

The introduction of needs assessments, and the 'trust in numbers' relative to practically grounded judgement of humanitarian actors, indicates a

---

[4] Interview, Official Hum Org UK, January 2012.

change in the humanitarian field about sources of authority to govern: humanitarianism has become professionalized, where judgements on what to do and how to do it are increasingly seen to flow from a professionally agreed-upon knowledge base that includes standards, guidelines, and best practices. Indeed, what is at stake in the field is the identity of humanitarian actors as moral agents with the necessary skills to make decisions based on their practice-based judgement rather than mere appliers of standards and pre-defined results. Nowhere is this clearer on display than in the MSF's justification for why it opted out of Sphere in 1998. In explaining MSF's withdrawal from Sphere, then president of MSF James Orbinski said:

Proximity for MSF means that we wish to be and remain in solidarity, in actual physical contact with the populations in danger that we serve, and whose suffering we seek to address. Volunteerism for MSF means that we are not a professional organization (Orbinski 1998: 2).

For MSF, the development of standards for relief work and relying primarily on 'technical' needs assessments run counter to MSF's ideals because 'standards of any kind must not become a cover for masking the active or passive failure to achieve humanitarian principles '. Referring to WFP in Sudan, MSF reports that WFP has distributed sufficient food in Sudan to meet its targets, but that it has to be done by focusing on targets that are relatively easy to access, that 'Technical standards appear to have been reached, but not humanitarian principles or goals' (1998: 4). A similar critique was launched by *Groupe URD*, a French think tank on humanitarian issues. The authors assert, for example, that Sphere standards 'ignore the diversity of cultural, political and security contexts', and they can 'support a consumerist attitude of affected populations' (Dufour et al. 2004: 126). Just as with MSF, Groupe URD are sceptical of the link forged in Sphere between rights and needs. At stake here is, as Orbinski discusses it, what kind of governance subject (humanitarian actors) emerges from this way of defining the governance object:

Sphere standards are, and must remain firmly embedded in the principles of international humanitarian law that entrusts disinterested – and I emphasize 'disinterested' – neutral, impartial and independent agencies with the responsibility to assess needs, and provide and monitor assistance. This will be a challenge against a growing trend among some governments or donor agencies that themselves seek to identify need, define response, and essentially sub-contrast a technical response (Orbinsky 1998: 5).

Sphere not only offers a list of what constitutes needs but defines these needs as inhering in rights: i) right to life in dignity, ii) right to receive humanitarian assistance, and iii) right to security and protection. Needs here become constituted through a checklist where the presence/absence of certain features is to be assessed against a set of professional criteria (WatSan, Shelter, Nutrition, and health). As humanitarian actors – committed to the imperative of protecting basic rights – it follows that this must be done under the principle of non-discrimination since all have a right to humanitarian assistance and this right should be protected equally. Sphere can be said to commit humanitarian actors to a set of standards, thereby – in the eyes of its critics – reducing the scope for what constitutes 'humanitarian practice'. Those organizations that have their strength in operational capacity (such as CARE) have typically supported Sphere to showcase such capacity to act, while MSF – as seen above – has always advanced a distinct profile where *temoignage* (witnessing) goes hand in hand with identification with and proximity to intended beneficiaries.

Conclusion

Beyond the issue of organizational differences over Sphere, there is the broader question of the re-configuration within humanitarian relief that has resulted from the introduction of needs assessment and evidence-based humanitarian action. An evaluation of the use of needs assessments after the Haiti earthquake concludes by privileging the authority of seasoned humanitarian actors to apply sound judgement in determining the 'needs' in question:

[I]n a highly volatile context such as the Haitian (and, one may argue, any other complex scenario), it is difficult to replace the experience and know-how of humanitarian practitioners on the ground with even the soundest of needs assessment methodologies. Thus, in the current process towards the creation of a common approach to needs assessment at the Inter-Agency Standing Committee level, it is extremely important to avoid falling into the trap of obsession with data and to remember that, without a proper understanding of the situation that comes from experience and communicating with people, an abundance of information and tools will not automatically be reflected in a more effective humanitarian response (Stoianova 2010: 10).

I attribute this ambivalence towards needs assessment to a tension between the professional authority of field operatives, on the one hand, and the professional authority that has grounded abstract knowledge and operationalized as codified practices and scientific techniques to measure and present 'needs'. The increased reliance on these methods serves to ground humanitarian *organizations'* legitimacy or trust with donors, while humanitarian *professionals* see these methods as cumbersome, prone to politicization, and a threat to their way of asserting control over how to allocate and deliver relief (Darcy et al. 2013; Dijkzeul 2013).

The relative marginalization of the status of humanitarian actors' practice-based judgement is significant for the identity of the humanitarian object of governance, and for the identity of humanitarian subject: the insistence on humanitarianism as an apolitical stance follows from commitment to these substantive values – independence, impartiality, neutrality, humanity, etc. They also persist despite humanitarians' gradual expansion, over the course of the last two decades, to also act on the causes of conflict and become 'alchemic' actors (Barnett 2011). The contestation over Sphere has also to do, finally, with needs assessments becoming the major advocacy tool, effectively removing the broader components from humanitarian advocacy: it is no longer enough to say 'we are here'. Advocacy is to be done through a particular set of techniques, using numbers, to convince broader audiences (Broome and Quirk 2015).

Notes

Interview, former senior OCHA Official. January 2011. Oslo.
Interview, OHCHR Official. December 2010. New York.
Interview, senior NRC Official. December 2010. Oslo.
Interview, UNHCR Official. December 2010. New York.

6 The Ford Foundation
Building and Domesticating the Field of Human Rights

Wendy H. Wong, Ron Levi, and Julia Deutsch

Since the late 1990s, scholars and policymakers have identified the role of non-state actors – and in particular, non-governmental organizations (NGOs) – in shaping the trajectory of the international human rights regime (Keck and Sikkink 1998, Risse et al. 1999, Welch 2001, Bob 2005, Carpenter 2010, Wong 2012a). Yet despite what is now a large literature on the role of NGOs, there remains a surprising lack of attention to the organizations that fund these actors – be they states, intergovernmental organizations, or private, philanthropic foundations (Cooley and Ron 2002, Sell and Prakash 2004). Among these, the funding provided by private foundations remains largely black-boxed.[1] This blind spot is surprising in many ways, considering both the amount of money that private foundations distribute in the name of "human rights," their active role in promoting and developing NGOs, at least in the US context, their relative lack of constraints in the way that they spend their money, and the looser oversight mechanisms with how they spend their money, especially when compared to democratic states.

Yet what we do know about the role of foundations emphasizes the matching process for funders in selecting recipients that can reflect and extend the needs of their domestic battles and constituencies. This is embedded in what Dezalay and Garth (2002b) refer to as the "internationalization of palace wars" – namely that investments in local organizations, ideals, and individuals abroad are part of a relational process of import/export, through which actors such as private foundations *export* their own ideals and strategies, and while actors such as local NGOs *import* these very strategies in an effort to gain resources and global legitimacy, and with it influence over professional fields and the state itself (see also Stroup and Wong 2017).

[1] Others have looked intensively at the interaction between foundations and state policy, specifically US foreign policy (Dezalay and Garth 2002b, Parmar 2012a, 2012b).

82

Understood from through this lens of international strategies, private philanthropic foundations are key players in defining the scope and practice of human rights, and in determining which organizations are regarded as legitimate and professional players in the field. This process of norm socialization is what Dezalay and Garth (2002b: 7–8) are most attuned to when they emphasize how international strategies are often "learned strategies," such that education, scholarship, and training – including the efforts of private philanthropic foundations – combine to set the foundational terms of the debate domestically and internationally.[2]

Within the human rights regime, this foundational moment occurred in the aftermath of World War II, when human rights emerged on the global scene as a key concern for international politics. With the United Nations taking up human rights as a fundamental pillar of its activities alongside peace and development, and – over time – allowing for NGOs to directly engage with this normative infrastructure and its own agencies (Jenson and Levi 2013), seemingly limitless opportunities for human rights funders and NGOs appeared on the horizon. Into this vacuum stepped actors who were seeking supporters for specific agendas and concerns. Unlike the current environment of NGOs and funders working along clear-cut guidelines of human rights expectations delineated by a growing body of international law and organizations and developing mechanisms of monitoring civil society effectiveness, funders and recipients had a harder time *finding* one another and successfully *matching* their interests in the beginning of the human rights project. During these unsettled periods, institutional habits and networks were unstable (Swidler 1986), and funders enjoyed a great deal of influence in defining the scope of issues and of legitimate actors that would fall under the umbrella of "human rights," a regime that was only starting to develop a vocabulary to operationalize the Universal Declaration of Human Rights of 1948.

Local NGOs offer opportunities for these funders, since the foundations enjoy significant material and symbolic power by controlling the issues they want to fund *and* the types of actors they select to pursue them – to thus extend their networks and export their positions globally. Our goal in this chapter is to understand how this supply-side of money and legitimacy shapes the human rights agenda. Following Seabrooke and Henriksen (Introduction to this volume), we identify a two-level network at play in how issues and organizations get "selected" into the world of human rights: we explore this two-level network by attending to the interaction between organizations such as private foundations and the NGOs that are the recipients of their attention (and who in turn vie for

[2] See also Finnemore (1996).

their support). A key contribution of this chapter is the emphasis on material resources in shaping the authority and reach of foundations. Through their grants, foundations play an important role in determining the NGOs that gain traction in global politics. We thus demonstrate how material resources have formed the backbone of ideational dissemination in the human rights field, thereby creating a "stamp" of approval for what ideas and kinds of NGOs become legitimated, certifying certain kinds of ideas about human rights (and excluding others), and providing a professional training ground for a particular view of human rights practitioners.

In this chapter we focus on the work of Ford Foundation (Ford) in shaping international human rights. We consider how Ford has orche-strated the human rights field, so to speak, through its distribution of funds. Of course, Ford played a key role in the establishment of many of the well-regarded human rights NGOs we know today – Human Rights Watch (HRW), Human Rights First, and the International Commission of Jurists – and for many years after World War II, it was the only game in town on human rights before the end of the Cold War.[3] Ford began working in earnest on "human welfare" in 1950 (Korey 2007: 11), and its role directly influencing Latin American countries on the issue of human rights is well documented (Dezalay and Garth 2002b). Yet what is considerably less well known are the *patterns of funding* Ford distributed from its turn toward human rights issues, from 1950 to 1989 (Dezalay and Garth 2002b: 156). This period is particularly important for the development of international human rights, where both the ideas were nascent and under contention between states and non-state actors, when most international law we know today governing human rights simply did not exist yet (or was coming into existence), when funding was still relatively rare, and "what" human rights sought to achieve was still relatively in flux (Moyn 2010). During this time, Ford's role in domes-ticating the mass of ideas and NGOs through its funding patterns would shape the development of human rights ideas and also the groups that would become the internationally recognized "gatekeepers" (Bob 2005) of human rights politics.

Foundations and Professionalization

Much of the work to date on the development of international human rights has focused on the role of NGOs (Korey 1998, Bob 2005, Carpenter

---

[3] The Carnegie Corporation, MacArthur Corporation, and the Rockefeller Foundation also funded human rights, but Ford was far and away the most generous funder of this group (see Ovsiovitch 1998).

2010, Murdie and Davis 2012, Wong 2012a), international organizations (Joachim 2003, Mitchell and Powell 2011, Helfer and Voeten 2013), states (Simmons 2009, Forsythe 2012), or some combination of these actors (Neier 2012), largely leaving the role of foundations unexplored.[4]

Exploring the role of these philanthropic organizations is central to understanding how ideas take hold at both domestic and international levels. After all, foundations provide the money that others apply to specific projects, but they also serve as institutions that "define realities, concert resources, enhance or frustrate the power of those who work through them and with them, and generally help shape their environments" (Hammack and Anheier 2010: 6). Foundations choose the groups that "deserve" funding, and that choice is laden with all sorts of important values that the organization hopes to impart onto the world.

In this way, some see private foundations as a de facto extension of the American state in particular, given the work done by US-based foundations since the early twentieth century (Vogel 2006, Parmar 2012a, 2012b). Foundations such as Ford can thus be considered alongside other human rights-related institutions that formed around legally trained activists working in NGOs, the academy, or think tanks (Dezalay and Garth 2006, Hagan and Levi 2007, Levi and Hagan 2008). All these contribute to social policy through investments in research as well as policy transfer, brought together in what Stone (2001: 355, 2010) refers to as an "emerging international market of expertise" of global social policy.

The challenge is often in delineating the differences between the work of such organizations because of the lack of "firm boundaries" (Stone 1996) or "demarcation" between Foundations, think tanks, and other institutional players (Medvetz 2012).

Foundations, we argue, stand out in their own right. Because foundations identify recipients, they engage in global social policy indirectly, through the networks they develop and sustain (Stone 2013), working as "meta-NGOs" (Bach and Stark 2002). As Stone's (2010) analysis of The Open Society Institute (OSI) shows, foundations can be thought of as private charitable organizations, enabling others to do things with their philanthropy. Foundations forge paths toward new norms (Stone 2010: 276), often operating on an "impact-investor model" (Salamon and Burckart 2014: 167–168). They can also provide an air of neutrality and legitimacy to organizations that they fund, such as think tanks (Stahl 2016). The "norms, knowledge, and networks" they provide can, in turn, enable local actors to expand their reach worldwide (Stone 2010: 277, 282). In this way, foundations can work as "dominating

---

[4] But see Dezalay and Garth (2002b), Korey (2007), Ovsiovitch (1998), and Stone (2010), noting the role of foundations in establishing major human rights NGOs.

institutions" across different professional fields, by changing the relationship of some players rather than engaging exclusively in content development (Khurana et al. 2011). Larger foundations such as Ford can amplify these effects loudly through their sizable funding capacity.

In contrast, think tanks often occupy national positions that are closely aligned with domestic political stakes, so that their work and activity are generated in political relation to one another. As a result, they can be caught between and within field struggles, trying to distinguish themselves from universities or advocacy groups while also maintaining proximity with them to gain expertise and credibility on issue areas (Medvetz 2012).

These elements of foundations make them salient for analyzing how professionals engage in issue control and in "defining what matters." Drawing on Seabrooke and Henriksen (this volume), we can evaluate the relationship between organizations and professionals via five criteria: scope, autonomy, resources, hiring patterns, and degree of knowledge centralization. As "professionalizers", foundations serve as training grounds for human rights professionals and as vetters of human rights causes, thereby professionalizing applicants (and often providing them with avenues to gain legitimacy and professional credibility) through their funding patterns. In short, we argue that foundations provide two professionalization functions.

First, they provide jobs and platforms for professionals – lawyers, analysts, policymakers – interested in a particular cause such as human rights (Quack 2010). Foundations provide offices that review applications; they allow grant officers to examine hopeful projects, perhaps all equally deserving of funding; and they make decisions on the amount of funding to be allocated. Grant officers are interested in the ideas that underlie applications, as well as the ability of an organization to complete a proposed project. Foundations are therefore engaged in a process of normative valuation that evaluates both the nature of the project proposed and the effectiveness of the proposer. As is well documented, professionalism generates with it the capacity to attract financial support for NGO activities – a professionalism that matches standards that funders seek, such as offices, dedicated staff, or mission statements (e.g., Boulding 2012, Massoud 2011, Watkins et al. 2012). For instance, in her study of health NGOs in Bolivia, Boulding (2012) demonstrates that Bolivian groups require the capacity and infrastructure to inspire confidence in others. Thus, to become legitimate as recipients of financial support, local organizations must strive to "look the part" to gain the support of foreign funders (Bob 2005, Cooley and Ron 2002). This process of *evaluation* is deeply embedded with the setting of *values*: foundation professionals vet causes and organizations, and in the process they encourage a structured competition, differentiation, and struggle among those actors who enter the field and take on its stakes (Fourcade-Gourinchas 2006).

Second, this vetting process sets the agenda that helps to delineate the legitimate boundaries of the field itself, providing some activists in some countries the opportunities to continue their work while denying others (Medvetz 2012). As patrons, foundations therefore also teach NGOs and other organizations how to be successful at attaining support for their work (Watkins et al. 2012). This may come in the form of having material capacity, but it also, importantly for us, shapes the ideas that are perceived as successful. Foundations fund projects that fall within their mandates and are compatible with their strategic goals and national investments. This of course includes input from the "domesticated" NGOs in terms of how foundations provide resources, and what projects are (or should be) important for an issue area. In the proposal submission process, NGOs signal the significance of certain ideas, concerns, and geographies – and foundations equally tailor their projects to these local contexts (Dezalay and Garth 2002b: 33). As foundations choose successful NGOs, they also build transnational networks that provide coherence to a particular topic, and help to solidify their raison d'être (Parmar 2012a: 14).

In an environment characterized by few foundations interested in investing in human rights and hopeful recipients working on the topic, foundations take on an even more important role in agenda-setting. By being the major funder of human rights projects, Ford built and maintained the human rights market, professionalizing human rights from an organizational and ideational perspective. Without its decisions regarding which projects mattered and which did not, human rights activism may have gone in a different direction than it did. An important example highlights Ford's focus: it denied Raphael Lemkin's application for assistance on a major genocide project in 1957 (Korey 2007: 21). While Ford was very prominently involved in Eastern Europe and Latin America during the Cold War (Korey 2007), looking at the "big cases" in this instance fails to capture the pattern of Ford funding that would herald the post-Cold War shift in human rights focus.

In these two ways, foundations "domesticate" both the nature of the agents that apply for money and the ideas that are able to secure funding and potentially grow as a result of NGO projects. This influence of funders is well known to scholars and professionals in the field, where much turns on being considered a *professional* rather than a *voluntary* organization (e.g., Winston 2001, Brown 2001, Hopgood 2006, Wong 2012b).

In the case of Ford specifically, many of its efforts were specifically directed at professionalizing the field of human rights and social justice activism (Dezalay and Garth 2002b: 69). Partly as a result, human rights practitioners and scholars know anecdotally that Ford was critical for the growth of the human rights regime, and in particular, civil and political rights. It funded important NGOs and bankrolled resistance against apartheid and the Soviet regime. Its most prominent progeny, HRW, refused to work on civil and political rights until the 1990s, only looking to incorporate them into its framework after a thorough review funded by Ford. Even so, HRW's approach to economic, social, and cultural rights frequently mirrors the approaches used to explore civil and political rights of finding a wrongdoer, a victim, and a remedy (Roth 2004). These prominent projects are part of what Ford was doing with its human rights work, particularly after the 1970s. We show in the next section just how they did so, and how their efforts professionalized a range of human rights work worldwide.

The Ford Foundation

In the US context, private foundations – with their leaders closely connected with the industrial, corporate, and political sectors – emerged as elite platforms for extending domestic elite battles abroad (Dezalay and Garth 2002b, Parmar 2012a: 2). These sometimes reflected and sometimes contested state policies: but as unaccountable to shareholders, electors, and at times market forces, the power of foundations lies in being "blocs of concentrated venture capital generating political ideas" (Parmar 2012a: 31). Much of this was targeted to domestic social policy: early twentieth-century foundations such as Rockefeller and Carnegie, for instance, were principal sources of domestic social and welfare reforms in the wake of mass industrialization (Dowie 2001: 6, Parmar 2012a: 36–40).

For its part, Ford emerged as a perhaps unlikely actor in the international human rights scene. It was not fueled by romantic ideals of "world peace" (Gaither 1949: 52, Korey 2007: 9), but was instead established to lessen the tax burden on the Ford family by having the Ford Motor Company's non-voting shares bequeathed to the Foundation (Korey 2007: 4). The Foundation's 1936 mandate explicitly adopts the statutory language of a tax exemption from the federal tax code, namely "to receive and administer funds for scientific, educational and charitable purposes, all for the public welfare" (Fleishman 2007: 224). The Foundation's wealth continued to grow as Edsel Ford, heir to the Ford Motor Company, continued to transfer his wealth to philanthropic purposes in order to mitigate tax concerns, so that by Edsel Ford's death in 1943, the Foundation held almost three million shares of the Ford Motor Company (Korey 2007: 4–6). The activities of the Ford Foundation were modest (Ferguson 2013: 5), and the Foundation remained a discreet, one-man operation with files contained in a double-drawer cabinet with no published annual reports (Korey 2007: 6).

A significant transformation of Ford occurred after 1948, during a realignment of the Foundation in a time of massive financial, personal, and national change. From 1948 to 1951, the Foundation grew to hold a $2.3 billion endowment as a result of massive bequests of family-held stock by Henry Ford II, Edsel's son, who had taken over the presidency of Ford Motor Company in the years following his father's death (Korey 2007: 7, Ferguson 2013: 5). On the national scene, this positioned Ford with a foundation wealth that towered over both the Carnegie and Rockefeller Foundations (Korey 2007: 7, Parmar 2012a: 45). In the wake of World War II, Ford had become one of the richest institutions in the world at a time when world order was shifting decisively toward American ascendancy (Korey 2007: 7, Parmar 2012a: 35).

While Edsel Ford himself made significant financial contributions to the arts, Henry II ever more actively embraced the sense of *noblesse oblige* that came with this foundation wealth. Henry II understood the Foundation to be a *public* responsibility and promptly tasked Horace Rowan Gaither to conceptualize a mandate for it (Fleishman 2007: 224). Gaither had close connections to both industry and the state, with leadership positions in the burgeoning field of defense-oriented research: a distinguished California lawyer and banker, Gaither was also an original trustee of the Rand Corporation and an assistant director of the defense-centered Radiation Laboratory at MIT – indeed, the Ford Foundation had provided funding for the 1948 reconfiguration of the Rand Corporation from its originally exclusive connection with the Douglas Aircraft Company (Hounshell 1997: 242).

Gaither was asked to straddle the line between what other foundations had achieved and "what men need to live more fruitful lives" (Korey 2007: 8), and his report came to highlight five program areas that mirrored Gaither's own elite connections and expertise: (1) the establishment of peace and a world order of law and justice; (2) the bolstering of democracy and freedom; (3) the strengthening of the economy; (4) general and civic education; and (5) expansion of knowledge of human conduct (Gaither 1949: 49–99, Fleishman 2007: 225, Korey 2007: 9).

The Ford Foundation's growth into fields such as law and justice then – and its growth into international work alongside it – reflects shifts occurring within the Ford family and in a reconfiguration of the US state in the years following World War II. Investment in public policy of this sort was fostered by increased links between non-profit organizations research in social science, industry, and government (Dowie 2001: 5), with individuals such as Horace Rowan Gaither representing the interface of these dimensions.

Enthusiastic about the Gaither report and seeking autonomy to take on potentially controversial approaches to problems internationally, Paul Hoffman – president of Studebaker and at this stage the administrator of the Marshall Plan for Europe after World War II – drew on Gaither's vision to expand Ford's operations to developing nations in Africa, Asia, Latin America, and the Middle East (McCarthy 1997: 131). Hoffman himself would focus much of his interests on foreign affairs and civil liberties, and in expanding US influence beyond Europe (Raucher 1985: 81–88) – and indeed would later become administrator of the UN Development Program. After his term, Rowan Gaither and then Henry Heald would replace Hoffman, with ever-greater expansion of efforts on foreign institutions and economic development, and with the influence of new directors in McGeorge Bundy and Franklin Thomas from the mid-1960s onward, ever-greater support of advocacy groups, civil rights, and social justice (Dezalay and Garth 2002b). Through them, Ford would further expand its bureaucracy, and in turn become a platform for a new class of "philanthrocrats" (Dowie 2001: 7) who supported contemporary social movements and became key nodes in funding and professionalizing the field of human rights.

Findings

While the influence of Ford on the human rights field is well known, the allocation of its funding over time – and with it, the shape it has given to the field through the supply of resources and the professionalizing of its NGO recipients – remains to be throughly investigated. The data informing our analysis come from forty years of Ford budget data, from 1950 to 1989, the central moments in the development of the field of international human rights and social justice, both within the United States and internationally. We rely on line-item budget data from the Ford Foundation Annual Reports, categorizing each entry that speaks to the broad field of human rights and social justice. While we took a conservative approach to including grants that might be within the field of human rights and social justice, we also rely on contextual information from the prose of the Annual

Reports, thereby remaining attuned to the fact that work in these domains was often done by multiple actors – including, for instance, university training programs in Latin America (Dezalay and Garth 2002b) – and we thus take an approach that recognizes that the contours of the field of human rights and social justice were themselves being shaped by this funding process.

We identified all grants within this field, whether these targeted civil and political rights or economic social and cultural rights. As a result, these grants could span issues of poverty, health, education, equality, and participation, or justice and civil rights. Grants were further identified as funding legalistic approaches or as highlighting social or economically based strategies. Finally, determining whether a grant was domestic or international required identifying the primary beneficiaries of the grant and their location.

In emphasizing these financial flows, we develop three broad findings in the analyses that follow. First, we find that the funding of human rights and social justice projects has been *strategically timed*, such that it allocated significant percentages of its funding to human rights and social justice projects at key time periods, including in its early entry into the field and then growth in funding this domestic and international field throughout the Cold War. Second, we find that over time there has been greater *convergence in the type of rights* – domestically and internationally – being promoted and developed through Ford funding. And third, we find that there are geographic patterns that suggest Ford has often *diversified its investments in politically contentious locations*, to include attention to civil and political rights as well as to economic, social, and cultural rights. We briefly turn to each of these findings below.

Strategic Timing

The 1950s and the 1960s were a busy era for the Foundation as it entered this field. Internationally, Ford was involved in large-scale development projects in southeast Asia (during the era of decolonization, as strategic funding for development in countries that could counter the political strength of communist China) (Heydemann and Kinsey 2010); and domestically, efforts toward funding civil rights, urban matters, and public interest law also figured prominently on the Foundation agenda. What one sees in the early years of Figure 6.1, then, is Ford's own efforts at securing its footing in this field – with massive human rights and social justice investment in times of major domestic and international change, at times upward of 60 percent of the total budget, precisely in an effort to fund those partners and alliances who were building the foundations of

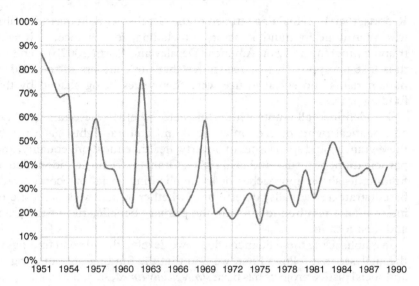

Figure 6.1 Funding for Human Rights Field Percent of Ford
Foundation Grants Budget

the human rights field of the era (Dezalay and Garth 2006). From our lens on professionalization, we identify these early years as foundational to setting the agenda and investing in activists and organizations.

More stable patterns, by contrast, emerged in the 1970s through the 1990s. While there are always annual fluctuations in funding decisions – partly as a result of multi-year projects that are developed and promoted – the key point is that the trend in allocation of Ford funding toward rights and justice increases steadily over this time, from a low of 20 percent of the Ford budget to rates of over 40 percent in the 1980s.[5]

Although we do not detail it here, with this funding (Figure 6.2), a key part of what Ford has successfully done since the late 1960s has been to generate connections and protégés internationally for US elites, particularly as a generation of younger reformers came to invest in the human rights field as a way to stake out new positions domestically (Dezalay and Garth 2002b). As others have noted through biographical analyses of Ford presidents, the decision to invest domestically or internationally maps closely onto Ford's organizational leadership. Similarly, there is evidence to suggest that institutional priorities between domestic and international funding map

[5] We focus here on percentages of the total Ford Foundation budget, rather than on precise dollar amounts, since these of course vary depending on the total budget available annually.

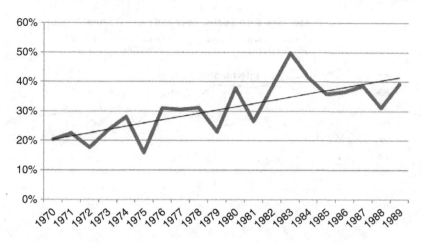

Figure 6.2 Funding for Human Rights Field, 1970–1989

onto the US political field more generally, with Ford funding being spent to fill in perceived political gaps both domestically and internationally (Dezalay and Garth 2002b, Korey 2007, Heydemann and Kinsey 2010).

Substantive Convergence

Yet if there is apparent consistency in regional allocations, this does not tell us much about the *content* of what is being funded. After all, much has been made about the cultural mitigation of universal rights (Goodale and Merry 2007), and textbooks on human rights all refer to the notion of cultural relativism and whether human rights are "Western" (Donnelly 2002, Forsythe 2012). Within this framework, "Western" values often take the guise of civil and political rights (CPR), whereas economic, social, and cultural rights (ESCR) are often touted as "non-Western" rights. In our study, we find convergence on the *type* of rights-based activity that has been underwritten by Ford funding over the key years of 1970–1989. Our data show that there has been significant convergence over whether to fund CPR or ESCR, such that when comparing spending in the United States and internationally, we find a similarity over time in terms of the percentage of the human rights budget that is spent on each type of right.

We see a broad trend toward convergence in the types of rights being funded and promoted. In contrast to simple accounts of Americanization, by following the flow of Ford funds we see instead a process of consensus building that has been occurring across the human rights field. Echoing

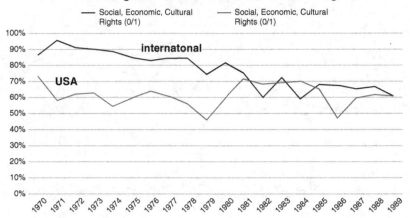

Figure 6.3 Percentage US Dollars on Social, Economic, and Cultural Rights

some of what Thérien (2007) calls the "new grand compromise," what we see below is that whereas the human rights funding envelope has increased over time, the percentage of human rights funding spent on ESCR has decreased internationally, so that the domestic and international trend lines now meet at an approximately 60/40 allocation between these types of rights (Figure 6.3). This convergence, in our view, demonstrates the importance of following trends in funding patterns over time. The domestication of the field that we see is one in which international and domestic projects alike come to mirror each other in general approach – so that we see an emerging consensus on which sorts of projects and activities are to be funded. If the Foundation is having an effect, then, it is one that is mirrored in both its domestic and international work.

This convergence is also met with an increasing "legalization" of the field of human rights and social justice from 1970 to 1989, both within the United States and ever more so internationally (Figure 6.4). When we compare the relative allocations within human rights and social justice funding themes, we see that projects with a more lawyerly focus – courts and legal assistance, for instance, compared with categories such as development or social advocacy – gain greater attention over time.

Location

There remain, however, different agendas for Ford in different parts of the world. As Figure 6.5 illustrates, from 1970 to 1989, Ford did not

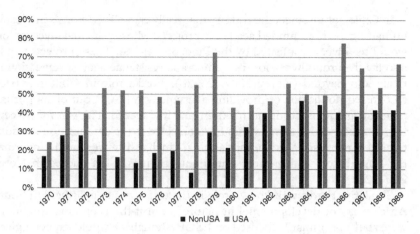

Figure 6.4 Legalization of the Human Rights and Social Justice Field

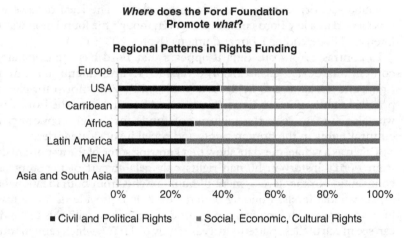

Figure 6.5 Regional Distribution for the Promotion of Different Rights

support ESCR and CPR projects uniformly across regions. Rather, ESCR funding dominates in some contexts (Asia and South Asia, Middle East and North Africa, Latin America, and Africa) but reaches near-parity in the Caribbean, the United States, and Europe. These patterns stand out in particular because of the role we know Ford played in notable instances of its influence.

In Chile, for instance, the country that really crystallized Ford's interest in human rights, Ford funded academic projects, whose principal investigators would be adversely affected by the Pinochet regime. These projects would also lay the groundwork for the democratic resistance against repression in Chile and beyond (Korey 2007: 25–28). Ford's role in Chile has been recognized not as one of providing assistance on ESCR but of supporting political dissidents, academic freedom, and free speech. This was the perception so much so that some within Ford objected to the organization's actions to protect repressed academics, claiming, "such assistance would 'jeopardize the Foundation's other more important activities.'" (as quoted in Korey 2007: 28).

Similarly, Ford's well-known role in the resistance to apartheid in South Africa was not developmental in nature (even if the economic conditions were stark) or primarily focused on ESCR, though we would expect it given the funding patterns of the Foundation in the region and the level of inequality between whites and blacks under apartheid. Early work in the 1950s emphasized research, exchange, and building positive racial relations. In the 1960s, Ford supported projects providing legal aid to blacks accused of violating security laws used to sustain apartheid. The legal defense work was viewed as a key Ford contribution, even though the foundation was also interested in defending labor and unions (Korey 2007: 172).

In contrast, from our data it appears that Ford has – particularly in contentious locales – strategically diversified its investments in the human rights and social justice field. As a result, while well known for civil and political rights efforts in Latin America and South Africa, the Foundation was also sure to seed the majority of funds for social, economic, and cultural rights in the human rights and social justice categories.

Taken as a whole, our data show that knowing some of the important cases from Ford's history in human rights only gets at part of the story of its contribution to the development of human rights from both ideational and organizational levels. Funding patterns over time provide us some insight into what we are looking for; and as we develop below, with this in hand we can see much of these patterns in a case study of HRW, which remains one of the most prominent examples of the Foundation's work in shaping this field as a whole.

HRW

HRW as we know it today started as two other organizations – The Fund for Free Expression and the Helsinki Watch Committee. Both of these were funded by Ford (Korey 2007). As the NGO achieved political salience as a proponent of rights in defense of the 1975 Helsinki Accords,

Basket III agreements (which included human rights), it began expanding into other areas, first Americas Watch, and then later Watches in Asia, the Middle East, and Africa (see Brown 2001, Wong 2012a). In the 1990s, as its founding director faced increasing criticism and was departing, Ford played an active role in providing support and advice for the transition to future leadership. The relationship between Ford and HRW in its various iterations was positive and mutually enforcing, and thus it is appropriate to examine just how Ford's influence affected the trajectory of HRW's work. Ford has recognized its own role in providing support for the international human rights movement, as one of its former vice presidents writes,

through its extensive network of overseas offices, the foundation has been a critically important source of sustained support for scores of human rights NGOs in Africa, Asia, and Latin America ... Russia and Central Europe ... the importance of the Ford Foundation's role in the human rights arena derives ... from the disturbingly fragile nature of the financial underpinnings of most human rights NGOs (Carmichael 2001: 248).

In some ways, the fate of HRW was a stroke of good timing. In 1974, Ford staff pointed out that the way the foundation had pursued its international agenda – through cooperation with governments, as well as building university programs in-country – could not be the only way to do business, given the political context in many of their countries of interest (Latin America being a particularly troubled region at the time). As dissidents faced government repression, it was clear that external actors needed to get involved in many of the cases Ford was interested in. Two years later, then Ford President McGeorge Bundy endorsed a move to begin supporting activity and research by NGOs and other groups based *outside* of countries in question (Carmichael 2001: 251).

As one of two NGOs that received long-term Ford support,[6] HRW offers an interesting case for thinking about the role of the foundation in producing a human rights organization. An especially enlightening study (Korey 2007) consults Ford's archival holdings in fine-grained detail, which we use here to illustrate the power of Ford in shaping the types of human rights NGOs that would emerge. Ford played a seminal role in providing seed funding (at times, supporting very large requests, see Korey 2007: 79–82), ensuring that the Watch groups could become sustainable projects.[7] The Fund for Free Expression was founded in 1975, and with a change in agenda and Ford support, it became

---

[6] The other is Human Rights First, what was then known as the Lawyer's Committee for Human Rights.

[7] HRW now has a long-term partnership with George Soros' Open Society Foundation, see www.nytimes.com/2010/09/07/business/07gift.html (Accessed 25 November 2013).

Helsinki Watch in 1978 (see Laber 2002). Nearly at the same time, Bernstein had selected Aryeh Neier to lead the Watch project, and the link became official in 1981 with the proposal and creation of Americas Watch. Together, these two Watch groups formed the backbone of what we now know as HRW. While what won Ford over initially was the ability of the Watch committees, and in particular Americas Watch, to deliver the engagement of political and social elites on human rights issues, Ford also bore a heavy imprint on the professionalization and trajectory of the NGO. Not until the mid-1990s did the HRW we know today – comprehensive legal documents, wrapped neatly in an "HRW brand" – emerge, and that emergence came from a fundamental rethinking and restructuring that took place with essential Ford support (Korey 2007: 116–117).

Perhaps more importantly, Ford's decision to throw its weight behind the Watch projects and not other proposed alternatives at the time is extremely telling. As Korey writes, "[HRW was] an American NGO that was virtually created by the Ford Foundation" (Korey 2008: 92). Although the Watch committees would eventually be seen as fulfilling the ambitions of top Ford brass (Korey 2007: 93), at the time, the backing of the Watch proposal, and certainly the amounts requested, was far from a bygone conclusion. Before Helsinki Watch was funded, there were two other organizations that requested support for related, Helsinki-watching purposes. The first was an organization called the National Conference on Human Rights, which approached Ford in 1977 to fund an NGO conference of like-minded civil rights and other groups, with the idea of forming a larger, Helsinki-focused NGO (Korey 2007: 94). This group had the backing of major groups, including Amnesty International. Ford's human rights officers were not enthusiastic, especially about the Conference's backing from anti-communist groups such as Freedom House (Korey 2007: 95). Furthermore, the lack of fully articulated plans, plus skepticism toward the Accords themselves, led to the rejection of the proposal. The second project Ford considered at the time was headed by a professor at Catholic University, Mort Sklar, who had founded his own local Helsinki watch group and was interested in domestic compliance with the Accords in Eastern Europe. Although this proposal seemed impressive to officers at the time, it was also rejected (Korey 2007: 95); it did, however, continue to come up as a contender as it became clear that the Watch project was gaining steam.

McGeorge Bundy, then Ford president, had a meeting with Ambassador Arthur J. Goldberg, who had represented the United States at the Belgrade Conference on Human Rights in 1977. Goldberg wanted to adopt a more confrontational position with Moscow with regard to its human rights policies and practices in light of the Helsinki Accords, but was finding his position limiting; there was open rejection of his tough style at the meeting in Belgrade and beyond (Korey 2007: 97). Goldberg sought a way to use the media, among other things, to shape US public opinion about Soviet human rights practices. Bundy tapped Bernstein, who at the time was receiving Ford money for the Fund for Free Expression and had a track record for taking on repressive regimes. Moreover, Bernstein's publishing contacts and links to wealthy and powerful people fit well with Ford's elitist strategies (Korey 2007: 98). Even so, there was resistance to the Watch project, and doubts about the human rights expertise of Bernstein and his team (Korey 2007: 100), especially from Bruce Bushey, who was the Ford human rights program officer at the time. Although Bushey actively compared the Bernstein proposal to others, his skepticism was overridden by the advantages the Watch project seemed to bring to the table: "publicity" to "focus attention on Helsinki issues" (Korey 2007: 101). Given Bernstein's wealth of personal contacts among the media and elite in the United States, Ford's top leadership threw its weight behind the proposal and created Helsinki Watch. Nonetheless, the leash for the new organization was very short, as "[Ford's] principal staffers would be in constant touch with Bernstein and his professional staffers" (Korey 2007: 105). Bushey and other staff essentially overhauled the Watch committees' decisions, offering ways to rethink and reshape the priorities of the organization (Korey 2007: 107).

The HRW account demonstrates the close interplay between foundations and NGOs in generating the ideas that become prominent internationally. Bernstein's team had the backing of the Ford president, and the Watch Committee enjoyed the support of senior leaders because of its potential to replicate a more confrontational style and its access to wealth and power. The Watch project fits closely with an ever more legalistic approach to the human rights field that is also apparent from the Foundation's own budget direction throughout the 1970s and 1980s (Dezalay and Garth 2006). These two priorities fit snugly into what Ford sought at the time in its human rights agenda. The symbiosis of HRW (and its predecessors) and Ford helped mutually reinforce their reputations as vital to the US and international human rights movements.

Conclusion

As professionalizers, foundations provide both the money and the content for movements such as the international human rights movement. Through its spending patterns in the latter half of the twentieth century, Ford directed money toward certain types of rights and to certain regions of the world. Because of its position both as the most consistent and most generous human rights funder in the immediate post–World War II period up to the end of the Cold War, Ford was unique in its ability to shape our concerns about what human rights to focus on non-US countries. The convergence of the distribution of funding between ESCR and CPR over time demonstrates the relative weighting that Ford assigned to each respective group of rights in its domestic and international projects. Similarly, the Foundation's spending on human rights and social justice tracks US foreign policy interests, particularly when looking from 1970 to 1989. This is a process that Dezalay and Garth (2006: 69) equally identify in articulating the Foundation's role, even when it at times worked outside of the interests of the CIA, as being central to the strategies of the US foreign policy establishment and its vision of "creating friends of America" through rights- and justice-based approaches. The effects are far-reaching: it is in this very period that NGOs such as HRW launch their forceful critiques against states, including the United States, for their human rights practices, and it is in this period that Moyn (2010) argues that human rights replaced nationalism as the dominant orienting narrative for states and societies.

Within all of the action around human rights, Ford stands out as having shaped not just states but also the actors it funds. What we demonstrate here is that following the money yields interesting patterns that are made more intriguing by their confluence around certain issues and areas of the world. As a case study, we see how HRW – a creation of the Ford Foundation that has come to be a dominant voice in the field – received its funding and support precisely because of its "fit" with Ford's geographic and institutional priorities, including in its growing attention to a legalization of the field, but also in terms of style, approach, and substantive resonance with a priority on civil and political rights. The trajectory of human rights and social justice ideas is deeply connected with the supply of funds and the professionalization of NGOs on the terms set by these foundations, and through them, we see the dominant contours of the language and practice of human rights practice.

7 Accounting-NGO Professional Networks
Issue Control over Environmental, Social, and Governance Reporting

Jason Thistlethwaite

The strategic use of accounting expertise to standardize corporate environmental, social, and governance (ESG) reporting in mainstream financial disclosure has emerged as a popular strategy in transnational environmental governance. Several initiatives have embraced this strategy, including the Climate Disclosure Standards Board (CDSB), the Sustainability Accounting Standards Board (SASB), and the International Integrated Reporting Committee (IIRC). Each of these accounting-led private governance (APG) initiatives are private standard setters supported by a partnership between non-governmental organizations (NGOs), financial report preparers (i.e., publicly listed firms), accounting professionals, and investors. In theory, APG reporting standards are designed to increase the information available that investors can use to shape capital allocation decisions in ways that increase returns, but also incentive publicly listed firms to improve their ESG performance (Kolk et al. 2008; Macleod and Park 2011).

Despite this potential, the growing role of professional accountants in ESG reporting has been met with opposition from civil society and corporate actors. Among civil society actors, there is a concern that professional accountants could weaken accountability by privileging market or neoliberal discourse that fails to reveal the true social and environmental impact of corporate behavior (Andrew and Cortese 2013; Malsch 2013). At the same time, many corporate stakeholders worry that professional accountants may abandon their technical neutrality by expanding disclosure to capture "non-financial" information that privileges civil society interests, increases costs, complexity, and even liability (O'Dwyer et al. 2011). These concerns suggest that the accounting professions' influence over ESG reporting represents a trade-off between civil society and corporate or "market" organizational logics that is often described in the literature on private environmental governance (Falkner 2003; Levy and Newell 2002; Pattberg and Stripple 2008).

This debate, however, has yet to assess APG, which provides an important opportunity to analyze an empirically consistent strategy for deploying accounting expertise to shape ESG reporting. In addition, this debate has yet to engage recent research on issue control among transnational professionals and their organizations (Andrew and Cortese 2013; Lovell and MacKenzie 2011).[1] This research suggests that when professionals participate in processes of issue control they can distance their interests from those "logics" embedded within their organizational environment, such as corporate support for free-markets or civil society interests in accountability (Seabrooke and Henriksen, Introduction). By embracing this analytical lens, this chapter will reveal how APG initiatives are competing for issue control over ESG financial disclosure in ways that blur the dichotomy between market and civil society logics. More specifically, APG initiatives seek to become "epistemic arbiters" (Seabrooke 2014a) for the requirements necessary to report ESG in financial disclosures by forging a professional logic that borrows but also contests aspects of both market (financial reporting) and accountability (ESG reporting) logics. A new professional logic is necessary to generate authority for APG reporting as a legitimate alternative to existing ESG reporting and regulated financial disclosure requirements.

To support this argument, the chapter will first explain the organizational logic behind ESG reporting, the emergence of APG initiatives, and a perceived trade-off between the interests of a civil society "ESG reporting logic" and corporate sector "financial reporting logic." The second section will describe how APG initiatives adopt the use of a "two-level" professional nexus to facilitate "epistemic arbitrage" and establish issue control over a new ESG reporting logic. The final section will conclude by summarizing the chapter and its implications for transnational professional networks, specifically the risk that epistemic arbitrage becomes politicized, limiting APG efforts to establish issue control.

The Evolution of Environmental, Social, and Governance Reporting

Corporate ESG reporting first emerged in the 1970s as a civil society strategy to leverage consumers and financial markets as agents of social

[1] Andrew and Cortese and Lovell and Mackenzie are exceptions as they have examined the CDSB's approach to deploying accounting expertise. But this research has not explored how the accounting profession is a part of a broader effort to influence ESG reporting involving groups such as the IIRC and SASB. In addition, research has not examined the technical standards produced by these initiatives that reveal how processes of issue control are shaped by competing approaches to ESG, accounting, and financial reporting expertise.

change (Brown et al. 2009). Disclosure on a firm's environmental and social impacts was identified as a useful tool that could help these agents pressure a firm into improving its performance (Gupta 2008). Information on these social and environmental impacts was released in a public document, usually an annual corporate social responsibility (CSR) report, which stakeholders including shareholders, consumers, and NGOs could use to track a firm's progress. It is important to note that voluntary disclosure emerged alongside a range of other "private governance" approaches designed to fill gaps created by weak or non-existent government regulation, including principles, codes of conduct, environmental management systems, and markets for trading environmental commodities (Clapp and Thistlethwaite 2012; Clapp and Utting 2009).

The Coalition for Responsible Economies (Ceres) was the first NGO to recognize that disclosure could also be used to leverage the influence of investors by measuring corporate environmental performance as a business risk or opportunity. By dictating that access to capital is contingent on effective environmental risk management, investors can "informally govern" corporate behavior by introducing incentives to reduce environmental impacts (Kolk et al. 2008). This approach to disclosure was distinctive by trying to communicate social and environmental performance as a measure on a firm's financial value, rather than its ethical reputation (Macleod and Park 2011, 56). To generate this type of disclosure, the Ceres Principles were developed as a standard benchmark that firms could use to communicate their ESG impacts to investors (MacLeod 2010, 55; Pattberg 2007, 176). In 1997, Ceres launched the Global Reporting Initiative (GRI) designed to standardize the disclosure of corporate ESG information. According to Brown et al.'s history of the GRI, it was designed to "create a global common framework for the voluntary reporting of the economic, environmental and social impacts of corporate and gradually other organizations" (Brown et al. 2009, 189).

During the early 2000s, the idea of attracting investors to ESG disclosures grew in popularity as a means of strengthening corporate accountability. In 2002, Tessa Tennant and Paul Dickenson, two policy entrepreneurs with relationships to the London-based investor community, initiated the Carbon Disclosure Project (CDP) to develop a standard reporting framework for publicly listed companies' exposure to climate change risks (Macleod and Park 2011). Investors, concerned about the long-term impacts of climate change on their portfolios, agreed to work with the CDP to encourage corporate preparers to disclose their risks. The CDP now represents the world's most widely used climate change risk reporting framework by companies listed on the Financial Times Stock Exchange and S&P 500, and is supported by over 722 investors that collectively manage $84 trillion in assets (CDP 2013, 2010, 1).

Ceres followed the CDP by inviting a group of institutional investors to join the Investor Network on Climate Risk (INCR). The INCR developed a "Global Framework for Climate Change Risk Disclosure" in 2006 as a standard that preparers could use to measure and communicate their climate change risks. Although a smaller initiative than the CDP, the INCR has managed to recruit one hundred institutional investors representing $11 trillion in capital (INCR 2013). The United Kingdom's Institutional Investor Group on Climate Change (IIGCC) and the Australian Investors Group in Climate Change (IGCC) also promote climate change risk disclosure, but have not developed their own disclosure frameworks (IIGCC 2005, 2010).

Despite a significant expansion in the amount of disclosure, research on its effectiveness reveals a gap between information on ESG and investor decision-making. According to research on climate change risk disclosure, for example, information is inconsistent and not comparable, which creates "an imperfect and incomplete picture in what is said and in the rules dictating what should be said" (Smith et al. 2008, 2). Similar conclusions have been made about the social and environmental disclosures through the GRI, where "smaller enterprises find the Guidelines too complicated and demanding while potential users of GRI reports find them insufficiently specific or standardized" (Brown et al. 2009, 196). For these reasons, it is difficult to find evidence that information is helping preparers, civil society actors, or investors improve their decision-making (Ceres 2013; Kolk et al. 2008, 741).

Analysis on the effectiveness of ESG financial disclosures reveals a gap related to the complexity and costs involved in providing and interpreting disclosure on "non-financial" information that is difficult to measure using a standard approach. In other words, there is a conflict with the organizational logic of civil society groups seeking disclosure on ESG information that may not be relevant to the organizational logic of investors who seek financial information to improve shareholder value.

Accounting-led Private Governance

To bridge the gap between non-financial information and investor decision-making, stakeholders supporting the existing patchwork of standards approached the accounting industry for its advice on how to standardize and improve the disclosure. This outreach resulted in the establishment of the CDSB, the IIRC, and the SASB. Each of these initiatives are examples of "private governance" involving a partnership between

NGOs, corporations, investors, and accountants designed to provide a public good that states currently do not provide (Green 2014; Pattberg 2007). In this case, the public good constitutes a set of financial disclosure standards that adequately capture and measure ESG information.

The CDSB was formed in 2007 in London by several organizations already involved in measuring and communicating social and environmental impacts, including the CDP, Greenhouse Gas Protocol, Climate Registry, Ceres, and the International Emissions Trading Association (IETA). Its mandate is to standardize the reporting of climate change risk disclosure in mainstream financial reports, specifically accounting standards legislated by international and national regulators. The founding organizations are members on the "Board," which has the final decision-making authority over the CDSB disclosure framework called the Climate Change Reporting Framework (CCRF) (CDSB 2013a). The framework was developed through a standard setting process that began with input from a Technical Working Group (TWG) composed of experts from accounting firms and professional organizations (CDSB 2010a). Once the TWG approves standards, they are released as an "exposure draft" to generate feedback from any interested stakeholder, which is then integrated back into the draft. The Board approves the draft for release once a consensus on its key components is approved (CDSB 2010b).

The IIRC was first established in 2009 after a meeting between the GRI and Accounting for Sustainability, a group of professional accountants supporting sustainability initiated by the Prince of Wales. In 2012, the IIRC formed a secretariat that is located in London, UK (IIRC 2013a). Unlike the CDSB, the IIRC is designed to generate a set of standards that captures more than climate change impacts by facilitating integrated reporting, which combines both sustainability and financial information in one report (Eccles and Krzus 2010, 3). In December 2013, the IIRC released the first version of its International Integrated Reporting Framework (IIRF). This framework was developed using a similar standard setting process as the CDSB. A working group composed primarily of accounting firms and organizations, investors, and NGOs developed an exposure draft, which was then exposed to a public comment period to gather feedback (IIRC 2013b). Feedback was then incorporated into the framework and approved by the IIRC Board (2013c).

The SASB was formed in 2011 with a mandate to develop "sustainability accounting standards" that could be used by "publicly listed corporations in disclosing material sustainability issues for the benefit of investors and the public" (SASB 2013a). Standards are designed to be sector-specific, which differentiates its approach from the IIRC and CDSB, which have developed cross-sectoral standards. This approach is based on research conducted at Harvard University's Initiative for Responsible Investment, which currently hosts several SASB Board members. To date, the SASB has completed a set of standards for both the health care and financial industry. These standards emerged through a similar decision-making process as the CDSB and IIRC. An industry working group develops and releases an exposure draft for feedback before the Board approves the final version of the standards (SASB 2013b, 2013f).

All of these initiatives share a mandate to align ESG reporting with the organizational logic behind financial disclosure, specifically the "financial reporting model." The objective of the model is to standardize the way financial reports reduce information asymmetries between investors and their investments and improve the efficiency of capital allocation (IASB 2013). Accounting regulators and professionals use this model to identify financial information that must be disclosed, and it has been widely adopted by international and national accounting standard setters (IASB 2013; SASB 2013c). The model stipulates that information on a firm's social and environmental performance must be "material" for investors, but also "cost-effective" for preparers (IASB 2013). Financial information is considered material if its omission from a financial statement would affect investor decision-making. Since this concept is open to interpretation, investors and preparers could find a great deal of financial information that should be disclosed. But as the quantity of information increases, the costs of both disclosure for preparers and interpretation by investors increase. For this reason, the financial reporting model also requires that disclosure is "cost-effective," meaning "the benefits of reporting" must "justify the costs incurred to provide and use that information" (CDSB 2012, 18).

The objectives of financial reporting reveal a similarity with ESG but also a key tension. Whereas financial reporting is designed to increase transparency and accountability for shareholder value, ESG is designed to increase transparency and accountability for civil society interests. As a consequence, there is a risk that accounting expertise could translate information on ESG into economic data that narrows the potential scope of accountability. For some, this translation helps "enable the logic of the market to permeate policy conversations as if the market is natural and value free" (Andrew and Cortese 2013, 399). Indeed, professional accountants are even perceived to "displace the core regulatory functions (over issues such as working conditions and environmental sustainability) from the state to the corporate sector" (Sadler and Lloyd 2009, 613). For this reason, organizations such as the CDSB, IIRC, and SASB could be viewed as neoliberal agents trying to mobilize support for market-oriented governance at the expense of public accountability (Malsch 2013, 150).

On the other hand, APG initiatives believe the accounting sector's participation could increase accountability by aligning disclosure with the decision-making requirements of investors, which can be much more influential in shaping corporate behavior than civil society actors (Macleod and Park 2011; Schmidheiny and Zorraquin 1996). Optimists, such as long-time climate change advocate Jeremy Leggett, believe investor advocacy could result in policy makers "playing catch-up to the markets that are already cutting emissions for them by default" (Clark 2014). To achieve this outcome, however, financial and corporate actors must be convinced that expanding reporting requirements will increase the efficiency of decision-making, rather than privilege the measurement of "non-financial" information that increases costs and complexity.

Making this case for expanded disclosure is particularly challenging among preparers and accountants. Preparers often argue that expanded disclosure hurts competitiveness by increasing the risks of liability if they fail to provide accurate information, which is difficult to accomplish with non-financial impacts. The costs of additional training needed to implement alternative measurement approaches can also be quite onerous, especially for companies with complicated supply-chains or subsidiaries (Richardson 2002, 264). Accountants are also hesitant to support expanded disclosure as it can lead to accusations that the profession is acting on behalf of special interests, rather than maintaining a technical neutral perspective (O'Dwyer et al. 2011). Measuring "non-financial" information is also imprecise as ESG impacts can be long-term, uncertain, and as a consequence do not reveal a "present obligation" to a firm with a tangible outflow or inflow of assets (IASB Staff 2009).

This debate on the strategy adopted by APG initiatives as an attempt to either strengthen or limit accountability has yet to engage emerging research on processes of issue control among professional networks. This research questions the analytical dichotomy between market and civil society logics as an assumption that mistakes a mandate for rule-making for issue control (as Seabrooke and Henriksen argue in Chapter 1). The case may be that professional and organizational networks working on these issues may well be changing how the issue is understood at the transnational level, and who is viewed as most suitable to deal with it. APG initiatives are designed to establish issue control over ESG reporting that is distinct from the organizational logics traditionally linked with either the ESG or financial reporting community. Without distinct issue control, APG initiatives can be contested as favoring either the organizational logics of the financial or civil society communities. The following section will explore processes involved in establishing issue control facilitated by these initiatives.

Issue Control via Epistemic Arbitrage

The process to establish issue control over corporate environmental reporting is evident in the technical debates and decision-making facilitated by each APG initiative. Although the organizational logic of the corporate and civil society logics is clearly evident in these debates, APG positions particular aspects of these logics as relevant for the technical legitimacy of new reporting frameworks, while disputing other aspects. This decision-making process is an example of epistemic arbitrage whereby knowledge from existing "first-level" professional environmental, corporate, accounting, and investor organizations is used to supply a "second-level" professional network hosted by the APG initiatives (see Figure 7.1) (Seabrooke 2014a, 3). The objective of this strategy is to become an epistemic arbiter of environmental reporting knowledge by exploiting a "structural hole" between the environmental and financial reporting communities (see also Thistlethwaite and Paterson 2017). To demonstrate how APG initiatives facilitate epistemic arbitrage using a two-level nexus, this section will be divided into two subsections. The first subsection will review the debate generated through consultations between the financial and environmental reporting organizational logics. These consultations help generate accountability for APG decisions but also offer important expertise that can be used to help cultivate a technical consensus over reporting. The second subsection

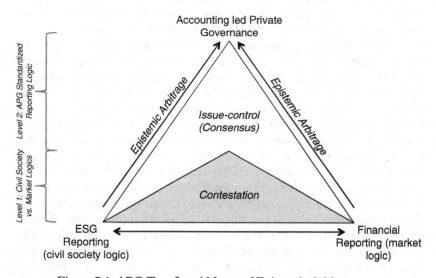

Figure 7.1 APG Two-Level Nexus of Epistemic Arbitrage

will explore how APG initiatives use epistemic arbitrage to draw on both logics in ways that generate a technical consensus on effective disclosure standards.

The Structural Hole: Financial vs. ESG Reporting Logics

Feedback to the SASB and IIRC reporting frameworks revealed significant concern that the financial reporting model would limit the disclosure of "non-financial" information, and should be expanded to capture less material ESG impacts. After consultations with stakeholders, the SASB admitted that materiality was limited as a measurement for issues such as climate change, resource constraints, and population growth that "would not be captured by a strict analysis of interest and economic impact, but could present significant risk over time" (SASB 2013f, 13). NGOs commenting on the IIRC's framework were less ambiguous in their concerns, arguing that financial reporting ignores the "societal perspective a corporation may be a net destroyer or expropriator of value" (Living Economies Forum 2013).

To address these constraints, measurement must be expanded beyond material information to include, for example, a company's impacts on the "stocks and flow" of a community's biosphere. Societal concerns about the environment, according to the NGO AccountAbility, should also be a benchmark for disclosure since organizations must adjust their business models in response to these perceptions (AccountAbility 2013). Climate change would fit into a category of information that may not be material given uncertainty around its impacts, but as a societal issue affecting business should be disclosed. This position was also supported by the European Coalition for Corporate Justice which questioned the value of "investor perception" as a benchmark disclosure compared to a broad assessment of impacts on a firm's organization, strategy, or business model (European Coalition for Corporate Justice 2013).

Even accounting organizations questioned whether the financial reporting model was a sufficient threshold to ESG information. Materiality and cost-benefit might unfairly emphasize impacts on financial capitals, which may not capture social or environmental information (ACCA 2013; Ernst & Young 2013). Although such disclosures would appease investor interests in efficient interpretation of information, it could sacrifice support from other stakeholders such as NGOs or regulators. Deloitte responded to these concerns in its comments to the IIRC, suggesting that financial disclosures of ESG information must explain how materiality "is distinct from materiality for other reports such as financial reports and how to handle the tension between application of materiality and achieving conciseness" (Deloitte 2013).

At the same time as stakeholders questioned whether the financial reporting model was effective at capturing ESG information, others argued that existing reporting standards are sufficient and any expansion to include non-financial information would be costly and inefficient. Ernst and Young responded to the IIRC's framework by disputing how expanded reporting on social and environmental impacts "would be truly different or significantly improved from existing corporate reporting in its broader context (i.e., financial reporting including the annual report and other communications with stakeholders)" (Ernst & Young 2013). Concern that expanding disclosure would just add redundant information was also expressed by industry stakeholders participating in the SASB consultations (SASB 2013e, 9).

To ensure reports do not become overcomplicated, the CDSB, SASB, and IIRC's frameworks all require that materiality is balanced with an effort to ensure conciseness (CDSB 2012, 10; IIRC 2013e, 21; SASB 2013f, 5). Accountants supported this idea by arguing that if disclosures were not concise, investors could oppose ESG financial disclosures that "are not yet completely convinced of the business case" (Ernst & Young 2013). Several stakeholders argued that establishing this balance would likely lead to reports burdened with too much information. Respondents to the CDSB questioned "the level of detail potentially required in response to the CDSB framework and how this could be managed through already overloaded mainstream reports" (CDSB 2010c, 4). BusinessEurope opposed the IIRC's framework because it "will not only create additional administrative burdens but will also add to the existing information overland that prevents stakeholders from seeing the wood from the trees" (BusinessEurope 2013).

Consultations on the CDSB, IIRC, and SASB's frameworks reveal a common tension between stakeholders concerned that the financial reporting model will limit effective disclosure, and those who believe it will expand disclosure, making it too costly. This contestation is, however, a key component in epistemic arbitrage that helps APG initiatives establish issue control over ESG financial disclosure. Feedback from these debates is incorporated into standards in the "second-level" by APG staff and working groups that leverage accounting expertise. This process is designed to facilitate technical consensus building over ESG financial disclosure among constituencies that APG initiatives need to establish issue control. The next subsection will examine this technical consensus-building process.

Issue Control over ESG Financial Disclosure

To establish issue control over ESG financial disclosure, APG initiatives integrate feedback from consultations into their frameworks but also produce a document that justifies their conclusions. These documents reveal how APG draws on both ESG and financial reporting logics to establish accountability among first-level stakeholders and technical legitimacy for their frameworks. After a framework has been developed, APG initiatives also engage in outreach among influential constituencies to encourage uptake of their standards.

The IIRC's International <IR> Framework was refined based on 350 consultation submissions. The incorporation of the ESG logic is evident in two decisions. First, the IR Framework expands existing disclosure requirements to include measurements of the impacts on natural, social, and relationship "capitals." These measurements include usage of water, land, minerals, forests, but also social impacts on communities and relationships with important stakeholders (IIRC 2013e, 12–13). Second, the IIRC relaxes requirements that disclosure is explicitly for the improvement of investment decision-making and must be considered material (IIRC 2013e, 7). Initially, the Framework argued that disclosures must be material, but the IIRC backed down after concerns that this requirement could "hamper application of the concept to non-financial information" (IIRC 2013e, 6). The Framework now includes a provision that disclosure must contain non-financial information that encourages "providers of financial capital to consider factors beyond financial capital alone" (IIRC 2013e, 6). While these requirements expand disclosure to include non-financial information, the Framework maintained the materiality provision in response to the financial reporting logic. The IIRC argued this was necessary to reduce complexity and that investors would ignore information not considered material, which would limit their incentive to hold firms accountable (IIRC 2013e, 6).

To appease concerns that materiality may limit disclosures, the SASB included a "forward-looking adjustment" in its standards that capture impacts that "fall outside the definition of materiality if, in spite of scientific evidence, the economic or financial impact on companies is not fully evaluated or may not yet have captured investors' interest" (SASB 2013f, 16). This adjustment proved contentious during the SASB's consultation over its health-care standards. Industry stakeholders complained that using this adjustment would force preparers to include non-material impacts such as pharmaceutical water contamination or the impacts of disease migration on demand. But the consultation also revealed that there was sufficient "scientific research on human and environmental health coupled with stakeholder concern" that these impacts could be material and should be included in the standard (SASB 2013e, 8). At the same time, the SASB agreed to limit disclosures on issues such as genetically modified organisms, which did not receive enough support from comment letters.

The CDSB's Climate Change Reporting Framework (CCRF) initially sided with the ESG logic by arguing that the cost-benefit requirement in the financial reporting model was unnecessary if climate change risk information is identified as material for investors (see also Thistlethwaite 2015). This choice was questioned by financial stakeholders that suggested a decision on whether to report information cannot be made unless a "cost-benefit analysis is performed" (CDSB 2010c, 4). The CDSB agreed with this position and decided to include the cost-benefit in addition to the materiality requirement to "keep the volume of mainstream disclosures manageable without losing the rigor and management responsibility that is appropriate to statements and disclosures made in mainstream financial reports" (CDSB 2010c, 30). While it is clear that the CDSB supports the financial reporting model, it also asks for disclosure content developed by "de facto" ESG frameworks, specifically the CDP and GHG Protocol (CDSB 2010d, 19). Physical and regulatory climate change risks in addition to greenhouse gas emissions must now be disclosed when using the CCRF, which expands disclosure beyond existing financial reporting requirements (CDSB 2010d, 20).

After frameworks have gone through a consultation, APG initiatives promote their adaption through strategic engagement designed to legitimize new reporting frameworks. This engagement largely focuses on identifying and addressing obstacles to adoption among preparers, investors, and regulators. The IIRC has developed several regional networks of preparers in Australia, Brazil, Germany, and Japan, in addition to a group of thirty-five investors representing over $4 trillion assets (IIRC 2013d, 11). The SASB has initiated a corporate roundtable designed to encourage uptake of its standards that requires participation from each firm's Chief Financial Officer. Accountants and Bloomberg officials participate in each roundtable offering advice on how to measure new social and environmental impacts in ways that align with the financial reporting model (SASB 2013d). The CDSB has also implemented a corporate, investor, and regulator engagement program designed to train end users and test its CCRF. Similar to its counterparts, the objective of this outreach is to gather "evidence of user demand for climate disclosures sufficient to justify adoption of the CDSB Reporting Framework by securities regulators and stock exchanges" (CDSB 2013b).

Analysis of APG technical debates' standard setting reveals two distinct professional-organizational logics that define the field of ESG financial disclosure. Some constituencies question whether such disclosure can be aligned with financial reporting, while others oppose this effort, citing concerns about costs and complexity. APG initiatives use consultations and engagement with these constituencies to facilitate epistemic arbitrage whereby aspects of both perspectives are contested but also integrated into a separate technical consensus that exploits a "structural hole" by aligning social, environmental, and financial reporting. The development of this technical consensus is contingent on the capacity of APG to enable a two-level professional and organizational nexus where contestation on the first level is used to develop new knowledge on the second level. Each APG initiative has committed to a process of continual refinement whereby this nexus will be maintained to encourage feedback that can be used to improve uptake of their standards, and over time establish issue control (CDSB 2012; IIRC 2013d; SASB 2013f).

Conclusion

The growing influence of accounting expertise in efforts to standardize ESG reporting in mainstream financial disclosure has fueled a debate defined by a trade-off between civil society and market interests. Civil society actors question whether this approach can adequately capture ESG information, whereas corporate actors express concern that expanded disclosure is redundant, complex, and will increase costs. This debate has yet to assess APG initiatives as a common approach for deploying accounting expertise, or recent research on issue control among transnational professionals. This chapter questioned this dichotomy by exploring how APG initiatives try to establish issue control over ESG financial disclosure. Issue control is dependent on APG initiatives assuming a role as an "epistemic arbiter" for the requirements necessary to report ESG in financial disclosures. This capacity requires the creation of a new professional logic that blurs aspects of both civil society and market organizational logics but is distinctive as a new form of expertise.

APG initiatives have embraced a two-level organizational nexus whereby feedback from preparers, NGOs, investors, and accountants on the first level is used to generate a technical consensus on the second level that supports the disclosure of ESG information in financial reports. This epistemic arbitrage leverages existing professional logics among each stakeholder group to generate a new logic as a means of establishing issue control over ESG financial disclosure. To date, each APG initiative has developed a set of disclosure standards that align ESG information with the financial reporting model. Analysis on these standards reveals how they balance market and civil society logics in ways that separate the interests of APG actors from their organizational networks as accountants, preparers, investors, or NGOs.

But, consultations on these standards also suggest that APG issue control has yet to emerge despite efforts to align ESG and financial reporting logics. Civil society and financial actors both have similar expertise over reporting that can challenge APG consensus-building, politicize their standards, and collapse the two-level network back into competing professional logics. The risk of politicization is particularly acute for two reasons. First, as the use of APG standards grow, competition is likely to grow between different frameworks, which can expose decision-making to further scrutiny by ESG or financial logics. The CDSB and SASB have recognized this risk by supporting a "third level" to the nexus that seeks the adoption of their standards by financial regulators (CDSB 2013a; SASB 2013a). While an effective approach for harmonization, influencing regulation creates a second source of politicization, as many more constituencies are involved in establishing mandatory reporting standards. Despite the risk, this strategy represents the ultimate test for APG issue control.

8   All the Trader's Men

Professionals in International Trade Policymaking

Matthew Eagleton-Pierce

The creation and legitimation of expert knowledge is the *sine qua non* of professional work. In the study of transnational governance, across many fields of enquiry, all persons that are commonly called experts seek the power to speak and be heard by relevant audiences. To different degrees, they diagnose, infer and treat problems of governance that are deemed important (Abbott 1988). Understanding how such knowledge is crafted is a central and enduring analytical challenge. In one major sense, it helps us to explain why and how particular theories and modes of reasoning acquire a legitimised power and who benefits from such privileging. Such analysis also informs our appreciation for how forms of social critique contest and, in certain cases, reshape the orthodoxies of the time. Yet the definition of what makes one type of expertise 'authoritative' and, by contrast, other visions less valid is a very difficult question to examine, one which necessitates attention to not only canonical bodies of thought, forces of economic materialism and processes of institutionalisation but also the working dispositions of the experts themselves.

Within the space constraints here, this chapter aims to unravel part of the nexus between knowledge and power in relation to a particular world of professionals: the policymaking surrounding international trade. Trade experts are scattered across many institutional settings across the world: from government ministries and international institutions, to academic departments and civil society groups. Among the prominent players on this stage are economists who preach the benefits of 'free trade', lawyers who launch into cross-national 'trade wars' and researchers from charities who campaign for 'trade justice'. Some of these experts are full-time members of the trade policy game; they are immersed in its histories, agendas and customs. Other professionals intervene less frequently or in a selective manner, before addressing other research problems removed from trade politics. Certain professionals work at the coalface of diplomatic policymaking, such as providing counsel to governments on their trade strategies or writing studies that are deemed 'policy-relevant'.

Others, by contrast, prefer to operate at a critical distance from such political processes, anxious perhaps of the (negative) connotations or duties that may come from being too close to power.

Drawing upon the conceptual framework of this book, this chapter seeks to ask how one becomes a professional expert on international trade policy and, in particular, what accounts for how certain NGOs have acquired a greater role in such debates. To accomplish this, the argument delineates a new ideal-type categorisation of experts on trade policy: (1) those conventional lawyers and economists, referred to as 'authorised experts'; and (2) a newer class of civil society groups called 'critical technicians'. My major objective is to examine some of the distinguishing qualities of these types of professionals and how they struggle among themselves for social and political recognition. These trade issue professionals exist within a two-level network, coalescing around their own professional networks to mobilise support for issue control, while also engaging with organisations and their strategies for issue control. In this sense, the researchers I aim to objectify may be commonly defined as policy-relevant, although this does not preclude such players engaging in activities that are more autonomous from political forces.

By building upon insights from the sociology of Pierre Bourdieu, the argument probes the different ways in which authorised experts and critical technicians work within the scope of their particular mandates, mobilise resources and argue for their particular interests. The chapter is organised into three sections. First, a brief conceptual discussion contextualises and unpacks the analytical value of Bourdieu's notions of field and capital. In the second section, through applying these conceptual tools, I explain some of the main attributes of the authorised expert and the critical technician in the world of trade policy. In the final section, to give added detail, I offer a dedicated illustration of a trade politics problem – the West and Central African cotton issue at the World Trade Organization (WTO) – and explain how particular critical technicians were instrumental in the agenda-setting phase of this initiative.

Conceptual Framework

As explored by Yves Dezalay and Mikael Rask Madsen (see Chapter 2), Bourdieu's conceptual arsenal offers a valuable point of inspiration for the contemporary study of professionals and their working practices. Building upon their discussion, I briefly outline here two notions designed by Bourdieu that can help to enlighten the ways in which professionals emerge, organise and struggle between themselves for authority: the idea of field and the concept of scientific capital as a form of power. As with any application of Bourdieu's thinking tools, some cautions are required. In one key sense, as I have argued elsewhere in a Bourdieusian-inspired political economy of diplomatic trade talks (Eagleton-Pierce 2013), the proof of the theoretical pudding always remains in its empirical eating. Thus, the deployment of these notions should be read here as an initial sketch and test, one that provides a basis for a richer investigation into the historical ties between expertise and power in the international trading system (Eagleton-Pierce, forthcoming).

Following Weber and Durkheim, Bourdieu characterises modernity as a process of differentiation into relatively independent and increasingly specialised spheres of social action which he calls 'fields' (*champ*), such as the legal field (Bourdieu 1987), the literary field (Bourdieu 1983, 1993b) or the bureaucratic field (Bourdieu 1991, 2004a). Four main conceptual properties can be noted. First, Bourdieu characterises fields as spaces of struggle over the control of valued resources. These resources can take many forms, but he underscores how economic power is not the only important object of struggle. Each field thus contains certain central stakes that orientate the activities of agents, notwithstanding their material or normative differences, which may be considerable. In contrast to others outside the field, who are not ensconced within its social games, the stakes may appear unimportant or unintelligible. Second, every field has an unequal distribution of power and this has consequences on how opinions are articulated and which speakers acquire legitimacy. This leads one to an examination of what 'chips' – such as particular world-views, theories or modes of reasoning – are considered meaningful to agents. Third, for Bourdieu, a field tends to impose upon actors specific contests, which they reflect and constitute. Often, agents become 'caught up in the game' and its investments, a sense of *illusio* as he puts it. They may fail to clearly see how field effects – to be precise, the objective sets of power relations between positions – shape their individual dispositions. Fourth, each field tends to be relatively autonomous in its relations with other fields, thus enabling agents to identify it. The question of autonomy points to an assessment of field boundaries, including the competition between related fields.

Due to the tendency of professionals to often justify their actions in rational and universal terms, the very suggestion that they marshal and wield 'power' may be met with opposition from such players. But if professionals are concerned with the ability to control knowledge and skill within an area of common work (Abbott 1988), then Bourdieu's concept of scientific capital can be offered as a vehicle for elucidating the labour involved in such processes. Bourdieu (2004b: 55) defines this notion as 'a set of properties which are the product of acts of knowledge and recognition performed by agents engaged in the scientific field and therefore endowed with the specific categories of perception that enable them to make the pertinent distinctions, in accordance with the principle of pertinence that is constitutive of the *nomos* of the field'.[1] How can this idea be unpacked? By connecting 'science' with 'capital' we are seeking to further politicise the knowledge production process and the agents – both visible and distant – who benefit from it. There are clearly degrees of politicisation in how policy-facing professionals work; the definition of any researcher's 'interest' is, therefore, neither purely 'political' nor purely 'intellectual'. In Bourdieu's view, scientific capital is a type of symbolic recognition which tends to acquire a social profit through two ways: (1) the originality of the knowledge (the degree of innovation in comparison with the norm), and (2) its visibility (exposure and citation of the knowledge by others in the field). Beyond a focus on individual researchers, it is important to assess the control over scientific capital within a designated field because each contribution shapes the overall structure of scientific authority, including all the conceptual frameworks, methods and arguing practices that are regarded as 'orthodox' (the 'correct', 'straight' interpretation) (Bourdieu 1975, 1977).

The extent to which the orthodox forms of scientific capital can change, particularly in response to 'heterodox' critiques, is a key subsequent question. As noted in the introduction, professionals that are established and consecrated often have a proclivity to block rivals from entering their networks who do not share their perspective or who could encroach upon their resources. This often presents considerable challenges to pretenders who want to enter the field and acquire the visibility to redefine the meaning of scientific capital. In other words, if one does not possess the dominant scientific capital, one will probably struggle to be heard, because heterodox opinions are not aligned with the principles of legitimacy in the field (Bourdieu 1975). In this chapter, I want to draw attention to this particular problem of how certain heterodox critics manoeuvre – often in an experimental and tentative manner – towards greater professional recognition for their agendas. It follows that since 'fields exist only through the properties that agents invest in them' (Bigo 2011: 239), the struggle between 'orthodox' and 'heterodox' forms of scientific capital has the potential to modify the structure of the field itself. The practical entry conditions into such professional games, the relative

---

[1] The idea of scientific capital is derived from Bourdieu's analytical construction of the 'scientific field' in his sociology of science. In my empirical application, the invoking of scientific capital is partly designed to foreground how positivist principles and methods are upheld by many researchers who are engaged in trade policy analysis and, thus, an epistemological affinity can be drawn with the natural sciences.

value of the tokens assigned to players and the strategies adopted in the struggle for control will now be explored in the particular context of international trade policy.

Professional Struggles over Trade Policymaking

The analytical construction of trade policy research as a 'field' in the Bourdieusian sense is not without its problems.[2] In the first instance, as noted, a field must have a core stake that all players gravitate around, providing each agent with an underlying *telos* or prize to fight over. Despite the range of organisational *milieus* from which these professionals are drawn from, I would suggest that all trade experts tend to be attracted together by a particular normative inclination: that maintaining a capitalist trading system is a valuable use of political and material resources. It is, in other words, a game that is 'worth the candle'. By way of initial reasoning, many of these professionals are often infused with liberal sensibilities, to different degrees, but especially a universalist and meliorist attitude, as captured in the belief that freer trade is generally beneficial or that trade works as a vehicle for national and 'global' development. Imagining trade policy-making as a field is thus defined through observing how such researchers share certain common dispositions, resulting in 'an objective complicity which underlies all the antagonisms' (Bourdieu 1993: 73). Thus, the professional struggles taking place in this social space are rooted in *the power to control the legitimate logic for understanding trade policy and how it may be politically prosecuted*. Although this point may appear rather self-evident, particularly to those experts under examination, it realises a greater importance when evaluating the scientific capital considered valuable by these actors in achieving such ends.

A central concern in this volume is to explore how 'issue professionals' can be grasped as an emerging category of actor for governing transnational political life, beyond, but not neglecting, the classic study of professions founded upon a tailored education and formal institutionalisation. As I will argue, this insight informs my argument in two ways. First, compared to the earlier post-war decades, and not ignoring the enduring disciplinary dominance of law and economics, the field of policy-facing international trade research now incorporates a more heterogeneous

---

[2] One risk, present even in Bourdieu's scholarship, concerns the potential to have an over-proliferation of 'fields', diluting the overall impact of the concept. With my application, it could be suggested that the looser expression of 'social space' may be more preferable rather than field (although both terms are used interchangeably here) or, alternatively, that the arena of trade policy struggles is merely part of a larger 'global' field of power. For some of the most careful discussion of such problems, see Bigo 2011.

range of experts with different social backgrounds. Second, the argument urges caution with imputing that the organisation to which the professional is attached to or, more generally, their class of organisation (state, NGO, international organizations, firm etc.) determines their normative interests and working practices. Rather, in keeping with the framework of the book, the discussion here reveals how these knowledge producers exist in a two-level network, forming their own professional networks to mobilise support for their efforts at issue control, while also engaging directly with prominent organisations and their strategies of control.

The Authorised Expert

Historically, particularly under the shadow of the General Agreement on Tariffs and Trade (GATT), a treaty-based order for organising international trade that ran from 1947 to 1994, the social world of trade experts took on an enclosed appearance. Not unlike other regimes in international relations which call for 'technical' knowledge to understand their political form and stakes, the esoteric, often impenetrably dry subject matter of trade – such as debating the finer points of non-tariff barriers or domestic subsidies – did not enhance the prospect of broader academic or public deliberation. When disagreements arose among these research professionals, it was anticipated that the process for managing disputes would be conducted with discretion, often insulated from not only larger social groups but other government ministries that were not specifically tasked with a trade remit. In essence, this was a 'self-referential' community (Weiler 2001: 336). The cultivation of such insularity led, in Robert Howse's (2002: 98) words, to the shaping of a particular 'elite', 'insider network' or 'epistemic community'. Although it would be wrong to depict the agents in this universe as either completely homogeneous in their normative outlook or organised according to some calculated and codified plan, there was still a broad liberal ethos and practical 'sense of the game' regarding what problems of international trade merited analytical attention and how they should be treated.

Who are the actors within this field today? In terms of organisational complexes, there are international civil servants, legal interpreters, economists and statisticians who work within the WTO Secretariat in Geneva. Prominent trade-related departments are also located in other international bodies, including the World Bank, the International Monetary Fund (IMF), the Organisation for Economic Co-operation and Development (OECD), the United Nations Conference on Trade and Development (UNCTAD) and the United Nations Food and Agricultural Organization (FAO). More diffusely, through intergovernmental channels, there are current and former governmental officials who have been given a trade remit and, thus, contribute to public and private dialogues. In the academy, the major trade knowledge producers have a background in economics or law, with international relations and political science as subservient third gateways. Some of these academics may work closely with the policymaking process, such as sitting on WTO dispute settlement panels or consulting for international organisations and governments. However, the majority of academics would still be removed from direct political involvement in this manner. Finally, one can also note private lawyers who advise governments and firms, such as White & Case and Sidley Austin, the two leading firms with international trade practices, both of which have Geneva offices.

To say that the professionals who work within these circles are 'authorised' is a deliberate label. In one sense, it implies that a process of acquiring authority has been undertaken, culminating in an actor that is held in esteem and appreciation by their peers. In another sense, it invokes the idea that the recognised expert can sanction and countenance other agents or propositions and, thus, reproduce particular processes of authorisation and not others. In economics, for instance, any aspiring authorised expert would be expected to gain mastery over certain foundational principles of trade theory, rooted in the classical insights of Adam Smith but given formal and mathematical expression post-Ricardo (Irwin 1996; Fine and Milonakis 2009; Fourcade 2009). According to professionals who fall within this broad tradition, it is claimed that trade liberalisation exists in a positive relationship with economic growth. Increasing trade provides access to worldwide resources and markets, enlarging the consumption capacities of a country and enabling scale economies. Trade helps to reward those countries that possess a comparative advantage, whether in terms of labour efficiency or other factor endowments. In turn, it is argued that with more growth, a country is in a better position to reduce poverty, as illustrated by the enlarged middle class in China and India. In the contemporary literature, these arguments have built upon a general critique against import-substitution policies which are claimed to foster biases against exporting. Among other undesirable outcomes, it is suggested that such policies can lead to the rationing and misallocation of foreign exchange, the empowering of 'special interests' and the weakening of national institutions (Sachs and Warner 1995; Dollar and Kraay 2004; Winters 2004).

A figure such as Jagdish Bhagwati of Columbia University is an emblematic authorised expert who has articulated and echoed such opinions over 60 years. In a foundational sense, he acquired and nurtured a significant volume of scientific capital: an education at Cambridge and MIT; research and academic positions at US, UK and Indian institutions; and a prodigious publications output, including contributions to trade theory, the results of which have been debated in three separate *festchrift* volumes (Feenstra et al. 1996; Balasubramanyam and Greenaway 1996; Koekkoek and Mennes 1991). But his making as an authorised expert on trade, and the manner by which he has moved within a two-level professional network, is more sharply revealed through his public and policy interventions. For instance, Bhagwati has held several high-level consultancy positions within the major trade bodies, including advising the former GATT Director-General Arthur Dunkel, serving on an officially sanctioned expert group that debated the future of the WTO and acting as an advisor to UNCTAD and other UN agencies. Elsewhere, he frequently writes media commentaries on a range of trade policy questions, including for the *Financial Times*, the *Wall Street Journal*, and *Foreign Affairs*. Although it would be wrong to overstress the influence that Bhagwati has had on some larger trajectories in trade policy – for instance, he has been a trenchant critic of the growth in preferential arrangements beyond the WTO, yet they continue to be negotiated at a significant pace – his consistent work at defending 'globalisation' (Bhagwati 2004) through distilling neoclassical theory into digestible forms has aided the legitimisation of a certain mainstream perspective.

Beyond Bhagwati, there are many other professionals who could also be called authorised experts on trade. For instance, since the 1960s, John Jackson, Professor of Law at Georgetown University and formally of the University of Michigan, has played a very important role in helping to tutor students in the study of international economic law, leading some commentators to suggest that he 'largely invented the field' (Kennedy 1995: 672). In one sense, Jackson has served as a kind of 'pragmatic conscience for liberal trade without becoming identified with any one issue or policy dispute' (Kennedy 1995: 673). Building upon his insights as a former member of the Office of the US Trade Representative, he has advocated a 'rules-based' international trading order, but conceived as a kind of 'management tool' for businesses and government officials, rather than a utopian narrative (Howse 1999; see Jackson 1997, for a landmark text). One of Jackson's signature policy achievements was helping to build political momentum for the creation of the WTO, first outlined in a Chatham House paper (Jackson 1990), before serving as a consultant for a sympathetic Canadian government who championed the idea and, ultimately, as an advisor to Peter Sutherland, the last GATT Director-General who, in 1994, shepherded the Uruguay Round of trade talks to a close (also see the recounting by VanGrasstek (2013: 50) who notes Jackson's status as the 'father of the WTO').

Nonetheless, most authorised experts are not as visible as Jackson or Bhagwati and, indeed, will never be able (or aspire) to build such volumes of scientific capital in the field. Their everyday forms of professional labour – from deploying computable general equilibrium models that aim to forecast future trade patterns to organising conferences that debate the finer ties between trade and other policy domains – may appear to outsiders as the trappings of a technocracy with its specialised agendas, codes and vocabularies. In the larger galaxy of transnational issue professionals, the authorised experts of trade policy contribute to the seemingly endless process of incrementally remapping the capitalist system around a liberal ethos. But to say that the research practices of all the authorised experts in trade operate within a bounded scientific 'orthodoxy' must always be treated with care since, importantly, the orthodoxy is not some rigidly imposed ideology. On the contrary, part of the efficacy of trade orthodoxy lies in how it adapts to heterodox criticism, even if in a partial or distorted manner (Eagleton-Pierce 2013). In this respect, perhaps the distinguishing quality of an orthodoxy centres on how it reacts to, and fortifies itself against, other *potential orthodoxies*; opinions that are positioned as heterodox by virtue of having a marginalised status (Berlinerblau 2001). This brings us to consider my argument regarding how the authorised expert has faced competition from other professionals who are more sceptical about the liberal trade project.

The Critical Technician

Since the 1990s, the trade policy has witnessed the emergence of certain critical voices that, I would suggest, have partially disturbed and redefined the logic of what can be considered under the category of trade politics. This is commonly acknowledged by noting the rise of different NGOs, operating at national, regional and international levels, which have campaigned on trade-related questions (see Hopewell 2015). The contemporary seeds of this activism are found in farming collectives and union protests against the GATT Uruguay Round in the 1980s, before morphing into opposition against the North American Free Trade Agreement (NAFTA) and, onwards, to the alter-globalisation movements that coalesced around the turn of the century, including prominent protests at the Seattle WTO Ministerial in 1999 (Murphy 2010; Lang 2011). My interest here is not in those actors who conduct 'street-level' mobilisations (although I do not discount that the study of these actors remains important) but, rather, in those NGOs that have heavily invested in research on trade policy, a focus that has received only limited attention (Tussie 2009; Hannah 2014). I suggest here that the cultivation of this social critique – where rigorous research is pursued with a contrarian disposition – has forged a new type of professional expert in the world of trade policy, labelled here as the critical technician.

Understanding how the critical technician has entered the trade policy field is a difficult problem to unpack. I would argue that this type of professional began to emerge in the 1990s within a more contestable intellectual environment on trade policy. These field dynamics were partly generated from a small number of prominent empirical economists who were sceptical about the orthodox case for free trade. Thus, work by these authors featured more cautious claims about what international trade policy could accomplish, especially in terms of the linkages between trade, growth and poverty. For instance, in one prominent analysis, Francisco Rodríguez and Dani Rodrik (2000: 266) critiqued the econometrics underpinning some major studies, arguing that the relationship between trade 'openness' and growth was not 'general' and 'unambiguous' but most likely 'contingent' and 'dependent on a host of country and external characteristics'. Other more forceful critics, such as Ha-Joon Chang (2003), argued that Western countries only became rich through high tariff walls in earlier phases of their development, contradicting the dominant narrative that border restrictions always lead to regressive outcomes. By the 2000s, such ideas had dovetailed with an examination of how trade policy changes are connected to industrial organisation, domestic institutions and the so-called 'sequencing of reforms' (Rodrik 2006). Such thinking was given renewed focus when rules under negotiation at the WTO appeared, from the perspective of some writers, to be narrowing the 'development space' for poorer countries to defend their economic interests (UNCTAD 2002; Wade 2003; Gallagher 2005).

The confluence of these forces – rising popular discontent surrounding the perceived harmful effects of 'globalisation' combined with some important interventions by such economists – created more attractive conditions for research-led activism on trade policy. In a Bourdieusian sense, therefore, the boundaries of the field were becoming slightly more porous, facilitating entry points for emerging critical professionals to increase their recognition, but on terms partially of their own making. The work of certain leading figures within Oxfam International can be highlighted as an interesting illustration. In 1991, Kevin Watkins joined Oxfam from the Catholic Institute of International Relations, rising from a Policy Analyst up to the position of Head of Research. One of the major lessons that Watkins took from the 1980s and early 1990s, when the Uruguay Round established the rules for the new WTO, was that activists on trade policy were left significantly behind the main action that shaped the global agenda: corporate lobbying of Western governments (also see

Wilkinson, 1996).[3] Without solid research into monitoring how trade law tended to be framed in favour of the powerful and how, in turn, to propose new agendas that could encourage social and economic justice for all, Watkins argued that Oxfam would not be able to make a major impact. But research alone was insufficient. One also needed strong partnerships with different organisations, including other civil society groups and government ministries (some of which may be ambivalent about Oxfam's role). Finally, the research had to be fused with a third element: the design of tailored campaigning material that would resonate with different targeted audiences, including particular governments, international organisations, the media and the wider public.[4]

But what forms of scientific capital were considered valuable to professionals such as Watkins as they built a research agenda on trade policy? Oxfam is clearly a diverse confederation of organisations with many competing voices seeking to shape how the resources of the group are deployed. On trade policy, however, Watkins, among others, encouraged a more macro perspective that was not fundamentally 'anti-trade' or 'anti-growth' (stronger attitudes that were common within internal Oxfam debates in the 1980s) but, rather, sought to explain how discriminatory rules of international commerce could be reformed in favour of the poor.[5] This political choice is important to underline because it returns us to Bourdieu's (1993b: 73) point about how a deeper 'complicity' can bind agents together within a field, despite often intense competition between such figures on the surface. If one did not commit to such a starting principle – that the world trade system is a game worth fighting for – Watkins, along with other critical technicians, would not be able to enter the trade policy field and engage with authorised experts. This should not be taken to mean that critical technicians of different colours do not imagine or desire a different capitalist system, or a world beyond capitalism but, rather, that they tend to publically commit to working within the parameters of dominant institutional agendas.

Three major professional tasks confront the critical technician in formulating research that could be potentially resonant. First, since the strength of any scientific capital is partly derived from its distinctiveness from the norm, the choice of what trade issue to examine is crucial. In terms of scale, no trade-related NGO or research group, including even larger policy hubs such as the Geneva-based International Centre for Trade and Sustainable Development (ICTSD), has the resources to

---

[3] Kevin Watkins, former Head of Research, Oxfam International, interview with the author, Oxford, 13 June 2011.
[4] Ibid.   [5] Ibid.

outcompete the operations of the World Bank, the OECD or the WTO Secretariat. At the same time, many trade issues, such as those involving rules on origin or anti-dumping codes, have a labyrinthine complexity that is not easily translatable to the many audiences NGOs wish to address. In one sense, therefore, the Oxfam trade 'mandate' is partly structured through which issues can be digested relatively quickly. In particular, if one can find a pertinent and topical 'trigger issue' that illuminates a larger cause – which may be framed under 'social justice' or 'sustainability' – then resources could be better mobilised.[6] According to Watkins, and reiterated by his predecessor Duncan Green, this decision is often formed through a range of difficult deliberations over if the issue is 'winnable', that is, the extent to which a positive policy adjustment could result from the research. These judgments are, however, always tentative, speculative and founded upon trial-and-error experiences of past research projects.[7]

Second, in terms of actual outputs, and further revealing the 'technician' side of their identity, Oxfam reports are often grounded with strong empirics. Explanations may include unpicking the legal inequities within trade rules or using economic modelling and statistical analysis to prove cause-and-effect linkages, that is, deploying similar methodological tools that are legitimately prized by many authorised experts. In addition, the research frequently incorporates punchy quotes from persons 'on the ground' in poor countries – farmers, labourers or other producers – who are claimed to be impacted by the problem under investigation. By combining these sources of evidence, the critical technician is able to appeal to different logics of legitimacy: the rigours of the 'impersonal' scientific method are implicitly respected, yet the numbers are politically interpreted through 'common victims' that are presumed to speak a more 'authentic truth'. Third, a series of other concerns surround what could be called the style or presentation of the critical technician. Here, the appeal to 'killer facts and graphics' (Green 2012) is particularly important as a way to quickly communicate a sense of injustice to the media and political officials. For instance, one of the most memorable 'killer facts' composed by Oxfam was the following: 'Every EU cow receives over $2 per day in support and subsidies, more than the income of half the world's people.' According to Duncan Green, composing effective killer facts and graphics can be key to encouraging different audiences to read the associated report.[8]

---

[6] Ibid.

[7] Duncan Green, Head of Research, Oxfam International, interview with the author, London, 27 May 2011.

[8] Ibid.

Illustration: The WTO African Cotton Initiative

In this final section, a particular trade policy issue can be briefly high-lighted as a way to explain how Oxfam, as a prominent collective of critical technicians, worked within a two-level network of professional organisation to problematise a neglected trade topic. The case centres on a coalition of West and Central African (WCA) countries – Benin, Burkina Faso, Mali and Chad – who began campaigning in 2003 at the WTO for the liberalisation of cotton trade. These countries are highly competitive in cotton production and sought greater access to foreign markets, particularly China, in order to enhance their livelihood standards. They argued, however, that their access was being impeded by highly subsidised US cotton farmers whose own competitiveness was artificially inflated. The issue quickly became a contentious touchstone and absorbed a considerable portion of the WTO's negotiating energy, including spawning a major, related dispute settlement case by Brazil against the United States (Eagleton-Pierce 2013).

Oxfam, along with a network of other civil society players, played a significant role in the very creation of 'African cotton' as a political issue that needed WTO attention. Although it is often tricky to identify the relative significance of these contributions and how, in particular, WCA officials interpreted their activism, it is safe to say that the initiative would not have been the same without such input. In the first place, the work of Watkins needs to be credited with mainstreaming the empirical connection between US cotton subsidies and WCA livelihoods. His 2002 report, *Cultivating Poverty* – backed by strong statistical analysis, a political critique of US cotton policy and quotes from WCA farmers – had a key impact in terms of increasing information awareness (Oxfam International 2002). As *Cultivating Poverty* became more widely read and cited, Oxfam's Geneva-based advocacy team plotted how cotton could be articulated in the WTO context. In particular, researchers such as Céline Charveriat and Romain Benicchio consulted with lawyers and analysts based at ICTSD.[9] The latter group became important in terms of building solidarity between African missions in Geneva, as well as connecting ambassadors with other relevant actors, including a Senegal-based network called Environment and Development Action in the Third World (ENDA or L'organisation inter-nationale enda tiers-monde).[10] Finally, a consultancy in Geneva called the

---

[9] Romain Benicchio, Advocacy Officer, Oxfam International, interview with the author, Geneva, 26 September 2006.
[10] El Hadji A. Diouf, Programme Coordinator, Africa Trade Programme, International Centre for Trade and Sustainable Development, interview with the author, Geneva, 29 September 2006.

IDEAS Centre, led by a former Swiss Ambassador, Nicolas Imboden, deserves attention. Imboden's work has been noted by many actors close to the initiative.[11] One of the differences between the IDEAS Centre and other civil society players was the quality of Imboden's social network: he had the political contacts and acquired expertise to meet regularly with high-level government officials in the region, notably through the Economic Community of West African States (ECOWAS).[12] Indeed, according to some insiders, Imboden was intimately involved in the drafting of the first official dossier that would be submitted to the WTO (also see Sneyd 2011; Blustein 2009).

If this mobilisation among critical technicians represents one level of professional labour, how did such players interact with the WTO directly? Here, in broad terms, I would suggest that Imboden, along with ICTSD experts, played broker-type roles in order to translate WCA cotton into the WTO negotiating mandate. In order to create a political rupture, but in a manner that would not be easily rejected by defenders of WTO norms and rules, two arguments were advanced. First, despite WCA producers adhering to orthodox trade practices – historically promoted by the United States – their efforts were being nullified as a result of discriminatory WTO rules that allowed for excessive subsidisation. Second, Imboden consciously argued that the cotton problem should be read through the frame of 'development', now a highly legitimate term in WTO lexicon due to the latest trade round being labelled a 'development agenda'. By 2004, through a series of arduous political negotiations, this twin approach eventually proved effective at institutionalising WCA cotton as a discrete trade issue in the WTO mandate (Eagleton-Pierce 2013). Thus, to return to a common theme of the book, this example reveals how action among critical technicians was the impetus for an agenda-setting process that would later crystallise into WTO law. At least initially, issue control was not directed by the WTO, other international organisations or member states, but derived from other policy-facing professionals. In time, however, as cotton became a 'normal' concern, debates became increasingly bureaucratised, including closer involvement of other authorised experts, especially linked to the World Bank (John Baffes) and the WTO Secretariat (Chiedu Osakwe).

---

[11] Imboden's contribution was recognised by WCA policymakers, including Ambassador Samuel Améhou at the Benin mission in Geneva (until 2007); Jason Hafemeister, former Deputy Assistant US Trade Representative for Agriculture and lead negotiator on agriculture during the Doha Round (until 2007); two officials at the WTO Secretariat who declined to be named; and another trade analyst who also wished to remain anonymous.

[12] Nicolas Imboden, Executive Director, IDEAS Centre, interview with the author, Geneva, 27 September 2006.

Conclusion

This chapter has sought to explore how the professional strategies of policy-relevant experts on trade policy can be better grasped through a Bourdieusian conceptual lens. In their efforts to shape issue control, these professionals navigate within a two-level network: mobilising around their own immediate social *milieus* and, in certain interventions, engaging with established organisations and their attempts at issue control. As stressed at the beginning, the categories of the authorised expert and the critical technician are ideal-type formulations; further empirical enquiries are needed to substantiate the analytical form and value of such notions. A particular emphasis has been placed on explaining some of the common practices of the critical technician, including the scientific capital that is valued by such figures. On the one hand, many critical technicians target the tensions, inconsistencies and contradictions within the orthodoxy reproduced by authorised experts. In the words of Luc Boltanski and Eve Chiapello (2007: 495), they are frequently found 'tightening up' the 'tests of justification', that is, to make whatever is the test of the moment ('liberalisation is good', 'the WTO enables fair negotiations', etc.) 'stricter'. In short, they make the management of power more demanding for the privileged. On the other hand, however, the critical technician always runs a risk that, in pursuit of multiple goals, of which the reproduction of their own networked field position is a key one, they may become overly cautious and stray too close to the more orthodox arguments expressed by the authorised experts. This anxious dance – between a creative ethic that seeks a greater 'good' and the need to appeal to power – lies at the heart of the professional conduct of such players.

9   Professional Activists on Tax Transparency

Adam Baden and Duncan Wigan

This chapter explores contestation over one aspect of the international corporate transparency agenda, company reports. Recent legislation in the United States and the European Union impose a new financial reporting standard on firms in specific sectors. The OECD's Base Erosion and Profit Shifting initiative (OECD 2015) instigated by the G20 and pushed at the G8 has addressed how to upgrade governance in the area of taxation, including country-level MNC reporting. These changes and initiatives dilute what has been the dominance of the International Accounting Standards Board (IASB) over the transnational governance of the corporate financial reporting regime and go some way in meeting the agenda of a large transnational activist network (TAN) seeking greater corporate transparency. We investigate the role of the NGO community in contesting expertise on corporate reporting and defining this shift. One organization, the Tax Justice Network (TJN) has been central in defining campaign targets and catalyzing action in the NGO community and policy environment (Seabrooke and Wigan 2015). In impacting an issue area, this specialist research and advocacy organization deployed professional expertise within an environment where such expertise is scarce. TJN leveraged professional resources to become a key broker in the process leading to the adoption of the new legislation and international guidelines and conventions, providing a broader activist network with the professional knowledge necessary to intervene in the parameters of the possible in terms of what a new reporting standard could demand. Work on TANs draws our attention to the importance of issue characteristics, political strategy and political salience in determining issue adoption, non-adoption and control (Carpenter 2010; Keck and Sikkink 1998; Wong 2012). This chapter highlights the importance of professional knowledge, organizational form and the

The research for this chapter was supported by the European Commission 2020 Framework Program project 'European Legitimacy in Governing through Hard Times (#649456-ENLIGHTEN)'.

interactions between organizational logics and professional logics in issue definition, activation and control. In this case issue professionals and network brokerage have trumped formal authority and rule-making, changing issue content and shifting the location of issue control.

We scrutinize the process leading to the emergence of a new corporate reporting framework, country-by-country-reporting (CBCR). The analysis is based on a three-year observation period and repeated semi-structured interviews with members of the NGO community working on the issue and other stakeholders, including firms, professional bodies and policy makers. We focus on how TJN and the issue professionals that inhabit it gained influence within the NGO network pushing for greater transparency among firms in the extractives sector and on the policy process leading to EU legislation and an urgent and much broader policy debate within the G8, the G20 and OECD on generalized CBCR and unitary taxation.[1] Increased political salience has led to an intensification of competition over global tax policy, with regulators, practitioners and activists weighing in on who has the expertise to address these highly technical policy issues. TJN propelled its agenda into the heart of this policy debate and hard law.[2] Through the contesting of credible expertise on financial reporting, IASB issue control has been diluted and an international tax agenda has been grafted onto a narrower corporate transparency agenda. We draw on the two-level network imagery (see Figure 1.1) from Chapter 1 (this volume and Seabrooke and Wigan 2016) to map out key professionals and organizations active on the issue of corporate reporting, with professionals deploying contrasting professional logics and contesting expertise to define the issue on the lower surface and organizational competition on the upper surface over where the issue is controlled.

The chapter is structured as follows. The first section contrasts the current framework for geographical reporting in IASB accounting standards with CBCR. We point to the significance of conflicting definitions of CBCR, which mirror professional logics at play and mark the struggle to define the reporting framework's emergence. One basis on which to identify the influence of TJN is the interplay between these conflicting definitions. The second section describes the two-level network in which the issue is addressed to identify the specificity of TJN's position and how

---

[1] The more radical proposal for unitary taxation promotes a system wherein firms are taxed on the results of global operations, and the revenue is divided between countries on the basis of 'real economy' indicators such as employee numbers, capital invested, sales and turnover. This would be an international tax regime anchored on CBCR information.

[2] For instance, the Fourth Capital Requirements Directive (CRDIV), implementing Basel III in Europe, requires European banks to provide full contextual data for country-by-country reporting.

TJN combines organizational form, professional knowledge and network position to impact issue definition on the lower surface of the triangle and policy innovation and change on the upper surface. A third section demonstrates TJN's role in the promotion of a particular notion of CBCR and the transformation of the demand for transparent reporting in the extractives sector into a debate about the technical specification of CBCR in European legislation and the work of the OECD. As specialists working on tax issues, TJN was able to graft an agenda onto that of the broader activist community seeking higher levels of transparency in corporate reports. Further, we reflect upon our analysis and the ongoing journey of CBCR at the G20, G8 and OECD's Base Erosion and Profit Shifting initiative to demonstrate how the issue of corporate financial reporting and CBCR is now addressed and contested in multiple venues, challenging the IASB's former issue control. In the Conclusion we reflect upon how professional attributes, organizational characteristics and network position can be navigated and deployed in transforming transnational governance for corporate reporting.

Country-by-country reporting

Corporate reports reflect the ongoing performance of a firm in relation to other firms and established benchmarks. In recent decades corporate reports have proliferated and now cover labour standards, corporate social responsibility and environmental performance (see Thistlethwaite, this volume). Reports empower or serve the interests of different constituencies and are mandated to pursue a defined purpose. Environmental reports empower civil society groups to monitor contributions to greenhouse gas emissions. Equally, governments will seek knowledge of environmental performance to inform regulatory innovation. The dominant mode of corporate disclosure is annual reports. These contain company accounts, the key market performance metric. Financial reports have been understood and designed to prioritize and protect the interests of investors, taking the form of a consolidated (global) overview of firm performance. In the case of multinational corporations (MNCs) this encompasses and amalgamates the performance of numerous related entities across multiple jurisdictions.

That MNCs are not required to break down their financial position geographically makes it difficult to specify a firm's activity in a particular jurisdiction and masks arbitrage between variegated national tax systems. International Financial Reporting Standard 8 (IFRS 8) on 'Operating Segments' addresses geographical disclosures by corporations. Despite initial opposition from European interests, IFRS 8 became effective in 2009 (Büthe and Mattli 2011: 99–101) and provided a choice between two definitions of an operational segment. The 'Line of Business' method allows a corporation like Apple to report financial information according to product lines such as tablets, phones and laptops, while the 'Geographical Segment' method reflects geographical performance. However, segments are not defined at the country level and might be 'Europe' or 'Asia-Pacific'. In consequence, even if a company opts to disclose its financial information by geographical segment, the IFRS 8 framework does not require a breakdown by country.

The MNC is an economic, not legal category and consequently appears as a series of separate entities incorporated in distinct jurisdictions (Picciotto 1992). While accounts reflect the global economic integration of the MNC, the 'separate entity principle' enables MNCs to navigate the international terrain so as to allocate profits, losses, costs and assets in various jurisdictions and potentially minimize overall fiscal contributions. MNCs may channel profits to subsidiaries in low tax jurisdictions and concentrate costs and losses in higher tax jurisdictions. For instance, only 6 per cent of Apple's 2010 global pre-tax global income was allocated to jurisdictions other than Ireland and the United States (US PSI 2013). The disjuncture between the fiscal capacity of the state and mobile capital has risen up the political and public agenda (Eccleston 2012; Morgan 2014; Seabrooke and Wigan 2014, Seabrooke and Wigan 2017), leading to an effort to graft issues of international taxation onto narrower corporate transparency agendas as the means and ends of corporate reporting have become subject to intense debate.

CBCR requires companies to provide reports to reflect performance in each jurisdiction in which they operate. The purposes of CBCR impact the technical specification of the CBCR framework. Lesage and Kaçar (2013) refer to 'maximalist' and 'minimalist' frameworks of CBCR. While both seek to widen the group of stakeholders benefiting from corporate reporting by rendering corporate operations in different jurisdictions more transparent, they differ in terms of the information to be disclosed and the purposes for which this information can be used. While the 'minimalist' version serves a more restricted development and anti-corruption agenda, the 'maximalist' version embeds this in a wider systemic agenda seeking to ameliorate the effects of corporate international tax planning. This second agenda distinguishes TJN from the broader civil society network.

A minimalist version of CBCR demands that corporations disclose, for each country of operation, payments made to governments. These payments include taxes, royalties, dividends and bonuses. Such disclosure enables civil society groups and other stakeholders to hold governments accountable for the revenue they receive from MNCs. The target of these transparency demands is predominantly government in resource-rich countries, in which corruption related to the extractive industries is perceived to have impeded social development. Distinctive from the maximalist demand for full contextual data, minimalist CBCR requires the disclosure of nominal amounts flowing from companies to governments on a country-by-country basis. The minimalist version has to date been targeted solely at the extractives and forestry sectors and as such does not represent a call for a broad transformation in the content and purpose of company accounts. This version sits squarely in a development logic that emphasizes the interplay between corruption and the resource curse, or the failure to benefit from resource wealth due to opaque governance and illicit payments.

A maximalist version of CBCR, on the other hand, starts from the recognition that any data must be contextualized to be meaningful. Just as the evaluation of profit rates requires contextual data on capital costs, costs of sales and turnover, the taxes paid by corporations are impossible to compare to statutory tax rates, unless full contextual data are provided on the financial performance of the reporting entity in the jurisdiction in question. Hence, the maximalist CBCR demands that MNCs disclose in all the countries where they are operational company names, pre-tax profit, tax payments to the government in question, sales and purchases split between intra-group transactions, labour costs, employee numbers and external transactions (Murphy 2012). The maximalist framework places reports for each operational jurisdiction in the context of all the operations of the MNC, allowing stakeholders to capture the impact of internal transfers on tax payments in any one jurisdiction. The target of the maximalist version of CBCR is systemic, not specific to any group of countries or sectors. Maximalist CBCR seeks to realign where corporate profits are booked with the location of profit-producing activities across all sectors and re-calibrate the relationship between the fiscal state and mobile capital in the form of the MNC.

Professions and Organizations on Geographical Reporting

This section addresses the constellation of and dynamics between professionals and organizations that have delimited the evolution of the issue of geographical reporting. Strategic interaction between professional and organizational networks is preconditioned by professional attributes and organizational attributes. In combination, networks and attributes define the locus of issue control and allow for an understanding of what seems a remarkable paradox. The international financial reporting regime is an extraordinary example of transnational issue management being almost exclusively controlled by the private sector and expert-led standard setting body, the IASB. The IASB develops and issues international rules for accounting in the form of IFRS, which are now required or permitted in more than one hundred countries. The European Union defers on accounting to the technocratic authority of the IASB (Büthe and Mattli 2011; Porter 2005), transposing IFRS into EU hard law through an institutionalized endorsement process. This well-resourced and relatively insulated organization displays a very close alignment between its organizational tasks and the skills of the issue professionals – mainly accountants and lawyers – involved in its activities (Perry and Nölke 2006). As such, the IASB maintains a strong authoritative claim to issue control, mirrored in its organizational form and circumscribed by a commitment to provide capital market participants with information to guide investment decisions. Despite this strong basis for IASB issue control and the limited resources of TJN, direct influence on debates surrounding the form and social purpose of company reports has been exerted by TJN. By acting as a broker between a large NGO network, Publish What You Pay (PWYP), the European Union and the OECD, TJN has been able to circumvent IASB issue control.

TJN was formally established at the British Parliament in March 2003 as a single issue organization seeking to raise the level of awareness about offshore finance, promote links between interested parties across the developed and developing world, stimulate and organize research and debate and encourage national and international campaigning activity. The network focuses on research and high-level advocacy work and in doing so relies on a specific set of professional skills held by its core members. TJN1, the Network Director since 2004, was formerly a trust and estate planner in Jersey and served for ten years as Economic Advisor to the States of Jersey in the British Channel Islands. An economist with direct experience working in a leading 'tax haven', TJN1 is well positioned to lead a research and advocacy organization working on an issue characterized by complexity and therefore posing considerable barriers to entry. TJN2 is a UK-based Professor of Accountancy with prior commercial experience at a large oil major in London. TJN3 is a Harvard graduate who has worked as Chief Economist for McKinsey & Co and served as business development manager in the chairman's office at General Electric under Jack Welch. He is the author of five monographs, three of which focus on money laundering, tax evasion and capital flight. TJN3 is a member of the New York Bar and managing director of a technology-focused private equity firm and consultancy. TJN4 has been a Professor of Law since 1992 and was a Commonwealth Fellow at the Chicago School of Law. He is the author of key texts on international business taxation and business regulation. TJN5 is a chartered accountant who trained at Peat Marwick (subsequently KPMG) in London, became senior partner in a London-based firm of accountants and has been Chair, CEO or finance director of a range of entrepreneurial companies.

The professional attributes of these core members enable the network to navigate and confidently address a complex and multifaceted issue. To comprehend and address issues of international tax governance requires high-level competencies in law, accounting, tax, business and economics. In aggregate this core membership, bound by a singular normative vision, encompasses these competencies and as such is able to provide research and advocacy based on professional knowledge and logics to service an increasingly large NGO community seeking to campaign on tax-related issues. While the NGO community is replete with passionate and skilled campaigners, it suffers a relative scarcity of the professional competencies necessary to successfully intervene on the multifaceted issue of tax justice or confront the orthodoxy on the fundamental building blocks of corporate reporting. This is the specific role of the professional critic, insiders turned outsiders who can furnish a network with the scarce resource of expert critique. Notably, of the core members we identify, only the Director is employed by the Network (until 2007 he was the sole employee), while the others maintain independent careers. The peculiarity of TJN's professional profile is reflected in the specificity of the organization's attributes.

As the introduction to this volume contends, organizational characteristics may be more significant than the formal designation of an organization in determining how professionals and organizational logics interact and are strategically deployed to pursue organizational goals. It might be expected that organizations that are able to harness networks for their goals and exert control over an issue through a network will be large, well-resourced and institutionally embedded either with a strong formal mandate of control or a strong normative mandate constituted on the basis of the claim to represent a significant constituency. Large NGOs would meet these criteria for a powerful and efficient organization. TJN singularly fails to do so, but has accrued network centrality and issue control despite this. An examination of the characteristics of organizations with an interest in the issue of corporate reporting makes this clear. Notably, TJN is a professional network with a singular focus on tax justice, considerable autonomy, high barriers to entry, a high degree of knowledge centralization and few resources. For TJN, resource scarcity is compensated by expertise and the traversal of the professional logics of accounting, business,

Table 9.1 *Contrasting Organizational Attributes*

Characteristic / Organization	Scope	Autonomy	Hiring	Knowledge Centralization	Resources
Oxfam	Broad	Moderate	Open	Low	High
IASB	Narrow	High	Closed	High	High
PWYP	Narrow	High	Open	Low	High
TJN	Narrow	High	Closed	High	Low

economics and law on the one hand and the organizational logics of development and the market that define the broader TAN and the IASB on the other (Table 9.1).

The third organization central to the policy evolution we analyse is PWYP. Established in 2002 as a single-issue campaign, PWYP supports national coalitions that campaign for mandatory disclosure of company payments and government revenues from the oil, gas and mining sector. The coalition is comprised of 800 organizations, including large NGOs such as Oxfam America, Transparency International, Human Rights Watch, Global Witness and the George Soros-funded programme Revenue Watch. PWYP operates across seventy countries and is well resourced. While PWYP has considerable expertise in issues pertaining to the 'resource curse' and development more broadly, it confronts considerable hurdles in appreciating the full ramifications of alternative accounting technologies. Low levels of knowledge centralization and low barriers to entry condition a narrower focus on payments to governments by corporations in the extractives sector. This narrow focus reflects the development logic of the TAN and contrasts with TJN's argument that the resource curse is not solely an outcome of errant company and government behaviour in developing countries but a result of systemic deficiencies in the international governance architecture for taxation.

The organizational configuration surrounding the issue of corporate reporting places in tension two distinctive organizational and professional logics, the market logic of the IASB and the development logic of PWYP. TJN is positioned to broker within the TAN and between these logics on the basis of professional capacity and organizational autonomy that allows the organization to fill a structural hole in the network surrounding financial reporting. This position and capacity have enabled TJN to graft onto the development agenda of PWYP a broader international tax agenda and loosen the hold of the IASB on the issue of corporate reporting.

Expanding the World of CBCR

The first governance initiative to introduce a reporting framework which mandates country-level disclosures by MNCs was the Extractive Industries Transparency Initiative (EITI), launched in 2002 by UK Prime Minister Tony Blair in response to intensive campaigning by the PWYP coalition. The EITI resonated with a shift in the development discourse around the turn of the millennium, often referred to as the Monterrey Consensus.[3] This recognized that mobilization of developing countries' domestic resources offered a more viable route to development than international aid. Specifically, the EITI was set up as a global program designed to combat the 'resource curse' – the experience of corruption, conflict and underdevelopment common to many resource-rich developing countries, despite their endowment of natural resources. Governments that sign up to implementing the EITI standards are required to publish a report on the revenues received from the extractive industries while all extractive companies in that country must disclose the payments made to governments. These reports are then compiled into an EITI report by an independent administrator, which compares the results and whether there is congruence between what companies say they pay and what governments say they receive. Hence, the EITI initially constituted a minimalist CBCR regime for the main purpose of improving resource management and reducing government corruption.[4]

TJN5 originally published CBCR in January 2003 in the form of a template for an international accounting standard (Murphy 2003). This emerged from a meeting between three subsequently core TJN members in Jersey. The meeting addressed the impact of Jersey's offshore strategy on the island and more broadly in the developing and developed world and the question of the best means to tackle tax injustice. TJN5 suggested country-by-country reporting. This marked the advent of a new accounting concept, campaign vehicle and advocacy target. CBCR as promoted by TJN was intended as a reporting framework that would increase the level of transparency in the activities of cross-border firms and provide the information necessary to ensure these firms made due fiscal contribution in host states. The framework targeted all sectors in all countries.

TJN in 2004 began cooperating with PWYP. Crucial here is that the broad network understood the resource curse through a development

---

[3] Established at 2002 International Conference on Financing for Development in Monterrey, Mexico.
[4] See Haufler (2010) for analysis of the evolution of the EITI and corporate transparency agenda.

logic that conceptualized the underlying problem as corruption. As such, the demands of PWYP, transparency as to payments made to host governments without any corresponding accounting data or contextual data, may shed light on corruption and stark incongruities between payments to governments and levels of investment and extraction. However, the demands, if met, would not reveal sufficient data to surmise what the correct level of payment should be or how a cross-border firm was using the international tax architecture to minimize taxes paid across its global activities. The EITI standard would not deliver the data necessary to evaluate whether payments were commensurate to the activities of the firm in the host country or data which could be aggregated to isolate cross-border tax avoidance. In the early 2000s, the geographical corporate reporting demanded by NGOs targeted developing country corruption, and was only manifest in concrete form, in the EITI standard, as a voluntary compliance mechanism. Both the demands of the PWYP network and the EITI standard did not constitute a full-blown accounting technology that would be capable of ameliorating international tax arbitrage.

PWYP picked up the concept of CBCR in 2005 after Global Witness, one of the lead organizations in the network, published 'Extracting Transparency – The Need for an IFRS for the Extractive Industries'. This had been drafted by TJN5 and marked the insertion of the TJN agenda into that of the broader network. For the first time PWYP reporting demands included information on commercial performance as well as the prior demands of absolute payments and reserves (Global Witness 2005: 1). By 2005, PWYP was campaigning for CBCR to be introduced in IFRS 6 for the extractive sectors, and subsequently pushed for its inclusion in IFRS 8. Despite setting up a sub-group on the topic of CBCR, the IASB took a largely obstructive stance with regard to the demands of PWYP. This stance has not since shifted:

The IASB has also been asked to consider adding 'country-by-country' reporting requirements to its agenda. Feedback from the 2011 Agenda Consultation strongly and consistently highlighted that this should not be a priority for the IASB. In the light of this feedback the IASB has decided not to undertake proactive work in this area for the next two years. The IASB will review its priorities again in 2015 (IASB 2013: 22).[5]

Blocked at the IASB and frustrated with the EU endorsement of IFRS 8, which expanded the options for segment reporting but did not mandate

---

[5] Notably, the IASB resisted the arguments presented by TJN in its submission to the EU public consultation on CBCR for MNCs that public accounts should by definition serve the interests of a wide range of stakeholders (Murphy 2010: 8–9).

country-level geographical reporting, the PWYP coalition and TJN pushed for members of European Parliament to take a critical stance. Sven Giegold, a European member of parliament in the Group of the Greens and European Free Alliance, was a founding member of TJN and provided a portal between TJN, PWYP and the parliament. In 2005, Giegold arranged for TJN5 to visit the parliament and give an address on the promise of CBCR. The campaign resulted in a 2007 European Parliament resolution calling for country-by-country disclosures by extractive companies. Important here is that the organization with formal authority in this area resisted pressure from the NGO community to reform its standards, only to be bypassed by the network. The epistemic technocratic authority of the IASB waned as reporting for extractives became a hot political issue.

The April 2010 BP oil spill in the Gulf of Mexico added momentum to the political process. Informants suggest that the spill, in conjunction with post-crisis enthusiasm for regulatory innovation, led to a curious inclusion in the July 2010 Dodd-Frank Act (see Christian Aid 2010: 3). Section 1504 of the Hiring to Restore Employment Act requires all US-listed companies to disclose payments (conforming with 'minimalist' EITI specifications) on a country-by-country and project-by-project level. It is interesting to note that the subsequent policy process in Europe was distinct from that leading to Section 1504 in that the US process did not incorporate a debate of what type of data should be required. In the absence of this debate, it might be reasonable to conclude that the US policy process and hence legislation were not impacted by a tax justice agenda. However, it seems that Section 1504, as in areas of emergent policy innovation in the tax area,[6] increased the political space in Europe for policy innovation. The European Parliament adopted a report on an effective raw materials strategy for Europe, calling on the European Commission to 'establish legally binding requirements for extractive companies to publish their revenue payments for each project and country they invest in, following the example of the US Dodd-Frank bill' (European Parliament 2011).

In October 2010, the European Commission launched a public consultation on the possible requirement for CBCR from EU companies. Crucially, the Commission posed this possibility in terms of a choice between a Directive that would require that all companies, whatever sector, reveal data on a country-by-country basis and one which would be restricted to the extractives sector and mirror the Dodd-Frank 1504 and the EITI initiative (EC 2010). We argue that the input of TJN to the NGO

---

[6] The extra-territorial reach and international adoption of the US Foreign Account Tax Compliance Act is a case in point (see Palan and Wigan 2014).

network and policy debate accounts for this. Notably, the consultation process surrounding the legislation bears witness to the definitional role of TJN in the agendas of a number of organizations seeking to influence the final outcome. For instance, the PWYP submission explicitly defers to TJN on maximalist CBCR: 'For all sectors, including extractives, we concur with the analysis of the rationale for such disclosure as proposed by the Tax Justice Network' (PWYP 2010). TJN effectively lent these organizations and the broader network the knowledge necessary to understand the implications of making a distinction between data on payments to governments as opposed to full accounting data and data for the extractives rather than across all sectors. The European Commission's impact assessment report concluded that the target was to support the EITI and create a level playing field with regard to Dodd-Frank. Thus, the Commission considered that a requirement for information on revenue, profits, intra-group trading and effective tax rates was disproportionate in addressing the problem of government corruption (EC 2011).

In consequence the instruments chosen, the amended Accounting and Transparency Directives, require the disclosure of payments to governments and not the disclosure of contextual accounting data, which would enable an evaluation of whether these payments are appropriate relative to companies' levels of profit and how far a particular company was avoiding making due fiscal contributions across its global operations. Hence, while TJN promoted CBCR as a general instrument to address corporate transparency and prosecute its wider tax justice agenda, this did not translate into amendments to the Directives. TJN broadened the agenda of PWYP and instigated a debate within the network over the apposite data to demand, but it seems the original, 'minimalist' anti-corruption and development agenda of PWYP prevented an unequivocal shift in the direction of the broader tax justice agenda. However, TJN inserted an accounting agenda into the network and promoted 'maximalist' CBCR as a parameter in both public and policy debates. Both PWYP and the EITI standards now promote and incorporate requirements for contextual data. PWYP has advocated for 'maximalist' CBCR since September 2012 and the EITI incorporated contextual data into its standards in May 2013. The network stance confirms that CBCR as accounting data now defines the boundaries of the possible.

Following public outcry against the tax planning of firms such as Google and Amazon in the spring of 2013, CBCR has been picked up by a diverse range of actors. This led to the inclusion of maximalist CBCR in CRD IV on European banks. By the time the Accounting and Transparency Directives were agreed upon, maximalist CBCR had become a default parameter in discussions on financial reporting reforms as a new international standard with the potential to address issues of corporate transparency and tax compliance. The spring of 2013 witnessed a wide array of politicians and institutions promoting country-by-country reporting. Michel Barnier, European Commissioner for Internal Markets and Services, strongly promoted the expansion of CBCR:

I welcome today's vote by the European Parliament on the new Accounting and Transparency Directives. Financial reporting obligations have been modernised and costs reduced, in particular for SMEs. With the new rules on country by country reporting, we have created a framework where businesses and governments must disclose revenues from natural resources. This framework will also contribute to the fight against tax fraud and corruption.

But we must go further now and take measures on more transparency on tax for all large companies and groups – the taxes they pay, how much and to whom. I think it should be possible to introduce rules for the publication of the information on a country by country basis, similar to those approved for banks in CRD IV, or in the Commission's proposal on improving the transparency of certain large companies on non-financial reporting, adopted in April (EC 2013).

This turn to maximalist CBCR was reflected in a proposal from the Commission to amend the new Directives to incorporate maximalist CBCR in line with CRD IV. In the same month as Barnier's statement, the 2013 Lough Erne G8 Leaders Communiqué included what was considered a major breakthrough within the TAN working on financial reporting. The leaders of the most powerful nations committed to a common template for CBCR:

Comprehensive and relevant information on the financial position of multinational enterprises aids all tax administrations effectively to identify and assess tax risks. The information would be of greatest use to tax authorities, including those of developing countries, if it were presented in a standardised format focusing on high level information on the global allocation of profits and taxes paid. We call on the OECD to develop a common template for country-by-country reporting to tax authorities by major multinational enterprises, taking account of concerns regarding non-cooperative jurisdictions. This will improve the flow of information between multinational enterprises and tax authorities in the countries in which the multinationals operate to enhance transparency and improve risk assessment. (G8 2013: 6)

A remarkable shift is unfolding[7] wherein the issue of corporate reporting is now understood to be central to a widely shared agenda to re-engineer

---

[7] The shift in the direction of the TJN agenda is stark considering that in the final May 2011 Declaration of the G8 Summit in Deauville governments committed to the 'minimalist' agenda of 'setting in place transparency laws and regulations or to promoting voluntary standards that require or encourage oil, gas, and mining companies to disclose the payments they make to governments' (G8 2011: 16).

the international tax architecture. The OECD invited TJN4 to discuss a unitary taxation system requiring aggregate financial results to be apportioned to fiscal authorities on a geographical and real economy basis. CBCR is a necessary component of this proposal and a key parameter in the OECD Base Erosion and Profit Shifting initiative (OECD/G20 2015). This initiative was premised on the admission that the international tax system is unfit for purpose and pushed the debate on CBCR from a discussion of whether to use CBCR at all to one on precisely how to use CBCR. Item 13 of the OECD's 'Action Plan on Base Erosion and Profit Shifting' called for the development of 'rules regarding transfer pricing documentation' and demanded the inclusion of 'a requirement that MNEs provide all relevant governments with needed information on their global allocation of the income, economic activity and taxes paid among countries according to a common template' (2013a: 23). The subsequent OECD Discussion Draft (2014) on transfer pricing and CBCR supported a 'maximalist' CBCR with a CBCR template that provides income and tax details on each entity in an MNC global group organized by country, each entity's revenues and profits, income and withholding tax paid, stated capital and accumulated earnings, intra-group transfers and indicators on the location of economic activities, including tangible assets, employee numbers and salary expenses.

In November 2015, the G20 agreed on the OECD's BEPS Package. Action 13 of the package, 'Guidance on Transfer Pricing Documentation and Country-by-Country Reporting' (OECD/G20 2015), includes requirements for the disclosure of much of the contextual data demanded by TJN. However, the report containing CBCR information is not to be made public and is exclusively to be provided to the tax authorities of the parent firm's home state. This excludes many countries, investors and civil society from its potential benefits and narrows the range of stakeholders able to use CBCR to hold MNCs to account. The OECD is, however, the anchor of transnational tax governance, and while the mechanism of information sharing might be inadequate and the potential beneficiaries limited, comprehensive CBCR disclosures are now being integrated into the framework of a rapidly transforming international tax system.

Conclusion

The narrative of the expanding world of CBCR confirms much of the analysis provided in the opening chapter of this collection. Issues of international standards for corporate financial reports have traditionally been the preserve of accountants in the guise of a market-orientated IASB. The IASB represents an almost archetypal manifestation of private transnational authority insulated from public pressure by a strong

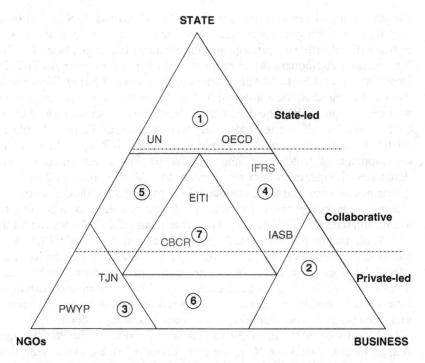

Figure 9.1 The Organizational Triangle on Global Tax Policy

claim to a technocratic expertise and authorized via a professional logic that rests on fulfilling a market function. The TAN working on issues of corporate transparency has until recently singularly focused on the developmental implications of corporate activities within developing countries in an effort to ameliorate the resource curse and associated corruption. TJN by virtue of the professional experience of its core membership and organizational attributes was able to fill a structural hole in the network surrounding corporate transparency, bringing into the network knowledge of the tax implications of financial reporting and confirming the 'strength of weak ties'. This knowledge supported a bridge between a development TAN agenda and the market agenda of the IASB. Figure 9.1 follows Levi-Faur and Starobin (2014) and locates the key organizations involved in global tax policy on the organizational plane.

As stated in the introductory chapter to this volume, this surface sits on top of professional networks that compete over issue definition and control. While TJN may be seen superficially as a garden variety NGO, it is a loose organizational form through which particular professionals with specific skills coordinate to push forward an activist agenda on global tax policy (Seabrooke and Wigan 2016). In our case, this capacity rests to a large extent on professional expertise and the deployment of expertise across different network domains. The professionals associated with TJN utilized its position in a structural hole exercising brokerage capacity to engage a broader NGO network, notably PWYP, and substantially alter their conception of effective corporate reporting. TJN has grafted its agenda into the political sphere bypassing the traditional transnational authority, the IASB, and instilling CBCR as an alternative form of corporate reporting for taxation purposes. TJN was able to draw upon a skill set scarce among the wider NGO community and commensurate with the skills of those traditionally tasked with crafting accountancy standards and tax law. For the extractive industry, the introduction of CBCR in a minimalist form moved the location of issue control from Zone 4 to Zone 7, from the IASB to the EITI. In the centre of the triangle issues are more contested and politicized, with technocracy sharing the table with civil society and politicians, accountable to and having to account for both. Figure 9.1 also locates the key standards (italicized) in IFRS and CBCR and where they sit in reference to states, NGOs and business. Issue control has been wrested from the traditional authority and the issue has been re-defined.

The activists pushing for CBCR suggest that remaining inadequacies in design and implementation may generate a ratcheting effect. Absent information and weak implementation may lead to calls for a more comprehensive CBCR as the engine of a radically new international tax system. Indeed, as CBCR unfolds on the ground and professionals continue to battle over its ultimate content and mode of implementation, it may be that the current juncture is no more than a mid-way point. The long-term aim of the activist professionals addressed here is unitary taxation and the effective end of the discrepancy between the legal fiction and economic reality of the MNC.

The chapter has provided an account of how an NGO mobilized professional attributes to become a key broker in and impact the terms of a critical issue in political economy: corporate financial reporting. It contributes to the TAN literature by demonstrating the salience of professional attributes, organizational characteristics and the interactions between organizational logics and professional logics in issue definition and control (see also Seabrooke and Wigan 2016; Baker and Wigan 2017). It demonstrates the applicability of the two-level network proposed in the introduction to this volume. While the analysis points to how activist and market agendas intersect in transnational professional battles, the role of state actors and logics and state-professional interactions remain to be explored more fully. This is especially relevant as CBCR moves from the object of transnational policy contention to the subject of state administration and implementation.

Part III

Professionals and International Organizations

10 Esteem as Professional Currency and Consolidation
The Rise of the Macroprudential Cognoscenti

Andrew Baker

Professional interaction is heavily shaped by the search for and subsequent allocation of esteem. Esteem is understood in this chapter as the positive regard or estimation of one's performance by significant others, within one's immediate peer or reference group (Brennan and Pettit, 2004). Consequently, professional networks are often characterized by a seemingly invisible supply of and demand for esteem. This in turn produces a series of systematic interactions determining the allocation of this 'intangible' good, based on continuous aggregations of evaluation and ordinal rankings of individuals, groups and even organizations' ongoing professional performance. The supply of, demand for and competition for esteem thus results in an unspoken social professional world, which the existing literature on professions has told us relatively little about. This chapter identifies how esteem can also become a resource or currency that can be used by those who possess it to exercise professional control and influence, and crucially to consolidate a group of professionals hold on a particular issue. Esteem played a particularly important role in the rise to prominence of macroprudential regulation following the financial crash of 2008. For some professionals this meant making macroprudential arguments at a time when they knew the climate of professional opinion was against them, sacrificing short-term esteem for longer term gain, by retrospectively appearing prescient. The rise of macroprudential regulation has in turn consolidated the control of a group of regulatory professionals connected to central banks, and their series of transnational regulatory networks, over financial governance, expanding the range and scope of central banks' regulatory powers, and simultaneously casting these very same regulatory professionals and their technical expertise as the primary features of this new macroprudential regulatory project.

Professionals are defined by the editors of this volume as individuals with abstract higher-level learning and specific skill sets to address tasks. In this regard, the launch of a new macroprudential regulatory project in the aftermath of the financial crash has created a raft of new prospective skilled tasks, creating a whole new growth industry for economists connected to the central banking community. Macroprudential is therefore the very definition of professional consolidation and renewal following a period of professional stress and duress. The volume as a whole employs the concept of a professional-organizational nexus in which professionals draw on organizational and professional domains at the same time, building alliances and drawing on resources from both domains as they seek to control issues and how they should be treated (Seabrooke and Henriksen, this volume, Chapter 1 and Chapter 18). The editors conceive of this as a two-level network in which professionals and organizations interact often in complex cross-cutting ways. This chapter demonstrates that both professional and organizational dynamics, interactions and considerations were at play in the rise to prominence of macroprudential regulation and in the resulting institutional and policy outcomes. In the macroprudential case, organizations act as key nodal points in transnational central banking networks. These networks are a mutually beneficial resource for the members of those networks and the organizations they represent to draw on. Central banking as a transnational profession and the central banks themselves, as well as a number of other related international organizations, have been direct beneficiaries of the macroprudential ideational shift (Baker, 2013a), in ways which have consolidated the professional hold of central bankers over financial governance and carved out new roles for a number of related organizations. Moreover, all of this is justified in terms of the expertise of key central banking professionals, their capacity to develop and hone new techniques for the measurement and control of 'systemic risk' and the pivotal position of constituent organizations, which have access to market data, information and have now had new research budgets and capabilities assigned to them for this very task by governments.

First, the concept of esteem and its relevance for understanding professional interaction is briefly sketched. Second, the organizational and professional logics involved in the rise to prominence of macroprudential regulation are assessed. Third, the professional and organizational consequences of these developments are evaluated.

Esteem and Professional Social Interaction

Professions are not homogenous social spaces and systems devoid of topography. Rather they have their own internal ecologies and social systems, which need to be more fully sketched and discerned (Seabrooke and Tsingou, 2009; Seabrooke and Tsingou 2015). Such efforts at analysis need to outline and examine the incentive structures and systems of social interaction that constitute the internal wiring of professions, allocating goods, resources and social standing within the profession, albeit within evolving organizational and institutional contexts (Bell, 2011). In this respect, professional status is linked to several factors: organizational posi-tion and formal office; strategic positioning of peer or in groups; and individual performance and the evaluation of that by significant others in one's reference group. Esteem refers to social standing based on an aggregate positive estimation of an agent's character, behaviour and performance. Office, affiliation and nationality can matter in transnational networks, such as those that operate in central banking, meaning that esteem allocation is not a symmetrical process that takes place on a level playing field. Certain individuals receive more attention because of the office they occupy and the country, or central bank, they represent. Office and to an extent access to research resources will magnify central bankers' capacity to be esteemed, but also their potential to be disesteemed by their peers, because their own views and actions are of far greater significance and therefore subjected to closer attention. A good example is the former Federal Reserve Chair Alan Greenspan, who attained the status of the 'maestro' during the great moderation, but has since attracted considerable (implicit) criticism from central bank peers for being dismissive of alternative modes of thinking in the decade prior to the crash of 2008.

Esteem allocation is a fluid form of social interaction that involves constant performance acts and evaluation of those acts by others. It is therefore subject to fluctuations and recalibrations. This is particularly so in the financial regulatory world, where volatile market performance and financial disasters and crashes can leave regulatory approaches and those professionals associated with them looking hugely inadequate. Esteem and the degrees in which it is allocated therefore have implications for the all-important question of how professions shape and control policy ideas and proposals. Esteem therefore becomes an important form of professional exchange and currency that is a crucial resource in its own right. In particular, changing patterns of esteem allocation were particularly important in the rise to prominence of macroprudential regulation and will be equally important in determining how macroprudential policy development proceeds.

Brennan and Pettit's magisterial account holds that esteem is an evaluative attitude that involves one actor rating another; a comparative attitude, because in most cases it depends on how the person compares with relevant others in the ratings given; and a directive attitude because an individual has the capacity to respond by improving their performance. Notably, esteem involves the grading of people against one another on a more or less continuous scale. Esteem is therefore allocated or supplied in degrees, and the degree given will be sensitive to the comparative performance of relevant others (Brennan and Pettit, 2004). On the demand side, professional networks are characterized by an almost subliminal competition for esteem amongst individuals, as the desire for the regard and approval from one's peers is a long-standing human motivation and the prestige or social status that comes with that (Veblen, 1905; Ricoeur, 1965, p.168; Smith, 1982; Brennan and Pettit, 2004, p.1). On the supply side, esteem is not a good that can be given away or traded in an ordinary manner, because people have to work to acquire esteem, rather than buying or selling it (Brennan and Pettit, 2004). Professional networks are therefore characterized by a system of social interaction that resembles an economy of esteem, involving both the supply of and demand for esteem, or social standing, as well as continuous rolling evaluations of individuals' conduct and performance over time, resulting in a systematic allocation of esteem across professional networks (Brennan and Pettit, 2004).

Esteem, as presented by Brennan and Pettit, is a quiet but powerful force, influencing and informing social interactions, which in turn distributes and allocates esteem as a good, or a resource. Existing literature has largely overlooked how esteem can be used as a resource. In this sense, an esteemed actor will have improved access to key decision-making processes within a social system, as well as having an enhanced voice, on the basis of their expertise, standing and past performance, which will increase the number of actors who willingly listen to and digest their views and pronouncements. This can take the form of deference to argumentation, based on wisdom, experience, expertise, previous performance, or to the office that an individual holds. Access is a key indicator of esteem in central banking. This is not just the question of who speaks but also who listens and is not listened to, or is ignored. The strength and supporting evidence for an argument is one determinant, but so too is a previous track record of high-level performance, and demonstrated ability to predict and explain events.

Individuals who stand outside of a prevailing professional consensus and established knowledge and truths may at first be actively disesteemed in a professional environment, but persistence in the presentation of arguments and the accumulation of evidence to support an earlier position can change that. If the predictive and explanatory capacity of an individual is seen to increase, so their social status and access within the peer group will grow, as they are listened to and esteemed by fellow professionals to an increasing extent. This is particularly the case if the analysis offers potential solutions to previously unseen problems. In this sense, an individual who is widely esteemed will see an increase in their potential to steer and influence the wider social whole. Consequently, esteem can be conceived of as a resource that can enable an actor to more easily shape and influence debate in a given area. The rise of macroprudential regulation after the financial crash of 2008 provides a good illustration of precisely that kind of process, as a position or set of arguments that were previously dismissed, or went largely unheard, moved to the centre of the policy agenda. The social and political dynamics of esteem allocation were a key element of that process.

Explaining the Macroprudential Ideational Shift

The rise of macropudential regulation after the financial crash of 2008 is an instructive one in terms of how professional cultures and systems allocate esteem and how that in turn shapes how governance issues are conceived of and dealt with. The story of macroprudential regulation is essentially that a small inner circle of professional *cognoscenti* (quite literally those in the know, with superior or specialized knowledge), connected to the world of central banking, developed macroprudential arguments and analysis in the pre-cash period. Some of these individuals found that when they tried to push these ideas in central banking networks they were actively disesteemed. Others chose to remain publicly silent about their ongoing work because they anticipated such a reaction and calculated there was little point in pursuing such arguments in public settings (Confidential interview, 10 November 2013). After the crash, however, early macroprudentialists appeared prescient as the best-performing individuals in their immediate peer group. Recognizing that the wider context was now much more amenable to their arguments, macroprudentialists used the crash of 2008 to engage in inter-organizational and professional networking to promote macroprudential ideas and analysis with some success. Essentially, the inner circle of the macroprudential cognoscenti exercised an insider's coup d'etat, deposing and discrediting the prior consensus (in part derived from the efficient markets hypothesis) and successfully established macroprudential as a primary post-crash interpretative frame. The Bank of England has created a new Financial Policy Committee (FPC) to execute macroprudential policy and oversight. Likewise, the United States has created the Financial Stability Oversight Council (FSOC) and the European Central Bank has the European Systemic Risk Board (ESRB) for similar purposes. After years of disinterest, the process of building macroprudential regulatory regimes has begun in earnest.

Macroprudential is a set of ideas about how to regulate the financial system, which emphasizes that the unstable nature of financial markets is due to time (procyclical) and cross sectional (complex interconnectedness) dimensions, and the endogenous, dynamic and systemic nature of financial risk (Borio, 2011a). Consequently, macroprudential regulation (MPR) argues in favour of macro-level top-down interventions to contain and manage systemic risk. Pre-cash orthodoxy essentially devolved risk management to individual private institutions' own Value at Risk (VaR) models, based on a belief that financial markets were on the whole efficient information processing and co-ordinating mechanisms (most of the time), possessing a risk management capacity based on increasing mathematical and computerized sophistication. Consequently, the embrace of macroprudential represented a significant ideational shift with important policy implications, including growing levels of central bank intervention in markets after thirty years of regulatory easing (Baker, 2013a, 2013b). One interpretation is that macroprudential policy should moderate credit supply over the cycle, tightening policy in a boom and lowering it in a bust, through instruments such as countercyclical capital buffers, countercyclical liquidity requirements, sectorial capital requirements and leverage ratios (Bank of England, 2011; Aikman, Haldane and Kapadia, 2013; Haldane, 2013a). This focus on the macro-stability of credit supply requires interventionist central banks, and the development of new policy instruments, data sets, concepts and policy techniques. Empowering regulators to engage in technical calculations and judgements to constrain systemic risk is precisely the prescription of the macroprudential regulatory project. Macroprudential has become a growth industry in its own right. It requires skilled professionals and simultaneously empowers those professionals on the basis of their expertise.[1] It also requires them to have a certain degree of policy autonomy, enabling them to take action to stem inflating financial bubbles, free from political and popular pressures that inevitably take hold during boom periods (Reinhart and Rogoff, 2010[2]; Haldane, 2013b).

Following the financial crash of 2008, macroprudential regulation became the central interpretative frame (Blyth, 2002; Widmaier, Blyth and Seabrooke, 2007) that would be employed to redesign financial regulation in the post-crash era (Borio, 2009, 2011a; Baker, 2013a). The anchor concepts of the approach, such as fallacy of composition (Borio, 2011b), procyclicality (Borio, Furfine and Lowe, 2001; Borio and White, 2004; BIS, 2006; White, 2006), herding (Hellwig, 1995; Persaud, 2000) and complex fragility (Haldane and May, 2011) challenged many of the basic tenets of the simplified version of the efficient markets hypothesis that had become part of a wider 'institutional DNA'

---

[1] For an argument that equates this with an evolving form of neoliberal governmentality, see Konings, 2015.

[2] Some jurisdictions have assigned some macroprudential powers to finance ministries and regulatory agencies; however, central banks dominate and there is a growing consensus that macroprudential policy is best performed by an independent central bank (Aikman, Haldane and Kapadia, 2013; Haldane, 2013b).

in the pre-crash period (Turner, 2011; Baker, 2013b). After the financial crash, reflexive critical intellectual reassessment and learning were the order of the day in elite regulatory networks such as the Financial Stability Forum (FSF) (later to become the Financial Stability Board (FSB), the G20, the Basle Committee on Banking Supervision (BCBS), the G30 and amongst national regulatory agencies and central banks. A spate of specialist technical reports calling for the establishment of macroprudential regulatory regimes were published (Brunnermeir et al., 2009, G30, 2009, 2010, FSF, 2009, De Laroisiere 2009, FSA, 2009). In the language of International Relations scholars this spate of reports resembled an irresistible 'norm cascade' (Finnemore and Sikkink, 1998).

Crucially, however, as one of the leading pioneers of the macroprudential perspective, Claudio Borio, of the Bank for International Settlements (BIS), has pointed out that macroprudential ideas and concepts were not always popular in central banking and regulatory professional networks.

A decade ago the term macroprudential was barely used and there was little appetite amongst policy makers and regulators to even engage with the concept, let alone strengthen macroprudential regulation ... .This swell of support [for macroprudential regulation] could not have been anticipated even as recently as a couple of years ago. The current financial crisis has been instrumental in underpinning it (Borio, 2009, p.2 and p.32).

What Borio was giving expression to was how macroprudential ideas have moved from relative obscurity in certain enclaves of the BIS to the centre of the policy agenda, dominating and driving the post-crisis financial reform debate, in the international community of central bankers and associated transnational governance mechanisms, so that in Borio's own words, 'we're all macroprudentialists now' (Borio, 2009, p.1).

The macroprudential shift involved officials from the BIS, some officials from national central banks, together with some well-networked private sector and academic economists such as Charles Goodhart, John Eatwell, Avinash Persaud, Hyun Song Shin, Markus Brunnermeir, Martin Hellwig, Jose Ocampo and Stephanie Griffith-Jones (Hellwig, 1995; Persaud, 2000; Goodhart and Segoviano, 2004; Griffith Jones and Ocampo, 2006; Brunnermeir et al., 2009), effectively exercising an 'insider's coup d'etat' (Turner, 2011; Baker, 2013b). Crucially, virtually all of the figures involved in instigating this insider's coup d'etat were economists that had not entirely bought into the pre-crash consensus associated with 'great moderation' notions that inflation targeting and permitting institutions to rely on their own sophisticated risk models were sufficient to produce financial and macroeconomic stability (Borio, 2011b, 2014). Many of them were highly critical of the Value at Risk (VaR) models adopted by large banks because of their procyclical nature (Hellwig, 1995; Persuad 2000; Goodhart and Segoviano, 2004). In this respect, macroprudential was very much an intellectual project developed by professional economists in a series of overlapping networks. As explained by Claudio Borio of the BIS, macroprudential had been 'evolving quietly in the background, known only amongst a small but growing inner circle of cognoscenti' (Borio, 2011a, p.1). Following the financial crash of 2008, this inner circle saw their status and social standing rise, which not only resulted in an ideational shift in a macroprudential direction but also empowered many of these very same professionals or immediate colleagues and associates with a range of new powers, also creating new research programmes to support and sustain this new policy direction.

Esteem and the Macroprudential Ideational Shift

Explanations of this macroprudential ideational shift have to acknowledge how a comprehensive regulatory agenda chimed with public sentiment and the rise of populist politics seeking punishment for the banking sector following the crash of 2008. This climate created incentives for politicians to open debates about financial regulation to include broader social externalities (Thirkell-White, 2009). Intellectually, reasoning derived from efficient markets thinking also appeared to have broken down and was having difficulty explaining the collapse in asset values and financial market distress (Baker, 2013a). An important background facilitating factor, however, that is often overlooked, but which made the macroprudential ideational shift possible, was the change in esteem allocation in central banking networks.

In the pre-crash period, macroprudentialists, mainly at the BIS, publicly made macroprudential arguments, but these made little headway, partly because a wider context of financial success and rising asset prices meant that their analysis was often ignored and overlooked. The prevailing social and political context meant that BIS staff found themselves isolated in their promotion of MPR. In several well-documented exchanges at the flagship event in the annual central banking calendar, at Jackson Hole, Conference of the Kansas City Federal Reserve in 2003, and at later meetings of central bankers at the BIS headquarters in Basel, Federal Reserve Chairman Alan Greenspan was notoriously dismissive of the macroprudential analysis and arguments of both Borio and William White, who were warning of the dangers of an inflating financial boom. Other central bankers at these meetings largely agreed with Greenspan (Balzil and Schiessl, 2009), or remained silent. In relation to this latter point, the Bank of England had an in-house financial stability team working on macroprudential issues, but chose to avoid publicly discussing these matters, because of the prevailing climate of opinion, and a recognition there was little point in putting this analysis to play in such a context (Confidential Interview, 10 December 2013).

Despite receiving backing from sections of the BIS, therefore, MPR remained relatively unpopular in the lead up to the crisis of 2007–09, and officials who had tried to promote these ideas and this approach found themselves professionally marginalized as economists out of step with prevailing sentiments. White, for example, was ironically derided at the Federal Reserve as 'merry sunshine' due to his repeated warnings of an inflating financial boom (Balzil and Schiessl, 2009). In other words, the social context in which White and Borio operated was shaped by the allocation of considerable esteem to Greenspan, while their own levels of esteem suffered in the short term because they challenged a prevailing consensus. Those who choose to lean against the wind of financial market, professional and public sentiment, do so at considerable social cost to themselves. This was certainly the case for White and Borio. White and Borio were effectively disesteemed by some of the loudest and most prominent voices in central banking networks in the years prior to the crash of 2007–08. Social pressures created by the dominant consensus, and the patterns of esteem associated with that, resulted in a reluctance to hear or listen to contrary analyses, and this combined with a social construction of White and Borio as 'Cassandra' figures in the central banking world, particularly at the Fed. Long term, White and Borio's willingness to stand outside of and challenge the dominant consensus did, however, result in considerable esteem gains. White and Borio most certainly were not inhibited by concern for their short-term esteem. Borio has revealed that he felt they could not miss the opportunity of presenting their arguments at Jackson Hole and announced this to White, urging him to go ahead and present their paper in 2003 (Balzil and Schiessl, 2009); see also Tsingou et al. 2017. Borio and White were led by a sense of the correctness and importance of their analysis, or 'ideational commitment' (Finnemore and Sikkink, 1998). While a short-term calculation of esteem would have led Borio and White in the opposite direction, they pushed the issue out of a conviction that it was the correct thing to do (Balzil and Schiessl, 2009). Organizationally, it was far easier for them to do this as officials connected to the BIS – an effective freestanding pool of expertise, which central banks could avail of or ignore. In contrast, officials at national central banks such as the Bank of England felt inhibited and avoided putting their macroprudential ideas to play, because they thought there would not be much of an audience for them, both within the Bank and also outside, particularly in the United States (confidential interview with official, 10 December 2013).

In this sense, behind the scenes of the financial crisis of 2008 were a subtle series of social processes that went largely unnoticed. As macroprudential norm entrepreneurs were peddling furiously in a variety of professional networks, they found the interactions and social relations within those networks were far more responsive to them than had previously been the case. As an event, the financial crash appeared to verify many macroprudential arguments. Retrospectively, macroprudentialists appeared prescient. Consequently, it became much more acceptable to make macroprudential arguments, as these positions were associated with high-performing individuals in the central banking community during the pre-crash period. Moreover, macroprudentialists made concerted efforts to mobilize and work together in the aftermath of the crash to promote macroprudential thinking and policy proposals. According to one prominent BIS official, 'most of the push for macroprudential came from BIS staff and UK academics (Charles Goodhart, John Eatwell), some of whom then went to the US (Hyun Shin and Markus Brunnemeir having left the LSE for Princeton)' (confidential correspondence with official, 6 January 2012). Goodhart, Eatwell and Persaud spoke informally with Adair Turner as he became head of the UK Financial Services Authority (FSA) about macroprudential thinking, and Turner became a leading macroprudential advocate in both the FSF and the G30 (confidential Interview, 15 March 2010). He was joined by Bank of England staff, who were prepared to be much vocal and public of their support for macroprudential than they had been in the pre-crash period. In the words of one Bank of England official, 'when the balloon went up, we already had the ideas in our knap sack. We had already discovered religion' (confidential interview, 10 December 2013). Tiff Macklem, Senior Deputy Governor of the Bank of Canada, also played a key role by chairing the key G20 Working Group, 'Enhancing Regulation', which was pivotal in cementing the macroprudential approach as the way forward internationally amongst the official community (confidential correspondence with official, 6 January 2012). William White meanwhile had retired from the BIS, but during 2009 briefed the Canadian and German G20 team. He was also being cited by Bank of Canada governor of the time, Mark Carney, as one of the leading prescient figures amongst the fraternity of economists who predicted the crash of 2008 (Carney, 2008). White also became one of the most in-demand speakers at central banks throughout the world during 2009 (Balzil and Schiessl, 2009).

In this sense, the esteem of both macroprudentialists and macroprudential ideas rose after the financial crash of 2008. Crucially, macroprudentialists who had been warning about the build-up of systemic risk, complaining about procyclical patterns in financial markets and pointing out that macro-level systemic risk management was the missing ingredient in the existing regulatory architecture, appeared to have performed well in the pre-crash period. In subsequent debates about the failure to recognize or predict the crash amongst economists and the official community, and the small numbers of voices who did recognize what was happening, White is frequently presented as a leading prescient figure (Carney, 2008; Balzil and Schiessl, 2009; Persaud, 2009). The common ground between individuals who emerged from the crisis with 'credibility' and esteem for performing well in relation to their comparator reference group of economists and financial analysts was that many or most seemed to favour forms of macroprudential analysis and policy. The financial crash of 2008 provided an opportunity for Borio's inner circle of cognoscenti to not only offer up their ideas, but also gave them new-found levels of recognition and status, which was given further momentum by mutual association.

Central bankers such as Bank of Canada Governor Mark Carney began advocating MPR, citing the importance of White's contribution (Carney, 2008). By esteeming White, and associating with his ideas, Carney was also effectively enhancing his own credibility and esteem by attaching himself to the macroprudential label. Individuals infected one another with both their mutual esteem and various repeated iterations of macroprudential ideas and arguments. Simultaneously, the 'esteem cascade' produced by the mutual association of macroprudential advocates also produced a norm cascade (Finnemore and Sikkink, 1998). Persaud, for example, repeatedly highlighted the contribution of White (Persaud, 2009), while White often cited Eatwell and Goodhart as pioneering macroprudential thinkers (White, 2004). Goodhart in particular, along with colleagues Hyun Shin and Markus Brunnermeir as academic economists highly regarded in the central banking world, having occupied policy positions, teamed up with figures from the central bank world, Andrew Crockett, ex-general manager of the BIS and financier Avinash Persaud, to publish the Geneva Report (Brunnermeier et al., 2009). This report was particularly important in establishing intellectual credibility for the macroprudential perspective (confidential interview, 27 March 2014).

This example of the Geneva Report is illustrative of how academic economists and central bankers obtain mutual gains from their interactions and associations. For academic economists, a stint at a central bank can be good for their CV, lends prestige and demonstrates policy relevance or 'impact'. For central bankers, association with and approval of academic economists lend authority, rigour and credibility to their work and projects. The Bank of England, for example, hired Hyun Shin, professor of finance at the LSE and later at Princeton as a consultant, to help develop the Bank's macroprudential thinking in the pre-crash period, and Shin later became a head of research at the BIS (confidential interview, 10 December 2013). In this respect, central banking is increasingly characterized by an observable process of scientization, a striking intellectualization of the world via formal analysis and mathematical abstraction (Marcussen, 2006). Modern central bankers make epistemic alliances with other members of the scientific brotherhood; their research departments finance their own scientific journals and conferences as scientific credentials enhance careers for central bankers, who increasingly possess doctoral and postgraduate degrees in economics and engage directly with the scientific community (Marcussen, 2006, p.9).

Central bankers and leading macroprudentialists such as the Bank of England's Andrew Haldane obtain enhanced prestige by collaborating with academics, and not just economists, but also natural scientists, such as Zoologist Robert May, publishing in leading science journals such as *Nature* (Haldane and May, 2011). One consequence of this 'scientization' is that central banks' organizational, territorial and cultural boundaries are blurring as co-equal central bankers work closely together from project to project (Marcussen, 2006, p.10). From this perspective, central banking is increasingly comprised of 'knowledge communities' constructed around inter-paradigmatic discussions about theory, methods and data. We have seen how this was evident in the rise of macroprudential regulation as a number of economists and central bankers worked together to effectively exercise an insider's coup d'état and to highlight the problem of the existing consensus and approach by building a coalition of supportive voices arguing for a macroprudential approach to financial regulation. Such a strategy was eased and facilitated by these individuals' rising esteem, and of the ideas and concepts they carried.

Organizational and Professional Consolidation

Following the financial crash of 2008, central banks, economists and their networks, resembled a policy community under stress (Tsingou, 2010). Pre-crash regulation came under scrutiny, and there can be little doubt that the pre-crash approach focused on the adequacy of microprudential supervision and private risk management models failed, not least because the macroeconomic effects of the crash were considerable – equivalent to a year's lost output in the United States and the United Kingdom (Haldane, 2012a). As existing studies have pointed out, a reflexive critical approach from within the established regulatory and central banking policy community opened up the regulatory debate by critiquing the existing approach (Engelen et al., 2011). Crucially, however, this reflexive approach and critique also allowed elements from within the existing transnational central banking policy community to not only exercise an insider's coup d'etat but also consolidate the hold of central bank professionals on financial regulatory policy and carve out new roles for their constituent organizations (Konings, 2016).

Macroprudential is resulting in the institutionalization of new forms of macroprudential expertise, involving a new expert division of labour (Abbott, 1991), entailing routine data collection on financial market activities and new macroprudential modelling (expertise in commodities in Abbott's language), expertise encoded in organizations and bureaucracies – primarily the research divisions of central banks and at the BIS and FSB, and through new macroprudential policy committees (FOSC US, ESRB, EU and FPC, UK). Macroprudential knowledge formation is now a priority and efforts are underway to more fully develop relevant data sets and policy instruments. Key professionals in these networks repeatedly emphasize that the science in this area is at an early stage, needs to be developed and remains largely untested (Aikman, Haldane and Nelson, 2011; IIF, 2011). When the BIS, the FSB and the IMF submitted a report to the G20 on the progress of the macroprudential project in November 2011, they cited twenty-four policy and research papers with a macroprudential theme produced by those institutions alone since the start of 2010. In Spring 2010, the ECB and the European System of Central Banks (ESCB with its twenty-seven members) launched the Macroprudential Research Network (MaRs) to develop, over a three year period, core conceptual frameworks, models and tools that provide research in order to improve macroprudential supervision and research. The MaRs involved more than 180 researchers from all EU national central banks and the ECB. They worked on 126 individual projects and 2 joint cross-country projects involving multiple central banks. Academics participating in MaRs activities were not just confined to European universities but include a range of staff from Ivy League US institutions. The MaRs network also encouraged teaching and research in universities to reflect macroprudential concerns, particularly assessments of macroprudential regulatory instruments. Meanwhile, the Bank of England has launched its own macroprudential research division and strategy team. Macroprudential knowledge formation is consequently a professional growth industry at central banks and the effects of the macroprudential ideational transformation have also been to change professional norms and activities. This change has itself, therefore, been constitutive of the professional environment.

The rise of macroprudential regulation propelled by 'an inner circle' of cognoscenti is in this regard a tale of professional reconfiguration. This has involved prominent macroprudentialists calling for change in the economics profession more generally. The Bank of England's Andrew Haldane, for example, has argued that economists succumbed to an intellectual virus of theory-induced blindness and has called for an intellectual reinvestment in models of heterogeneous, interacting agents, following in the footsteps of other social sciences (Haldane, 2012b). Adair Turner has talked of the need to reconstruct economics as a discipline challenging the free-market simplicities of rational expectations and efficient markets hypothesis, which in the policy world translated into a simplified version of equilibrium theory, with market completion seen as the cure to all problems and mathematical sophistication decoupled from philosophical understanding as the key to effective risk management (Turner, 2011). Crucially, being critical of their own home discipline – economics – and seeking to address identified intellectual failings have indirectly allowed a new cadre of macroprudential economists to keep control of debates on financial regulation. Ultimately, no rival profession launched a bid to become ascendant in financial regulation, following the financial crash of 2008, and central bank economists, in conjunction with some academics, maintained their ascendancy by critiquing factions of their own profession and the VaR modelling undertaken by private sector financial risk professionals.

Macroprudential has become a new professional activity in its own right. With this has come a potentially much more expansive role for central banks. The immediate beneficiaries of the macroprudential project are often the very central bank officials and economists who have pushed for it. In this sense, the macroprudential project essentially seeks to empower a new cadre of technocrats and price engineers (Baker and Widmaier, 2014). Countercyclical capital buffers, for example, require regulators who have the capacity and capability to identify normalized paths of credit to GDP and deviations from that path, based on extrapolations from previous evidence and data. Further, they would also be required to reach judgements on the precise calibrations of new macroprudential policy instruments and how they should be scaled up or down to reflect particular identified phases of the credit cycle. Such a process clearly depends upon the technical capacity of regulators to reach such calculations, the data sets and data collection techniques they have at hand and some discretionary powers to reach judgements on how policy should be adjusted. Empowering regulators to engage in such technical calculations and judgements is therefore one of the outcomes of the macroprudential project. As Andrew Haldane reflects, 'if there were a benign enlightened regulatory planner, able to redirect competitive forces, this could potentially avert future tragedies of the financial commons. Fortunately there is' (Haldane, 2012a, p.12). 'Technocratic mastery of financial markets', driven by a desire to open new possibilities for control of complex adaptive financial networks, through mathematized control technologies is, therefore, an objective of the macroprudential project (Erturk et al., 2011). Consequently, central bankers are currently wrestling with multiple, intersecting issues concerning measurement, mapping and devising new practices of intervention. Transnationally, this has meant that central banking networks such as the Basel Committee on Banking Supervision (BCBS) have remained central in the development of international notions of best practice in macroprudential regulation. Likewise, the Financial Stability Board, as a collection of international and national agencies, in which central banks and economists have a dominant presence, has been charged with the task of reporting to G20 leaders on the development of macroprudential policy. Organizationally, the macroprudential ideational shift has allowed central banks and their constituent networks to retain control over post-crash regulatory governance. The macroprudential ideational shift has therefore resulted in a process of professional consolidation. Such a process of professional bureaucrats crafting new areas of expertise for themselves is not entirely new to scholars of International Relations (Barnett and Finnemore, 2004; Konings, 2016; Johnson, 2016). What is more striking about this particular case is how the staff of international organizations, academic economists, some market participants and the staff of central banks interacted, exchanging ideas and analyses to enable macroprudential to become a new orthodoxy in a period of just over six months. Macroprudential became a respectable new normal supported by highly esteemed experts supporting one another's ideas.

Professional consolidation has also been accompanied by organizational consolidation. Central banks are at the centre of the new macroprudential policy frame and have new policy responsibilities as a consequence, at a time, when they could have been severely criticized for failing to use monetary policy to stem credit expansion. In part they have the BIS to thank for this as the BIS is the international organization to service and support central banking, and macroprudential was a concept that grew out of the BIS. Staff from the BIS were early macroprudential pioneers and as an organization the BIS did more than any other to drive the development of macroprudential concepts and analysis. As histories and literature reviews of macroprudential reveal, the BIS is indelibly associated with macroprudential and has some claim to institutional ownership of the concept (Clement, 2010; Galati and Moessner, 2011). The rise to prominence of macroprudential has organizationally consolidated the BIS's role as a source of analysis and support to central banks precisely because of this. As the organization with the most experience of macroprudential analysis and concepts, and as home to a number of the most highly esteemed macroprudential experts, the BIS has emerged from the crash with its collective esteem enhanced, as one of the best-performing organizations, because of its pre-crash analytical track record.

Conclusion

This chapter has shown that esteem and its allocation are a key professional currency and resource. The rising professional esteem of individual macroprudentialists after the financial crash of 2008 enabled an inner circle of macroprudential cognoscenti to exercise an insider's coup d'état, critiquing and displacing the prior efficient markets consensus. In its place a new macroprudential ideational frame has emerged, which has spawned a new growth industry at central banks and their constituent networks. Energies are now focused on constructing the policy instruments, techniques, data collection and research programmes to make macroprudential regulation operational. One interpretation of this spate of activity is that macroprudentialists have essentially invented and manufactured new areas of expertise. Macroprudential technocrats framed the financial crisis in terms of the intellectual failures of the efficient markets position and a failure to understand systemic dynamics. In this way they forced open the argument about the re-regulation of finance through carefully assembled arguments and persuasion (Engelen et al., 2011, p.199). With this has come a potentially much more expansive role for central banks. The immediate beneficiaries of the macroprudential project are the very central bank officials and economists who along with their associates did most to push for it. The macroprudential project essentially empowers a new cadre of technocrats and price engineers. The rise of the macroprudential cognoscenti consequently represented a classic case of professional consolidation and strengthening, at a time when that profession was potentially under crisis, stress and duress.

11 Treating Market Failure
Access Professionals in Global Health

Adriana Nilsson

This chapter focuses on the issue of access to medicines, a problem that went from being regarded as one aspect of primary health care concerns in the 1970s to a transnational policy area of its own at the turn of the millennium. Since 2001, the issue has been the recipient of one international agreement (Doha Declaration), a Global Strategy, and three distinct expert groups at the World Health Organization (WHO) alone. This process has involved a multi-disciplinary and multi-organizational debate involving intergovernmental organizations, NGOs, firms, states, and foundations. The establishment of the topic in the public domain and international agenda, which started in 1994 with the signature of the Trade Related Aspects of Intellectual Property (TRIPS), has been widely attributed to vigorous political activism, epitomized in the Access to Medicines campaign ('t Hoen 2002; Matthews 2002; Sell and Prakash 2004). Activism alone, however, cannot explain its continuity as a distinct policy area.

In this chapter, I argue that the permanence of the issue in the transnational agenda is closely connected to the emergence of a transnational professional, called here access professional. The main task of these experts is to design supranational solutions able to induce needs-driven innovation on drugs and medical technology while ensuring widespread access to them. Drawing on Abbott's ideas of objective and subjective elements of tasks, and on Seabrooke and Henriksen's conceptualization of two-level networks (Chapter 1, this volume), I show: (1) the process in which changes in the objective nature of the problem, initiated at transnational level, was seized by professionals with a distinctive type of career patterns, allowing them to reinterpret its subjective qualities and claim jurisdiction to diagnose, infer, and treat problems involving access to medicines, IP, and innovation; (2) how control is increasingly attached to the ways the issue is treated, with strategies involving the activation of inter-personal networks that allow access professionals to carve organizational space for action that addresses the problem transnationally, rather than at the national level.

To illustrate the first point, I retrace the problem since its origins, in the 1970s, focusing particularly on the changes brought by TRIPS; for the second point, I use the case of the Medicines Patent Pool (MPP), a licensing agency for HIV/Aids drugs launched in 2010 in Geneva, to illustrate how the mobilization of personal networks enabled a group of access professionals to navigate and circumvent organizational and political resistance (see also Nilsson 2017).

The chapter contributes to the literature on professions in transnational governance by connecting the interactions between tasks and issues that support jurisdictional claims to career patterns, at the same time as it teases out their impact on outside-in strategies of control. A distinctive mix of quantitative and qualitative research methods supports these findings. Between 2012 and 2015, semi-structured interviews were conducted with 34 experts working on the issue based at IOs, NGOs, industry, governments, and foundations. This process led to the identification of a group of transnationally active experts whose main task is defined as providing access to medicine and enabling needs-driven innovation. Once this group was identified, data on their educational and career trajectories were compiled and analyzed with the sequence analysis software TraMineR (see Chapter 4 for a discussion of this approach). Educational and career trajectories of 65 IO-based experts involved in the trilateral WHO-WTO-WIPO report on access to medicines, IP, and innovation (2012) were also collected and analyzed.

The chapter starts with a brief overview of the literature and connects it with the trajectory of the problem of access to medicines, before and after the TRIPS agreement. The second section offers an overview of the educational background and professional patterns of access professionals, as well as of the knowledge patterns developed up to the Doha Declaration. The third section covers the organizational environment linked to issue, including changes of mandates and hiring patterns at the WHO, WTO, and WIPO. The fourth and last part of the chapter focuses on the outside-in strategies used to establish the Medicines Patent Pool in a context of two-level networks.

Linking Tasks and Professionals: The Emergence of the "Access to Medicines" Issue

Andrew Abbott (1988) defines the tasks of professions as "human problems amenable to expert service" both for individuals and groups. Links between tasks and professions, however, change continuously. This happens because problems, and tasks, have objective and subjective characteristics: the former related to natural, organizational, and technological objectives and facts; the latter related to culture. Objective elements are more resilient to reconstruction than subjective ones, but both elements are vulnerable to change. Objective foundations for professional tasks can, for instance, be organizational foundations such as teaching and the educational system. Subjective qualities, on the other hand, are the way the profession currently in charge of the jurisdiction defines the problem. Abbott uses alcoholism as an example: alcohol consumption is the objective element, while the subjective components have been constructed through time as biological (GPs), mental (psychiatrists), moral and spiritual (clergymen), or legal.

Subjective elements, therefore, support claims to diagnose, to infer, and to treat, acts that Abbott see as the "cognitive structure of a jurisdictional claim" (Abbott 1988, p.40). Diagnostics brings information in the system of professional knowledge, treatment brings them back out from it, and inference connects the two, taking into account the client's characteristics and chances of success. While analytically distinct, some professions run these together, in a different order, or diagnose by treating. Narrowness in the type of information and evidence required for diagnoses, too much or too little need for inference, and failure to treat or measure success leave jurisdictions vulnerable. Moreover, Abbott sees control over treatments as central for jurisdiction control – the more specialized a treatment is, the more a profession can retain control over it (Abbott 1988, p. 46).

In the framework proposed in the introduction to this volume, Seabrooke and Henriksen upscale Abbott's definition to transnational governance, to argue that tasks professionals perform and the control of issues go hand in hand in technical and narrow areas of governance. When different professionals assign tasks to problems, however, there is more space for contestation and cooperation. As a consequence, professionals will devise strategies to explore vulnerabilities in other jurisdictions and reinforce their control over issues. One way to do so is drawing support from both professional and organizational networks, a context referred to as a two-level network, in which actors build alliances from both domains in an attempt to control issues (see Chapter 1). These strategies are particularly suitable in transnational environments, where organizations cannot hold issues too tightly and continuous management is required.

The emergence of the access to medicines as a transnational governance issue reflects both changes in objective and subjective elements of tasks, with jurisdictional claims supported by particular career patterns and strategies of control increasingly aimed at treatments. In much of the 1970s and 1980s, the problem was part of the tasks of health professionals, usually medical doctors and pharmacists, working for governments and the WHO building effective primary health care systems and securing efficient management of pharmaceuticals. Diagnostics on the reasons for poor access pointed at unreliable systems and poverty, and the treatment prescribed was based on tackling irrational use of drugs and poor drug quality, a set of tasks tightly controlled by public health experts. By 1975, the World Health Assembly at WHO introduced the concepts of national drug policy and essential medicines, with the first Model List of Essential Medicines, identifying more than 200 individual drugs for communicable and non-communicable diseases, published in 1977[1] to help countries to identify priority medicines for their health needs (Quick, Jonathan et al. 2002).

While the list was and still is a very important tool for access, cooperation with developing countries would soon start to show it was not enough. This opened space for health economists to claim jurisdiction by improving the efficiency of national systems through the study of patterns of production and consumption of health and healthcare, as well as pricing, as suggested in an expert interview:

When I arrived at the WHO, in the 1970s, there were only two health economists. And for many years it was very hard to make a case for economics in the area of medicine and access. Economists talking about medical issues would be abused immediately. But working on the ground, with countries, we started to see that whatever they did with prices of drugs and drug systems was essential for access. It is now a established expertise inside the WHO.[2]

The reconstruction of the subjective aspects of the problem to accommodate jurisdictional claims of health economists, therefore, was tightly linked to the incapacity of previous treatments to solve the problem at national level. The emergence of the access professional, however, is linked to a transnationally induced change in the objective element of the problem: the signature of TRIPS, a legal agreement that requires World Trade Organization (WTO) members to translate into domestic law the IPR standards stipulated in its 73 articles. The result of a US business campaign (Drahos and Braithwaite 2002; Matthews 2002; Sell 2003), TRIPS was described as "a revolution in the history of IP protection" (Deere 2009), providing the enforcement powers missing in the previous 1883 Paris Convention for IP protection by bringing the Dispute Settlement Mechanisms of trade into IPRs (May 2000).

---

[1] Its 18th edition was released in April 2013. Information about the process can be found at www.who.int/features/2013/essential_medicines_list/en/
[2] Interview 1.

The Agreement extends patent rights to 20 years and establishes conditions in which compulsory licenses can be issued.

IPR rules impact R&D and innovation decisions, as well as pricing of drugs and medical technology. Geographical expansion and standardization of this institutional environment objectively impact the task of providing quality medicine at affordable prices to meet health needs. Attempts to understand the new scenario and the exact consequences for public health had the effect of connecting the many different professional and organizational networks linked to the problem. A milestone in this process was the Bielefeld meeting, organized by the Health Action International (HAI), in October 1996. The selection of speakers in that meeting illustrates the diversity of expertise the subject now required: the five panellists invited had training in economics, health economics, law, and medicine/pharmacy and represented health and consumer groups, as well as the WTO and the WHO (HAI 1997). "I remember this first workshop, when James Love explained to me what a patent was and how it was linked to prices. And he was talking about compulsory licenses and that the US used it all the time. I had no clue about that."[3]

This period, in which a better understanding of the aspects of the problem and its political dimensions was developed, led to the support of a different paradigm that considers uniformly high IPR protection in itself a barrier to access to medicines (Kapczynski 2008; Muzaka 2011; Sell 2013). Large part of the technical work by access professionals in the first five years after TRIPS was on the understanding of the agreement itself: its legal requirements and flexibilities, particularly the mechanism of compulsory licencing. The first international meeting focusing on HIV/Aids drugs took place in 1999 ('t Hoen 2002). "Between 1999 and 2002 I was very much involved in trying to work with countries to create compulsory licenses, change their patent laws to make it easier to get access to inexpensive drugs, a lot of this in relation to AIDS. But a lot of people talking about compulsory licensing had not come close to one."[4] This work unearthed the technical and political difficulties for countries to use TRIPS flexibilities and, combined with a robust civil society campaign and a rampant HIV/AIDS epidemic, supported the need of legal clarification obtained with the Doha Declaration (WTO 2001).

By the time the Doha Declaration was signed, professionals working on the issue had fully integrated the changes in the objective element of the problem into a convincing reconstruction of the subjective elements of the task. In this new cognitive structure of jurisdictional claims, IPRs are considered a key reason for lack of affordability and needs-driven

[3] Interview 2.   [4] Interview 4.

innovation. With the complexity of circumventing the new rules at national level, there is a need to combine health, legal, economic, and political knowledge to diagnose IP-related blockages and design mechanisms able to solve the problem at the transnational level. The next section reviews the characteristics of the access professional.

Characterizing the Access Professionals

The cohort I call access professional is different from experts whose role is to provide specific technical assistance regarding legal, economic, and medical aspects of the policy area, a group that includes influential academics (Morin 2014). The access professional, as mentioned above, has a very clear aim of diagnosing IP related obstacles to access, as well as developing and implementing solutions to the problem at transnational level. After Doha, as mentioned above, the focus had moved to the production of TRIPS compliant diagnostics and solutions that can help provide access to medicines and innovation to developing countries but do not necessarily imply the use of flexibilities.

Throughout the 2000s, access professionals have taken part in the different committees and expert groups, usually hosted by the WHO, but have also been board members for different organizations and foundations, working closely with both NGOs and governments/governmental agencies. These activities peaked at the time of the Global Strategy and Plan of Action on Public Health, Innovation, and Intellectual Property (2008), approved in 2009 by the WHO. The Global Strategy is in fact the result of two working groups: the Commission on Intellectual Property Rights, Innovation, and Public Health (CIPIH 2006); and the Intergovernmental Working Group on Public Health, Innovation, and Intellectual Property (IGWG), whose job was to draft the Global Strategy from the Commission's recommendations. A further report by an expert group on finance and innovation was released (2012).

Using the language platform R (R Core Tream 2014) and the sequence analysis package TraMineR (Gabadinho et al. 2011), I analyzed a group of 24 people self-identified or identified by peers as access professionals presently working within the Geneva hub. The main aim here is to explore their training background and career patterns since the late 1980s. In terms of the former, these professionals have undergraduate degrees in health (medicine and pharmacy), economics, law, science, and humanities. The most recurrent in this pilot group is health, with ten professionals, followed by humanities (6), economics (4), and law (2) and science (2). Out of 24 professionals 22 have postgraduate degrees, nine of them at PhD level. Postgraduate degrees are mostly in the same area of the undergraduate

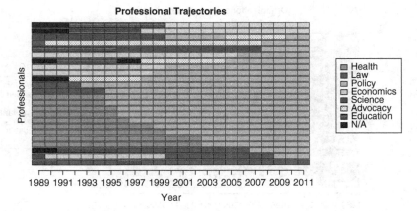

Figure 11.1 The Career Trajectories of Key Access Professionals (for full colour images please refer to www.professionalnetworks.org)

studies, with four people seeking complementary expertise in law (3) and economics (1). Out of 10 professionals with background in health, 9 started their careers on the ground as field doctors and pharmacists. Four of the six individuals with undergraduate diplomas in humanities have career trajectories involving advocacy for non-profit and profit organizations, with the two remaining completing PhDs in law and health economics.

Looking at career patterns, 13 out of 24 were leading research and/or teams working directly on access by 2003, an activity coded here as "policy." Ten years later, 21 were involved in these tasks.

Figure 11.1 Illustrates the main tasks performed by access professionals throughout their careers, with most turning to policy/access related activities after TRIPS in 1995.

Professionals working with health related activities progressed quicker to policy positions than people working in law, economics, and advocacy. Organizational trends are also very clear: most access professionals in this group have moved between institutional settings throughout their careers and four have engaged in revolving doors activities between the public and private sectors (Seabrooke and Tsingou 2009). Six, however, have spent their whole careers in governments and IOs, while one has only worked for the non-profit sector.

Figure 11.2 illustrates access professionals' trajectories in relation to institutional affiliation, with most moving between different types of organization at least once

Regarding current employment, the slight majority works for governments and IOs (12), with eight based at NGOs and four in academia. A not uncommon background summary goes as follows:

Organisational Trajectories

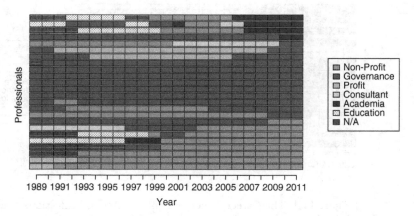

Figure 11.2   The Organizational Trajectories of Key Access Professionals
(for full colour images please refer to www.professionalnetworks.org)

I am a strange kind of animal, a doctor by training, with experience treating patients, but also background in administration and public health, as well as a former regulator of medicines. Moreover, I have been exposed to legal issues during my time in the Ministry of Health and was also my country's focal point for the translation of the Doha Declaration into European regulation.[5]

These professionals, therefore, have educational backgrounds that include at least one of the three disciplines linked to the issue: health, economics, and law. Their most distinctive characteristic, however, is linked to career patterns that include multiple organizational environments and professional involvement in different aspects of the problem. This factor, complemented by the strong cooperative activities across organizational boundaries that characterized the first years after TRIPS, have two important consequences: it reinforces jurisdictional claims that exposure to different aspects of the problem trumps technical knowledge produced within formal disciplinary barriers in the complex case of access; and facilitates two-level network interactions that support strategies of control increasingly targeting the treatment aspect of professional practice. The latter is particularly important for access professionals because attempts to challenge jurisdictional claims have tried to blur the clear linkages between IPRs and access embedded in the subjective

[5] Interview 3.

construction of the task. Against this criticism, control of treatment, and measurable success, automatically confirms the diagnostic.

The next section includes a short overview of organizations linked to the debate, how their mandates are connected to the issue and the changes in their hiring patterns in response to them before moving to the implementation of the MPP.

The Organizational Framework

Since the signature of TRIPS, the issue of access to medicines has ceased to pertain only to the WHO, whose mandate is to promote and protect health, to become the subject of a trilateral cooperation between the WHO, WTO, and WIPO in the late 2000s. As feasible solutions to the problem of access and innovation have to comply with TRIPS, access professionals depend on expertise within the WHO, WTO and WIPO to diagnose and treat the problem.

The WHO was the first international organization to evaluate the impact of TRIPS on public health, responding to member state request. The first reports were published as part of the WHO working force on health economics series (Kinnon 1995; Correa 1997). The "Globalization and Access to Drugs" report (1997), also known as the red (and then blue) book, was authored by a health economist and a lawyer and aimed at public health professionals. Because of its mandate, which has been broadened and strengthened 12 times by member states since 1996,[6] WHO experts are in constant interaction with other networks of humanitarian, governmental, and non-governmental bodies working on health, turning the organization into a focal point for access professionals based at different organizations. As a result, WHO was the most likely place for the housing of three expert committees and the Global Strategy and Plan of Action on Public Health, Innovation and Intellectual Property. In response to new responsibilities identified in these reports, the health agency has continued to provide key expertise in traditional areas such as public health in low- and medium-income countries, but also entered new terrain by hiring experts in subjects such as pricing and evidence based selection of medicines. "WHO and Health Action International have made a standardised protocol to measure medicine prices. It has been done in 70 countries and is now standard but

---

[6] Since concerns were first raised in the World Health Assembly in 1996 (WHA49.14), 12 resolutions focusing on the foment of policies that increase access through the availability of generics, local manufacturing, targeted R&D and development of new products were approved by the WHA. An overview and link to all WHA resolutions can be found at the Department of Public Health, Innovation, Intellectual Property Division and Trade of the World Health Organisation www.who.int/phi/documents/en/index.html.

ten years ago the WHO was not allowed to measure prices. We were not allowed to touch it."[7]

The WTO, like the health agency, is a member-driven institution. Contrary to the WHO, however, it did suffer a backlash from its membership when it strayed from the substantive analysis of the TRIPS legal framework and entered the debate about solutions for access to medicines and lack of innovation, pushed by the civil society campaign of the late 1990s. As stated in an interview, the external influence was significant:

Back in 1999, 2000, it was maximum pressure on us to do something. Everyone was blaming the TRIPS Agreement so, under the leadership of Michael Moore, we started the debate and we had workshops, presentations, we talked about differential pricing and different kinds of financing. All became totally focused on patents. We had only started the conversation when member countries said: this is none of your business, this is for other agencies. You have to talk about IP and access to medicines within TRIPS. That led to the negotiations on the Doha Declaration.[8]

In its second attempt to influence the debate, the WTO's focus is on management of IPRs, and the range of possibilities for this work within TRIPS.[9] Both changes enhance WTO's "arbitrageur" control over the dilemma of providing public goods under a system that prioritizes the protection of private rights. The expertise supporting these activities is mainly on the legal side: of the 15 WTO employees contributing to the trilateral report, at least 11 have an undergraduate or postgraduate degree in law.[10] But the Intellectual Property Division, which provides services for the TRIPS council and dispute settlement, among other duties, is increasingly hiring experts with hybrid backgrounds. As conveyed in an interview, hybrid skills are important as "Basically what's going on in IP policy-making generally is that you find that lawyers are having to learn the economics and that the economists are having to learn the law. IP is really an exercise in practical economics as carried out through legal mechanisms".[11]

The move towards broader expertise is also clearly seen at WIPO, the third organization closely involved in the issue of public health and IP. Albeit a formal collaborator of WTO since TRIPS, WIPO has undergone substantial changes in the past five years. The reshuffle is a response to developing countries' request for the restoring of the public policy aspects of IPRs (May 2007), the so-called Development Agenda, established in 2007. Since the arrival of Francis Gurry as Director General, in 2008, a new division entitled Global Challenges, focusing on global health,

[7] Interview 5.   [8] Interview 6.   [9] Interview 8.
[10] Compilation of publicly available CVs   [11] Interview 8.

climate change and food security,[12] was created with very specific hiring patterns. Advertising in *The Economist* for the position of director of the division, WIPO asked for "professionals responsible for anticipating/ addressing IP issues arising from global challenges and ensuring an effective contribution from WIPO in the collective search for solutions by the UN and the international community" (cited in Okediji 2008, p.84). An analysis of publicly available CVs of WIPO staff contributing to the trilateral report shows that, of the 11 participating experts hired after 2009, two have PhDs in Economics and worked as economists for other intergovernmental organizations, one comes from the pharmaceutical industry, one is a medical doctor with industry and NGOs experience, and two are senior experts on public-private partnerships. The six new employees with legal background have experience on trade, public private partnerships, developing countries and licensing. This contrast with other 12 WIPO experts named in the report hired between 1992 and 2008, in which nine are lawyers specialized in more general IP issues. "Historically WIPO has implemented the treaty, looked at legal and patent infrastructure. The Global Challenges Division is a change of culture to make WIPO relevant in global issues, providing fact based, pragmatic contribution to the debate."[13]

The next section illustrates how access professionals engaged with these organizations, making use of organizational and personal networks to set up the Medicines Patent Pool, an entity designed to solve procurement and innovation problems. Successful implementation and measurable results, in turn, reinforce issue control in two ways: it confirms the diagnostic by treating the problem; and places access professionals in charge of the process of steering the creation of information and knowledge previously unavailable or inexistent.

The Medicines Patent Pool

The Medicines Patent Pool was established as a Swiss charity in August 2010 under the sponsorship of UNITAID, a WHO agency. The idea of using the concept of a patent pool to induce the manufacturing of inexpensive generic drugs, at the same time creating at a big enough market, was developed by James Love, from the NGO Knowledge Ecology International (KEI). Love's solution speaks to a concern that is central to access professionals' jurisdictional claims: the prospect that new drugs now under patent world-wide will be unavailable for large

[12] www.wipo.int/about-wipo/en/activities_by_unit/units/global_challenges.html.
[13] Interview 9.

numbers of patients. In the case of HIV/AIDS drugs, this could re-create the crisis of the early 1990s. While companies were putting forward voluntary licenses and donation programs to fend off intervention, the worry is that this kind of initiatives can turn into a patent dustbin, where the right patents on the right molecules were not available.[14] For a patent pool to work properly, it would have to be linked to particular health needs. MSF teamed up with KEI to promote the pool and the group pitched the idea to series of supranational agencies, including the WHO, without success.[15]

The use of personal networks to navigate organizational logics and establish collaboration was central in at least two moments in the case of the MPP: the initial introduction to UNITAID; and during the task force phase, when the Pool had to be justified in terms of medical and clinical needs.

The lack of response from potential sponsors, as mentioned above, was a serious barrier circumvented when UNITAID, the international drug purchasing facility funded by the governments of Brazil, Chile, France, Norway and the United Kingdom, was established. As a senior access professional directly involved in the process explained: "As soon as UNITAID decided to focus on children's formulations and second line HIV/AIDS and TB drugs, a group of NGO experts I have worked with requested support for this idea that had been used in agriculture, IT, but not health. I invited them to pitch it to the board because I believed we would be able to take that further."[16] Besides the inter-personal connections, the Pool's aim of making new lines of HIV/AIDS treatment affordable in the medium and long terms fits well the purposes of UNITAID, an entity searching for innovative market-shaping solutions. Moreover, UNITAID functions under the umbrella of the WHO, with direct access to in-house expertise, but answers only to its own board, composed of founding countries and foundations.

The final decision to establish the Pool was taken in November 2009, three years after the first presentation. It followed a legal review (Gold et al. 2007), a multidisciplinary expert group (UNITAID December 2007), and a task force led by Ellen t'Hoen, who left the MSF to join UNITAID and would be the first executive director of the MPP (2009). Some countries were worried about the pool harming their own prerogative of issuing compulsory licenses and being narrow in its scope while others were under pressure by their pharmaceutical industry; other board members were unsure about the problems the pool would solve.[17] The latter was a particularly sensitive point and moving the debate forward depended on

[14] Interview 10.   [15] Interview 4.   [16] Interview 16.   [17] Interview 11.

having a technical justification for why a patent pool would be able to solve the problem at hand. A crucial moment in the process was the establishment of a clear link between the proposed activities of the MPP and global health needs, particularly in connection to the development and production of new drugs. Prompted by the need to provide a final push to convince the UNITAID board, senior experts based at the WHO linked the tasks of the MPP with the Model List of Essential Medicines through the compilation of an official wish list of the medicines that are needed but do not exist. The list was endorsed by the WHO 17th Expert Committee on the Selection and Use of Essential Medicines (2009). Here, again, trust on the professional judgment of personal network members was crucial:

Ellen 't Hoen, who was in charge of implementing the MPP, is a very well known person to us, a very trusted professional and individual. So if Ellen says it is a good idea, we look very carefully into it and most probably support it. I was the one pushing for a link with the Essential Drugs list and the argument was that WHO has a positive list for important medicines but we have a second dimension to it, which is the missing essential drugs, the ones that do not exist yet. That was the 20% addition to the 80% already existing argument to support the pool. It provided a clear medical background to the new entity.[18]

Establishing the MPP depended on the ability of access professionals to acquire information produced by the WHO, WTO and WIPO and turn it into relevant and useful knowledge. In relation to the most effective design for the MPP, WTO experts analyzed issues of anti-trust and competition rules from transnational and national perspectives[19], and a wide range of practical IP management mechanisms that could be deployed were extensively debated with support of both WTO and WIPO.[20] The wish list provided by the WHO, mentioned before, was also indispensable. Once the Pool was given the go-ahead and a budget by the UNITAID board, the continuous collaboration with these transnational organizations started to feed directly into the capacity of access professionals to control the issue. WIPO was requested to assist the Pool in the identification of the legal status of 35 patent families (i.e. searching where in the world key patents are valid) and, after this first stage, to expand the list to identify relevant patents for potential new products, a so-called state of the art search.[21] The work on a patent database containing data landscape from different countries had already started with the help of external consultants[22], but without WIPO as an intermediate it would be very difficult to reach regional and local offices to retrieve information.[23] WIPO has also organized a workshop on terms

---

[18] Interview 5.   [19] Interview 7.   [20] Interview 8.   [21] Interview 13.   [22] Interview 14.
[23] Interview 11.

and conditions of patent pool licenses, bringing groups of experts from all over the world to discuss how the licenses could be structured.[24]

In this process of instigating the production of information and creation of knowledge, the MPP itself has become a central node of the technical and political networks connected to the issue of access, innovation and R&D. The patent database, for instance, is a first of its kind, containing data for pharmaceutical products from over 70 countries. Although it was compiled and is regularly updated primarily to inform the Pool's negotiations with companies, it has become publicly available to assist the work of other procurement agencies such as UNICEF and the Global Fund. The Pool has continuously established technical collaborations with different experts and organizations and has increasingly provided technical-legal advice to other agencies and individuals, both on patent law generally and on specific patents in the database.[25] Collaborations are also created in response to issues that arise from the negotiations with companies, for example, the stronger interaction with WHO's Qualifications Programme, or the establishment of a working relationship with the European Medicines Agency.[26]

The other side of the coin is the firm links of the MPP with NGOs working on the issue, many with particularly important insights on different elements of the problem, from medical expertise to logistical information on treating patients in developing countries. Many access professionals are members of its executive and advisory board. There is, however, a clear concern of not positioning the MPP as an advocacy group fighting for access but an expert entity catering for global needs, as communicated in an expert interview:

From the MPP perspective it is important to be known broadly throughout the community: academia, international organisations, civil society, national governments. To be know as an expert, very knowledgeable in a number of areas, particularly in the are of patenting of HIV medicines, which is what we are tackling at the moment, and the issues surrounding licenses, also a key focus, but more broadly on global politics of IP and access to medicines.[27]

The establishment of the MPP has spurred reaction from other organizations attempting issue control. The patent status and state of the art search conducted by WIPO to the MPP became a pilot case and the service is now on offer to developing countries, NGOs and other IOs in the area of global health.[28] In 2011, a few months after the MPP was established, WIPO launched Re:Search, an upstream patent pool for malaria and tuberculosis. In July 2009, when the MPP was already sending letters

---

[24] Interview 15.   [25] Interview 12.   [26] Interview 15.   [27] Interview 12.
[28] Interview 13.

introducing UNITAID and the future pool, GlaxoSmithKline announced the establishment of its patent pool for neglected tropical diseases. It is now a partner of WIPO RE:Search.

By the end of 2015, the MPP had negotiated licenses on 12 priority anti-retrovirus drugs from seven different patent holders and had more than 50 product development projects in the pipeline. Its generic partners have distributed 3 billion doses of low-cost products to more than 100 countries and it is estimated that the MPP will help the international community save between 1.2 and 1.4 billion dollars over the coming years. It is still early to accurately measure the success of the MPP, as many of these promises have not materialized yet, but the Pool has certainly gone a fair bit in confirming the diagnostics, and the legitimacy of the access professionals behind its implementation.

Conclusion

This chapter argues that the establishment of the issue of access to medicines in the international agenda cannot be solely understood as a result of political activism, but is directly linked to the emergence of the access professional, an expert whose main task is to design supranational solutions able to induce needs-driven innovation on drugs and medical technology and ensure extensive access to them. Using Abbott's (1988) conceptualization of professional tasks as containing subjective and objective elements, I show that changes in the objective nature of the problem by the signature of TRIPS led to intensive collaboration across professional and organizational networks, which, in turn, allowed a group of professionals with a distinctive type of career patterns to restructure the subjective elements of the task to claim jurisdiction. This was done through the creation of a multi-disciplinary linkage of access to medicines to intellectual property and innovation that had the effect of placing the professional practice acts of diagnosis, inference and treatment at supranational level.

Attempts to control the issue, on the other hand, are better understood using the lenses of the two-level network proposed in the introduction of this volume. The process of implementation of the Medicines Patent Pool details how outside-in strategies to create organizational space for action involved the activation of inter-personal networks that allowed access professionals to instigate the production of information confined within organizational boundaries previously inaccessible to create knowledge that support their control of the issue.

Supported by a novel combination of qualitative and quantitative methods, the chapter contributes to the literature on professions in transnational governance by providing empirical evidence on the ways jurisdiction claims are built upon subjective elements of tasks, in line with Abbott's ideas, but also highlights that the ability to restructure these elements can be related to professional experience that stems from career trajectories. The chapter also advances knowledge in relation to outside-in strategies of control by providing an account of how professionals, using personal networks, are able to engage organizations and their experts to produce information that can reinforce their own control of the issue.

Cited Official Sources

WHO (1996). Revised Drug Strategy. W. H. Organisation. WHA 49.14.

WHO (2008). Global Strategy and Plan of Action on Public Health, Innovation and Intellectual Property, World Health Organisation.

WHO (2009). The Selection and Use of Essential Medicines. WHO Technical Report Series, WHO.

WHO (2013). Financial Report and Audited Financial Statements. WHO, WHO.

WHO/WTO (2002). WTO Agreements and Public Health, WHO, WTO.

WHO/WTO/WIPO (2012). Promoting Access to Medical Technology and Innovation: Intersections between public health, intellectual property and trade.

WTO (1995). Agreement on Trade-Related Aspects of Intellectual Property Rights – Annex 1 C. W. T. Organization.

WTO (1995). WTO-WIPO Cooperation Agreement. W. a. WIPO.

WTO (2001). Declaration on the TRIPS Agreement and Public Health. O. World Trade. WT/MIN(01)/DEC/2.

WTO (2003). Implementation of paragraph 6 of the Doha Declaration on TRIPS and Public Health. W. T. Organization.

List of Interviews

Interview 1: economics background, NGO based, interview conducted in Cape Town, December 2014.

Interview 2: medical background, NGO based, interview conducted in Cape Town, December 2014.

Interview 3: medical background, WHO based, interview conducted in Geneva, March 2012.

Interview 4: economics background, NGO based, interview conducted in Geneva, March 2013.

Interview 5: medical background, WHO based, interview conducted in Geneva, May 2013.

Interview 6: legal background, WTO based, interview conducted in Geneva, October 2013.

Interview 7: legal background, WTO based, interview conducted in Geneva, March 2012.

Interview 8: legal background, WTO base, interview conducted in Geneva, March 2012.

Interview 9: science and law background, WIPO based, interview conducted in Geneva, March 2012.

Interview 10: legal background, NGO based, phone interview conducted in March 2012.

Interview 11: medical background, government based, phone interview conducted in December 2014.

Interview 12: legal background, 'anonymous', interview conducted in Geneva, May 2013.

Interview 13: science and legal background, WIPO based, interview conducted in Geneva, March 2012.

Interview 14: legal background, NGO based, phone interview conducted in June 2013.

Interview 15: policy background, MPP based, phone interview conducted in March 2012.

Interview 16: medical background, UNITAID, phone interview conducted in December 2013.

12 Professions and Policy Dynamics in the Transnational Carbon Emissions Trading Network

Matthew Paterson, Matthew Hoffmann, Michele Betsill, and Steven Bernstein

This chapter explores the role of professions in the politics of diffusing emissions trading (ET) as a policy instrument to deal with climate change. It builds on an existing analysis of the transnational expert network through which ideas about ET have diffused (Paterson et al., 2014), by introducing the question of professional ties and identities. It approaches this question in two ways. First it explores the sorts of pre-existing professional identities that served to constitute the transnational ET network as ET was being initially developed. Second it explores, in a more preliminary way, the emergence of what might be called a "carbon market profession." This is in line with what Seabrooke and Henriksen (this volume) term "issue professionals," professionals whose identities form around the issue itself and the practices associated with it. We suggest that what we may be seeing at the moment is that the diffusion process for a new generation of ET systems is functioning rather differently than in an earlier era – through this professionalization of carbon market activity rather than (or at least alongside) via the pre-existing professions that made up the earlier network. Figure 12.1 provides a visual representation of the argument of the chapter.

Professional ties and identities are important in the first phase of the diffusion of ET because the individuals involved in the initial transnational network were trained in specific professions and disciplines and worked in organizational settings that framed their activity in terms of particular professional norms and habits. These professions therefore explain, in part, the development of ET as a crucial aspect of climate policy, with people in the initial network making connections to others in part because of prior professional association or shared epistemic practices arising out of this professional context. But they also explain the particular sort of framing of ET as a policy issue, with competing professions seeking to engage in

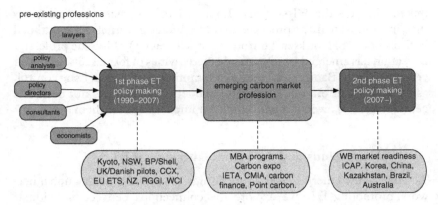

Figure 12.1 Professions and Emissions Trading

"issue control" (Seabrooke and Henriksen this volume) over how ET was to be understood and implemented. To explore the diffusion of carbon markets and the role of professions, we apply social network analysis methods supplemented with interview and archival data to identify how policy ideas travelled between ET venues, and in particular to how the structure and distribution of professions across the network can add to our understanding of this process of diffusion. In contrast to a specific organizational setting like the IMF (e.g., Seabrooke and Nilsson, 2015), our network in the initial phase is constituted in a number of different geographic settings, with members employed in a wide range of organizations, and thus the conditions within which specific professions come to participate in the network are rather different. Carbon markets exist simultaneously in local and transnational spheres. Their transnational existence has no natural organizational home (beyond the general UNFCCC process, which can only loosely be regarded as an "organization") and is instead a network of individuals and organizations that have promoted the use and spread of emissions trading in a number of different venues.

Professional ties and linkages may be even more important in the current phase of ET policy making because of the emergence of a carbon market profession. As ET has become institutionalized at the global level and as mechanisms for standardizing ET policy have emerged, issue control may now be shared among the political jurisdictions that decide to undertake ET and the carbon market profession. In particular, carbon market professionals and the specialized knowledge they possess and deploy may now be indirectly regulating ET by setting the general parameters that make carbon markets work (as markets) and allow individual emergent markets to link to other, existing ET systems.[1] Important to recognize in this process is that, in contrast to many processes of transnational governance (as outlined in Seabrooke & Henriksen's introduction, Chapter 1), this issue professionalization has emerged largely outside the activities of formal IOs. In recent years the World Bank can be seen as attempting to engage in issue control, as we detail later on, but the carbon market profession has not been one centered on IOs, even if it has significant implications for them.

Professions and the Initial Diffusion of ET

To analyze the emergence and functioning of an initial transnational network promoting ET, we explore the connections between individuals participating in eight policy venues that were involved in the early development of emissions trading.[2] Three of these venues form a "germination" period in the early days of climate governance where the idea of emissions trading emerged: Project 88 in the United States (a bipartisan sponsored expert-based initiative focused initially on developing the policy case for market mechanisms for US domestic clean air policy), OECD/UNCTAD (both of which sponsored reports on emission trading), and the Annex I Working Group (AIXG), the principal forum for discussing emissions trading in the UNFCCC negotiations before Kyoto in 1997. The other five venues are specific instances where emissions trading was considered and designed. These include Kyoto/Marrakesh (UNFCCC negotiations in Marrakesh produced the 2001 Marrakesh Accords, in which parties finalized the rules of implementation for the 1997 Kyoto Protocol) and four venues that are or were operational – the UK, EU, RGGI, and WCI.[3] Research on these eight venues uncovered 130 individuals who were part of

---

[1] In ET, the commodity being traded (carbon permits) is created by a policy decision to cap emissions and divide the cap into permits to emit greenhouse gases. Entities that emit less greenhouse gases than their allowance can sell their permits to those entities that emit more than their allowance. Over time the cap ratchets down and through this mechanism, theoretically, emission reduction efforts are driven to where they cost the least. The original vision for using ET to address climate change was to have an integrated global carbon market associated with the Kyoto Protocol. However, because of gridlock in the global negotiations, the originally envisioned single cap and trade system has fragmented into multiple, distinct ET venues (Bernstein et al., 2010; Betsill and Hoffmann, 2010). These venues emerged in diverse places (primarily in the industrialized world) and political jurisdictions (from the global to the local) and include both the public and private sectors.
[2] For a full description of the network mapping methods used in this section of the chapter, see Paterson et al., 2014.
[3] The UK ran a pilot emissions trading system between 2003 and 2005. For the WCI, the precise start date for the ETS is not yet completely decided, but at the time of writing, California will begin trading in 2013 with British Columbia, Québec, and perhaps Ontario to follow at an as yet undisclosed date.

the "transnational" network – individuals that participated in more than one venue.

We collected biographies for these 130 individuals and coded their professions inductively from this data. We used both the discipline of the highest degree received, and the principal positions during the person's career, to arrive at a judgment about the profession for each individual.[4] The professions we identified in the network are economists, lawyers, policy analysts, policy directors, and lobbyists/consultants/traders. A brief description of how we see each of these operating as professions, and how we understand the distinctions between them where this may be ambiguous, is in order:

- Economists are identified as people trained as economists and still working as economists professionally – either in universities or in think tanks or similar research positions. They are close to some of the policy analysts in their policy work but orient themselves to the task of policy analysis as economists.
- Lawyers are trained as lawyers and still identify their role as lawyers. They may work in government, private firms or NGOs, but present themselves as lawyers.
- Policy analysts/advisors are people who have a range of disciplinary backgrounds and whose identity as a group is centered on their focus in their work in the analysis of emissions trading policy, and perhaps climate change policy more generally. They differ from economists in drawing on a broader range of disciplines in analyzing policy. They differ from policy directors in being relatively separate from the formal decision-making process. They differ from consultants in that the research they do is not directly to advance particular positions but rather to advance debate on policy. They may work in government, NGOs, think tanks or business.[5]

---

[4] In future work we aim to unpack their careers temporally. What we expect on the basis of reading the biographies is to find a very considerable fluidity in professional situation across their careers, compared to other professional networks. For example, in Seabrooke and Nilsson's article (2015) on IMF staffing the career trajectories of network members appear for the most part highly stable – they involve a hierarchical trajectory from junior to senior, within a similar organizational framework and thus set of professional norms and habits. In the ET network, there is much greater fluidity, with actors moving from private trading organizations, to government bureaucracies, to NGOs or think tanks, and back again. This will add considerable richness to our analysis of professions in the ET network, but the work remains to be undertaken.

[5] We accept that the boundary between economist and policy analyst as we have constructed it is difficult to identify with great precision. Certainly, people we have coded as policy analysts use economic forms of analysis and discourse in their articulations of ET as a policy project. However, it is in our view a useful distinction to make as we have defined it here. For example, looking at Figure 12.2, the prevalence of policy analysts in transmitting ideas about ET into the UNFCCC process is important. Key actors like Michael Grubb (PhD in engineering, working then at the Royal Institute of International Affairs as

- Policy directors are people whose professional career has mostly been spent at high-levels of decision-making about ET. Most are in national governments but some are in private sector organizations involved in direct governance of ET (e.g., the climate registry) as well as at the UN.
- Lobbyist/consultant/traders are people who are primarily involved in ET in a commercial capacity. They are either traders who have been involved in the policy process, or lobbyists for particular industries. The consultants are those hired directly by companies to produce reports to advance their cause. The consultants are close to some policy analysts but the distinction is about any research they do being directly of interest to funding parties.

With data on individuals and the emissions trading venues that they participated in, we turned to network analysis. We defined the network by treating individuals as nodes and common participation in a venue as the link (edge) between nodes.[6] If John Smith and Mary Jones participated jointly in RGGI discussions they are linked by a tie. The edges are presented as value-free (i.e., no difference between a link that represents common participation in a single venue and a link representing ten venues participated in common). In a number of the graphs below, node size is a function of the betweenness score – a measure of centrality that captures how important a node (individual or organization) is to the connectivity of the network.[7] Professions are represented by node color.

Examining the transnational network with information on professions included reveals a number of interesting dynamics in the diffusion of ET over time.[8] First, a pseudo-epistemic community dedicated to ET for climate change emerged in the late 1980s and early 1990s that provided intellectual foundations for a global ET system. This community was dominated by economists who offered the initial intellectual foundation and justification for pursuing the development of emissions trading.

---

a researcher on climate policy) brought to ET debates arguments about feasibility in international negotiations and global justice in distributing the burden of reducing GHG emissions in ways that those trained in economics only rarely do.

[6] Focusing on individuals or organizations as nodes downplays other ways that information can flow – e.g., through citations. In addition, while we concentrate on individuals or organizations that participated in the venues, this does not mean that other kinds of links between individuals are not also important.

[7] There are multiple measures of centrality for nodes. Betweenness measures the importance of nodes for network connectedness and nodes with high betweenness scores can play roles as brokers (because removal of high betweenness nodes leaves the network fragmented). One could use other measures like degree centrality (the number of links a node has to other nodes) or closeness centrality (the length of the path from one node to all other nodes). However, betweenness has more relevance for our project because of its association with a brokering role.

[8] For a full discussion of diffusion dynamics, see Paterson et al., 2014.

However, from the beginning, diffusion of these ideas took two paths – one North American and one European – thus defying conventional wisdom about how ET for climate change resulted from the externalization of US experience with emissions trading for sulfur dioxide (e.g., Damro and Luaces Méndez, 2003; Ovodenko and Keohane, 2012; for a fuller critique see Paterson et al., 2014).

The international policy diffusion literature has limited insight here because it seeks to explain how and why policies in one or a few political jurisdictions get emulated or reproduced in other similar units, or how an idea promoted internationally – say through a treaty or an international institution – becomes state policy (e.g., Finnemore, 1996; Füglister, 2011). The focus is almost exclusively on government actors as sources and targets, explaining how or why they select similar policy instruments or institutional forms in different jurisdictions (e.g., Dobbin, Simmons, and Garrett, 2007; Ovodenko and Keohane, 2012).

Second, and in contrast to the traditional diffusion literature, we observe that the diffusion of ET both (re)constituted and flowed through an emerging polycentric governance structure, where diffusion of transnational policy ideas do not find immediate homes in already existing polities like nation-states (Paterson et al., 2014). ET was never designed holistically for climate change – there was never a focal organization that had authority to control the issue of emissions trading transnationally or globally. On the contrary, some venues picked up and began to work with ET in anticipation of a larger system, gaining experience and shaping what ET applied to climate change would look like. After 2001 when it became clear that a global ET system would not materialize, the fragmentation of ET accelerated as different venues engaged with ET for a variety of reasons and the distribution of specific professional involvement in particular venues varied significantly. No one profession dominated in the fragmentation of ET.

This structure for the "global" issue of emissions trading makes the role of professional networks a complex one. Professions can play a role at two levels. Within the transnational network (explored here), professions can influence how the idea of emissions trading circulates. However, professions may play an even larger role within individual venues, with cooperation and competition among professional networks playing a key role in how emissions trading systems are designed and implemented locally. Unfortunately, an analysis of professions' involvement in each individual venue is beyond the scope of this chapter.

Finally, the growing diffusion of ET in this post-2001 period was again largely a transnational phenomenon, shaped by the two paths that developed in the early days of ET discussions. While the network diagrams show a dearth of connections between the early epistemic community and the later operational venues, the distinct European and North American pathways are still evident and are shaped by different distributions of professions who connect these venues to the transnational community.

Two Roads to Emissions Trading

To examine the emergence of emissions trading in the climate change arena, we first created a network map of the two expert venues (Project 88 and OECD/UNCTAD) along with the venues that considered the place of emissions trading in the UN negotiations (AIXG and Marrakesh). What is immediately apparent is that the early pseudo-epistemic community, while dominated by economists, is actually bifurcated into two distinct clusters with relatively loose connections. One cluster emerged in the United States organized around the Project 88 initiative and another in Europe, organized in particular by UNCTAD and the OECD (Figure 12.2). In Figure 12.2 the square nodes represent these early venues and the circles are individuals who participated in these discussions (only those individuals who also participated in at least one additional venue are included) (find a version of the network graphs where the nodes are colored according to their profession at [www .professionalnetworks.org). This illustrates the separation between the two sites in which emissions trading discourse emerged in climate change debates. Only two individuals (Tom Tietenberg, an academic economist, and Dan Dudek, the senior person at US-based Environmental Defense Fund, which strongly promoted ET in this period) participated commonly in Project 88 and in the OECD/UNCTAD reports. Notably, both are non-state actors. Further, Project 88 has fewer connections to the UN venues (AIXG and Marrakesh) than does the European oriented OECD/UNCTAD. The US network is also more dominated by economists than the European/IGO network, while the actors that connect these early venues to the Annex I working group (where ET was discussed prior to Kyoto) and the Marrakesh venue (the venue that decided the principal rules for the emissions trading features in the Kyoto Protocol) are for the most part not economists but policy analysts. This suggests that very early on, the intellectual foundation for emissions trading mechanisms were developed, not surprisingly, by one profession (economists). When emissions trading became a political issue (i.e., when it was taken up by the UN negotiations), however, another profession (policy analysts) provided the translation into the policy process. Given that these two network clusters are the principal sites for early discussions of emissions trading for climate change, we unpack the character of the discourse at each site and how it emerged since this is an important context for understanding the observed variation in emissions trading systems.

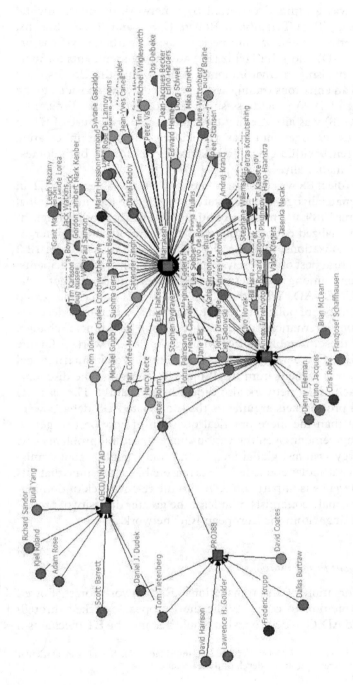

Figure 12.2 Network Graph of Early Venues and the Kyoto-Marrakesh Process (for full colour images please refer to www.professionalnetworks.org)

Project 88 was an initiative started by a network of environmental economists (e.g., Tom Tietenberg, Robert Hahn, and Robert Stavins, who was the project director) and policy-makers (particularly Senators Timothy Wirth (D) and John Heinz (R)) advancing arguments for market-based mechanisms in environmental policy within the US. Its work led directly to an emissions trading system created by the revisions to the Clean Air Act of 1990 to address sulfur dioxide emissions. Project 88 (1988, pp. 17–18) was also the first to suggest the possible use of ET to address climate change, and was particularly important in creating a strong preference within US policy-making circles for ET both domestically and internationally.

But while Project 88 was the first to mention the possible use of ET in relation to climate change, the idea started to gain broader international currency during 1989 as a number of others, mostly from other English-speaking industrialized countries but working in Europe and in intergovernmental organizations, took the idea and ran with it. As Figure 12.2 shows, they were at best only loosely connected to Project 88 participants. The discussions among this network were coordinated by both the OECD and UNCTAD. What the figure also shows is that this group contained a number of policy analysts that served as a bridge to developing ET within international expert discussions of climate change. A number of these, notably Corfee-Morlot and Jones, worked for the OECD and IEA. These policy analysts, institutionalized in international organizations, were absent from the Project 88 network. The discourse adopted by each initial network also differed significantly. The classical efficiency and pro-markets arguments that dominated US debates were less important than the more practical question of how best to get an international agreement given the various huge structural problems (the inertia of energy systems, global inequalities, uncertainties about emissions trends in particular countries).[9] It is reasonable to presume that this discursive difference is in part connected to the relative lack of domination by professional economists or at least the greater diversity of professions participating within the European/IGO network.

Emergent Fragmentation

The early bifurcation of the transnational ET network foreshadowed further fragmentation to come. While the Europeans worked through the OECD and AIXG to develop what would become the ET mechanism

[9] Interviewed by Paterson, 17 December 2007 (Cambridge UK). See also in particular Grubb (1989), where he explicitly develops these arguments.

in the Kyoto Protocol, US refusal to ratify the protocol doomed the possibility for a globally integrated market. What resulted was the development of autonomous ET systems at the national and subnational level. The transnational network would still serve as important linkages between these autonomous venues, but the impact of specific professions was lessened at the transnational level because the politics turned local.

Figures 12.3 and 12.4, where links between nodes represent common participation in one or more venues, shows that the continued relative separation between the US and European network clusters continued once ET moved to the operational phase. The early networks already discussed appear in the top left of the picture (Project 88 and UNCTAD/OECD) and in the dense cluster in the middle in Figure 12.3 (AIXG).[10] The two clusters in the bottom of the picture are RGGI (left) and WCI (right). The clusters on the right are the UK pilot scheme (top) and the EU ETS (bottom). The size of the node indicates an actor's betweenness score. Larger node size means that node is more central to the network in the sense that removal of the node would have a relatively large effect on breaking up the network. Indeed what is even clearer in Figure 12.4, when Kyoto is taken out of the picture is that US-based network participants only participate in US venues and the UN process – they do not participate at all in non-US venues at national or regional levels. This fragmentation lessened the impact of any transnational professional cadre because centers of authority are emerging with relatively sparse individual connections between them and with relatively few direct individual connections to the intellectual foundations or global design of ET. Professions may well have been important in shaping the development of the individual venues, but the transnational realm was much sparser.

At this broad level there is relatively little by way of patterned professional engagement. Policy analysts play the biggest single role in connecting venues, and economists the smallest role, but all five professions identified are involved in such connections. We can identify one or two patterns at particular venues. Notably, the US venues, in particular RGGI, are the only ones where lawyers play a significant role, not surprisingly perhaps given what is known about the law-driven culture of US policy-making. The UK and RGGI also appear as the most lobbyist intensive venues. (In the UK at least, this was explicit – the UK Emissions Trading Group, which is the source of our data for the UK venue, was constituted explicitly as a forum for policymakers and affected industries to discuss and develop ET policy.) It is also

---

[10] The picture looks largely similar if we add in the Marrakesh network. It is very close to the AIXG network and we leave it out for clarity.

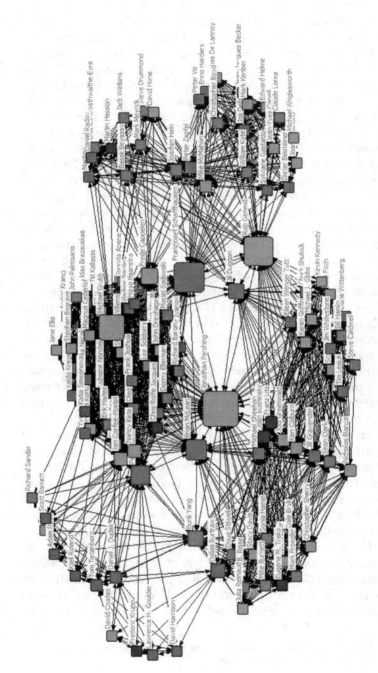

Figure 12.3 Network Graph of Early and Operational Venues (for full colour images please refer to www.professionalnetworks.org)

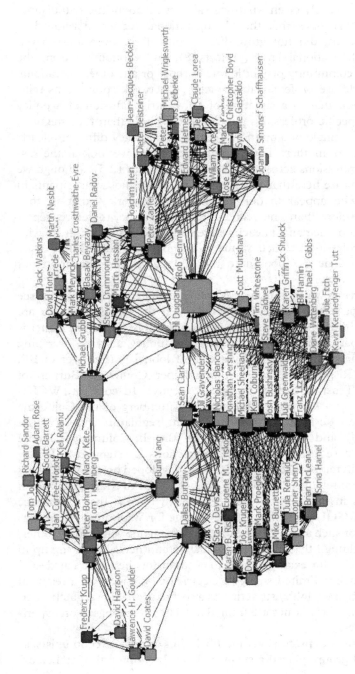

Figure 12.4 Network Graph of Early and Operational Venues (Excluding Annex I Working Group/Kyoto) (for full colour images please refer to www.professionalnetworks.org)

noteworthy, especially given what was said earlier about the two distinct sorts of ET discourse, that the US operational venues, developed at subnational levels, did not grow directly out of the economist-driven network at the national level (project 88), and economists from the transnational community play little role in those or any other operational venue. This diffuse professional character of network connections reinforces the point that in a situation of polycentric diffusion of a policy instrument, specific professions play a less clear role than they might in a situation of a single organizational structure or policy diffusion clearly from one site to another. This is reinforced when we look at the distribution of professions across each venue (see Figure 12.5), although we need to emphasize here that this is based solely on those participants in each venue who appear in our transnational network – that is, they participate in more than one venue. This may not be, therefore, representative of all participants in each venue (we hope to follow this up with coding by profession at each venue – although we have 2,000 or so individuals to code as opposed to the 130 or so who appear in our transnational network).

However, when we explore specific venue connections in detail we see a few more patterns. Figure 12.6 shows that the two US venues are connected to the UN process very differently. RGGI (on the right) is connected, apart from Reinaud and Pershing (policy analysts – Pershing at WRI, Reinaud at the IEA), by a wall of lobbyists (Proegler of BP, Stilwell and Risse of the International Paper Company, Burnett of the Climate Trust, a carbon trading company). In contrast, WCI is connected by two key policy directors – Wittenberg of the California Climate Action Reserve (a NGO developing regulatory infrastructure for the WCI) and Tim Lesiuk of the British Columbia Climate Secretariat. These different types of connections are suggestive. It may be important in temporal terms (RGGI was developed before WCI), so it may be that the relative closeness in time of RGGI to Marrakesh meant that lobbyists involved in the former decided to take that experience directly into RGGI, while the passage of time for WCI meant there was less impetus for such a transfer of experience from one venue to the other. This may (although this is rather speculative and needs following up in further research), for example, help to account for the particular design of RGGI, which is limited solely to electricity emissions, as a result of industrial lobbying – lobbyists acting as a sort of professional gatekeeper/ diffuser, shaping how issues are framed at a later venue based on experience in another.

The initial story of professions and ET is thus one where economists, as a professional group, played a strong role in developing the intellectual

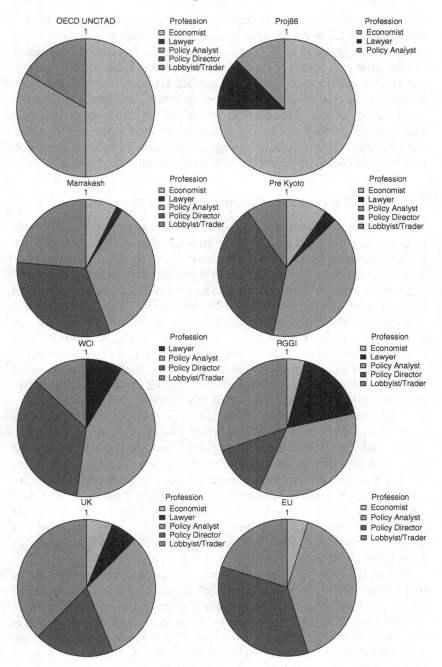

Figure 12.5 Distribution of Professions by Venue (for full colour images please refer to www.professionalnetworks.org)

foundations of this particular climate policy, and the distribution of professions in the US and European clusters may provide insight into the very different development of ET in these regions. Very quickly the influence of particular professions was muted at the transnational level because of the rapid fragmentation of ET and climate governance more generally. Specific venues must be examined to see the influence of professions on the development of ET. However, as we discuss in the next section, the influence of professions at the transnational level was not finished. On the contrary, the nascent emergence of a carbon market profession may be a significant development in the continuing diffusion of ET.

The Emergence of a Carbon Market Profession

While the emergence of ET systems in the period from the early 1990s through to the mid-2000s was stimulated by the existence of a transnational expert network whose members came from diverse professional backgrounds and worked in many different organizational settings, what we see emerging since the middle of the 2000s is a process of emergence of what Seabrooke and Henriksen call "issue professionals" (see introduction, this volume). Specifically, we contend that we can see the emergence of a "carbon market profession" during this period. This process is ongoing and far from complete. In particular there is nothing in existence like in other professions (accountancy, medicine, for example) that creates strict barriers to entry without going through specific accredited training. But there is a set of inter-related practices, which we contend means that those involved in carbon markets – both their day-to-day market operation and the policy design – are becoming more homogenous in their training, daily habits, and collective identity. And we can discern at least at a general level, the sorts of issue control that these emerging carbon market professionals engage in, specifically to reframe carbon markets as markets first and climate policy second, and thus to seek to remove what they see as obstacles to the continued expansion of carbon market activity. A number of processes are involved in the emergence of this professional identity and practice, and this section sketches this historically.

First is the emergence of a number of organizations that operate as representational sites for carbon market actors. These are the earliest to emerge, with the Asia-Pacific Emissions Trading Forum (AETF) founded in 1998 and the International Emissions Trading Association (IETA) created in 1999 around the process of the Kyoto Protocol. Another such organization, the Carbon Market Investors Association (CMIA), was established much later, in 2008. These organizations have operated principally as

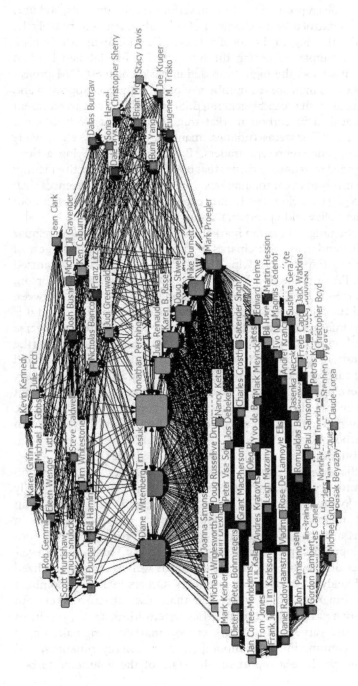

Figure 12.6 Network Graph of Marrakesh, the WCI, and RGGI (for full colour images please refer to www.professionalnetworks.org)

lobby organizations representing actors in various carbon markets, and thus engage in issue control over the character of key carbon markets, notably the EU ETS and the Kyoto Protocol's Clean Development Mechanism (CDM). For example, regarding the latter, IETA has lobbied hard to remove what it sees as the high "transaction costs" of the CDM project approval process to increase the numbers of projects that get approved and thus market activity that can be generated. Some (IETA) aim to represent both firms engaged in carbon market trading activity as well as those regulated under ET systems (utilities, manufacturing firms, etc.), while others (CMIA) only represent traders. But alongside lobbying activity they have engaged in various activities that build a sense of collective identity among those involved in carbon markets – organization of conferences such as Carbon Expo (see below), providing expertise for members about both carbon market policy and operational issues (IETA, 2013).

Second is the range of carbon market conferences that are now regular parts of the calendar for participants in carbon markets. The largest of these is Carbon Expo, started in 2004 (IETA n.d. a), and organized jointly by IETA and the World Bank (see Descheneau and Paterson, 2011 on Carbon Expo). It is held annually, alternating between Cologne and Barcelona. Around 3,000 people attend annually, and it is a mix of a conference and networking event, with panels on diverse aspects of carbon markets from specific aspects of market operation (the design of a carbon offset contract, a new sort of structured finance model for bundling carbon market "assets") through to specific contemporary issues (the development of an ET system in a specific jurisdiction). Point Carbon (see below) also runs an annual global conference, and there are a great many regional conferences, such as the Carbon Forum North America, Carbon Forum Asia, and so on, that fulfill similar networking, community-building, and market-constructing activities.

Third is the development of specific news services for the carbon market operators. The best known of these is Point Carbon, originally run out of Oslo but with an office also in Washington DC. It started as an independent organization but was bought up by Thomson Reuters in 2010. It runs a daily news service comprising information about both market developments (prices, new commodities, etc.) and policy development issues of relevance to market actors, as well as more specialized research and analytic services to subscribers. Others include Bloomberg New Energy Finance, which is broader than just carbon markets but produces daily news. Less frequently, Ecosystem Marketplace produces broader periodic surveys of different carbon markets (originally on its own, now in conjunction with Bloomberg New Energy Finance), and annually, they produce a report on the state of the voluntary carbon

Table 12.1 *Carbon Market Graduate Programs*

University	Program	Website	Notes
Edinburgh, Business School	MSc Carbon Finance	www.business-school.ed.ac.uk/msc/carbon-finance	
Edinburgh, Business School	MSc Carbon Management	www.business-school.ed.ac.uk/msc/carbon-management	
Edinburgh, Business School	MBA, specialization in Carbon Management	www.business-school.ed.ac.uk/mba/full-time/programme-structure	
University of East Anglia	MBA Strategic Carbon Management	http://business.uea.ac.uk/programme-details	Established 2009
Columbia Business School	Carbon finance strategies program		2009. Collaboration with Point Carbon*. No longer appears to be running.
London School of Business and Finance	Global MBA (Carbon Management)	www.lsbf.org.uk/programmes/masters/mba/lsbf-mba/specialisations/mba-carbon-management.html	
Danube University Krems	Professional MBA Energy and Carbon Management	www.donau-uni.ac.at/en/studium/energyandcarbonmba/	

* "MBA courses respond to change in carbon landscape," Financial Times 25 November 2009.[11]

markets (e.g., Peters-Stanley and Yin, 2013), while through to 2012 the World Bank produced an annual report on the state of carbon markets as a whole (Kossoy and Guigon, 2012).

Fourth, there has been the development of a number of MBA programs designed specifically to train people in the ways of carbon markets, and carbon finance more generally. Table 12.1 below gives the main ones that have been developed. Many more business schools now have individual courses on carbon finance, accounting and management.

Finally, institutions have emerged aimed at training a future generation of ET policy professionals. The World Bank's Partnership for

[11] Available at www.ft.com/cms/s/0/9c3607e4-d9d7-11de-ad94-00144feabdc0.html #axzz2jng9sRH0.

Market Readiness Programme,[12] and the International Carbon Action Partnership are the main two here, although IETA has also played a role in this.[13] Both of these have developed to institutionalize the diffusion of ideas and the development of capacity for both policy development and for market activity among private sector actors from countries where ETS had already been developed. ICAP, established in 2007, focuses on organizing regular workshops to train policy professionals in questions of design of ET systems, with an express aim to try to make future carbon markets consistent with existing ones so as to enable linking. The World Bank's program focuses more on grant funding and consulting on the design of ET and other carbon pricing policies (for example, the carbon tax recently introduced in South Africa), notably ET systems being developed in Chile, China, Costa Rica, Turkey and Ukraine (Partnership for Market Readiness, 2013).[14]

As just one example, China launched seven subnational emissions trading pilot projects in 2014–15 and announced plans for a national system to launch in 2017. They have turned to the World Bank's program for capacity building assistance precisely because shared knowledge about the parameters that (should) make markets work has developed and relevant categories for developing carbon markets have been established in an institutionalized way. China, in seeking World Bank support, noted a need for capacity building

to take place on the establishment of a registration system of voluntary carbon emission trading, which aims to ensure justice, equity and transparency of the trading activities, to guarantee the healthy development of the market, to improve the trading efficiency as well as to reduce the trading cost. There is also a need for capacity building in those regions and industries which are able to experiment potentiality of carbon emission trading. To encourage and support carbon trading at these regions and industries, research on target setting, target allocating, trading platform development, establishment of monitoring and management system, and experimentation on trading practice are crucial.[15]

This is evidence of growing issue control being exercised by an institutionalized epistemic community – by a nascent carbon market profession. With the later involvement of the World Bank, it is also evidence of some attempt by IOs to coordinate and consolidate this emerging professional activity, but also of the relative autonomy of this professionalization

[12] www.thepmr.org   [13] ICAP, www.icapcarbonaction.com
[14] In the wake of the 2016 Paris climate agreement, the World Bank is looking to further consolidate this role and issued "Emissions Trading in Practice: A Handbook on Design and Implementation." https://openknowledge.worldbank.org/handle/10986/23874, viewed 11 March 2016.
[15] www.thepmr.org/system/files/documents/China_EoI_January_31_2011_0.pdf

process from states and IOs. Collectively, we see these as part of a professionalization of carbon market practice. Notably, this emerged first not within policy-making processes, but within the markets themselves as they have developed on the back of the first generation of carbon market policies – among the traders, accountants, auditors, lawyers and financiers who make up the daily life of carbon market activity. But we suggest that this may well have started to have an effect on the way that ET policy development has occurred since around 2008–9. Rather than being diffused via a range of diverse pre-existing professions that make up the transnational networks we analyzed earlier, it is increasingly being effected through a more homogenous set of "carbon market professionals," notably via the World Bank and ICAP.

Conclusion

Examining the professions of individuals in the transnational ET network enhances the understanding of polycentric carbon market governance and offers some intriguing lines of further research. First, there is a clear handoff from one profession (economists) to another (policy analysts) once emissions trading moves from being an idea to a negotiating agenda item. To be sure, both policy analysts and economists participated in the early development of the intellectual foundations of emissions trading, but in our network it is the policy analysts who dominate the connections between the early intellectual venues and the operational venues that followed. This analysis thus suggests that early stages of diffusion are distinct and have a good deal in common with learning and elite network dynamics, whether or not they are formal epistemic communities and that academic economists dominated here. Second, the fragmentation of carbon markets suggests that professional networks may play a very different role in the transnational and local spheres. A key area of future research is the examination of the participation of professions within the individual venues themselves to see whether and how different distributions of professional engagement in different ET venues explains the diversity we see in the design and functionality of ET venues.

Third, and perhaps most importantly, our analysis suggests that beyond the contribution of pre-existing professions, the politics of ET the field of carbon market politics are currently being influenced by a process of professionalization. The first stage of ET diffusion was influenced by a transnational policy network that helped the development of ET systems in various venues and was made up of multiple professions. More recently, a range of organized activities have emerged that are regularizing the operation of carbon markets and the next wave of their spread. Interest groups promoting carbon markets, new services dedicated to reporting on ET, specialized training of policy professionals in developing carbon markets, the development of MBA programs specifically in "carbon finance," "strategic carbon management" and "carbon accounting," recurrent conferences, and emerging standard best practices are important elements in the emergence of a distinct "carbon market" profession. There is some evidence that this nascent issue profession is seeking to control the issue of ET by standardizing the practices associated with ET. This standardization is already beginning to have an effect on the shape of carbon markets now developing and thus has the potential to significantly alter the trajectory of the global response to climate change. Understanding the contours and impact of this new carbon market profession is thus a crucial area of continuing research.

13 Quasi-Professionals in the Organization of Transnational Crisis Mapping

John Karlsrud and Arthur Mühlen-Schulte

The recent explosion of increasingly sophisticated mobile information communications technologies (ICTs) has led to the creation of new and complex networks and relationships. The fastest growth and adoption of mobile technologies is now in the developing world and often among populations facing development and humanitarian challenges. The entrepreneurial utilization of technological advances in these populations, combined with dispersed online networks in the developed world, is shaping global governance and the response of international organizations and governments in various ways. In this chapter we explore the particular phenomenon of crisis mapping that has arisen in the past five years out of the confluence of various technological advances and its combination with populations facing crisis. Specifically, we seek to analyze how quasi-professional crisis mappers or "mapsters" are shaping humanitarian action as an evolving professional field.

Humanitarian action has been going through a process of professionalization over the last two decades, responding to outside pressures to become more accountable vis-à-vis donors and beneficiaries, and inside pressures to establish criteria and guidance for what can be considered "good" humanitarianism (see also Chapter 5). Barnett argues that, as humanitarians no longer could rely "exclusively on moral authority, humanitarianism now had to demonstrate its competence. Accordingly, it began developing specialized knowledge, advanced training, bureaucracies with standard operating procedures, and rule books with guidelines" (Barnett 2011, p. 234). In a similar fashion crisis mapping has developed ad hoc in the last five years out of a combination of technologies brought together by the internet and social media platforms harnessing increasingly sophisticated open-source satellite imagery. The strategy of "crowdsourcing" information from affected populations through emails, text, and Twitter messages is now becoming rapidly integrated into the humanitarian sphere and driving the importance of ICTs in the creation of crisis information management (CiM) strategies for the UN system (Bott and Young 2012; Kahl et al. 2012).[1]

This chapter will look at the particular relationship of a specialized group of "mapsters" – the Standby Action Taskforce (SBTF) – and the UN Office for the Coordination of Humanitarian Affairs (OCHA).[2] Using the general theoretical framework of a two-level network analysis, we explore whether the mapsters in the SBTF can be analyzed as a group of loosely organized individuals threatening the jurisdictional claim of OCHA, whose existence and legitimacy in the humanitarian field is reliant on the effective organization and dissemination of verified information. In particular, mapsters threaten to circumvent and obviate the key function of OCHA as a hub for organizing and disseminating information, by providing direct and specialized data to humanitarian organizations at significantly higher speeds than OCHA has previously been able to do. Types of information include detailed maps and data concerning the where, when, what, and who of actors involved on the ground. We then look at the various strategies that OCHA has embarked on to adapt and mitigate the impact of crisis mapping by drawing upon the strengths of mapsters, using a strategy of cooperation, co-optation, and confrontation. In the chapter we follow the lead of Seabrooke and Henriksen (see Chapter 1) and analyze OCHA and humanitarians as issue professionals, where mapsters are volunteers from a wide variety of backgrounds and are seen as quasi-professionals.

We have conducted a review of relevant literature and a number of interviews with mapsters, the UN and member state officials. Both authors have also worked with the UN in conflict and crisis contexts, permitting participant observation of humanitarian processes and developments in adoption of new technologies.

The chapter will proceed by first analyzing the recent evolution and impact of ICTs in developing countries and populations facing crises. It is important here to try and differentiate the impact, as well as the particular type of technologies being adopted and used, from the broad sweep of grand statistics and hype often used to portray a technological revolution underway. The reform of the UN system in adapting and reflecting these changes in its ICT and CiM strategies is also important to understand as crisis mapping in the UN system is not in and of itself a new phenomenon.

---

[1] Crowdsourcing was coined by Jeff Howe as "the act of taking a job traditionally performed by a designated agent (usually an employee) and outsourcing it to an undefined, generally large group of people in the form of an open call" (Howe 2008, p. 99).

[2] Over time, the SBTF evolved into the Digital Humanitarian Network (DHN).

This can be seen in entities such as UNOSAT,[3] yet the engagement of loosely based networks such as SBTF, in collaboration with forward thinking entities in the UN system like OCHA, does represent a new dynamic outside traditional bureaucratic structures.

Secondly, it is necessary to look at the context of crisis mapping and the formation of the SBTF as fourth-generation mechanisms for both early warning and response (Letouzé et al. 2013). Here it will be seen that the issues resulting from data collection, in particular verification and visualization, have led to the development of crisis mapping through a combination of deployments in both political crises and natural disasters. Yet with the expansion and use of volunteer-based crisis mapping, UN organizations have been forced to quickly retreat from its deployment and use in conflicts due to issues of privacy and individual protection stemming from open-crowdsourcing under harsh political regimes. Here we see the engagement with OCHA as part of the formalization and professionalization process in humanitarian action structuring the engagement of quasi-professional mapsters and we identify an increasing pressure to establish codes of conducts, guidelines, and other forms of rules organizing the behavior and engagement of mapsters.

Third, we will look at how the coordination of humanitarian action is being transformed by quasi-professional mapsters. We argue that while the natural tendency of international organizations such as OCHA is to gradually adopt and include capacities considered to be central for their mandate, the nature of crisis mapping makes this near impossible, as it requires large amounts of human data processing. OCHA is forced to choose a cooperation strategy with SBTF and the crisis mapping community. Yet the reverse is also true for SBTF, which also relies on OCHA to symbolically and actually validate and legitimize the information they produce, as well as disseminate it to humanitarian actors within and outside the UN system.

Finally, we conclude that the relationship between OCHA and SBTF can be considered as a two-level network relationship of mutual dependency where issue control must be shared. Both levels consist of groups who make dedicated efforts to professionalize their fields to achieve issue control. On the individual level, a relatively small number of crisis mappers are moving through revolving doors and act as consultants for various international organizations, member states, and NGOs (for more

[3] UNOSAT is the United Nations Institute for Training and Research (UNITAR) Operational Satellite Applications Programme.

on revolving doors, see, e.g., Karlsrud 2016; Stone 2013a; Seabrooke and Tsingou 2009). Looking at the relationship between OCHA and SBTF, it is clear that mapsters clearly operate beyond epistemic arbitrage and are able to significantly impact the agenda setting of OCHA issue control, showing a bottom-up source of influence by issue professionals.

The Revolution or Evolution of ICT?

In the past five years there has been a seismic shift in information communication technologies (ICT) from traditional hardware to the predominance of mobile phones, social media, cloud computing, and the advent of "big data" caches. Importantly, it is not only developed countries which now feed this deluge of data, mobile phone ownership in developing countries also now accounts for 56 percent of the world's 5.4 billion subscriptions (UNDP 2012: 13) and is growing with "smartphone" technology and adapting to ICT4D strategies (Kleine and Unwin 2009). The UN International Telecommunications Union (ITU) has declared that 38.8 percent of the world's population now has access to the internet, up from one-third in 2012 (ITU 2012, 2013) and is rising rapidly as smartphones are becoming increasingly cheaper and more advanced as networks expand. Affected populations are now able to engage directly with online platforms, signaling a profound change for the internal structure, management, and coordination of international organizations (IOs) by humanitarian professionals. This is clearly seen in the accessibility to geospatial mapping that began with Google Earth. Small groups of volunteers now possess the ability to gather information in real time through mobile phone texts, online media reports, and social media updates and then collate the information with satellite imagery of crisis areas. Until recently this was the domain of government intelligence agencies.

With the potential of using big data in this way, new questions also emerge. How can we ensure that important data from crises is shared while also ensuring the privacy of individuals? How is data that is generated from social media such as Twitter and Facebook being used, and how and by whom is the data verified? What particular vulnerabilities are volunteer organizations and the UN exposed to? On a more structural level, what impact does social media have on traditional actors in the field, such as NGOs, INGOs, including Red Cross, member states, and international organizations like the EU, NATO, and the UN? Despite, or perhaps because of, the amount of unstructured data that can be analyzed, new ways of informing multilateral efforts for conflict prevention and international security have rapidly increased.

The utilization of new technologies for crisis mapping results in part from what is often asserted as the "democratization" of the internet. While the nature of this democratization is debatable, it can be seen in the context of early warning and response mechanisms that there has been a definite devolution of control between the location and objectives with successive waves of new and increasingly open technology.

The first and most important crisis mapping platform to date is Ushahidi ("witness" in Swahili) that was created during the 2008 post-election violence in Kenya. Ushahidi developed from a platform using basic text messages to log and map eyewitness accounts of human rights abuses into a live multimedia collaborative platform using smartphone technology and social media through Twitter and Facebook. Using such crowdsourcing techniques, it has also created some 20,000 maps across 130 countries (Meier 2015). In 2010, crisis mapping attracted the attention of the UN and governments when, after the Haitian earthquake, volunteers mapped responses to 10,000 text messages with an average ten-minute delay per message during the initial days of the crisis (Meier 2015). Furthermore, the translation of each message from Creole into English was achieved by mobilizing more than 1,200 members of the Haitian diaspora through online social media in the same short space of time.

The volume of information was described as "trying to drink from a fire hose" (HHI 2011: p. 17). Despite various emergency responders significantly improving their management tools and processes over the previous decade, the volume of information gathered through mobile phones, as well as the processed information from mapsters and other voluntary and technological communities (V&TCs), dramatically increased the flow of information from the affected population. In record time, mapsters "turned a blank spot on the map into one of the most accurately mapped countries in the world" (HHI 2011: p. 30). This challenged traditional bureaucratic structures such as the UN and mandated professionals working in a hierarchy.

VTCs used flattened, decentralized structures with decision-making and conflict resolution mechanisms that were adapted from online communities like Wikipedia and opensource software development projects. As a result, the VTCs moved far faster than larger players in nearly all circumstances – *and perhaps faster than established protocols* (emphasis added) will allow. It is here – in the politics and tempo of this new volunteer capability – that the bottom-up, grassroots structures need protocols to work with the top-down systems within large organizations.[4]

---

[4] www.gfdrr.org/volunteer-technology-communities-open-development.

What was happening was a paradigm shift, according to the World Bank – "decentralized VTCs were faster and more adaptable than centralized bureaucracies," and used days rather than months to build a new map (World Bank 2011: p. 15). However, there were also serious concerns about the veracity of the information provided and the inability to ensure this independently at the speed required. This was thus the start of an ambivalent relationship – on the one hand, there were obvious advantages emerging from cooperation with mapsters, but OCHA also felt there was a need to make sure that mapsters were aware of, and subscribed to, the core principles of humanitarian action, such as impartiality, neutrality, and operational independence, making sure that support given did not inadvertently harm those in need.

Crisis Mapping and the SBTF – 4th Generation Humanitarian Technology

Following the Haiti earthquake it was recognized that the UN faced an information overload with the advent of new information technologies and volunteering communities such as the crisis mapping community (HHI 2011). While the UN and other major disaster relief organizations wanted to make use of the information available and ensure its veracity, it did not have the necessary expertise or processes to do so. Yet with crowdsourcing a number of challenges also emerge, in particular the verification of information and bias among those providing it. These are acknowledged within the crisis mapping community that is working to enhance tools to improve verification (Letouzé et al. 2013). The importance of these new technologies and data innovation can nonetheless be seen in the pressure they create for the UN to adapt and learn.

The UN has engaged with the crisis mappers community since 2010,[5] and the Standby Task Force also supported OCHA by crowdsourcing crisis preparedness data for South Sudan, collecting "a total of 1,767 unique rows of data and 15,271 unique pieces of information" in three days.[6] The UN therefore recognizes the need for improved efforts in crisis information management that could support the endeavors of " 'One

[5] UN, "Crisis Information Management Strategy." Available at: http://ict4peace.org/wp-content/uploads/2012/07/High-level-meeting-on-CIM-Strategy-July-2012-FINAL-1 .pdf: p. 4.
[6] Standby Task Force, "OCHA South Sudan Deployment: Curating Data for Disaster Preparedness." Available at: http://www.standbytaskforce.org/2012/07/16/ocha-south-sudan-deployment-curating-data-for-preparedness/

UN' and better coordination within the UN and the international community in general."[7]

One of the volunteering communities that contributed with information to disaster relief organizations was the SBTF, a specialized offshoot of the crisis mapping community with limited membership based on CVs and verification. As stated by the SBTF, it "is not an organization, it is a platform, a shared space for those who have skills to offer ... to assist crisis affected communities through the use of crowdsourcing and mapping technologies."[8] As such the SBTF often deployed with other organizations, and although it isn't directly funded by them, it did take in-kind donations. Five key partners listed by SBTF included the Digital Humanitarian Network (DHN), "which provides an interface between formal professional humanitarian organizations and informal yet skilled-and-agile volunteer & technical networks like the SBTF ... DHN can also activate the SBTF on a deployment, either alone or with other DHN partners"; GISCorps, a GIS, remote sensing, spatial and nonspatial data cleansing function that also develops web-based mapping applications (desktop and mobile); Humanitarian Open Street Map (HOT OSM) that coordinates the creation, production, and distribution of free mapping resources to support humanitarian relief efforts in many places around the world; ESRI, which provides software, data coordination, technical support, and other GIS assistance to organizations; and UN Volunteers (UNV) who are advocates for volunteerism globally, encouraging partners to integrate volunteerism into development programming as well as mobilizing volunteers through the UN system.

At the time of writing, SBTF had a membership of some 1,110 mapsters, predominantly based in North America and Europe, assigned to five key teams dealing with verification, geo-location, data mapping and analysis, research and support tasks, and finally monitoring and evaluation. Members were assigned to teams according to their education, professional background, or expertise, and each team can accordingly take further training modules or "webinars" in order to be assigned greater responsibility during deployments. These trainings were increasingly becoming mandatory and were simultaneously facilitated and taken also by UN staff.[9]

---

[7] Swiss Mission to the United Nations, "Report on High-Level Dialogue with UN Member States on the status of the UN Crisis Information Management Strategy (CiMS) using inter alia social media tools, crisis mapping and crowdsourcing." New York: Swiss Mission to the United Nations, July 10, 2012. Available at: http://ict4peace.org/wp-content/uploads/2012/07/Report-on-Swiss-Mission-HL-Luncheon-on-the-status-of-the-UN-CiMS.pdf.

[8] SBTF, "About." Available at: http://www.standbytaskforce.org/

[9] http://techchange.org/online-courses/technology-for-conflict-management-and-peacebuilding/

In order to further analyze the conceptual aspects of crisis mapping between professional and quasi-professional coordination, four core areas of concern were identified by the community of crisis mappers which need attention. Firstly, *data acquisition* – how do UN agencies govern data acquisition from quasi-professional volunteers? Secondly, *visualization* – how is the visualization of emergency responses mediated by UN agents and quasi-professional volunteers? Thirdly, *analysis* – how are verification and due diligence procedures mediated by UN agents and quasi-professional volunteers within the analytic process behind emergency response? Fourthly, *response* – how are governing roles and authority delegated from the UN agents to quasi-professional volunteers once analysis leads to action? (Ziemke 2012). The relatively recent professionalization of humanitarian action and the expanding structure of UN humanitarian coordination are instructive in this regard.

The Professionalization of Humanitarian Action

The convergence between mapsters and humanitarians began as a bottom-up process, first on the ground in Haiti and then through more institutional arrangements in Libya where OCHA mediated a mapping exercise with a combination of around 300 SBTF and UN Online Volunteers.[10] In the UN system, OCHA is a comparatively small organization with only around 1,900 staff globally in 2013.[11] It became OCHA in 1998 with the merger of the Office of the United Nations Disaster Relief Coordinator, created in 1972, and the Department of Humanitarian Affairs, created in 1991. The organization gained respect during the 1990s and 2000s for being able to act as a neutral ground between humanitarian actors, both from the UN and outside, including political and military actors. The creation of the Central Emergency Response Fund (CERF) in 2005 was also important as it gave the relatively small agency an important role in soliciting needs through national and global so-called consolidated appeals processes (CAPs), matching these with funding from donors. OCHA also managed to emerge as an actor and central node in the humanitarian world – voicing the concerns of humanitarians and facilitating the training of troops participating in peacekeeping operations on the need for "humanitarian space."

As humanitarian organizations value their independence highly, OCHA also has to carefully manage its role and reputation to maintain its position

---

[10] See http://www.volunteeractioncounts.org/iyv/content/unv-world-volunteer-web/con tent/feature-stories/Libya-crisis-map.html.

[11] UNOCHA, "Who We Are." Available at: www.unocha.org/about-us/who-we-are.

as the central node in the UN system for coordinating and sharing information. Humanitarian action has during the last 20 years gone through a rapid process of professionalization, and there are now a number of guidelines and codes of conduct established for practitioners,[12] as well as training and dedicated academic programs at the masters and PhD level focusing on humanitarian principles and action,[13] including an international biannual World Conference on Humanitarian Studies.[14]

This professionalization drive is led by a combination of internal and external pressures. Externally, donors have been pressing for greater accountability and more efficient and effective use of funds. Internally, the professionalization process has been driven by a need to define and control what can be considered humanitarian issues. Furthermore, funding for humanitarian purposes has been comparatively easier to access than peacebuilding and development, for example, and there has thus been a drive to define the tasks and criteria for humanitarian action to achieve issue and funding control.

A similar trend is discernible in the more rapidly developing crisis mapping community (Meier 2015). By March 2016, the crisis mapping humanitarian technology network had 8,264 members and some 2,000 organizational and institutional affiliations across government, universities, and the private sector (Crisis Mappers 2016, 2012). The community has also set up an annual conference starting in 2009 and established course syllabi for academic institutions over the last few years.[15]

Two-level Network

OCHA and other relief organizations, whether multilateral, bilateral, or NGOs, have embarked on a steep learning curve to better understand how they can make use of the large amounts of information that modern communication technologies and mapping offer. In this process, some of the key actors in the volunteering community have played a pivotal role and become "multiple insiders" (see Chapter 1). They are being hired as consultants to help draft background documents, concept notes, and strategies, and sit on advisory boards (OECD 2012; Letouzé et al. 2013; Mancini 2013).[16] Multiple insiders can gain status by being able

---

[12] For example, see: https://corehumanitarianstandard.org/
[13] NOHA, "What is Noha?" Available at: http://www.nohanet.org/
[14] WCHS, "Proposed Panels/Papers." Available at: http://www.humanitarianstudiesconference.org/
[15] See www.crisismappers.net.
[16] In all of these publications one or more of the key individuals are hired as lead authors, have been brought in as members of advisory boards, or both.

to play the role as knowledge carriers and brokers between organizations and the quasi-professional crisis mapping community. These individuals are playing an important role in the formative stage of the relationship between the crisis mapping community and OCHA as well as other multilateral organizations. However, as more competency is gained within the organizations, and more professionals are emerging outside the organization that can offer the expertise needed, the relationship is gradually being transformed into a more institutional one.

From this view professionals are not loyal to their employers and organizations but respond to emergent professional ethics issues in their field. The crisis mapping community adheres to this analysis but with even greater heterogeneity. The membership of the crisis mapping network and the SBTF is an association of "quasi-professional" humanitarians; an eclectic cohort in terms of professional training, education and expertise, from academia, government, computer science, and geographic information systems (GIS). This is increasingly also reflected in the institutional structures of the UN and can be seen in examples such as the Information Management Working Group (IMWG) that advises the UN Country Team in Sudan and draws a membership of staff from the various UN Agencies, Funds and Programs (AFPs). Despite the members of the working group having specific institutional affiliations and coming in with varied roles in coordination, logistics, GIS, and communications skills, they specifically combine their expertise to conduct various forms of mapping and data analysis. Co-chaired by OCHA and the Resident Coordinator's Office (RCO) the IMWG not only acts to harmonize mapping and information functions within the UN Country Team but also seeks collaboration with private sector initiatives and provides capacity building and emergency mapping capabilities to the government on request.

As Seabrooke and Henriksen have outlined in the first chapter to this volume "issue professionals" are professionals who "combine knowledge and skills to enhance their attempts at control on a specific issue in transnational governance" (see Editors' Introduction). Issue professionals are less formalized and more loosely organized than traditional professional groups. We have chosen to use the term "quasi-professionals" here as mapsters are even more loosely organized than issue professionals, at what can perhaps best be seen as an embryonic stage of professionalization.

The crisis mapping community consists of a wide range of heterogenic members of volunteering communities. Humanitarian professionals, technological experts, and others who want to make a difference from their home computer a long distance away from crises areas, contributing with everything from an hour or two to full-time engagement for shorter or longer durations.

Yet the relationship between international humanitarian organizations such as OCHA and the V&TCs that SBTF is part of is a complicated one. On the one hand, loosely organized mapsters, through organizations such as SBTF, have been able to help significantly speed up the collection and dissemination of information, populating maps with important information. On the other hand, OCHA and other relief organizations, whether being multilateral, bilateral, or NGOs, have embarked on a steep learning curve in order to better understanding how they can make use of the large amounts of information that modern communication technologies and mapping offer.

This process has had some interesting effects. OCHA and mapsters alike understand that there are significant risks involved in the collection and dissemination of information. One of the cornerstones of humanitarian action has been the principle of "do no harm." Collecting and disseminating information, individuals or communities can be exposed and victims of retaliation, particularly in violent conflict settings as in Libya and Syria, but also when humanitarian crises and disasters are unfolding in urban settings or in politically unstable environments.

Hostile cyber groups can quite easily eavesdrop on or take control over computers used by OCHA and mapsters alike. During the Libya crisis, the crisis map was developed in cooperation between OCHA and the crisis mapping community, with an open and a limited access site. The limited site was updated in real time, while the open site was on purpose delayed 24 hours to avoid sensitive information falling into the wrong hands. Stottlemyre and Stottlemyre (2012) argue that the Libya crisis map constituted tactical military intelligence and was actively being used by NATO for targeting purposes. The site would also be vulnerable to hostile cyber groups that have capabilities that far outpace the protection capabilities of V&TCs (Scott-Railton 2013). Similarly, the Conflict Risk Mapping and Analysis (CRMA) unit of UNDP in Sudan had to intensively negotiate sensitive issues around data collection that aroused the suspicions of certain sections of government. Although ultimately gaining approval, it was subsequently deemed too high risk to continue with the project. There is thus a push to develop codes of conduct and guidelines to ensure that mapsters operate according to humanitarian standards and principles (OCHA 2013; IFRC 2013; Capelo et al. 2013) and informing V&TCs about how formal humanitarian organizations work and how they can cooperate (Waldman et al. 2013; Milner and Verity 2013). The Digital Humanitarian Network (DHN) planned to hire its first cyber security expert in 2013 (Interview with OCHA official, Istanbul, October 25, 2013), and OCHA has hired experts from the volunteer sector to strengthen their own capacity to interact with mapsters and the V&TCs, but also enable the organization to a larger extent execute the coordination of V&TCs. In 2014, OCHA released a report on *Humanitarianism in the Age of Cyber-Warfare*, pointing to the dangers of the collection and storage of large amounts of data by humanitarians and quasi-professional humanitarians, preparing for further discussions around the development of Codes of Conducts for organizations and individuals who are engaged in this field (OCHA 2013). Some of the security standards that are being developed by OCHA will effectively limit the number of participants that can comply with the Code of Conducts by raising the bar of the competence needed to qualify and enter the conversation (Interview with OCHA official, Istanbul, October 25, 2013).

Crisis mappers and SBTF have now made a formal decision not to be involved in countries where conflicts are ongoing, due to the risks involved:

The speed [at which] cyber groups [and] governments are developing offensive capabilities is frightening. People are dying because of that. The humanitarian community is several steps behind. Ironically, the digital humanitarian communities are perhaps more aware of this, but they are largely based on volunteers. Their code of conduct does not deal with the hard-end tech side of this. (Interview with OCHA official, New York, October 11, 2013).

The efforts of mapsters to ensure humanitarian principles will effectively heighten the bar for volunteers who want to engage in crisis mapping. The increased focus on data security will likewise effectively shut out some of the V&TCs from engaging in humanitarian action, as they will not be able to upgrade their equipment and software to ensure complete data protection in zones where this will be considered essential, such as in Syria (ibid.).

As pointed to earlier, the interaction between the UN and other large disaster relief actors and volunteering organizations such as the SBTF springs out of a mutual need. The SBTF can organize large amounts of information virtually in real time and make this available to organizations such as OCHA. OCHA can then share the organized information with other actors. To manage control of an issue, organizations tend to try to acquire the needed capacity during paradigmatic shifts, but in this case this is unfeasible, as SBTF relies on high numbers of volunteers to carry out its tasks. OCHA quite simply cannot acquire such a capacity and do the entire information processing in-house. On the other hand, SBTF benefits from the legitimacy that OCHA can bring – the information is validated and approved before being shared with the rest of the humanitarian community.

Conclusions

The Haiti earthquake gave impetus to a new set of actors in humanitarian action – crisis mappers, volunteering their services from far-away locations. Post-Haiti, crisis mappers have become an important constituency in national and international responses to crises. By forming volunteering and technological communities, crisis mappers have embarked on a steep learning curve, understanding that they operate in complex political economies where a number of considerations need to be kept in mind. Foremost they need to ensure that their support does not adversely affect those they intend to help – following the core principle of "do no harm" in humanitarian action. To do this, they also need to carefully consider when they can respond (Sandvik et al. 2014). With Libya, crisis mappers better understood that there were many groups operating in a complex crisis. This included groups with ill intentions and the capability of intercepting and misusing the dissemination of data and information as well as seeking to harm those that provided information to the outside world. Hostile cyber groups have the capability to, and have done so on many occasions, intercepted and taken control of information flows from humanitarian and human rights actors. They have used information to identify individuals and target them, or target specific neighborhoods from which a high concentration of reports of violations emanates.

The emerging humanitarian information infrastructure includes international organizations such as OCHA, NGOs, bilateral organizations, and volunteers such as the crisis mappers from SBTF. These actors are managing and sharing an ever-increasing volume of information in crisis and conflict areas. Understanding the need to better protect those that provide this information, they are now establishing codes of conduct and guidelines. This can be seen as a larger process of professionalization, and it is here we consider traditional humanitarian actors as issue professionals, along the lines of the introduction in this book. Although primarily driven by an urge to support and improve humanitarian action, mapsters and other members of the V&TCs are to some extent challenging the control of traditional humanitarian actors and their ability to manage information on disasters and emergency response. As these mapsters and other V&TCs are often performing these tasks in their free time, we have then developed the concept of quasi-professionals to describe their entry into the humanitarian field.

These quasi-professional mapsters interact in a two-level network with traditional humanitarian professionals. In this way communities of crisis mappers coalesce and fit a trajectory of issue control referred to as "yoking" (see Chapter 18), whereby the SBTF has mobilized mapsters, and challenged the professional boundaries of humanitarian agencies in the UN system, by yoking themselves to multiple UN agencies and other international organizations, thereby influencing the UN's emergency response to crises. While humanitarian organizations realize the net benefit of the skills and tools that mapsters bring, they also employ strategies to maintain their control of humanitarian tasks and ensure that humanitarian values and principles are respected.

We have detailed how OCHA and established humanitarian actors have embarked on a combined strategy of cooperation, co-optation, and confrontation. Experts from the crisis mapping community have acted similarly as multiple insiders and strengthened the knowledge in OCHA and elsewhere. These experts have also been hired as permanent staff at headquarters and field level, and develop policy papers on the interaction with mapsters and V&TCs. Yet the opportunities that the merging of modern technology and humanitarian action brings have also created unintended consequences for crisis-affected populations, resulting in a strong push to develop new guidance frameworks and codes of conduct. This can be seen as an effort both to strengthen knowledge of the key principles of humanitarian action, but also as a way of barring entrance to the field by those who pose a threat, those who have a high level of expertise but insufficient knowledge of the principles of humanitarian action (see also Chapter 5).

Part IV

Professionals and Market Organizations

14 Global Professional Service Firms and Institutionalization

James Faulconbridge and Daniel Muzio

The global professional service firm (GPSF) is now a significant agent in national and transnational political economies. Yet, in existing literatures on transnational governance the role of these firms is somewhat hidden by a tendency to place the professions at centre stage. Thus, whilst the literature recognizes how 'the professions in modern society have assumed leading roles in the creation and tending of institution' (Scott, 2008: 219), there has been less systematic attention to the role of GPSFs as institutional agents. In part this can be explained by the fact that the sociology of the professions traditionally does not recognize the analytically distinct nature or role of professional organizations within professionalization and broader institutionalization projects (Faulconbridge and Muzio, 2012). Yet, such a state of affairs no longer seems tenable. GPSFs have their own agendas, capabilities and patterns of activities that are both related to but also distinct from those of the wider professional communities to which they belong (see Faulconbridge and Muzio 2016). From prominent and politically charged cases such as the General Agreement on Trade in Services (GATS) (Arnold, 2005) and carbon trading markets (Knox-Hayes, 2009), to less-well reported and softer systems such as regimes around sustainable building design (Bulkeley and Jordan, 2012; Faulconbridge, 2013) and competition (antitrust) agreements (Morgan, 2006), GPSFs have been central actors in 'issue control' processes (Seabrooke and Henriksen, Chapter 1). Such compacts are of course important for those actors directly engaged in the issues in question. Perhaps more importantly, though, they also matter because, as Suddaby and Viale (2011) argue, through their actions GPSFs have wider spin-off effects on adjacent fields, whether that is the development of employment law as a result of trade agreements or property financing as a result of sustainable design regimes.

In this chapter we, thus, seek to highlight the importance of advancing the work that does exist on GPSFs in the institutionalization of transnational governance regimes through a more careful consideration of the identities, projects and effects of the firms in question. We contend that in their attempts to develop new markets, services and more efficient internal organizational models, GPSFs exercise far-reaching institutional effects as they challenge governance regimes, disrupt/create jurisdictions, and transform identities, practices and systems of regulation in the professions themselves. They do this, we suggest, through three strategies associated with scope of control, defining scales of knowledge resources and the production of ecologies of linked interests. These strategies involve developing strategic alliances with a range of other field actors such as academia, regulatory bodies, international organizations, national governments and professional associations as part of linked ecologies (Abbott, 2005). As such, GPSFs exemplify the process of professional strategy > organizational opportunities > issue control that Seabrooke and Henriksen (this volume) claim is central to the transnational realm. This chapter provides, then, a contribution to ongoing attempts to 'revisit theories of professionalism, which did not fully anticipate the shift of professional work to the context of large organizations' (Suddaby et al., 2007: 25). It also complements the following chapter by Boussebaa, outlining the institutionalizing effects of neo-colonial networks.

The GPSF in Context

It is important to begin by clarifying what exactly is meant by GPSF. Such clarification is important because we use the term GPSF to refer to two related but subtly different groups of organizations (on this differentiation and the debate it inspires, see von Nordenflycht, 2010). On the one hand, we have the 'old' professional service firms, old being used to indicate organizations employing professionals from long-ago established and state-recognized professions. Key examples are accountancy, architecture and law (for analysis of each, see respectively Cooper and Robson, 2006; Faulconbridge, 2010; Muzio and Faulconbridge, 2013). Whilst firms have existed in these professions for decades or centuries, they have acquired an increasingly global scale in the latter years of the twentieth century. In all cases these 'old' GPSFs exploit the monopolies over markets afforded to them by professional closure regimes which restrict the production and deliver of services to registered individuals and firms structured in line with clearly defined (usually by national professional associations) regulations (Faulconbridge and Muzio 2007).

On the other hand, we have the 'new' professional service firms. 'New' is used to indicate the rise of a series of occupations that have sought to mimic and claim the same status as the 'old' professions whilst developing new organizational forms and practices. Examples include executive search, management consultancy and project management (see respectively Faulconbridge et al., 2008; McKenna, 2006; Hodgson 2007; Paton et al., 2013). Distinctive about these firms is the absence of a clearly defined status for the 'professionals' employed (they are not part of a state-regulated profession), yet a tendency to present services as professional. Such attempts stress knowledge richness, ethical practice and fiduciary role mimicking the logics underlying the 'old' professions (Muzio et al., 2011).

Whilst there are important differences between the 'old' and 'new' professional service firms (as summarized by von Nordenflycht, 2010), we badge both as GPSFs as the two do share one important commonality: the last years of the twentieth and early years of the twenty-first century have seen these firms exert significant forms of agency designed to ensure control and influence over key issues such as corporate globalization, trade regulation, carbon markets, etc. This agency, which we examine in more detail in the next section of the chapter, emerges from important changes in the strategies of GPSFs over time.

Organizational Strategies and the Institutional Agency of GPSFs

Table 14.1 gives examples of both 'old' and 'new' GPSFs and their key organizational characteristics. GPSFs have not always been so large and

Table 14.1 *Magnitude of Key Professional Service Firms*

Accountancy

Company	Countries	Professionals	Revenues
PWC	150+	180k+	$31bn
Deloitte	150+	193k+	$31bn
Ernst & Young	140+	167k+	$24bn
KPMG	150+	152k+	$23bn

Executive search

Company	Countries	Professionals	Revenues
Korn Ferry	60+	2,500+	$532
Spencer Stuart	40+	? (300+ consultants)	$475m
Heidricks	50+	? (385 consultants)	$375m
Ray Bendston	40+	? (194 consultants)	$231m

Law

Company	Countries	Professionals	Revenues
Baker & McKenzie	45	4,000+	$2.3bn
DLA	30	3,700+	$2.1bn
Clifford Chance	25	2,500+	$2.0bn
Linklaters	19	2,100+	$1.8bn

Management consultancy

Company	Countries	Professionals	Revenues
A T Kearney	30+	2,000+	? ~$1bn
McKinsey	50+	9,000+	? ~$7bn
BCG	40+	6,000+	$3.7bn
Booz	300+	3,000+	$1.3bn

influential. In their earliest guise, which for some such as accountancy firms dates back to the late nineteenth century, GPSFs simply followed their clients. Overseas offices were established in locations where home-country clients had or were considering setting up operations (Beaverstock et al., 1999; Cooper and Robson, 2006; Bagchi-Sen and Sen, 1997; Faulconbridge et al., 2008). Globalization was, then, very much about providing a service to existing clients, and thus sometimes involved establishing offices but, in cases where client needs were sporadic, could also mean establishing best friend alliances with local companies.

Over time, the strategies of GPSFs have evolved. Initial forays overseas gave organizations a taste for new markets and highlighted the potential to acquire new clients. Hence, GPSFs became market seekers, particularly in the 1980s and 1990s as neoliberal reforms led to more and more clients globalizing their operations. This created an ever greater role for fully owned overseas offices (on this development trajectory see Bagchi-Sen and Sen, 1997; Faulconbridge et al., 2008). In terms of our discussion here, the initial two stages (client follower and market seeker) are, however, of less significance than a third stage, which we call market making. In this stage, which is associated with the last years of the twentieth and first decade of the twenty-first century, GPSFs became active agents in the institutionalization of new transnational regimes. This involves both the importing of already existing products and markets into new geographical contexts as part of efforts to reduce the complexities of transnational practice – exemplified by the cases of bankruptcy law (Halliday and Carruthers, 2009) and sustainable building assessment tools (Faulconbridge and Yalciner, 2015) – and the creation of supra-national compacts designed to govern activities outside of the nation state – as exemplified by GATS (Arnold, 2005) and competition agreements (Morgan, 2006). In the market making stage, GPSFs rely upon their owned offices to act as staging posts for forms of institutional work designed to shape rules, norms and logics in ways that locate GPSFs at the centre of new economic, political and social regimes (see Beaverstock et al., 2010; Smets et al., 2012; Suddaby et al., 2007). It is to the nature of this institutional work and its impacts, as an exemplar of what Seabrooke and Henriksen (this volume) call the 'professional-organizational nexus', that we now turn.

GPSFs and Their Institutional Work Strategies

This section examines key trends in relation to how GPSFs exercise institutional agency. This is in line with the recent focus in the sociology of the professions (Scott, 2008; Viale and Suddaby, 2011; Muzio et al.,

2013) on the agency of the professionals as 'the preeminent institutional agents of our time' (Scott, 2008: 219), who as 'lords of the dance' choreograph the broader transformation of societal and economic systems.

In this analysis, we adopt the concept of institutional work, introduced by Lawrence et al. (2009), to capture the diverse forms of GPSF action that have led to new transnational settlements relating to issues as diverse as climate change, international trade and the governance of the global economy. By institutions we mean the widely recognized rules, norms and cultural-cognitive schemes that govern everyday practice relating to particular issues (on this, see Scott, 2008); thus, institutions are the key structuring device of economies and societies. These institutional regimes are increasingly transnational in scale, in contrast to earlier periods in which national scale regimes dominated (Djelic and Quack, 2010). The concept of institutional work understands the process of institutionalization by which (transnational) rules, norms and cultures come to gain widespread recognition and influence to involve three forms of agency: creation, maintenance and/or disruption. We suggest disruption and creation are especially relevant to our story of the role of GPSFS in the development of transnational governance regimes, with agency being exercised to disrupt or create institutions depending on what is needed to protect the interests of the GPSFs in question.

In terms of the actual forms that agency takes, the institutional work literature draws our attention to the importance of a diverse array of strategies, from the overt such as lobbying (Greenwood et al., 2002) and the deployment of discourses to legitimize and inspire change (Phillips and Nelson, 2004), to the more covert, banal and often missed, such as the use of human resource practices, like recruitment and training, to produce suitable individuals which internalize appropriate values and norms (Faulconbridge et al., 2012; Pache and Santos, 2010), and the quiet role modelling of new institutional regimes which then organically diffuse and gain widespread influence (Smets et al., 2012). We suggest that all of these forms of agency are relevant to GPSFs and their attempts to develop transnational governance regimes.

As an illustrative case study, drawing on a series of published studies (Arnold, 2005; Robson et al., 2007; Suddaby et al., 2007), we use the example of Big Four accountancy firms. These have been selected because they are not only the most sophisticated GPSFs but are, as indicated by Table 14.1, amongst the largest and most global GPSFs. Furthermore, and crucially for our arguments here, they have been particularly significant within processes of institutionalization, interacting with nation states and supra-national entities like the EU,

WTO and IMF to reframe key institutions in ways that support their own professional projects. Crucially, these attempts at institutional work have had broader repercussions, as they reverberate through the transnational field affecting existing institutions such as local regulation and qualification systems, national markets and occupational jurisdictions, and established societal and corporate practices. In particular, we focus below on three interrelated examples: the role of the Big Four accountancy GPSFs in reframing established auditing practices and markets (Robson et al., 2007); their attempts to change accountancy qualification regimes to create a new transnational designation for business professionals (Suddaby et al., 2007); and their use of WTO procedures to challenge national regulations as part of efforts to develop and control a global market for their services (Arnold, 2005).

Three Examples of Institutionalization by GPSFs

Our first example of the institutional role played by Big Four accountancy firms refers to an issue which is at the heart of the accountancy professionalization project (MacDonald, 1995): the redefinition of auditing. Auditing has traditionally represented one of the economic cornerstones of the accountancy profession. Furthermore, as a highly visible example of what accountants do, it is one of their key sources of (self) identity, as well as one of the most persuasive justifications for their professional status as gatekeepers (Coffee, 2006) of public interest (the protection of investors, creditors and the general public through the certification of corporate accounts). Yet, despite its foundational role at the heart of the accountancy project, auditing fees have over the last few decades been under growing pressure. This reflects the increasing commodification and routinization of this area of practice as well as the reluctance of clients to pay for a regulatory service which does not directly add value to their business (Coffee, 2006). In this context, accountancy firms have been growing alternative and more profitable lines of business such as tax advisory and management consultancy services, with auditing divisions decreasing in economic and political significance within the firms which they historically dominated. Indeed, reflecting this development, during the 1990s the main strategy of the Big Four centred around the treatment of auditing as a loss leader to secure clients for more lucrative consultancy services, with auditing partners being rewarded for their ability to cross-sell the firms' broader expertise to their clients (Coffee, 2006; Robson et al., 2007).

Consequently, firms embarked on a project to redefine and reframe auditing practices through the development of Business Risk Audit

(BRA) methodologies (Robson et al., 2007). BRA expands the remit of the traditional audit to include a comprehensive focus on risk management and business assurance. In particular, audits are broadened to include the analysis of corporate strategies and business processes and the way these generate business risks which in turn affect financial statements. This repositioning of the audit was theorized by firms as important for clients not only because as a more holistic perspective it was more likely to increase the accuracy and reliability of audits but also because by enlarging its remit BRA methodologies redefine auditing from a 'compliance' to a 'value-creation' tool. By casting a wider perspective on the operations and activities of a firm, BRA generates valuable knowledge on its current performance, as well as future risks and opportunities. Thus, through the development of BRA large accountancy firms have effectively redrawn the boundaries between auditing, risk management and management consultancy; as a result auditors are empowered to advise clients on a wide range of matters pertaining to their business whilst the economic potential of auditing services is maximized. BRA thus serves the interests of large accountancy firms as they seek to control a wider range of issues and reap the economic rewards (see also Momani, this volume).

Our second example broadens our focus from the technical (i.e. auditing) to the regulatory. Historically, professions have developed within the confines of the nation state and professionalization processes have often unfolded as part of broader state-building projects (Burrage and Torstendahl 1990). In this context, national regulations tend to control both who can deliver professional services (control over the production of producers) and how professional activities can be legally organized, produced, traded and consumed (control over the production by producers) (Abel, 1988). This implies that whilst global professional services firms have invested to develop one firm models of management (Muzio and Faulconbridge, 2013) based on globally integrated structures and seamless service delivery practices, their operations are often disrupted and fragmented by national regulatory requirements (Faulconbridge, 2008). Big Four accountancy firms have responded to such national impediments by actively trying to subvert local restrictions to their activities, developing in the process a global market for their services as well as helping to consolidate emerging transnational governance regimes.

At the heart of the Big Four's attempts to change national regulations are WTO initiatives such as GATS article VI:4 and the Disciplines on Domestic Regulation in the Accountancy Sector, these being successfully used to challenge domestic regulations which restricted global accountancy firms' activities in specific jurisdictions. Thus, the autonomy of democratically elected institutions, such as national governments and professional associations, over traditionally domestic matter such as credentials, qualification regimes, ethical codes and standards of practice became subordinated to WTO-mandated tests of necessity and proportionality, as well as to analyses of their compatibility with international standards. The inability of Greece in the 1990s to resist liberalization and to re-regulate its own domestic accountancy profession, in face of opposition from large professional services firms and international organizations such as the OECD, represents a clear example of the effects of these measures (Caramanis, 2002). This point is also resonant of the role of GPSFs in reproducing neo-colonial regimes as described by Boussebaa (Chapter 15) and by Momani's analysis of management consultants in transnational governance (Chapter 16).

Our final example extends this analysis and indicates how large firms have been actively seeking to build a transnational training and qualification system around the new XYZ designation (Suddaby et al., 2007; Covaleski et al., 2003). This was intended as a transnational multidisciplinary qualification for global business professionals; an elite MBA for accountants which crucially sought to deliver international consistency, visibility and recognition in professional qualification pathways so as to support more effectively the requirements of GPSFs and their clients. XYZ effectively operated as a market-driven qualification whose legitimacy rested on its ability to add value to its holders, employers and users. This qualification effectively sanctioned a division between a business advisory elite which operated at a transnational level and the rest of the accountancy profession which continued to be embedded and constrained by national institutions, values and arrangements (Suddaby et al., 2007).

Efforts to institutionalize the XYZ qualifications were ultimately unsuccessful, in particular because not enough firms and professionals considered the qualification to be advantageous. Nonetheless, the XYZ project provides a clear example of a transnational professional qualification which was explicitly designed to support the requirements and activities of GPSFs. In doing so it would have provided Big Four accountancy firms with an effective way to short-circuit national systems for the regulation of the production of producers and to recruit individual practitioners educated and socialized into the realities and norms of transnational professional work. This points to the increasing role of GPSFs as sites of professional identity formation and regulation (Cooper and Robson, 2006) as firms deploy increasingly sophisticated HRM techniques, such as recruitment and selection, mentoring and corporate training programmes to mould the subjectivities of the professionals they employ in ways that best serve corporate priorities (Anderson Gough et al., 1998; Grey, 1998). As such, this example indicates how 'the historical regulatory bargain between professional associations and nation states is being superseded by a new compact between conglomerate professional firms and transnational trade organizations' (Suddaby et al., 2007: 334). In this context, GPSFs are hollowing out historical functions of the nation state and reframing these as part of new transnational governance regimes of which they are a key component.

GPSFs in Transnational Governance Ecologies

The three examples from the accountancy profession discussed above all point to significant forms of institutional change driven by GPSFs as they disrupt established institutions and create new ones to support their organizational strategies and activities. Thus, the traditional audit is transformed to cater for a broader range of business assurance functions and, in the process, helps to develop new lines of business. National regulatory systems are challenged and overhauled as part of attempts to legitimize the strategies and activities of GPSFs and to produce a global market for their services. Finally, new professional qualification systems and credentials are sought to support the needs of global practice, threatening to fragment established professional projects and institutionalizing divides between global professional elites and local practitioners.

One important thing to notice here is how the professionalization projects pursued by GPSFs trigger broader processes of institutionalization. For instance, it was the attempts by accountancy firms to circumvent the effects of the restrictions imposed by the Sarbanes-Oxley Act of 2002 and by auditing departments to raise their profitability and prestige within their firms that led to the transformation of auditing practices. Similarly, attempts by large accountancy firms to use WTO regulations to expand their markets contributed to the hollowing out of the role of the nation state and the consolidation of transnational governance regimes around the professions themselves. And, importantly, GPSFS were not isolated actors in the institutional transformations previously described. Rather, they acted as part of dense coalitions formed with key stakeholders in their broader field of practice. Thus, accountancy firms worked closely with academia to develop, diffuse and legitimize BRA, by funding research and teaching posts, providing case studies and other materials, co-authoring key texts (such as Bell et al., 1997 – which acts as the unofficial bible for BRA) and sponsoring as well as participating in relevant academic conferences (such as KPMG's Business Measurement Process Conference). Through these activities large firms have been able to shape the academic agenda and leverage this to help promote BRA methodologies, this being possible because of the desire of universities to reform their relationship with industry and their role in professional governance regimes.

At the same time, because BRA calls on a broad range of business skills and knowledge in areas such as strategy, operations and risk management, which go beyond traditional auditing curricula and qualifications, accountancy firms have developed close working relations with the professional associations who set and police standards, frameworks and regulations in the accountancy field. In particular, the delivery of BRA required the development of new curricula, qualification pathways and professional credentials. Professional bodies, keen to reproduce their role and importance in a changing political economy, had a clear incentive to cooperate with Big Four firms to affect institutional change. For instance, the Institute of Chartered Accountants of England and Wales (ICAEW) in its 1998 Green paper 'Creating the Added Value Business Advisor' promoted the development of new qualification pathways which explicitly targeted the development of the generalist business and management skills. Indeed, by the start of the new millennium, 25 per cent of the ICAEW training syllabus was concerned with business risk and assurance (William, 2001 cited in Robson et al., 2007). Importantly, such networks involve international organizations such as the International Auditing and Assurance Standards Board (IAASB) of the International Federation of Accountants, who, as part of its Audit Risk Project, revised international auditing standards to reflect and in turn endorse the new BRA agenda in auditing practice. In particular, these revisions, in line with BRA methodology, led to the mainstreaming of risk assessment standards, which had traditionally been separate and peripheral issues, as core concerns within regulations on financial statement audits (IAASB, 2002, 2003). Similarly, Big Four accountancy firms joined forces with international trade lobbies such as International Financial Services London (IFSL) and the US Coalition of Services Industries (USCSI), transnational professional networks such as the International Federation of Accountants (IFAC), multinational clients such as UBS, BT and DHL, and international organizations such as the WTO, the OECD and the EU Commission to drive their deregulatory projects (Arnold, 2005).

The intimate relationship between the institutional work of the Big Four and the allied projects of universities and regulators is supported by revolving door-style arrangements through which Big Four firms funded named accountancy chairs at leading universities (such as Ira Thomson's KPMG Professorship in Accountancy at the University of Illinois) and key staff moved from Big Four accountancy firms to key positions in professional associations and international regulatory bodies, and vice versa.

The impact of such links is to place GPSFs such as the Big Four accountancy firms in de- and re-regulatory compacts with groups who share a similar institutional agenda including industry and lobby groups (such as the Liberalization of Trade in Services Committee), neoliberal states (such as the US and the UK) and transnational institutions (such as the WTO) which actively seek to expedite and extend measures associated with the construction of new transnational governance regimes. As such, the institutional agency of GPSFs cannot be disconnected from wider forms of transnational political economic settlement and complex linked ecologies. GPSFs are, then, important stakeholders in the Washington Consensus and subscribe to its neoliberal vision of unfettered competition and open markets (crucially including professional services). This is perhaps unsurprising; after all, economic interest certainly ties GPSFs into a symbiotic relationship with the masterminds of the neoliberal agenda, as the new economic order delivers to them significant financial gains and opportunities whilst their services and expertise are essential to the smooth operation of transnational capitalism.

The Process and Impacts of Institutional Work by GPSFs

Reflecting the suggestion in the chapter by Seabrooke and Henriksen (this volume) that issues of scope, autonomy, resources, staffing and knowledge are significant in analyses of the role of professionals in transnational regimes, the discussion here reveals three important dynamics in the transnational institutional work of GPSFs.

Theorizing the scope of control. Exemplified by work associated with the institutionalization of BRA, we see GPSFs engaging in concerted efforts to expand the scope of their control over certain markets through a theorization process similar to that outlined by Greenwood et al. (2002). This process identifies both the problem at hand, and the solution GPSFs can provide to it. In the case of BRA the problem related to the reactive nature and the limited value-added of traditional auditing services, and the solution was provided by the integrated audit and risk assurance methodologies developed by Big Four firms. Through this theorizing firms were able to position themselves in a central position within the increasingly transnational field of business advisory services (Arnold, 2005; Barrett et al., 2005; Suddaby et al., 2007). Similar processes of theorization are present in other cases relating to the role of GPSFs in the development of transnational regimes – such as international bankruptcy and sustainable building design – yet to date the existing literature pays limited attention to the firms in question, something this chapter and the theoretical framing here developed can help to resolve.

Defining scales of knowledge resources. As part of efforts to secure influence in transnational markets and regimes, GPSFs engage in sustained efforts to detach their claims of knowledge and expertise from national jurisdictions and reattach them to transnational regimes. This is associated with broader evolutions in the basis of the knowledge claims of the professions (Evetts, 1998, 2011), particularly towards a transnational arena in which the state is just but one actor in governance regimes (Faulconbridge and Muzio, 2012). In the case of accountancy, this process is exemplified by the exploitation of the GATS regime to redraw national jurisdictions and challenge local regulations. This redefining of scales of knowledge in part means maintaining existing logics of professional practice – for instance, the fiduciary logic associated with accountancy (Malsch and Gendron, 2013) – and exploiting the associated knowledge in claims about the centrality of the profession in transnational regimes.

Transnational knowledges are, then, crucial resources for legitimacy claims. This often means rescaling onto the transnational level the knowledge resources that professions have traditionally deployed at the national level to accomplish their professionalization projects. This process is further exemplified by the attempted XYZ qualification in accountancy; this new qualification being designed to be operated and policed by transnational professional associations. Other examples of such resources include the protocols, deontological codes and principles of best (ethical) practice set out and monitored by transnational professional associations and networks such as the International Bar Association, International Union of Architects, the International Auditing and Assurance Standards Board and the International Competition Network (on such bodies, see Faulconbridge and Muzio, 2012; Hussain and Ventresca, 2010).

Forming and exploiting ecologies of shared interest. A key aspect of the institutional work performed by GPSFs is the strategic effort to collaborate with and piggy-back on the agendas of other stakeholders in emerging transnational regimes. In the case of accountancy (as well as other GPSFs), such an ecology of shared interest is exemplified by relationships with international organizations like the WTO, the World Bank and IMF, as well as neoliberal nation states (such as the UK and the US) and academic institutions. It is important to note that this is not an ecology that solely benefits the GPSF. At the same time they also serve the agendas of the collaborating organizations, with a mutual dependency developing. For instance, international organizations require the expertise of professional organizations to manage globalization processes and coordinate transnational governance regimes. Any illusions of professionals being separated from and impervious to commercial interest are, then, shattered in these emerging transnational ecologies where shared interest binds the GPSF to the neoliberal agenda of the Washington consensus (Morgan, 2006). This suggests that transnational regimes are the outcome of a strategic compact between parties that together seek to control issues that are central to the wider economic and social order.

Conclusions

We have in GPSFs a crucial locus of power and agency that is integral to the construction of the new transnational regimes that are transforming the system of the professions (Abbott, 1988) as well as the wider political-economy. Reflecting broader trajectories, GPSFs in various ways disconnect themselves from national professional projects and redefine their jurisdictions through three processes outlined in the previous section of the chapter. It thus seems crucial to more carefully locate GPSFs in debates about transnational governance, issue control and institutional change, transcending the established tendency to focus on professional firms and individual professionals in isolation, without consideration of the broader institutional context they inhabit and that help form.

In closing we propose three agendas for future research that would enhance understanding of the role of GPSFs in transnational regimes. First, it seems important to further unpack the organizational strategies of the firms in question. By this we mean the ways that individual GPSFs seek to enact the scope, knowledge resource and ecology strategies outlined in this chapter. To date we know little about the efforts made by individual firms as part of their corporate strategies to enact transnational institutional projects. Second, the heterogeneity in the successes of GPSFs and the regimes they sanction in different countries needs closer scrutiny. As Djelic and Quack (2003) highlight, transnational regimes are additional layers of governance that coexist with national regimes. Yet, little effort has been made to bring back in the national scale and consider how transnational compacts 'come down to the ground' and get operationalized in and through individual nation states, with implications for the role of GPSFs within different jurisdictions and political-economic systems. The development of the international bankruptcy regime exemplifies this (Halliday and Carruthers, 2009), as it involved negotiations and compromises in each country it is deployed in. It would thus seem useful to provide more comparative work focussed on the efforts and outcomes of the activities of GPSFs in different national contexts. Third, better specifying the ecologies of shared interest that GPSFs are part of would be helpful in better revealing the new kinds of compacts and networks associated with transnational governance. For instance, we know little about the way GPSFs in the same sector (e.g. law) come together to form alliances, how GPSFs from different sectors compete or collaborate, or about how GPSFs manage to insert themselves into the agendas of the WTO and other supra-national organizations.

There is, then, much to be done to further specify the role of GPSFs in transnational institutional processes, including the creation and operation of those regimes that are so central to the functioning of contemporary economies and societies.

15 Global Professional Service Firms, Transnational Organizing and Core/Periphery Networks

Mehdi Boussebaa

In the last few decades, global professional service firms (GPSFs) have emerged as major corporate players who not only provide services to clients worldwide but also engage in a range of governance issues that cut across national borders. They play a significant role, for instance, in constructing 'universal' economic laws (Halliday and Carruthers, 2009; Morgan, 2006); in spreading 'best' management practices (McKenna, 2006; Sturdy, 2011) and legal structures such as asset-holding trusts (Harrington, 2015) around the world; in setting 'global' accounting standards (Botzem and Quack 2006); and in reforming public services worldwide (Momani, Chapter 16). In addition to being implicated in external processes of transnational reform and standardization, GPSFs also engage in internal cross-national organizational design as a means of controlling and coordinating their work and resources across countries (Barrett et al., 2005; Boussebaa, 2009, 2015a; Greenwood et al., 2010).

Yet research on the role of professionals in transnational governance has paid little attention to GPSFs as analytically distinct actors, the main focus generally being on 'the professions' (see Faulconbridge and Muzio, Chapter 14). Importantly, the relevant research has tended to overlook the global power asymmetries and unequal exchange relationships that GPSF professionals (re)produce as they engage in transnational governance issues – externally (in the world economy) but also internally (within their own organizations). This is in part due to an underlying conception of transnational governance in which processes of cultural diffusion, isomorphism and adaptation are given primacy (see Drori, 2008). A problematic consequence of this at the level of the firm, which is my focus in this chapter, is a tendency to portray GPSFs as increasingly homogeneous and 'flat' structures in which the constituent subunits and the professionals within them operate under conditions of equivalence and equal exchange when in practice they do not.

This chapter aims to help in addressing these limitations. I argue that, in attempting to serve clients internationally, GPSFs are institutionalizing internal hierarchies that mirror the long-standing core/periphery hierarchy of the world capitalist system. This occurs because, I contend, GPSFs *in practice* operate largely as instruments of professionals located in 'core' nations. These core professionals occupy command posts, control key client relationships and design organizational arrangements with which to expand into, and manage operations in, the periphery. They present the firm's emergent structure as a neutral 'transnational' organizational design but, in practice, use it as a platform from which to (1) serve multinational clients in the periphery, (2) grow demand for their services in that zone, and (3) leverage core/periphery wage differentials. The overall outcome is a gradual cultural-economic colonization of the periphery and, concomitantly, an unspoken internal division of labour in which core professionals bolster their dominance and growth by utilizing firm-wide resources as a bridge into 'emerging markets' and as a source of 'cheap labour'. In advancing this argument, I hope to contribute to a better understanding of the role of GPSFs in transnational governance and, importantly, how the professionals within them come to (re)produce relations of domination and exploitation as the global level.

GPSFs and Intra-Organizational Transnational Governance

GPSFs are international market organizations that offer professional and quasi-professional services to a wide range of clients across an equally wide range of economic sectors and geographic regions. They have offices dotted all around the world and some are even more internationalized than the major multinational corporations which they serve (Greenwood et al., 2006). Typical examples are the prestigious strategy consultancies (e.g. Bain & Company, McKinsey & Company, Boston Consulting Group), the leading providers of consulting, technology and outsourcing services (e.g. Accenture, Capgemini, IBM),[1] the 'elite' law firms (e.g. Allen & Overy, Clifford Chance, Freshfields Bruckhaus Deringer, Linklaters), and the 'Big Four' accountancies (Deloitte & Touche, Ernst & Young, KPMG, PriceWaterhouseCoopers).

GPSFs not only deliver services globally but also put considerable effort into managing and integrating their geographically dispersed operations (Boussebaa et al., 2012; Greenwood et al., 2010; Jones, 2003; Klimkeit and Reihlen, 2016; Muzio and Faulconbridge, 2013).

---

[1] Historically, IBM was a computer manufacturing company but, in the late 1990s, it developed a consulting division alongside its traditional business, which it then expanded by acquiring, in 2002, the consulting arm of PricewaterhouseCoopers, one of the world's largest audit-focused GPSFs.

As part of this, they also put much energy into projecting an image of themselves as supranational agents of capitalism that transcend the "imagined communities" (Anderson 1991) of nations, national economies and nationalism' (see also Boussebaa, 2015b). A key driver behind such efforts are multinational clients: these require 'seamless' cross-national services and hence to push GPSFs to work on developing 'transnational' organizational and delivery capabilities such as shared work methods, procedures and standards. In addition, GPSFs seek to learn from the different countries in which they operate as a means of being more innovative than competitors and thus work to facilitate multi-directional inter-unit knowledge flows within the organization – in theory at least. They also aim to utilize their firm-wide human resources efficiently by, for instance, assigning staff to projects based on skill and ability rather than geographical and cultural homophily (Boussebaa, 2009).

These intra-organizational transnational governance efforts are now well documented in the management literature (for a summative review, see Boussebaa and Morgan, 2015) and, increasingly, also in sociological research on the role of GPSFs in transnational governance (Boussebaa and Faulconbridge, 2016; Morgan, 2006; Morgan and Quack, 2006; Suddaby et al., 2007). A key theme here is that such efforts are gradually leading to cross-national homogeneity within the firms. For instance, Spence et al. (2015) note how, in the Big Four:

[a]ll of the elements that strengthen the "corporate glue" and thus that are conducive towards homogeneity are more vociferously practised today than they were 20 years ago: standardization of knowledge sharing, training and service delivery are important means through which the Big 4 seek to manage their risk profile. [...] English dominates as the working language in these firms in a way that is viewed as unproblematic; [...] and national interests appear to have successfully converged around making as much money as possible. [...] Overall, Big 4 firms are more internationally coherent now than they were 20 years ago in the (then) Big 6 and therefore more able to transcend national boundaries.

There is recognition in some studies that important cross-national differences remain (see, e.g., Muzio and Faulconbridge, 2013, 2016) but, on the whole, the suggestion is that the firms are evolving an organizational space or identity that cannot be reduced to any single national rationality. However, as noted earlier, this account of the GPSF, in being mostly focused on processes of diffusion/isomorphism/adaptation, leads to a view of the GPSF as a flat structure, overlooking the global power asymmetries and unequal exchange relations that professionals (re)produce as they engage in intra-organizational transnational governance. It is these processes which I believe require attention and to which I now turn.

GPSFs as Subunits of the World System

GPSFs are capitalist organizations and so understanding them as agents of transnational governance requires an appreciation of the nature of the global capitalist system. A good starting point is world-systems theory and related research on uneven development (Amin 1976; Chase-Dunn, 1998; Wallerstein, 1979, 2000). This body of work conceives of the modern world economy as the product and continuation of centuries of unequal exchange between 'core' and 'peripheral' societies – i.e. between wealthy, dominant (neo)imperial states and market actors located (mostly) in the 'West', and poorer, weaker ones in the rest of the world. Prior to the 1960s, this relation manifested itself in a relatively simple international division of labour in which core nations specialized in manufacturing and exporting goods while peripheral societies – often colonies of European empires – served as a source of raw materials and food stuffs for core markets. Following the decolonization of much of the world, a 'new international division of labour' (Frobel et al., 1980) began emerging in the 1960s and 1970s as core nations (now labelled 'developed' economies) relocated segments of their industrial base to peripheral societies (now called 'developing' countries). In this new division of labour, the 'core' specializes in skilled (capital/knowledge-intensive) production using highly paid labour and the 'periphery' in unskilled or low-skilled (labour-intensive) production using low wage labour. The result is the continuation of a hierarchical world order in which the 'core' bolsters and sustains its dominance and economic growth by exploiting resources from the 'periphery'.[2]

This relationship is of course not static – consider, for instance, the rise of the BRIC nations.[3] Nor is it just economic in nature and necessarily always rationally articulated; it is also cultural, being framed by various norms (e.g., laws, regulations, standards, etc.) that core actors develop

[2] This international division of labour is generally seen as comprising of not two but three zones: a core and periphery but also a semi-periphery. Semi-peripheral societies occupy an intermediate position, with a combination of both core-like and periphery-like features and, over time, can transition in or out of the core. Like peripheral societies, semi-peripheral ones are commonly understood as 'developing' nations and the two groups are often described as the 'periphery'. In this chapter, for empirical reasons and also to aid exposition, I only refer to core and peripheral zones.

[3] Brazil, Russia, India and China.

and seek to universalize – knowingly or not – in the course of their global expansion (Carruthers and Halliday, 2006). Further, the core/periphery relation is not just a unidirectional export from the 'core' to the 'periphery' and a mere act of exploitation by the former – it is relational and mediated by collaborative (but also ambivalent and sometime resistive) peripheral actors. Comprador legal professionals in Asia and Latin America, for instance, have been key to the diffusion of neoliberal economics and a US conception of law in those regions of the world (Dezalay and Garth, 2002b, 2010b). Similarly, Eastern European actors have played an important role in spreading neoliberal forms of knowledge at home (Bockman and Eyal, 2002) and, indeed, their professional strategies have even led to a radicalization of the neoliberal paradigm (Ban, 2016). This, however, occurs in a historical context of *unequal* exchange, as postcolonial studies of global knowledge diffusion remind us (e.g., Frenkel and Shenhav, 2003, 2012). For instance, the diffusion of English in workplaces around the world, whilst pursued locally by indigenous professionals and other actors as a means of achieving international competitiveness, is structured by wider conditions of empire (Boussebaa and Brown, 2017; Boussebaa et al., 2014).

The core-periphery relation is reproduced through the work of a variety of different state and non-state actors, with intergovernmental organizations (e.g. World Bank) and multinational enterprises (MNEs) playing an increasingly central role since the 1960s (see Chase-Dunn, 1998). Whilst there is a dearth of research on core/periphery strategies *inside* contemporary MNEs, a few scattered studies offer some useful insights. They draw our attention to, for instance, how core actors continue to occupy top management posts in MNEs (Doremus et al., 1999); how they exploit and maintain core/periphery wage differentials through offshore outsourcing arrangements (Levy, 2005); how they promote their knowledge as universally applicable 'best practice' whilst delegitimizing that of the periphery (Frenkel, 2008; Mir and Mir, 2009); and how they seek to universalize their languages and enforce them as 'global' norms (Boussebaa et al., 2014; Vaara et al., 2005). I suggest that all these intra-firm core/periphery strategies are relevant to understanding the role of GPSFs in transnational governance. I unpack some of them in what follows, using the case of global management consulting firms (GMCFs) as an illustrative example.

Controlling Professional Norms

A key issue faced by GMCFs is the need to control professional norms (standards, procedures, processes, methodologies, etc.) on a firm-wide basis as a means of providing a consistent level of service to multinational clients. In order to understand the implications of this intra-organizational transnational governance issue, it is first important to place GMCFs in their historical context and specify who the 'global governors' are within them. To begin with, it is useful to recall that the management consulting profession originated in the USA and its spread to the rest of the world has occurred via the internationalization of US consultancies (Kipping, 2002; McKenna, 2006). Today, whilst a number of non-US GMCFs have emerged (e.g. Capgemini in France, Wipro in India), 'management consultancy as a global industry is still dominated by its North American origins, with most of the large firms continuing to have their operational headquarters located in the US' (Kipping and Wright, 2012: 168). Further, the firms' command posts are still largely controlled by US professionals, with UK professionals also typically occupying an important hierarchical position given their cultural and linguistic proximity to the US and their role in spreading US-style consulting around the world (Bower, 1979).

Thus, GMCFs are, on the whole, governed by professionals located in the 'core' of the world economy. This is also reflected in the fact that these core professionals typically control – 'own' – their firms' most prized client relationships and projects, namely those with *Fortune* Global 500 corporations (Boussebaa, 2015a). Being generally headquartered in 'core' economies, these major multinationals in effect provide an opportunity for core professionals to develop business relationships with clients whose operations span the globe. Consequently, core professionals find themselves in charge of numerous high-value 'global' client projects and since these projects are 'owned' not by 'the firm' but by the subunits – or indeed the individual consultants – which develop them, they inevitably come under the control of core professionals. In short, core professionals continue to control not just the firms but also key value-generating activities such as global client relationships and projects.

Global client relationship/project control in turn leads to core professionals playing a major role in producing and diffusing of 'global' norms within the firm (Boussebaa, 2015a). This is not surprising since global norms are crucial to effective global project delivery but also client retention and repeat business. As one UK partner at a major GMCF put it:

You have to build global standards. You have to be quite strict with global processes and global methodologies. I mean our clients are international so if somebody screws up a project in Spain, you'll find it very hard to sell a project in the UK because the Spanish have screwed it out and the English will say "we heard that the Spanish project wasn't very good". So you have to make sure that your quality is consistent. (cited in Boussebaa, 2015a: 699)

This consistency issue is typically presented as a 'global' issue but is in effect a core-related one. To address it, core professionals seek to control norms on a firm-wide basis through, for instance, training. This is then also presented as a 'global' matter but is, again, a core-related issue (and solution). In this way, the firms' 'global' norms come to reflect the 'local' norms of core professionals. This is perhaps most visible in the decision to impose English as the firms' official corporate language. Such 'global' norms are of course not mechanically reproduced at the local level (Boussebaa, 2015a) – there is always a degree of 'decoupling' – but nevertheless demonstrate how the issue of cross-national consistency is first and foremost an issue faced by core professionals, not 'the firm' as such. In this sense, 'global' norm building or rather the attempt to universalize core norms can be re-interpreted as a professional strategy used to shape firm-wide resources in ways that permit core professionals to provide the consistency required by their multinational clients.

Selling Into the Periphery

In addition to the issue of global consistency, core professionals seek to create international demand for their services and, in particular, to sell solutions to emerging-market clients. A key strategy here is to use the firms' global knowledge management systems (hereafter, KMSystems) as 'advertisement boards'. KMSystems are basically global databases designed, in theory, to help consultants codify their knowledge and make it available to others throughout the firm (see e.g. Ambos and Schlegelmilch, 2009; Boussebaa et al., 2014).[4] In the official 'transnational firm' discourse, the systems facilitate multi-directional cross-national knowledge flows, helping consultants around the world to learn from, and share their knowledge with, international colleagues – the view being that 'learning from the world' (Doz et al., 2001) leads to more creativity and more innovative solutions than can be achieved through local networks and ultimately to competitive advantage.

While (arguably) fulfilling their purpose to some degree, the systems are also being used by core professionals for a different purpose, namely to 'sell' services internationally, especially in peripheral nations. My own research into four major GMCFs from the perspective of UK-based consultants showed how core professionals used KMSystems primarily as a platform from which to advertise and promote their local skills and

---

[4] This approach to knowledge management is typically used in conjunction with approaches aimed at facilitating sharing through direct social interaction via, for instance, international networking and inter-office staff exchanges (see Hansen et al., 1999).

experience on a worldwide basis inside the firm (see Boussebaa et al., 2014). In so doing, they would attract the attention of peripheral professionals, get involved in their domestic projects and, ultimately, secure additional 'billable work' for their office. They rarely, if ever, used the systems to 'learn' from peripheral professionals and, indeed, tended to see themselves as 'specialists' that peripheral professionals would call on to win and deliver their own projects. Thus, UK consultants turned KMSystems to their advantage by using them not as 'global' learning and sharing mechanisms but as a means of selling into the periphery.

One implication here is that knowledge flows in GMCFs tend to follow traditional core-to-periphery lines. It can of course also flow in other directions – between the USA and the UK for instance (i.e. intra-core) – but the key point is that little tends to flow from the periphery into the core and that the periphery is viewed as a site for knowledge exports, not imports. Paik and Choi's (2005) study is particularly insightful here. The authors examined the KMSystem experiences of Accenture, one of the world's largest and most successful consultancies and a firm often seen as a pioneer in the area of knowledge management. Based on research in the USA (Chicago and Los Angeles) and East Asia (Beijing, Hong Kong, Seoul, Taipei and Tokyo), they found no evidence of periphery-to-core knowledge flow. In practice, the firm's US professionals largely disregarded the experience and expertise of their Asian counterparts and instead worked in ways that supported a 'unilateral flow of knowledge from the U.S. or Europe to East Asia' (p. 82). The authors highlight how 'very few U.S. consultants intentionally sought out management experiences from Asia' (ibid.) and that in fact 'most U.S. consultants were not aware of projects in Asia' (ibid.). As a result, 'many Asian consultants doubted that their knowledge was being sought or appreciated' (ibid.). This was in spite of the Asian offices being a source of useful knowledge and innovation:

Asian consultants had valuable knowledge that could be shared with the rest of the organization. For example, there was little doubt that Japanese and Korean experiences with wireless communications could provide interesting marketing and new product knowledge to consultants in the U.S. and Europe. Some project teams in the U.S. would have benefited from the various market data collected in Asia (ibid.).

Thus, in practice, core professionals circumvent the official discourse of 'global' learning and instead use the associated KMSystems as a platform from which to export their knowledge and do so, as the next section shows, at a very high cost for the periphery.

Leveraging Core/Periphery Wage Differentials

A third issue pursued by core professionals is that of global resourcing (i.e. the staffing of client projects through the firm's worldwide pool of professionals). In the official discourse, such resourcing is presented as a 'global' issue, which 'the firm' seeks to address through various organizational mechanisms. One such mechanism is what GMCFs describe as global scheduling systems (hereafter, GSSystems). These work off global databases that provide data on where consultants are located around the world, who is rolling onto an assignment, who is becoming available and what projects are coming through. The databases also store information on the professional background of consultants. The GSSystems are designed to support effective and efficient staffing on a worldwide basis and, in particular, to help in assembling project teams based on 'skill and ability' rather than geographic-cultural homophily.

My research in four GMCFs found that these systems were, as in the case of KMSystems, rarely utilized in the way originally intended (see Boussebaa, 2009, for the various reasons behind this). In practice, core (UK) professionals often used the systems in ways that leveraged – wittingly or unwittingly – core/periphery wage differentials. Here, it is important to note that major cross-national fee-rate differences existed within the firms, with UK consultants commanding rates that were generally significantly higher (sometimes 10 times) than those of peripheral professionals. This resulted in substantial wage differences and, in turn, meant that the use of peripheral resources by core professionals was a very attractive proposition, as the following comment by a consultant I interviewed demonstrates: 'A Poland resource is cheap; you could buy a doctor for a year for £3,000! If I had a project and I wanted Polish developers, I'd go on the phone straightaway because their salary rate would be £5000–6000 and I'd be billing them out at £10,000 a week' (cited in Boussebaa, 2009: 843). Thus, UK professionals often sought to lower labour costs at home by including in their project teams peripheral consultants. The fee rates negotiated with UK clients would generally be mostly based on the cost of employing UK professionals to run and deliver projects and so the use of peripheral consultants could significantly increase profit margins back in Britain. Moreover, fee-rate differentials meant that it was prohibitively expensive for peripheral professionals to draw on core consultants in delivering their own domestic projects, as the following example illustrates: 'In Poland, my project [a large Polish project for which assistance from the UK was requested] was £3.2 million and I think I accounted for about £750,000 of that £3.2 million – just one resource' (cited in Boussebaa, 2009: 843).

GSSystems thus not only provided a platform from which core professionals can lower their labour cost but also a means by which they can extract value from the periphery. This also means, in line with the above discussion on knowledge flows, that core professionals tended to serve as providers of skills and expertise whilst the periphery acts more as a source of 'cheap labour', thereby (re)producing the traditional core/periphery hierarchy of the world system. Peripheral professionals also proved useful – as local intermediaries – in helping UK consultants deliver projects in emerging economies on behalf of home-country multinational clients, 'a phenomenon not dissimilar to the practice of using indigenous elites as a bridge between the "natives" and the "sahibs" in colonial times' (Boussebaa et al., 2014: 1236).

Re-conceptualizing GPSFs as Neo-Imperial Spaces

The above analysis reveals how the current view that GPSFs are giving rise to (more or less) 'transnational' logics or identities within their organizational boundaries in response to various environmental pressures is an incomplete. In many ways, this account follows the causal logic highlighted and challenged by Seabrooke and Henriksen (Chapter 1 in this volume): *organizational strategy* > *authority type* > *rules and standards making*. Yet, in looking more closely at the strategies of GPSF professionals, we find a more complicated reality. We find that GPSFs remain the tools of professionals based in core nations (cf. Boussebaa, 2015a, 2015b; Boussebaa et al., 2012). These core professionals establish the firms, expand them across the world and then, by retaining control over command posts, key client relationships and professional norms, become one powerful and hegemonic set of players among several structurally less significant peripheral others – the core of the firm in other words. In this sense, GPSFs are similar to non-market international organizations; like them, they become 'boards of directors for ruling states' (Boswell and Chase-Dunn, 2000: 238).

From this central position, core professionals put themselves in charge of managing the firm and pursue three key issues which reflect such position: (1) the issue of cross-national consistency, (2) the issue of international sales, and (3) the issue of international resourcing. These are presented as 'global' issues faced by 'the firm' but are in practice core-related issues, reflecting the location of core professionals at the heart of the firm and the wider world economy. Such core-centrism is also reflected in the strategies that core professionals pursue to address the three issues. They attempt to universalize their 'local' norms to serve multinational clients consistently across nations and, in so doing, mould the 'transnational' organization in their own image. They also put in place various 'global' management systems, presenting these as means of facilitating cross-national learning and efficiency but then using them as opportunities or platforms from which to sell into the periphery and leverage core/periphery wage differentials. The overall outcome is a gradual colonization of the periphery by core professionals and, relatedly, an intra-organizational international division of labour which very much mirrors the core/periphery hierarchy of the world economic system.

These colonizing professional strategies and related governance outcomes suggest the causal logic highlighted by Seabrooke and Henriksen (Chapter 1) does indeed need challenging, with specific reference to intra-GPSF transnational governance in this case (see also Boussebaa, 2009, 2015a, 2015b; Boussebaa et al., 2012, 2014). The official discourse of the 'transnational firm' is in practice circumvented and manipulated by the GPSFs' national subunits and the professionals within them. In particular, the above analysis shows is that this discourse is itself a form of manipulation designed as a means to universalize the norms and interests of the core. Bourdieu (2003: 75) is useful here, reminding us how 'globalization' is 'the justificatory mask sported by a policy aimed at universalizing the particular interests and the particular tradition of the economically and politically dominant powers (principally the United States)' (see also Wallerstein 2000). The notion of the 'transnational' or 'global' firm (as a nation-transcending entity) and the various concepts associated with it ('global' client, 'global' norm, 'global' knowledge, etc.) can be interpreted along similar lines. Moreover, the universalizing process also serves to maintain and reinforce core/periphery power asymmetries and unequal exchange within the firm, and, by implication, also within the world economy.

The presence of such asymmetries and exploitative relationships also point to the importance of locating the 'professional-organizational nexus' (Seabrooke and Henriksen, Chapter 1) in the wider world political economy, as conceived of by world systems theory and other perspectives emerging from, or influenced by, it (e.g., Carruthers and Halliday, 2006; Dezalay and Garth, 2010b). In this vein, the observed dynamics also call for a re-conceptualization of GPSFs as 'neo-imperial spaces' (Boussebaa and Morgan, 2014). As noted earlier, current accounts tend to suggest that GPSFs are gradually evolving 'transnational' logics. Some see this as a *fait accompli* (e.g., Spence et al., 2015) while others point to how 'national' influences co-exist with transnational emergence (e.g., Faulconbridge and Muzio, 2012; Morgan and Quack, 2006). The analysis presented here suggests the need to go one step further to also include (neo)imperial influences on intra-GPSF transnational governance. This is important because the various countries across which GPSFs operate are not simply different institutional spaces; they are also 'societies that have been intertwined in a complex and shifting hierarchy of nations over centuries' (Boussebaa et al., 2012: 470). Thus, whilst it is true that 'no "island" or "islanders" [...] are spared the isomorphic global pressures that also infuse the local and problematize its authenticity' (Drori, 2008: 453), it is equally true that few, if any, islands are spared the imperialist forces that come to transform and exploit the peripheral local. The account of 'transnational' emergence obfuscates such forces and the significant power asymmetries and unequal exchange relationships which they produce within the firm, and, by implication, with the world society. It is my hope that this chapter has gone some way in addressing this problem.

In closing, I propose three key avenues for future research that would deepen and refine the analysis presented here and thereby enhance understanding of the role of GPSFs in transnational governance. Firstly, further research on the colonizing strategies of core professionals is needed, across different types of GPSF structure (e.g., partnership versus corporate) and different segments of the professional services sector (law, advertising, etc.). Secondly, and importantly, research is required on the strategies used by peripheral professionals in response to intra-GPSF transnational governance efforts. The argument I have put forward has been silent on such strategies and yet one can expect peripheral professionals to be neither 'cultural dopes' nor simply victims of economic exploitation but active agents in the core/periphery relationship. Thirdly, and related to the previous point, research is needed on how ongoing changes in the geopolitical balance of power (rise of the BRIC, etc.) may be influencing core and peripheral professional strategies. Relatedly, research is required on the strategies used by core and peripheral professionals in the new GPSFs that are springing up from the periphery (e.g., Infosys and Wipro in India).

16 Professional Management Consultants in Transnational Governance

Bessma Momani

Professional management consultants are increasingly being contracted to provide policy advice to governments, private market firms, and to international organizations on ways to improve their functions and operations. Global Management Consulting Firms (GMCFs) – such as McKinsey, The Boston Consulting Group, Bain and Company, AT Kearney, Booz and Company, Deloitte, Price Waterhouse Cooper, Accenture, and KPMG – have long played a key role in advising the private corporate sector on ways to alter their company policies (see also Faulconbridge and Muzio, Chapter 14, and Boussebaa, Chapter 15). Less well known is their growing role in advising governments worldwide, which is increasing their transnational governance footprint.

Over the years, management consultants have provided public policy advice to governments in a wide array of issue areas, including but not limited to fiscal and budgetary reforms that concern the civil service, health care, education, transportation, law enforcement, food security, taxation, energy, defense, and privatization of state-owned assets. Increasingly, they have been able to market their knowledge and advice as the "go-to" source for public policy advice on critical and pressing issues that concern governments. However, the critical question under-theorized by the academic literature studying professionals like management consultants is: What tools and strategies do management consultants utilize to control such a diverse set of policy issues that concern many governments? Following a discussion on the mixed-methods approach used in this chapter, the following section conceptualizes and identifies four tools and strategies: (a) management consultants market themselves as analyzers of unique knowledge leading to "Big Data"; (b) management consultants claim to identify the big picture to forecast trends and patterns amid growing uncertainty; (c) management consultants use a common language of positive messaging that inspires and offers a feel-good approach to problem-solving and; (d) management consultants simplify ambiguity and complexity into actionable items to empower clients.

In the subsequent section, this chapter examines why management consultants are successful at having governments lean on them to provide solutions to their concerns. Increasingly, governments are resorting to paying the very high fees of GMCFs in order to receive advice that may be available in-house or externally through the more cost-effective (or sometimes free) international organizations, as is the case with both the OECD and technical assistance of the IMF and the World Bank (Seabrooke & Nilsson 2015). It is argued that the success of these GMCFs is aided by an environment of international uncertainty and ambiguity, as well as by an unregulated transnational professional space for easy recruitment.

Methods, Data, and Approach

There are reportedly more than 1 million management consultant professionals operating in 2014. Currently, the largest management consulting firms have over 1,565 offices throughout the globe. Management consultants are professionals that cannot be ignored or overlooked; after all, the largest global management consulting firms earned more than $300 billion worldwide in selling their very expensive policy knowledge, skills, and expertise to their clients. To illustrate the magnitude of this industry's financial strength, the largest management consulting firms' combined revenue surpasses the national GDP of Saudi Arabia, Venezuela, and of approximately another 160 countries.

Significantly, and according to management consultants' own industry analysis, governments worldwide are among the fastest growing group of new clients, spending billions of dollars contracting management consultants to provide advice and solutions to important public policy issues. This implies that GMCFs have a significant role in potentially shaping domestic and transnational policy issues. While many management consultants are traditionally contracted by the public sector in developed economies, there has been a noticeable rise of governments contracting consultants in order to give advice in "nation-building" projects throughout emerging market economies. Again, this implies their reach is no longer isolated to private firms or to developed countries but that, in fact, management consultants have a global reach and have become a valued go-to professional group for governments seeking policy advice.

Using a mixed-method approach, including participant observation, personal interviews, and content analysis of management consulting firms' studies and materials, this meta-study broadly searched for strategies used to control the issue of creating "effective and better government." The three-day annual meeting of the International Council of Management Consulting Institutes (ICMCI) in Orlando, Florida, in October 2012, offered a unique opportunity to observe the proceedings, coaching, and discussions of management consultants who have provided advice to governments worldwide. The ICMCI is based in the Netherlands and operates as an umbrella organization that includes 47 national organizations representing all regions and countries. More than a dozen personal and semi-structured interviews were conducted with participants at the sidelines of the ICMCI meeting. Using a snowball method of creating additional contacts, I conducted another dozen phone interviews with management consultants in a variety of positions, locations, and levels of experience after the meeting.

Through participant observation of the ICMCI and personal phone interviews, I observed, questioned, and assessed management consultants' strategies in advising governments worldwide. Furthermore, at the ICMCI, approximately 180 attendees in a general session were asked to complete a written survey yielding a 26 percent response rate. A follow-up email was sent to all those who filled out the survey for further personal interviews. This method provided fascinating insights into understanding the strategies of control used by management consultants in their advice to governments worldwide, but the method did not explain governments' views and perceptions of management consultants, or provide insight into the quality of consultants' advice. Nevertheless, this anthropologically inspired method of understanding management consultants' strategies of control did elucidate a great deal of empirical and theoretical considerations in order to better our understanding of these transnational professionals (see also Chapter 3 on studying professionals in transnational settings).

In addition to participant observation and interviews, a thorough qualitative content analysis of GMCF's top flagship publications on public sector reforms was conducted. The management consulting industry is comprised of thousands of firms and a million or more consultants spread across the world, yet the industry is concentrated among a small number of very large firms. Among those top firms that have an established public sector division in their operations are McKinsey, Boston Consulting Group, Booz, Allen and Company, Bain and Co, AT Kearney, Deloitte, PriceWaterhouse Coopers, Accenture, IBM Global, and KPMG. These GMCFs collectively produce thousands of studies and reports. This study focuses on the top firms' flagship publications in a five-year period (2009–2013), examining 26 documents in which their core arguments and values regarding public sector reform are laid out. Using these 26 documents from these 10 large firms, there is a rich pool of data from which to analyze the communicative value or contextual meaning of their writings (*see* McTavish & Pirro 1990). This qualitative content analysis approach therefore provides a flexible means of analyzing text data – be it in print or online – by intensely examining the language and words used in GMCF reports to create an efficient number of categories that share similar meanings, be it explicit or inferred (*see* Weber 1990).

After careful reading of these documents – in addition to the personal interviews and participant observation carried out – categories of strategies for control were found to flow from the data gathered; no preconceived categories were used. Here, qualitative content analysis provided a research method for the subjective interpretation of the content of text produced by GMCFs, providing new insights to understanding the strategies used by management consultants to control issues of how to create better and more effective government. A total of 26 GMCF documents were read, word for word, to derive suitable codes that capture key thoughts or concepts that were then organized into clusters of categories that were reflective of more than one thought, idea, or concept (Patton 2002). Focusing on these GMCF studies and reports in the past five years provided a broad and yet selective content analysis of these documents, which effectively revealed management consultants' strategies for issue control. In other words, the language, text, and words found in the 26 GMCF documents were then coded into themes; and the pattern that emerged was the four tools and strategies for issue control described below.

Management Consultants' Tools and Strategies for Issue Control

Based on the mixed-methods approach described, I identified four tools and strategies that management consultants utilize to control the diverse set of policy issues that concern many governments. These are (a) management consultants market themselves as analyzers of unique knowledge leading to "big data"; (b) management consultants claim to identify the big picture to forecast trends and patterns amid growing uncertainty; (c) management consultants use a common language of positive messaging that inspires and offers a feel-good approach to problem-solving and; (d) management consultants simplify ambiguity and complexity into actionable items to empower clients.

Analyzers of Unique Knowledge Leading to "Big Data"

Professional management consultants often sell their expertise of strong analysis to government clients by noting their access to data and "big data" that no other institution is able to synthesize. The reports analyzed reveal a trend that explains GMCFs' perceptions as to why the public sector does not see the value in the data that they, the consultants, can so effectively synthesize. An IBM (2011a) report, for example, blames public sector apathy and blind spots, noting that:

Apathy is, perhaps, the biggest contributor to the relative lag in public sector analytics usage. Only a third of the participants in our study [public sector employees surveyed] felt the external environment is sufficiently disruptive and uncertain today – or would become so within the next three years – to require new courses of action. We believe several "blind spots" – structure, budget and skills deficits, discomfort – cause them to underestimate how a complex environment affects their operations (Ibid.: 5).

This is supported by the survey data conducted at the ICMIC. Of the management consultants surveyed at the ICMCI, 75 percent agreed that public servants do not have the required expertise that consultants have. A similar percentage agreed that public servants cannot problem-solve effectively; 71 percent believed that consultants provide a better quality of service. Similar arguments in business management studies suggest that private firms often contract management consultants because the latter are able to provide advice with "economies of scale," "economies of scope," and "economies of repetition" (Morgan, Sturdy, & Quack 2006). Extending this to explain how management consultants claim they persuade governments to hire them for knowledge ideas, it is often argued that management consultants can do it better and faster than in-house talent.

Through content analysis of the GMCF documents and studies, there is a clear signal to their clients – in this case governments – that GMCFs believe they can help bring together disparate pieces of information into an analytical framework that is useful and unique knowledge. Many GMCFs suggest that this knowledge is also a skill set that is innovative, fresh, and new. Moreover, these GMCFs suggest that the public sector is not ready, capable, or willing to make good use of the data contained within the public sector. For example, the following statement is indicative of this unique positioning that management consultants claim to have:

There is no substitute for talented people who can translate the context of issues into the right questions. These questions, in turn, become the data that matters. Success today requires increasingly sophisticated combinations of knowledge, technical expertise and insight ... many agencies have pockets of talented analytics professionals ... government and other public sector organizations will need to explore new talent management models for analytics skills. (IBM 2011a: 6)

This quote highlights a repeated theme found throughout GMCF studies – that is, that professional management consultants have unique knowledge in how to analyze large volumes of data that is not synthesized or understood by the public sector. Again, in a PriceWaterhouse Coopers (2013a: 10) report, the study noted: "The key to unlocking the potential power of this kind of [reform] framework is the right data, information and insight." Reading between the lines, management consulting firms claim they have the ability to identify a framework that will highlight sorely needed talent, be it internal or external, and help make the public sector's latent data into useful data for bettering government policies. Here, Deloitte (2010: 1) captures this point further: "Around the world, government leaders are beginning to understand that unlocking public data can fuel new levels of performance. In many jurisdictions, data are now being viewed as public assets to be leveraged by citizens, businesses, and communities." Another firm, AT Kearney (2013: 4), suggests ways that governments can capture this data:

Define the data required, not just what is provided . . . Take advantage of existing data sources. As noted above, much of the data is currently available—it is just a matter of getting the most out of it. Existing data to explore more fully includes financial data, program performance, and comparisons to similar programs. (Ibid.: 4)

One theme that resurfaces across GMCF studies as well is that this latent data is in the hands of citizens. The goal of government is to find ways of capitalizing on data that citizens hold. It does not take much deductive effort here to note, therefore, that theme is another way of suggesting a privatization of public data for economic gain. The potential controversy inherent within this AT Kearny (2011) proposition, for example, is indicative of how the GMCFs advise governments to raise capital from citizens' private data:

We recommend that governments consider giving appropriate incentives to individuals for sharing their data and facilitating citizen-focused services. One private-sector example is loyalty cards, popular in supermarkets that offer vouchers, discounts and preferential service in exchange for customer data. How would this work in the public sector? It might mean paying for parking or reducing waiting times for benefits claims in exchange for data about employment history with other departments. (Ibid.: 7)

The political concerns of sharing public data are noted in the AT Kearney study. Nevertheless, the marketing of public data for private gain is evidently a theme in a number of GMCF reports. While across the GMCF studies analyzed, there is this emphasis on the government's need to capture data, the prescriptions remain vague and undefined. Simply put, the firms suggest that the data is there, it is latent, untapped, and therefore easy for the public sector to capitalize on. The closest description of what to do with such data is the idea that this data simply needs to be refigured, re-gigged, or envisioned in a new manner. Here, AT Kearney describes ways to capitalize on data to trim public sector finances:

"The [public sector] program leaders wanted to improve cost transparency and understand what the specific sustainment activities and modernization capabilities were costing the program. The program had lots of data related to cost (for example, invoices, EVM data, and contract budget estimates), but this data had not been turned into useful insight. The data was often structured based on how contract and purchase orders were executed, not based on how work was actually organized and managed. As a result, truly understanding the cost and performance picture for a project required extensive effort and unique knowledge. By reorganizing and creating a drill-down structure that made sense to program managers, the government was able to analyze more effectively where money was spent and which parts of the program were in trouble and in need of additional attention." (Ibid.: 7)

The key message across the GMCF studies is that these firms have the comparative advantage to bring innovative and unique knowledge and ideas to public sector clients by finding ways to harness public sector data. Some management consulting firms bluntly note that they are collating this unique and interesting data, into what is often referred to as 'big data'. As McKinsey's chair Dominic Barton noted: "With the push of a button we can identify the top 50 cities in the world where diapers will likely be sold over the next ten years".[1] *The Economist* revealed that McKinsey "invests $400 m a year on 'knowledge development', and Mr Barton touts its 'university-like capabilities' to impart it to its consultants".[2] This new "big data" is a complement to the reconfiguration of latent data that management consultants impart on clients. Similar to Mr. Barton, IBM Chairman and CEO, Ginni Rometty also noted that: "Data promises to be for the twenty-first century what steam power was for the eighteenth, electricity for the nineteenth and fossil fuels for the twentieth – that is, the creator of enormous wealth and progress" (IBM Global 2013: 4). This quote by Rometty points to an important sales pitch or economic rationale to governments that hire their services – namely, that GMCFs can best synthesize public sector data in order to realize or ensure economic wealth and prosperity.

---

[1] Economist (2013) 'To the Brainy the Spoils', *The Economist* May 11, http://www
.economist.com/news/business/21577376-world-grows-more-confusing-demand-clever-
consultants-booming-brainy
[2] Ibid.

GMCFs argue that the ability to analyze and synthesize data into big data is also a key requisite for modern economic prosperity. Here, IBM (2013) articulates this as a domestic public good as well:

[A]t the heart of smart approaches to economic development, is *the harnessing of data and analytics* to address problems pre-emptively rather than reactively. The capture, integration and analysis of data (in all its forms) enables us to anticipate problem areas – whether it is congestion in the traffic system, pupils at risk of dropping out of school, or water shortages occurring as a result of leaks in the water system – before such issues manifest and embed themselves in our societies. (Ibid.: 8, emphasis mine)

The above quote is reflective of the first tool used to control the issues, analyzing and synthesizing data, but it also is indicative of the next tool to be discussed: how GMCFs also claim to have the big picture and the ability to predict and prevent government failures in an era of global uncertainty.

Identifying the Big Picture to Forecast Trends and Patterns amid Uncertainty

Through content analysis of GMCF studies, a strategy used by a number of firms to attain control on public policy issues of concern to governments is to claim to have access to big data that gives GMCFs a big picture that is sorely lacking in the public sector. Moreover, this big picture offers a comparative advantage in a world marked by excessive uncertainty and complexity. One Deloitte (2011a: 5) report, for instance, points out government failings to use "data analytics" in order to "leverage their existing information assets to make better decisions based on a more complete picture."

All of the GMCFs note their access to past consultations with a wide range of private sector clients as an asset in building their presumed knowledge base. For example, as the top firm in the industry notes: "McKinsey has been researching productivity in the private and public sectors for two decades, helping many organizations transform their performance. Building on that work, it is now set to embark on a comprehensive, international analysis of public-sector productivity in developed countries" (McKinsey & Company 2010a: 2). This claim, moreover, to cross-fertilization of knowledge and experience from the private sector and into the public sector, has no bounds. For example, one study by Booz Allen Hamilton (2002: 1) suggested that it was a GMCF that was "uniquely positioned" to give advice on bioterrorist threats, because of its "long history of work for both commercial and government clients; our many engagements in government security, and our broad based experience in waging wargames for government and corporate clients."

This birds-eye view gives GMCFs the advantage of seeing potential government policy flops that the public sector can – and in many GMCFs' views, quite often – miss. Again, here McKinsey explains that:

By analyzing competitiveness at the sector level, we reach conclusions that run counter to the way many policy makers think about the task in hand. Many governments worry about the "economic mix"—and assume that if they achieve the "right" mix, higher competitiveness and growth will follow; our analysis finds that solving for mix is not sufficient. (McKinsey & Company 2010b: 11)

As exemplified in the above quote, GMCFs claim public sector decision-makers are taking an economic view rather than a business view of growth and prosperity issues. Similarly, a number of GMCF studies take direct aim at macroeconomists' view of the world and at their failure to identify economic fault lines. The GMCFs, which are typically staffed by graduates of business schools and not economic departments, often pitch their knowledge in oppositional terms to traditional macroeconomists' view and diagnoses of economics and wealth. These macroeconomists also frequently staff the highest echelons of the public service with important decision-making influence like finance departments and central banks. As a McKinsey (2010b) report noted:

An important reason why government intervention in markets has been hit or miss is that action has tended to be biased on academic and policy research that has looked through an economy wide lens to understand competitiveness – in other words, whether one country is "more competitive" than another. The top down analysis has all too often failed to capture the fact that the conditions that promote competitiveness differ significantly from sector to sector. (Ibid: 9)

Again, and as noted in the same McKinsey report (2010b), GMCFs take aim at these traditional tools of diagnosing the health of economies: "It is no surprise that top down econometric assessments of what drives competitiveness have often proved inconclusive and that government intervention in markets has tended to be hit or miss" (p. 17). The McKinsey report also continues to explain how its knowledge differs from econometric approaches:

Over the course of nearly two decades, MGI [McKinsey Global Institute] has used sector-level research in more than 20 countries and 28 industrial sectors, employing microeconomic intelligence to build a picture of macroeconomic outcomes. We believe that this micro-to-macro approach is vital in answering the question of enhancing competitiveness. (Ibid: 17)

Claiming to provide a bottom-up business perspective to understand a top-down economic problem is another theme in many of the GMCFs studies. For example, KPMG (2010) argues in one of its reports that it looks at deficit reduction in the public sector by drawing on "international data from previous experiences of fiscal adjustment, economic research, insights from KPMG partners and directors around the world, as well as interviews with senior academics and public sector leaders in the US, UK, Germany, Canada and Spain" (p. 5). It is important to note here as well on the methods used by GMCFs in their analysis throughout the many reports analyzed. Specifically, GMCFs rarely rely on macroeconomic data to infer any of their arguments; instead, there is an enormous reliance on surveys of business leaders in order to ascertain their findings. Moreover, there is a great deal of referencing to anecdotal evidence in order to demonstrate success stories, but no context is provided and rarely is a feasibility study included in references to case studies.

There is an implicit urgency in many of the GMCF reports on public policy issues where they not only claim their access to big data provides them the bird's eye view of government concerns but that there is global or domestic urgency in having GMCFs assess and diagnose the "problems." According to one IBM (2012) report, for example:

[T]he economic uncertainty of the 21st century demands that government agencies take action ... Helping governments implement smarter approaches is something IBM has been doing for more than 100 years, from the 1890 U.S. Census, to the Apollo moon missions, to helping cities deal with issues related to crime control, traffic and water systems. (Ibid.: 4)

Public policy issues and government concerns have grown more complex, GMCFs often argue, which necessitates the use of the outside knowledge of management consultants. PriceWaterhouse Coopers (2013b), for example, further noted: "In our view, the world has become so interconnected and inter-dependent that there has emerged a clear and common agenda of actions for government and public sector organizations" (p. 37). The list of concerns and uncertainty facing government is seemingly endless. In another report, PWC (2013c) notes that "natural disasters, pandemics, terrorism, disruptive technologies – all of these and more are contributing to a world in constant flux. Governments will need to find new levels of adaptability and flexibility in order to be 'secure with insecurity' " (p. 10). Again, the prescription implied here is that GMCFs have the ability to provide greater security by imparting knowledge onto their clients. Not surprising then that CapGemini consulting firm claims it is contracted by the governments because "taxpayer expectations are intensifying. More and more – success comes from

Table 16.1 *Consultants' Buzz Terms*

Journey, road, navigate, forward
Innovative, creative, flexible, talent
Leveraging, enablers, facilitators
Opportunities, promise
Technology
Analytical
Integrate, convergence
Transformational, productivity

[public sector] being ready to respond to complex and unpredictable challenges" (CapGemini 2010b: 4).

The Power of Positive Talk

In combination with the strategy of providing government clients the big picture amid global uncertainty, management consultants often also use a common language of positive talk and affirmative messaging. According to one Deloitte (2013, p. 29) study, for example: "In government, it's not about competition. It's about fulfilling your mission. It's about helping citizens, business and society. Mobile can help you accomplish that. So ... what are you waiting for?" There is often a repeated "We Can Do It" theme to problem solving. These terms evoke these kinds of positive, feel-good synonyms that devolve a great deal of responsibility and accountability on the public sector to initiate change (see Table 16.1). Here, McKinsey (2010b, p. 45) goes as far as to devolve responsibility to individual circumstance, and glosses over global structural impediments or challenges: "There is no single right policy to boost growth of manufacturing sectors ... Policy execution, personal passion and drive, and luck, all play a part."

As many of the GMCF studies and reports concerning public policy issues were focused on means of reform, there was a high usage of common language that evokes positive talk and messaging on how these reforms were, in fact, opportunities. Booz Allen and Hamilton's Reform Playbook (2014) had perhaps the most upbeat wording and messaging throughout this particular study:

• "Even though it is not always a choice, reform is an opportunity for your agency to shine and achieve everything from incremental improvements to breakthrough change for the country" (pg. 4).

- "Once your change efforts are in full swing, maintaining a steady drum-beat of positive outcomes will keep critics at bay" (pg. 20).
- "Lean forward into reform with an open mindset that allows you to envision new possibilities and spark innovation" (pg. 22).
- "Successful reform is not about just trying to check the box on the mandated requirements; use it as the impetus to do something magnificent" (pg. 25).
- "There are peaks and valleys to the implementation of reform, but over time you learn to always climb up" (pg. 26).
- "Lean forward with everything you've got. The seeds of innovation are buried within the soil of reform—find those seeds and enable them to flourish" (pg. 23).
- "Reform changes the game, so shape the rules in your favour" (pg. 26).

The same kind of common language or messaging is prevalent in other GMCF studies where the emphasis is a "can-do" mantra on public sector reforms. One PWC (2013a: 7) noted, for instance, that "This is a time for courage, confidence and for taking risks in order to motivate others and bring communities, employees, and partner organizations together to build consensus around shared desired outcomes." The theme of government leaders taking courageous steps toward reform is one that is found throughout the many studies and reports analyzed. The PWC (2013c: 11) study, entitled *Future of Government*, is perhaps the bluntest with this statement: "Public bodies must decide if they want to consume the legacy left behind by predecessors, or create a new legacy for the next generation, while navigating some seismic shifts." Boston Consulting Group evokes similar references to bravery among government leaders and decision-makers who initiate reforms: "While transforming the service delivery may seem a daunting task, the size of the prize is enormous ... the principles outlined here provide a winning formula for leaders who are prepared to take the leap" (BCG 2011: 13). In its paper on public sector reform, McKinsey (2007: 24) similarly calls out government decision-makers: "In short, you can mandate 'awful' to 'adequate', but you cannot mandate greatness, which must be unleashed."

In addition to the theme of bravery, there is a common language referring to innovation and creativity. In many of the GMCF studies and reports analyzed there is a great deal of references to opening up the latent creative minds of the public sector. McKinsey (2007: 24), for example, notes that "achieving great performance in the public sector ... requires unlocking the initiative, creativity, and motivation of leaders throughout the system." Similar themes are promoted by PWC (2013b: 2): "In our view, partnering, co-venturing, co-creation and co-design are the new 'must-have' capabilities, and agility, innovation, connectedness, and transparency the characteristics and behaviours needed by the public bodies of tomorrow." Innovation is often put at the center of reform initiatives. For example, as Deloitte (2011b: 8) notes: "Governments at all levels need to incorporate 'innovation as strategy' ... [and] address more 'new ideas' that shape future capacity to deliver high quality programs and services. Public service innovation holds real promise for those governments willing to confront these challenges." If the public sector has latent creativity and innovation, what is the role of the management consultants? Accenture (2012: 2) claims that:

Our goal is to inspire and support public service leaders: to take a fresh look at the problems they face, to highlight innovative solutions to emulate, to present paths to progress they may not have considered, and to show how all of the pieces can fit together. But it's a hard road to go alone. That is why Accenture is pleased to inaugurate our *Delivering Public Service for the Future* program. (Ibid: 2)

One of the most interesting findings of this chapter's extensive content analysis of the GMCF studies was the repetition of key words and themes expressing "shared understandings" among management consultants. Images that evoke a journey, a road, a travelling ship are all too common in many of the GMCF reports and studies. This McKinsey quote – "to embark on the journey to the next level of e-government, public-sector organizations should" (McKinsey & Company 2009: 6) – is one that can be found in numerous other studies and reports. Deloitte refers (2011c: 2) to "the road to fiscal sustainability [where] Success requires navigation of three distinct phases that comprise one long journey to sustainability." Similarly, IBM (2011b: 1) states that "There's no turning back now – citizens' demands for openness are here to stay." This kind of positive talk and messaging used by GMCFs is an important strategy and tool to control policy discourse.

Simplify Ambiguity and Complexity into Actionable Items

The final strategy that management consultants utilize to control the many policy issues that concern governments is the simplification of ambiguity into actionable items, such as this statement: "How can middle-income countries like Mexico compete with China? By adding higher value" (McKinsey & Company 2005: 99). Throughout all of the GMCF reports, there is always a solution, even to complex governance challenges, and often without the need for increased financing. Consider the following passage by Diana Farrell, who leads McKinsey's Washington DC, and is cofounder of the McKinsey Center for Government:

Our research shows it is possible to make huge strides in addressing critical challenges, even without resolution of the many ideological and policy dilemmas. From government spending to tax collection, education improvement to health outcomes, and welfare reform to job creation, we see the potential for meaningful improvement, to do more and better with less. What is needed is government management by design, built to fit these difficult times: government that identifies the most critical, solvable problems, reorganizes where necessary to deliver the right solutions, and abandons the tools and approaches that no longer work. (McKinsey & Company 2012: 1)

Again, these solutions to complex policy issues are depoliticized in order to make them solvable and simple to address. Partnered with themes of brave government leaders who are also keen to innovate, there is a startling amount of simplification of real complex policy issues into bulleted lists or steps among GMCFs. The lists tend to be four must-do items to resolve incredibly complex issues and achieve remarkable results. The following quote is from a McKinsey report on increasing public sector productivity, reducing solutions to four steps: "The first step defines and measures productivity – a prerequisite for managing it. The second organizes the sector in such a way that there is pressure to improve productivity. The third identifies the most effective drivers of productivity, while the fourth secures sustainable transformation" (McKinsey & Company 2012: 1). All four steps are equally ambiguous, with rather vague terms and references to positive keywords and messages. McKinsey does not provide concrete directions, any references to feasibility studies, and does not suggest other measurements of effective implementation.

PWC (2013d) also has a three point list to boosting public sector productivity that is similarly vague: "Resolving the public sector productivity challenge relies on three focus areas, prioritization, measurement, and alignment. Each of these needs to be an area of focus for a modern public service" (p. 11). To increase government transparency, IBM (2011b: 15) offers its three-step plan: "Getting started—or taking the next leg of the trip – on the 'open' road is a series of three steps that are repeated progressively over time: step 1 – define and measure openness, step 2 – open up, and step 3 – capitalize on greater openness." Equally fuzzy is the Boston Consulting Group's report on improving public sector delivery: "Five Principles for Transforming Delivery. (1) Recognize that one size does not fit all (2) Realign the operating model (3) Apply an open-systems mindset (4) Self-fund the journey (5) Tackle the root causes of complexity" (BCG 2011: 6–7). Another BCG (2012: 5) paper notes that "Segmentation programs should not require a steep upfront investment in analysis ... we have identified six steps to developing and implementing an effective segmenting program" (p. 5). All of these examples demonstrate the simplification of complex policy issues into actionable lists that governments ought to be able to fashion into new policies.

Management Consultant Firms as New Go-To Partners in Advising Governments Worldwide

Evidenced by their growing global footprint in opening up new offices and increased revenue in gaining government clients, management consulting firms are becoming increasingly successful as go-to professional organizations for solutions to key public policy concerns. Why are management consultants successful at having government lean on them to provide solutions to their concerns? The success of management consultants is ever more puzzling, moreover, by the abundance of negative portrayals of their profession in popular magazines, films, and media.

In an article in *The Economist*, for example, management consultants were dubbed "power-point rangers," "brains-for-hire," and "insecure overachievers."[3] More often, negative popular accounts of management consultants have made them appear to be menacing "travelling merchants" (Czarniawska-Joerges 1990), "vague experts" (Seabrooke 2014a, p. 59), or as "the great folk devils of the business world" (Fincham 1999: 36). Popularized movies and television shows, like House of Lies on Showtime, portray management consultants as people who will stop at nothing to secure a deal through unscrupulous methods to retain and entertain clients. As Svensson (2010: 1) put it: "The consultant is often seen as 'the guy who borrows your watch to tell you what time it is." Mostly derived from books describing life in corporate America, a number of exposés have suggested that corporate clients can become captive to management consultants' ideas through the sinister machinations of corporate politics (see O'Shea & Madigan 1997; Argyris 2000). Yet, despite these negative news stories and popular culture references, management consulting firms are increasingly hired by governments to advise on public policy issues.

This section argues that the success of these GMCFs in advising international governments is aided by an environment of international uncertainty and ambiguity, as well as an unregulated transnational professional space that provides for easy recruitment.

Environment of International Uncertainty and Ambiguity

In numerous studies carried out by constructivist approaches to the study of knowledge actors, it is often noted how knowledge actors can

[3] Economist, op.cit. fn. 1, p. 1.

successfully cultivate their expertise by creating an allure around them. More to the point, in their interaction with public officials, Barnett and Finnemore (2004: 25–26) note how knowledge agents gain influence by being *in authority* (for example, by holding key positions, notable roles, and seats from which to exercise power), and from being *an authority* (for example, by having exclusive expertise, training, experience, and respected solutions to policy dilemmas). As noted above, GMCFs cultivate an image that they are providers of innovative solutions stemming from their unique knowledge. However, management consultants take this accorded role as professionals one step further. Management consultants do not just sell their knowledge as different or unique; they also mystify their knowledge in abstract terms that give them a distinctive allure.

Nevertheless, management consulting firms were not always the go-to source on providing policy solutions to governments, and in this sense of Seabrooke's and Henriksen's (Chapter 1) conceptualization of professionals, management consultants would be understood as "brokers" who are trying to change how public policy dilemmas are solved. But this is changing and the demand for management consultants' services by government clients is on the rise. What makes management consultants different from technical and scientific expertise and professionals like economists, lawyers, accountants, and others is that they are somehow selling common sense. This is why the adage of "The consultant is often seen as 'the guy who borrows your watch to tell you what time it is'" (*see* Svensson 2010: 1) is so telling. Management consultants do not bring knowledge that is hard to come by, technically and scientifically speaking, and yet they are able to sell governments on policy solutions that should have been intuitive. Management consultants can do this because they can convince public servants that the "McKinsey way" or the "BCG methods" are better than in-house ideas and proposals of the civil service. Tellingly, AT Kearney advises, for example, that "To improve the chances for success, we believe government leaders need to tear up their old rule books" (2011: 7). In organizational behavior literature, management consultants are aptly discussed as change agents (Sahlin-Andersson & Engwall 2002) because they are seen as coming to the rescue of the archaic public sector.

In a global environment of international uncertainty on policy issues of great concern to governments – a contemporary "globality" in which shifting power relations and global boundaries have left world leaders struggling to cope with (among other things) increased security threats, pressing environmental concerns (i.e., climate change), and the need to negotiate complex international trade agreements (i.e., the recent Trans-Pacific Partnership, or

TPP) – management consultants thrive on the enhanced ambiguity inherent in such an environment about what the right solutions to these (and other) core policy dilemmas are. As Jacqueline Best's (2012) work demonstrates, professionals utilize ambiguity to enhance their situational power. As she also notes, governments are generally anxious of ambiguity, such that the very *raison d'être* of its public service is meant to be "ambiguity-reducing machines" (Best 2012: 91). Markets, societal actors, citizens, and voters all want certainty in an age of globalization, fast-moving political developments, and hyper-connectivity. Management consultants offer a recipe for calm and certainty, and yet also re-enforce ambiguity through their vague policy prescriptions. As Best points out, however, it is not uncommon for professionals to claim solutions to ambiguity while creating ambiguity through the unintended consequences of offering provisional solutions to the same ambiguous issues in the first place (Best 2012: 100).

Why are management consultants more successful today than in previous decades in gaining governments as clients? On the one hand, it could be argued that some of this may be a result of excessive public downsizing in a global age of fiscal consolidation. With the increased scrutiny of public accounts, governments are challenged with having a lean workforce, and therefore often resort to hiring management consultants to compensate for the lack of in-house capacity. One could also add that this may be the result of the growing influence of neoliberalism and new public management in the public sector (O'Mahoney & Sturdy 2015). It is useful, however, to understand that management consultants do not control discussions on strategic policy issues by simply filling in the void of human resource cuts.

This chapter argues that management consultants are more successful today at providing their services to government clients because, more and more, governments want to grab on to the hope of certainty in an increasingly global age of uncertainty and ambiguity. In personal interviews with management consultations, many noted that the increase of global regulations has opened up a large demand for their services, where many governments are confused and want guidance on how to meet the plethora of regulatory frameworks. Not surprisingly, many GMCFs sell the notion that they offer a one-stop shop for policy ideas, data, knowledge, and greatly needed solutions. Helden et al. (2012) also concur in their study that governments hired consultants when they were looking for solutions to "well-defined practical and technical problems." It may be that management consulting firms are actually selling ambiguity in the form of vague policy prescriptions, but it is the promise of hope through tools like simplification of complexity, positive messaging, unique knowledge, and forecasters of trends and patterns that has successfully made GMCFs a go-to profession.

Martin's (1998) study of the Australian government use of consultants concludes that government officials believe that consultants bring "gravitas" to their proposals. The word "gravitas" captures the notion that management consultants have a unique way of packaging their ideas. It is less the substance (at times), than the method of delivery. Hence, we see *The Economist* referring to management consultants as "powerpoint rangers" – the delivery of the ideas is packaged in a way that accords management consultants considerable gravitas and allure. In this volume, Baker demonstrates how esteem – which refers "to social standing based on an aggregate positive estimation of an agent's character, behaviour and performance" (Chapter 10: p. 151) – functions as a central variable in the professional interaction of macroprudentialist central bankers. He details how an inner circle of macroprudential "cognoscenti" relied on esteem to push forward a new frame for financial regulation.

Management consultants and their GMCFs, albeit operating in a thinner (read: uncertain and ambiguous, discussed above) transnational space, possess a similar allure, which also has shaped their relationships within the organizational networks of international governments.

However, while the esteem discussed by Baker allows certain professionals (in this case, central bankers as regularly experts) to consolidate their control over a particular issue, the allure or gravitas of management consultants is more diffuse and amorphous: it is not limited to a specific network or domain of professional control but is rather spread out, as it were, across diverse policy issues and government clients. To be sure, business management studies have generally supported this view by showing that clients hire management consultants because clients want to recruit those perceived to be the "intellectual elite" of their respective fields (Armbruster 2004: 1259). A number of studies on the corporate sector have found that management consultants were noted as providers of "high-quality" ideas (Aharorni 2000: 128) and are often recommended by elite circles of "networked trust" (Glucker & Armbruster 2003).

Unregulated Transnational Professional Space in Recruitment

Management consultants are often also recruited from elite, ivy-league business schools. With most management consultants having MBA degrees from prestigious and rigorous business programs, the success of management consultants is further complemented by their assumed intellect. Many of those recruited from MBA programs are indeed the elite crop of graduates who are generally hard-working, committed, and critical thinkers. Many management consultants are confident, almost to a fault, and perceive problems as just obstacles of framing and understanding, and less as inherent structural failures that cannot be overcome by all the goodwill and determination of MBA thinkers.

Management consulting firms are successful because they operate what Seabrooke calls "thin transnational environments" with few professional regulations. There are few institutional obstacles that stand in the way of MBA graduates of elite schools who want to enter and exit the pool of professionals (Seabrooke 2014a: 15). This in turn gives professionals the autonomy to mobilize talent quickly in such a "thin transnational space," where there are fewer "jurisdictional battles" of professional syndicates and accreditation. Moreover, the ease of recruitment from a global talent pool helps many GMCFs to gain a wide breadth of talented individuals who do not have to comply with domestic professional certification. Being "de-coupled" from domestic concerns and practices augments the success of these professionals to operate on a transnational scale with greater ease (Seabrooke 2014a: 15).

It is important to point out that suggesting that management consultants are able to control the issues and gain traction in their ideas as a result of their allure, mystique, and gravitas does not mean that governments do not have the in-house capability of performing the work of GMCFs. However, management consultants and their respective firms have used these fuzzy qualifiers to build an image, rightly or wrongly, that they have *an* authority on a policy issue that is simply unavailable in the public sector. As Lindquist (2009: 5) notes in the case of the Canadian public sector, government officials "rely on consultants to deal with peak demands, and stories circulate about consultants doing the heavy lifting on strategic policy analysis." Consequently, as these stories propagate, government officials perceive management consultants as authorities on key policy issues. This explains why management consultants, as Lapsley and Oldfield (2001: 527, 531) also found, have, at times, been hired to legitimize internal decisions that were already made.

When management consultants propose ideas, they are regarded as being very convincing. Why is this so? Well, akin to how knowledge agents gain the respect, legitimacy, and admiration of civil servants through repeated contact, management consultants gain a reputation that allows them to convince governments of policy change. Christensen and Skaerbaek (2010) add that consultants have a unique "purification" role in working with government officials because they are able to persuade them to implement controversial ideas. When ideas are introduced within the public sector, there is an implicit suggestion that civil servants are more motivated by the incentives of their own bureaucratic structures than what is best for the public good: the Weberian notion that bureaucracies are inherently going to experience the iron-cage syndrome is a prevalent phenomenon in wider society. This opens space for GMCFs to be perceived as "subjective" and "outside" voices, and for management consultants to further cultivate their role as innovative providers of unique and independent knowledge.

Conclusion

Management consultants are professionals who have sold their services to corporate entities for more than a hundred years. Yet, today they are becoming the go-to professionals of governments. Their wide transnational footprint and their increased involvement in providing policy advice to governments is an indication of their growing influence in transnational governance.

More than ever, governments are paying high fees to management consultants to give them policy advice, competing with other professionals in the public service at the domestic level or in international organizations. This chapter conceptualizes and identifies four tools and strategies that management consulting firms utilize in order to gain control over a wide range of public policy issues: (a) management consultants market themselves as analyzers of unique knowledge leading to "big data"; (b) management consultants claim to identify the big picture to forecast trends and patterns amid growing uncertainty; (c) management consultants use a common language of positive messaging that inspires and offers a feel-good approach to problem-solving and; (d) management consultants simplify ambiguity and complexity into actionable items to empower clients.

Management consulting firms try to use these tools and strategies to become go-to professional organizations for solutions to key public policy concerns. Management consultants use the strategies described to control the conceptualization of the problem, and to increasingly control the key to offering solutions. Their success is evident in their growing global footprint in opening up new offices and increased revenue from government clients. Success of these GMCFs is aided by the reality of an environment of international uncertainty and ambiguity, as well as by an unregulated transnational professional space for easy recruitment.

GMCF Reports Consulted

AT Kearney. 2009. *How to Become a Citizen-Centric Government.*
AT Kearney. 2011. *Creating Cross-Government Success.*

AT Kearney. 2013. Making Sustainment Programs More Sustainable.

Booz, Allen & Hamilton. 2002. Bioterrorism: Improving Preparedness and Response.

Booz, Allen & Hamilton. 2014. *Reform Playbook*.

Boston Consulting Group. 2011. *Citizens, Are You Being Served?*

Boston Consulting Group. 2013. *Strength in Numbers*.

CapGemini. 2010. *Corporate Annual Report*.

Deloitte. 2010. Unlocking Government: How Data Transforms Democracy.

Deloitte. 2011a. The Path to Sustainability: Creating a Cost-Conscious Government Culture.

Deloitte. 2011b. Innovation in Government? Conversations with Canada's Public Sector Leaders.

Deloitte. 2011c. *Red Ink Rising*.

Deloitte. 2013. *Government Meets its Mobile Future: Seven Essential Strategies for State Leaders*.

IBM Global. 2011a. The Power of Analytics in the Public Sector: Building Analytics Competency to Accelerate Outcomes.

IBM Global. 2011b. Opening up Government.

IBM Global. 2012. *The Foundations of Efficiency*.

IBM Global. 2013. Improving Economic Competiveness and Vitality.

KPMG. 2010. *Meeting the Deficit Challenge: Strategies for Fiscal Sustainability*.

McKinsey & Company 2005. Beyond Cheap Labour: Lessons for Developing Economies.

McKinsey & Company. 2007. *Three Paradigms of Public Sector Reform*.

PriceWaterhouse Coopers. 2013a. *Redefining Local Government*.

McKinsey & Company. 2010a. *The Public-Sector Productivity Imperative*.

McKinsey & Company. 2010b. How to Compete and Grow: A Sector Guide to Policy.

PriceWaterhouse Coopers. 2013a. *A New Contract Between Business and the State*.

PriceWaterhouse Coopers. 2013b. *The Future of Government*.

17   Professional and Organizational Logics in Internet Regulation

David Kempel and James Perry

This chapter examines the new and emerging field of internet infrastructure regulation, now commonly referred to as 'net-neutrality', which concerns the regulation of how packets of data are moved across the Internet. Although this may appear to be a narrow technical question, it is in fact a broad and political one that defines the commercial opportunities available to firms whose business models are dependent on internet infrastructure. With the rise of cloud computing and the 'internet of things', the regulatory questions introduced by the net-neutrality debate play a significant role in defining what is profitable on the internet, who profits, and how much. The issue has been contentious within the American and European regulatory regimes for some time, and in the U.S. the Trump presidency has made its intention clear in reforming current net neutrality regulations.[1]

We argue in this chapter that net-neutrality represents a struggle for issue control at two levels. At the first, and most visible, level there is an organizational struggle between different types of firms. In the existing net-neutrality literature, the opponents in this struggle are often reduced to two types: 'infrastructure' and 'content'. *Infrastructure* refers to incumbent telecoms companies who own much of the internet's physical infrastructure, and who control the all-important 'last-mile' of cable or fibre that connects households and businesses to the internet. *Content* refers to the newer companies, who potentially own no physical infrastructure at all, and make their money from the provision of a range of content and applications delivered over the internet and paid for either by subscription or by advertising. Vodafone and Deutsche Telekom are typical infrastructure companies; Google and Facebook are typical content and application providers (CAPs).

The second level of the struggle for issue control in net-neutrality can, we argue, be usefully analysed as one that takes place between different 'professional logics'. We do not use this term to refer to any means by

---

[1] 'Net Neutrality Is Trump's Next Target, Administration Says', *New York Times* March 30 2017, see: www.nytimes.com/2017/03/30/technology/net-neutrality.html?_r=0

which the professions *directly* confront each other but rather to the conceptual frameworks they deploy, which have roots in their respective academic disciplines. Such professional logics are mobilized to legitimize the arguments made by organizations occupying different strategic positions, which often confront each other. Although our use of 'professional logics', defined as such, will be of interest to those researching the sociology of professions, this chapter does not attempt to examine the boundaries between professions, or the means by which the authority of a particular profession is established and reproduced. Nevertheless, by identifying and mapping the core professional logics embedded in the network-neutrality policy discourse, namely those of *lawyers, engineers, and economists*, we believe our investigation contributes to a broader analysis of how three of the most important professions in the international political economy interact with one another.

In this chapter we present empirical work surveying both of the above levels of contestation in net-neutrality. We do this by examining 136 official responses to the European Commission's 2010 Network Neutrality industry consultation (EC 2010). As we show, the three professional logics are deployed in the net-neutrality field by organizations in competition with one another in order to achieve issue control. The second section of this chapter introduces the net-neutrality problem; the third section presents the economic, legal, and engineering concepts surrounding the topic and forming the professional logics. This provides the necessary theoretical framework for our research project.

The fourth section presents our empirical findings. We first show that the responses submitted to the Commission revealed a contest at the organizational level, and demonstrate that this contest was indeed (and continues to be) organized around a split between 'infrastructure' and 'content' companies. However, we also identify some additional considerations that must be borne in mind when unpacking the latter category. In the second part of the section we employ an inductive approach to investigate those policy arguments that do not conform neatly to the above-mentioned split between infrastructure and content. Based on this, we develop a conceptual typology of the professional logics within the net-neutrality debate, which we present as a two-by-two matrix. Third, we trace the use of different professional logics by the respective organizations to reveal how professional logics were distributed and applied to attain issue control in the net-neutrality debate in the 2010 consultation. Our results provide an explanation as to why certain combinations of arguments focused on innovation did not gain very much attention in the regulatory debate. The final section of the chapter concludes with a discussion of our findings.

What is Network Neutrality?

Over the past two decades, as the internet has become an essential piece of commercial infrastructure, the question of 'network neutrality' moved from being a topic discussed by computer engineers to one at the centre of an increasingly heated policy debate in the European Union. Net-neutrality concerns the way packets of data are transported across the internet, who pays for their transport, and how much they pay. This is not merely a technical issue but, as this section explains, a key determinant of the power of several of the world's largest corporations, who are presently vying to be the main gatekeepers in the knowledge-based economy. As such it is also a key determinant of the continuing impact the internet has on broader society.

Just as containerization in the shipping industry was integral to the rapid globalization of production and trade of physical goods (Levinson 2006), the pricing and organization of data transport on the internet are now central to the so-called 'fourth transformation' in the production and trade of *non*-physical goods and services (Kushida and Zysman 2009). Contrary to popular perceptions, the internet is actually not a unified public network, but rather a collection of privately owned networks that, when interconnected in an open and 'neutral' manner, can be used *as if* they were a unified public network.

Despite the internet's essentially open character, the owners of its infrastructure nevertheless maintain control of potential 'bottlenecks' that can command monopoly or oligopoly rents. Net-neutrality is thus a classic issue for political-economic analysis, standing at the intersection of business, politics, and technology. Regulatory economists, national and supranational regulatory authorities, and the (few) political scientists (Hahn, Litan and Singer 2010) who have engaged with this topic, all tend to see net-neutrality as a struggle between telecoms infrastructure companies (hereafter 'telcos') on one side and internet CAPs on the other. This is true regardless of which side is taken: either CAPs are portrayed as 'free-riding' on the telcos' infrastructure (Clark 2009), or telcos are portrayed as rent-seeking oligopolists (Lee and Wu 2009). The more technical question of rationing scarce network capacity is sometimes mixed into the debate, but here again the ensuing analysis is structured around the same CAP versus telco dichotomy.

Telcos, like any company, want to avoid a situation where they make only 'normal' profits by supplying the commodities with which others go on to make 'supernormal' profits. Much of the struggle centres on whether telecoms companies are understood as merely renting out infrastructure, or are able to persuade consumers and regulators that they add differentiated value to individual products.

In many respects, the answer to this key question depends as much on ideational framing as it does on technical assessment. As Manuel Castells (2009) has argued, because of the way distribution has become decoupled from production, the pursuit of price discrimination (charging different prices to different people for the same product) is unavoidably a key feature of the network economy. The internet significantly increases the scope for customization and differentiation to disguise central production of locally distributed products customized for specific audiences on the basis of marketing models. Indeed, internet-based selling allows for individualized price-offerings to every consumer, raising the possibility for firms to capture much more consumer surplus than has hitherto been possible. That said, society has historically shown considerable distrust of such discriminatory pricing, despite its prevalence in other historically significant network sectors as canals, railways, shipping, and road transport (Odlyzko 2004). This is borne out by customs, laws, and regulations that have closely regulated, and indeed often prohibited, the practise regardless of economists' claims that it leads to more optimal resource allocation.

The basic structure of the internet is shown in Figure 17.1. A device at the edge of the network connects to the 'backbone' via a telecommunications company (telco).[2] This device can then communicate with other similarly connected devices, via the backbone, by sending and receiving packets of data that conform to internet protocol (IP). This same setup applies whether the device belongs to an end user or a CAP, such as Amazon or Facebook. The user of each device pays their telco for their own connection, and this payment entitles them to send packets of IP data to others, and receive packets of IP data sent to them by someone else.

Inherent to this structure, telcos charge their customers on the basis of how many data packets are sent and received, and all data packets are transported with equal priority. This is what is meant by 'network neutrality': The network is *neutral* with respect to who is sending or receiving data, and what the content of that data is. BEREC,[3] the European Commission's coordinating body for national telecommunications regulators, invokes US scholar Tim Wu's explanation as to why net-neutrality is desirable:

---

[2] Sometimes 'telcos' are referred to as an Internet Service Providers. However, 'telcos' is used in this chapter for clarity, e.g. to distinguish clearly from reference to 'internet services' such as streaming video, voice over internet protocol, etc.

[3] Body of European Regulators for Electronic Communications (BEREC). BEREC and its support office were created within the recently approved reform of the EU Telecom rules to improve the consistency of implementation of the EU regulatory framework.

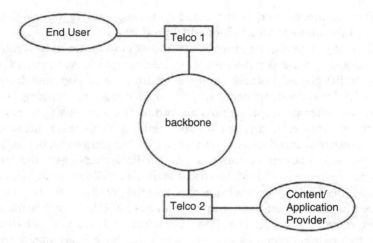

Figure 17.1 Basic Structure of the Internet (adapted from Schuett 2010)

The idea is that a maximally useful public information network aspires to treat all content, sites and platforms equally. This allows the network to carry every form of information and support every kind of application. (Tim Wu cited by BEREC 2011: 7)

Network neutrality, and its tariff structure based purely on quantity, was not a discretionary *choice* on the part of telcos, but rather was a design principle of IP, intended to make the network as flexible as possible and allow it to be put to unforeseen uses in future – thus fostering innovation.

When telcos first began offering internet access on a commercial basis in the late 1990s, they had no choice but to adopt IP because it had already been developed and deployed – although, as legal scholar Jonathan Zittrain (2008) remarks, if the telcos had realized back then how big the internet would become, they would have immediately tried to get IP changed to be considerably less neutral. Today, this is effectively what they are doing. Telcos can now circumvent net-neutrality while still offering IP connections. This is because the cumulative fall in the price of computer processing power over the past decade means that it became both technically feasible and commercially viable for telcos to use routers that can open every IP data packet as it passes and look inside to see what sort of data it contains. This technology is known as deep packet inspection (DPI), and is functionally equivalent to the postal service opening and 'skim-reading' every letter it handles, before delivering it. DPI opens up many new tariff opportunities for telcos since it offers them the possibility of discriminatory pricing on the basis of what kind of service or product is delivered in a stream of data packets as well as the crude volume being transported. However, because DPI changes the nature of a public infrastructure network, it also raises significant regulatory problems.

The Professional Logics of Network Neutrality

As mentioned in the introduction, we use the term 'professional logic' to refer to a resource that is mobilized through the legitimacy of the conceptual logic that dominates a profession. We use this term consciously in the very limited sense of seeing the logic as the application of pre-existing concepts; we do not use it to address the formation of professional networks or their status as actors. A professional logic can function across multiple social domains as it inevitably draws on a profession's tradition and historical influence, as well as the academic discipline that trains its members. In this sense the professional logic of an economist, lawyer, or engineer is the aspect of professional strategy that relates to *how* an issue is treated (Suddaby and Viale 2011 and Chapter 1 of this volume). While recognizing that professional logics have different policy preferences, we here posit the term as a resource to be drawn upon by organizations in the argumentative struggle over issue control. We do not assess the strength or validity of logics in question, but rather we analyse the tensions between those logics and the dynamics linking them to the organizational units in the regulatory arena.

The Economists' Professional Logic of Network Neutrality: Price Discrimination and Ramsey Pricing

Regulatory economists' literature on net-neutrality addresses the topic in terms of whether a telco should be allowed to segment its market by using a strategy of price discrimination. In combination with DPI technology, the use of price discrimination allows telcos to escape from being commodity providers of data connections and instead capture revenue from upstream segments of the value chain. The most commonly cited example of this is telcos using DPI to block Skype calls on 'regular' connections, and then sell a 'premium product' internet connection that allows Skype calls.[4] Many telcos were prompted to do this because the Skype application competed with their old business model of charging customers separately for phone calls. Discriminatory pricing by telcos is possible for most internet applications because a users' willingness to pay for a service is generally not proportional to the quantity of data capacity the

---

[4] This was a practice at Vodafone, for example.

application uses. Such discriminatory pricing has long been the norm in the telecoms sector, for example, the price of sending SMS/text data with a mobile phone is many multiples of the price for sending email data over the very same mobile connection (Odlyzko 2009: 5).

Some regulatory economists argue against restrictions on price discrimination by telcos and justify their argument on the basis that free markets maximize allocative efficiency (Cave and Crocioni 2011, Hahn et al. 2010). The justification proceeds as follows. On the one hand, consumers are willing to pay prices representing the relative value they place on goods or services. On the other hand, open competition among producers drives prices down to the marginal cost of production (which includes 'normal' profits). A market unencumbered by regulation finds a competitive equilibrium between consumers and producers such that goods and services are allocated to those who most value them, and are produced by those able to do so at lowest cost.

Regulatory economists arguing against mandated net-neutrality invoke the classic Ramsey pricing model (Sidak 2007). This model has long been used to design tariff structures for network industries in which there is a natural tendency towards monopoly or oligopoly and which are characterized by very large sunk costs. The classic problem faced in such industries is that sunk costs can only be recovered with extremely high prices, unless the firm is allowed to engage in differential pricing. This is because if the firm lowers prices to attract extra users and gain revenue, it simultaneously loses revenue on all the existing customers who were already paying the higher price. In a Ramsey model, price discrimination is thus allowed, but only in such a way that mimics as closely as possible what *would* happen in a competitive market.

When considering the merits of telcos being allowed to use discriminatory pricing strategies in selling internet connections, a further complication arises because price discrimination can be combined with DPI not merely to charge based on content but also to *prioritize* data packets based on their content. Customers who have been segmented onto a 'premium' tariff can thus be offered a prioritized delivery of data packets. Likewise, customers can pay for certain content or applications to be prioritized. Cave and Cracioni (2007: 672) argue that, in this sense, Ramsey pricing is also efficient in engineering terms – it is not simply a case of paying a telco to let you use Skype but rather paying them to make Skype work effectively.

Indeed, as new applications have been developed for the internet, it has become clear that the original practice of giving all data packets equal priority can be wasteful. To give two extreme examples, video transmission requires high-capacity connections because of the volume of data, but it is latency-tolerant since the transmission can be buffered to overcome delayed data packets. Phone calls require the exact opposite since they comprise a relatively small volume of data, but are highly sensitive to delayed data packets.

The Lawyers' Logic: Market Power, Innovation, and Freedom/Piracy

Net-neutrality is often presented as a clash of two corporate cultures. On one side is a telco culture that has grown used to operating in a relatively slow-moving, highly regulated, environment in which negotiations with regulators in Brussels and Washington are a routine activity. On the other side is the more innovative culture of the CAPs which comes from a completely different fast-moving, high-tech entrepreneurial culture whose heartland is Silicon Valley (Sidak 2007: 378, 388). However, there is an alternate framing of net-neutrality in which it is not telcos who are threatened by upstart CAPs but rather the internet itself is threatened as a platform for innovation and growth.

The key question in this regard is: What is it about the internet that has made it such an effective platform for innovation and economic growth over the past two decades? Seeking an answer, Johnathan Zittrain has labelled the internet's key characteristic as *generativity*. This is defined as 'a system's capacity to produce unanticipated change through unfiltered contributions from broad and varied audiences' (Zittrain 2008: 70). According to Zittrain, the generative character of the internet was essential for the ease-of-experimentation and low-entry barriers that enabled start-ups such as Skype, Google, Amazon, Facebook, Salesforce, and so on to emerge and grow. Enthusiastic individuals with technical knowledge were able to make the internet's basic protocols do things that its inventors in the early 1980s had never anticipated (see also Oudshoorn and Pinch 2003). Furthermore, the established firms whose business models were negatively impacted (either directly or indirectly) were unable to stop them, even when those firms owned some of the infrastructure that the upstarts depended upon.

Zittrain links his concept of generativity explicitly to Christensen's model of interaction between *disruptive innovations* and business models, in which cohorts of firms come and go with the generational transitions of technologies (Christensen 1997, 2003). More broadly, the concept can also be understood as a 'knowledge economy' update to Schumpeter's dynamics of creative destruction (Schumpeter 1950). A less remarked-upon antecedent of generativity is the work of Thorstein Veblen (1921) on the transformation of US capitalism at the start of the twentieth century. Through his *business–industry* dichotomy,[5] and his analysis of

---

[5] Or, in different terms, his scarcity–efficiency dichotomy.

how the former *sabotages* the latter in order to survive, Veblen provides a structural model for explaining the evolving power relations between vested interests in different economic sectors. Despite Veblen's key industries being railways, iron, coal, and crop milling, he was nevertheless writing about the *politics of generativity* using an institutional approach that would be more familiar today for legal scholars than for economists.

Besides generativity, legal scholars focus on the democratic aspect of free information. Since the birth of the commercial internet there have been calls for and celebration of the democratic nature of the technology. People and organizations could now connect and share outside the entrenched routes of communication and across vast distances. The design of the internet allowed for this free exchange but, with the rise of piracy and other low-value traffic, profit-seeking stakeholders have begun challenging the model. Piracy and other illicit traffic are sometimes used as an argument for increasing control over what is transmitted, although lawyers have frequently raised concerns about the extent to which this also curtails freedom of information and other legal rights (Cherry 2011).

The Engineer's Logic: Internet Protocol and End-to-End Network Design

In technical terms, the generative characteristic of the internet can be traced to the way its different functions are arranged. In this regard, the internet has until now been built according to what engineers call an 'End-to-End' design: The network's intelligence is located at the ends of its connections where the users and content providers are, while the connections themselves remain as 'dumb' as possible. Engineers refer to today's internet having applications and data at the 'edge', while the 'core' comprises a simple set of protocols and equipment that just send packets of data between end-points (an end-point can be, for example, an individual user's computer or a web server that generates web pages). Because its protocols and equipment are standardized to incorporate as few assumptions as possible about the data they are moving, the internet has proved very flexible, allowing for continual innovation in the applications at the edge without the need to change anything else.

To put some familiar terms on the technology we can unpack the multiple *layers* between the core and the edge of the internet (Kurose and Ross 2009). Each layer has a specific responsibility, and its own set of protocols. The application layer at the 'edge' has protocols with well-known acronyms such as HTTP for transferring web pages, POP/IMAP for email, FTP for

Table 17.1 *The Internet Protocol Stack*

Layer	Example Protocols
Application	HTTP, POP/IMAP, FTP
Transmission	TCP/UDP
Network	IP
Link	Ethernet, Wifi
Physical	PPP, PPPoE

Source: Authors' interpretation based Kurose and Ross 2009: 48–56.

file transfers, and so on. 'Lower' layers have responsibility for other functions that are further from the user. This is commonly called the internet protocol stack:

This layered structure and end-to-end design of the internet have important implications for the power relations between companies owning assets associated with particular layers. Perhaps most importantly, it means that new innovations can be deployed at the application layer without the need for any modification of other layers in the network. For example, when Skype is added as an application to a user's computer, it allows that user to make phone calls without the need for any changes anywhere else in the protocols or physical links that subsequently carry the calls. This is possible because a Skype phone call appears as a standardized stream of data packets which behave no differently from data packets containing parts of a webpage or email.

Crucially, this also means that companies owning the physical links of the internet (i.e. telcos) have been unable to block developments at the applications layer. Before the development of DPI techniques they had similarly been unable to charge users extra for using new applications (or even identify which applications their subscribers were using). This is why we can talk of 'free' phone calls on Skype and 'free' instant messages on MSN, etc. Of course, Skype calls are not free because each user pays for their access to the internet. However, from the point of view of the telcos, the call is free because it does not attract revenue in line with their old business models, which concerned charging per minute and per distance, rather than per kilobyte.

New innovations can be deployed at any layer of the internet, not only the applications layer. For example, it was possible to add Wifi connections and cellular data connections to the internet without any technical adjustments being required elsewhere. In short, technical design of the internet has created a polyarchy in stark contrast to the hierarchies of the closed-proprietary networks[6] that preceded it (Zittrain 2008: 69). The internet offers a level playing field for its users; there is no possibility for strategic network behaviour or for the privileging of certain applications over others (Lemley and Lessig 2001).

The European Commission 2010 Consultation on Network Neutrality

Framed as a telco versus CAP dichotomy, policy on net-neutrality amounts to a political decision over how much revenue each of these sectors deserves to collect from monetizing the internet. In many respects, this boils down to a pro-regulation versus anti-regulation debate with CAPs supporting the former position, and telcos the latter. In the first section of this chapter we demonstrate this empirically.

In the second section we show that there is, however, a second level of the net-neutrality contest. This second level is revealed by examining the content of the arguments put forward by stakeholders. Here we find that there are two additional and distinct dimensions to either side of the contest, and thus there are four 'positions' that can be taken. In the third section we then suggest that a fruitful way of understanding how these four positions gain traction, or fail to gain traction, provided by considering how different professional logics are contained within these positions. In particular, the positions among which there is the strongest debate are those that contain overlapping professional logics.

The EU Consultation as a 'Vote' on Whether to Regulate Network Neutrality

The issue of network neutrality became the subject of political debate in the United States several years before it did so in the European Union. In 2005, the US Federal Communications Commission (FCC) adopted four principles of net-neutrality, which were worded in terms of consumer entitlement to
- Access any lawful internet content of their choice
- Run applications and use services of their choice
- Connect their choice of legal devices that do not harm the network
- Competition among network providers, application and service providers, and content providers.

---

[6] Traditional telephone systems or videotext precursors to the World Wide Web.

In April 2010, Neelie Kroes, then vice president of the European Commission, and incoming Commissioner for the Digital Agenda, explicitly aligned herself with the FCC's principles, adding:

Every player on the value chain should be free to fairly position themselves to offer the best possible service to their customers or end users. Any commercial or traffic management practice that does not follow objective and even-handed criteria, applicable to all comparable services, is potentially discriminatory in character (EC 2010: 5).

This statement, following on from 2009 amendments to the EU Telecoms Framework which required national telecoms regulatory to promote 'the ability of end users to access and distribute information or run applications and services of their choice',[7] led many net-neutrality proponents to anticipate EU legislation mandating some form of net-neutrality.

However, in April 2011 Kroes published a long-awaited report stating that the European Commission's position was that telcos should be allowed to engage in prioritization, and 'determine their own business models and commercial arrangements' (EC 2011: 7). The report argued that this was necessary in order to manage network congestion. It also expressed confidence that media scrutiny and pressure from consumers in Europe's competitive telecoms market would be sufficient to protect an 'open and neutral' internet.

What caused this apparent U-turn in policy direction? In between the Commissioner's April 2010 pro-regulation comments and the Commission's 2011 decision not to regulate, there was a EU public consultation on net-neutrality. This took place in June 2010 with a questionnaire dedicated to 'the open internet and net neutrality in Europe' (EC 2010).

In the remainder of this chapter we analyse the responses to consultation at two levels: professional logics and organizational interest. The results we present are both quantitative and qualitative, but the underlying data are fundamentally qualitative in nature (Bernard and Ryan 2009). Firstly, the opinion on the issue of net-neutrality as framed in the EC questionnaire was distilled from the responses and quantified into three positions: (1) proponents of net-neutrality, (2) opponents of net-neutrality, and (3) responses that are balanced either in terms of weighting both arguments equally or simply by not having a clear opinion on the issue. The responses were then coded twice in order to locate them

---

[7] Article 8(4)(g) of the Framework Directive.

relative to a mean position. Secondly, we identified themes emerging from coding the documents inductively using qualitative data analysis (QDA) software. The themes reveal several interesting cleavages in the net-neutrality debate and illuminate a number of perspectives, which we discuss in the following section.

The responses to the consultation provide a view on the positions and arguments identifiable among the stakeholders in net-neutrality regulation in Europe. Respondents included stakeholders from private companies, interest organizations, and national regulatory agencies. The responses differed in type in several ways. Most were direct answers to the questionnaire while some were essays and short statements. The responses also differed in quality. Some replies engaged in serious and detailed analysis and argued a particular intellectual position in the debate; others repeated well-worn slogans of established positions; some tended to focus on their narrow business interests.

We categorized respondents as
- ISP
- CAP
- 'Activists'
- Business organizations.

The EC classified sixty-eight responses as either 'NGOs' or 'industry organizations', which we found confusing because some 'NGOs' were in fact thinly disguised business organizations, whereas others were radical political organizations such as the Pirate Party. We therefore re-categorized these using the four categories listed above. Our categories of CAP and ISP now include, in addition to profit-seeking firms in these respective sectors, special interest-organizations which were either directly funded by CAPs or ISPs, or lobbying their interests, or both. 'Activists' and 'business organizations' encompass a group of responses which were unaligned with either the CAPs or the ISPs, and are distinguished according to whether or not they represent profit-making entities.

To a large extent the CAP/ISP cleavage is evident from the data. An overwhelming majority of telcos rejected the notion of net-neutrality being a problem that required (European) regulation. Surprisingly, CAPs were more divided on the issue with only half of the respondents claiming there was a net-neutrality problem in the European Union. As is clear from Figure 17.2, the telcos saw no existing threats to net-neutrality and argued against regulation in that spirit. The CAPs, as anticipated, were broadly in favour of net-neutrality regulation.

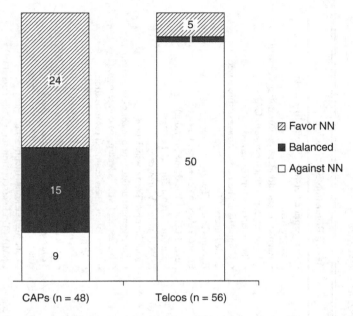

Figure 17.2 CAP and ISP Stakeholders on the Issue of Net-Neutrality as Defined by the EC Questionnaire
Source: based on data from EC Consultation on Net-Neutrality and the Open Internet (2010)

The Content of the EU Consultation: Beyond the CAP–Telco Split

There is a caveat in our claim of a CAP–Telco cleavage. Firstly, some CAPs were *not* in favour of NN regulation. This was true for providers of content with specific latency requirements such as IPTV, but also for a category of CAPs who were vulnerable to piracy and saw peer-to-peer file sharing as an extension of NN. Secondly, a number of large CAPs appeared to be taking advantage of the NN debate by blaming telcos for degrading the internet via non-neutrality, while simultaneously rejecting any suggestion of mandated neutrality in their own applications arena. These observations confirm the CAP–Telco cleavage was an important dimension to the net-neutrality debate. However, they also problematize this cleavage and invite us to apply analysis from an alternative perspective.

By looking at the EC Consultation responses (2010) it was possible to inductively locate the opinions and interests of the stakeholders in the debate. Cleavages between interests emerged on two levels. Firstly, they differed in their overall framing of the term *innovation* as related to either

Table 17.2 *Map of Opinions and Stakeholders on the Innovation–Efficiency Cleavage*

	Favor Regulation/Open Internet	Against Regulation/Free Market
Innovation	• Open internet means low entry barriers • Consumer access • Discrimination by Telcos • High switching-costs • Telcos profit from undercapacity • Lack of competition among Telcos Bonnier (Media company) The Number (Directory service) Skype (Voice over IP provider) Writer's Guild of America, West (Trade association) France Télévisions (National Television Broadcaster)	• Competition between Telcos/ Broadband market competitive • Regulation should focus on promoting competition • Vigorous competition between CAPs • Transparency for consumers • Competition should be infrastructure based Cable Europe (Telco) Eircom Group (Telco) France Télécom (Incumbent Telco) Level 3 (Tier 1 backbone provider) Vodafone (Transnational Telco) ZON (Cable TV provider) Cable Europe (Trade association)
Efficiency	• Management will lead to degraded public internet • Priority internet and Public internet in rivalry • Opaque interconnection agreements • Traffic prioritization discourages investment • Bundling (walled gardens) • Censorship • Vertical Integration TV4 Sweden (Television Network) European Game Developers Federation (Trade association) Netherlands Public Broadcasting (Public Television Broadcaster) Cogent Communications (Tier 1 internet transit provider) International Confederation of Music Publishers (Trade Association)	• Management needed for avoiding congestion • Increasing traffic is leading to congestion • High-latency services need prioritization • All players in value chain should fund investments • Telco business model no longer profitable • Lack of incentive to use network resources efficiently Telia Sonera (Tier 1/IncumbentTelco) Huawei (ICT equipment and solutions provider) Deutsche Telekom (Incumbent Telco) GSMA (Trade association for mobile operators) UK Music (Trade association)

the open-internet or to the free-market. Secondly, they differed in their prediction for the future *efficiency* of the internet.

The differences in the framing of innovation illustrate an overall dis-agreement within the net-neutrality debate. On the one hand, certain respondents pointed to the development of new products and services based on the internet as a 'free' market. Prohibiting the delivery of high-end (i.e. differentiated) internet services dampens innovation in this area. On the other hand, some respondents highlighted how the open internet and the end-to-end principle were the key drivers of the benefits accruing from IP. The open-ended engineering of the internet is what allowed its success and penetration into a range of previously 'offline' sectors. We refer to these arguments as *innovation-based*.

With regard to the scenario for the future efficiency of the internet, the cleavage becomes wider. Some stakeholders argued that increas-ing traffic required internet provision to allow the prioritization busi-ness model. Their rationale was that charging for prioritization will pay for investments in the internet infrastructure and thus avoid a scenario of degradation of the service for all internet users. Another set of stakeholders proposed that prioritization would instead lead to the degradation of the less profitable public internet. Their argument was that offering prioritized services will erode the incentive to invest in the public internet which will become slower and will lack connectivity to certain services. We refer to these arguments as *efficiency-based*.

These are concerns which revitalized the net-neutrality debate as a debate about structural deficiencies in the institutional environment for innovation and efficiency in Europe and also posited the cleavages in a more nuanced light.

Professional Logics and the Net-Neutrality Debate

Based on this insight we extracted the key arguments and located their supporting logics in the academic literature on network neutrality, and network policy more broadly. We develop a typology derived from our inductive coding of cleavages between consultation responses (Figure 4) mapped onto deductive reasoning based on the arguments made by different professions in the academic literature (Table 17.3).

Table 17.4 connects the spectrum of arguments to the underlying professional logics. With each quadrant labelled A-B-C-D, we attribute combinations of concepts to professions as follows: Lawyers' professional logic occupies the left side of the table (quadrants A and C); economists' occupies the right side (quadrants B and D); engineering logic occupies

Table 17.3 *Underlying Arguments of Professional Logics*

	Favor Regulation	Oppose Regulation
Innovation	The *generativity* of an open internet drives innovation. Generativity refers to a technology which has leverage, scope, usability, accessibility, and transferability (Zittrain 2008).	If no market failures are present competition will drive innovation. No regulation needed unless economic discrimination/unfair practice is evidenced. PD (Ramsey pricing) and 2-sided markets can optimize welfare (Hahn et al. 2010).
Efficiency	Network-economics and the lean computing of peer-to-peer technology maintain the efficiency of the internet. Network-economics refers to the positive-feedback effects of an additional peer (Katz and Shapiro 1994).	Paid prioritization and 2SM maintains the efficiency of the internet. Technologies and business models for handling the increasing traffic volume and value generation ensure the efficiency (Faratin et al. 2008, Crocioni 2011).

Table 17.4 *Connecting Professional Logics to EU-Consultation Responses on Net-Neutrality*

	Favor Regulation (LAWYERS)	Oppose Regulation (ECONOMISTS)
Innovation Framing	A. Open internet	B. Free Market
Efficiency Framing (ENGINEERS)	C. Degraded public internet	D. Differentiated services

the bottom half of the table (quadrants C and D), and thus engineers overlap with economists and lawyers.

In order to further investigate the connections between responding organizations on one side and professional logics on the other, we coded the most elaborate responses (sixty-one in total) and mapped them, in considerable detail, to the three professional logics of lawyers, economists, and engineers. This produces a matrix for comparing the use of professional logics by organizations. From this matrix a number of expected and unexpected nuances arise.

Our first finding is that the economists' logic (quadrants B and D in the matrix above) dominated telco responses. Thirty-two per cent of the substantial replies from telcos conveyed an argument with roots in the economic logic. Considering the economists' logic emphasizes non-intervention and freedom to operate, it is unsurprising that telcos employed these types of arguments. These arguments opened a discursive space for the telcos to support the status quo in areas where they already control the marketplace. As infrastructure provider *Everything Everywhere* wrote in its consultation response, 'there is at present nothing to suggest that the market is not functioning effectively and competitively'. Furthermore, these arguments allowed telcos to support price discrimination in areas where they were losing control. Telia Sonera, a Swedish infrastructure owner, explained, '[t]here is a need to incentivise end-users, as well as content and application providers, to be more efficient ... That could be achieved by innovative offerings such as certain services being included or excluded from a particular internet connection offering.'

Our second finding is that CAPs draw very little on the economists' logic, with only 4 per cent of their arguments falling in this rubric. CAPs instead favoured a legal logic emphasizing efficiency (quadrant C in Table 17.4), with 60 per cent of them making arguments using this logic. For example, the European Broadcasting Union feared that 'there is a risk that investments would be diverted from the public internet towards managed services' (2010: 3), with the latter being said to reduce the efficiency of the internet. Only a minority of CAPs (16%) suggested legal intervention on the basis of innovation (quadrant A in Table 17.4). This was unexpected from the perspective of the traditional cleavage in the net-neutrality debate, where CAPs were seen as being principally concerned with the neutrality of the internet. Among the few replies conforming to this, we found the European Game Developers Federation writing, '[t]he success of innovation can be traced back to the original architects of the internet, who intentionally created the internet as an open system which allowed distributed innovation and freedom for entrepreneurs'. In contrast, many CAPs employed the legal-engineering logic (quadrant C in Table 17.4) to express concerns over piracy and, by extension, the neutrality of low-value traffic such as peer-to-peer. Some, such as the International Federation of Film Distribution Associations, dismissed net-neutrality regulation on this basis: 'transmission of audio-visual content illegally made available on the internet will threaten the quality of service'.

Finally, the engineering argument was trumpeted by activist organizations and by business organizations. Fifteen per cent of activists' arguments and 13 per cent of business organizations' arguments emphasized the engineering logic (quadrant C and Ds in the matrix). The Internet Society, an activist group, remarked that 'those who create internet protocols need to develop them in such a manner as to account for the use of the protocols within the greater internet environment'. Interestingly, activist and business organizations were also the most outspoken when it came to voicing arguments supported by the legal logic on innovation (quadrant A). Among the activist groups, 21 per cent of arguments were in this category and for the business groups the share was 25 per cent. The activist group *Internautas* feared that without regulation to support innovation it 'will inevitably lead to an internet like a walled garden, where each ISP [telco] will boost their own services' at the expense of competing, innovative services.

In sum, analysing the net-neutrality debate in terms of professional logics reveals that regulatory innovation concerns were mostly represented by rogue game developers or outsiders in the form of lobbying and interest organizations that had no ties to the for-profit firms in the sector.

Conclusion

In this chapter we have introduced net-neutrality as a crucial aspect of internet regulation and analysed it from the perspective of the logics of three professions. Net-neutrality concerns the profitability and distribution of gains in the internet economy. We presented the professional logics, and the arguments they map onto, in this regulatory arena. Our empirical investigation of the net-neutrality debate, based on the biggest EC consultation to date in this field, reveals that the traditional CAPs–telco cleavage indeed is informative as a lens, but we also found that additional nuances to this cleavage were shaping the outcome of policy. We argue that understanding issue control in this policy arena requires a mapping of the (competing) professional logics and careful attention, particularly to 'positions' where these logics overlap.

While net-neutrality was the initial aim of EU regulation in this arena, the apparent U-turn that followed in 2011 was, we argue, a reflection of the fact that few influential stakeholders were willing to stand up for net-neutrality as a case where legal-based support for innovation was required. Only non-profit organizations, of both business and activist types, were vocal about innovation as a legal problem or about engineering efficiency as a concern in itself.

In contrast, the CAPs were surprisingly unwilling to expend efforts on innovation-based arguments and instead, inasmuch as they deployed legal arguments at all, they did so in regard to issues of anti-piracy and market structure. Likewise, telcos primarily applied the economists' logic to try and retain issue control in areas where they were losing influence.

The case of NN illustrates how issue control can be attained by organized interests when employing professional logics as resources to back their argument. In the case of NN we have not seen a unified stance from each profession, but rather the economists, the lawyers, and the engineers have been hired as spokespersons for particular organizations.

The chapter has, with the two-level approach to organizations and professions, demonstrated that the NN debate not only revolved around a telco–CAP split. The arguments of economists and engineers were used to support incumbents' interests while the regulatory expertise on innovation remained the domain of outsiders and activists, leaving innovators weakened against incumbents.

Looking at the NN debate through the lens of the dynamic between professions and organizations, we propose that professional logics were employed successfully as resources in the struggle for issue control. Policy-wise this raises questions about the quality of public consultations in terms of giving sufficient voice to the disruptive innovators, who are supposed to be the lifeblood of the 'knowledge economy'.

18 Issue Professionals and Transnational Organizing

Lasse Folke Henriksen and Leonard Seabrooke

This volume identifies why professional strategies matter for institutional change in transnational governance. We offer some key concepts on how to think about why this is important. In the Introduction we set out the first conceptual contribution of this Volume, which serves as the analytic device that asks authors to consider institutional change via two-level professional and organizational networks, where organizations and professionals wrest for issue control. The second important conceptual invention is to argue that issue control is, in itself, important. Issues are thematically linked social facts that are subject to particular treatments. The delineation of what is included within an issue, and what is excluded, is a consequence of professional competition and claims by organizations to particular mandates. Issue control is to have predominance in how issues are treated and how that treatment is changing. This leads to our third key conceptual contribution – the "issue professional." We suggest that a world of professions holding on tightly to their formal training and professional associations is less important for transnational governance. Transnationality permits more freedom of movement for professionals to develop strategies in their attempts at issue control, and to partially—not completely—decouple from domestic professional associations and institutions. Professionals tied to powerful states may use their embeddedness in domestic institutions as a means to leverage their power in the transnational realm (Dezalay and Garth 2016). We suggest that in the transnational realm the one identified as knowing best does not necessarily follow established professional hierarchies. Competition and cooperation center on competing conceptions of how to treat issues that are derived not only from formal training but also from experience and from the deployment of skills on particular issues. In short, this volume posits that issue professionals are our actors, issue control is what they want, and a two-level professional-organizational network is their context of action.

This book explores a range of methods to identify professional networks in transnational governance. Our contributors use network analysis, sequence analysis, content analysis, semi-structured interviews, surveys, and ethnographic work to assess how professionals and organizations operate in the context of action – that is, two-level networks. There is much to be done to further these methods, especially in fostering greater cross-fertilization across traditions and disciplines.

This concluding chapter is divided into two sections. The first is to reflect on the diverse range of professional-organizational dynamics presented in the previous chapters, which cover a wide range of cases across different issue areas and a range of organizational types. Below we identify trajectories of change that can be harvested from the case contributions in this book. These trajectories direct us back to thinking through our key conceptual interventions on actors, control, and context. The second section discusses methodological innovations in this volume. We reflect on the methods used in this volume, as well as what lies ahead for future research. Our view is that as knowledge in the social sciences is not automatically cumulative, it is important to continue to ignite these conversations rather than assume that particular methods should be dominant (Bendix 1984; Abbott 2001; Shapiro 2005).

Professional Strategies and Trajectories of Issue Control

Professional strategies vary across the chapters, in how centralized and distributed they are, with some professional strategies aligning well with organizational strategies, while in other cases professionals actively work around organizations in their attempts at issue control, or view organizations as arenas for their activities. We hasten to add that organizational opportunities are determined by organizational strategies to dominate an issue.

Figure 18.1 depicts abstract conceptions of trajectories of issue control. These are drawn from the various contributions to this volume. The illustrations are abstract, depicting organizations as black circles and professionals as white circles, with the process of change indicated by the directed arrows.

The first identified trajectory of issue control is *decoupling*. Here the process starts from interaction between a known organization and an established professional group. This professional group then fractures and decouples, and then seeks to influence an organization that is more responsive to its demands for issue control. We have two examples from the volume of decoupling. The first can be seen in Dezalay and Madsen's chapter (Chapter 2). Reading from left to right, a well-known and established legal profession is embedded with the state (the initial organization here), as the classic literature would suggest (Saks 2015). The transformation of the profession occurs as cosmopolitan law becomes a more tempting area of work for some. In playing their "double game" they partially decouple from

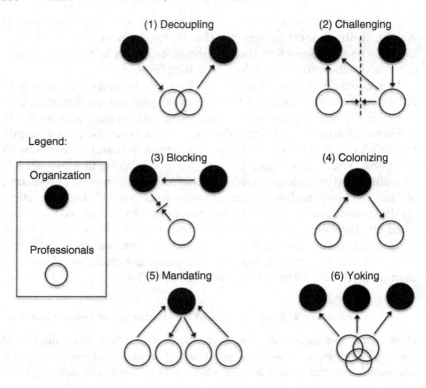

Figure 18.1 Trajectories of Issue Control

a nationally based legal profession and from the state to become a professional group informing European human rights law and other areas of international law, such as trade and arbitration. This professional group then influences how international organizations and international courts operate (the second organization), including the European Court of Justice, the World Trade Organization (WTO), and others. A second case can be found in Thistlethwaite's investigation of environmental and social disclosure in accounting (Chapter 7). From left to right we have accounting firms as organizations and the accountancy profession as an established group. Within this group are professionals who decouple from "purist" accountancy to foster the use of the environmental and social reporting standards. To do so they engage in "epistemic arbitrage," playing off differences in knowledge between accountancy firms and NGOs (Seabrooke 2014a). They then use this strategy to directly inform how NGOs treat environmental and social reporting issues.

Faulconbridge and Muzio provide a different example of decoupling in accountancy in their discussion of global professional service firms (GPSFs). Faulconbridge and Muzio outline how seemingly rigid national professions, such as historic pacts between states (the first organization) and the accounting and auditing associations (the first professional group), fractured as professionals sought to become transnational market seekers (in Chapter 14). As a consequence the creation of GPSFs provides a new form of organization that places stress on professional value as organizational competence rather than national-based occupational training, and which actively seeks to reshape professional identity construction at the transnational level.

Challenging is our second trajectory of change. Here a parallel professional group and organization form to push and criticize established issue treatment. The parallel professional group is not decoupled in the sense of creating a new dimension of professional work. The friction between professionals in *challenging* is more about normative tensions and what is deemed appropriate knowledge for issue treatment. It is also about carving out organizational alliances that provide professionals with resources and a platform for critique. We have three cases of *challenging* in the volume. The first is Eagleton-Pierce's chapter on "critical technicians" on international trade policy and transnational standards (Chapter 8). Eagleton-Pierce details how a parallel system exists that engages the WTO (the first organization) and its associated experts (the first professional group). With support from Oxfam (the second organization) a group of critical technicians (the second professional group) was formed to actively contest trade experts and to inform the WTO on issue treatment. In contrast to decoupling, this process of calibrating is about the political mobilization of professional tools to alter a normative agenda. The second example is from Baker's study of macroprudential "cognoscenti." Here the financial crisis ushers in serious questioning of the microprudential basis for financial regulation, which exacerbated the crisis by freezing financial systems when all banks behaved the same way in a manner that was individually rational but systemically disastrous (see Chapter 10). The microprudential consensus was encouraged by the Federal Reserve, the G30, and others (the first organization in the figure) and established issue professionals (the first professional group) in financial regulation (Tsingou 2015; Seabrooke and Tsingou 2014). During the crisis a range of macroprudential professionals emerged to disrupt issue control (the second professional group). Many of them were tied to the Bank for International Settlements (the second organization) that had previously found it difficult to find voice on this issue and was also deeply implicated in the microprudential consensus. Baker explains how the

intensity of the challenge was heightened as the macroprudential cognoscenti acquired more esteem among their professional peers, which helped
them to increase their influence on issue treatment in the post-crisis
period. Also on financial issues, Wigan and Baden's chapter provides
a different case of challenging, where those confronting are expert-
activists (Chapter 9). In this case an established relationship between
the International Accounting Standards Board (the IASB, the first organization) and professionals involved in financial reporting, such as
accountants (the first professional group), is challenged by expert-
activists associated with the Tax Justice Network (the second organization). These professionals challenge the IASB on how multinational firms
working with extractive industries report their taxable income. This effort
directly informs the creation of the Extractive Industries Transparency
Initiative and provides a fundamental pillar of global tax reform.

Our third trajectory of change is *blocking*. Sending's chapter on humanitarian professionals provides a clear case of this dynamic (Chapter 5).
In his chapter Sending details how an international organization (the first
organization) is under pressure from donor states (the second organization) on humanitarian issues, especially for professional work in the field
to be standardized to make it more efficient and accountable to them.
The international organization then seeks to place pressure on the issue
professionals (the professional group of humanitarian workers) who resist
and block change by appealing to a different standard of professional
behavior. For these humanitarian workers "bearing witness" is more
important than top-down efficiency measures. Cohesion within the professional group allows them to block change.

Colonizing is our fourth trajectory. This can be found in Boussebaa's
chapter on the role of knowledge management systems and their use by
Global Management Consulting Firms (GMCFs) (Chapter 15).
Boussebaa describes how Western professionals (the first professional
group) work through GMCFs (the organization in the Figure 18.1) in
a unidirectional manner that imposes defined forms of issue treatment.
These are replicated and enforced through knowledge management systems and the cultivation of internal professional hierarchies.

Our fifth and sixth trajectories cover a range of cases in the volume and
speak to general phenomena. Fifth is *mandating*, where professional
groups (on the far left and far right in the figure) work to impose particular
forms of issue treatment on other professionals (the center professional
groups) via organizations. Examples of mandating from this volume can
be found in a number of chapters. Momani, for example, discusses how
management consultant professionals enter public organizations to
advise policymakers on best practices (Chapter 16). The styles and

language they use to do so have a comical edge to them, but they are nevertheless powerful and tell us a great deal about the spread of this way of organizing as a source of professionalism. Paterson et al. provide a case of mandating in their study of carbon markets (Chapter 12). In the early phase of carbon market establishment policy analysts played an important role as brokers while the general population contained more economists and lawyers (the professional groups on the far left and far right). They establish the terms for carbon markets, which vary according to regions and organizations (the organization in our abstraction). In a later phase the organizations claim the mandate for how carbon markets should operate. They delegate much of the authority to the private sector for evaluation and certification. The shift in professionals doing the work changes to operations via policy analysts and policy directors, as well as lobbyists (the center professionals). The latter phase also includes the professionalization of carbon markets through management training and education. Wendy Wong, Ron Levi, and Julia Deutsch provide a different case of mandating that talks to the expansive literature on transnational advocacy networks (Chapter 6). In their story legal and banking professionals (those on the far left and far right in the figure) seek to minimize Edsel Ford's tax liabilities through the establishment of a philanthropic organization and act as a platform for "philanthrocrats." They detail how the Ford Foundation's (the organization) claim to a mandate on human rights leads to funding programs that track American foreign policy interests. The selection of issues to treat also strongly informs professionalization within the NGO sector (the center professionals).

Our final trajectory is *yoking*. Yoking is when a new professional group is created from boundary interactions between different established groups. Yoking can occur when established professional boundaries are delegitimized or when new boundaries are accentuated (Abbott 2001: 272–73; Eyal 2011). Nilsson's chapter traces an emergent group of professionals, "access professionals," amalgamating professional skills from law, public health, and economics (the lower professional groups) and drawing on experience from a range of different organizations (Chapter 11). This group has been instrumental in pushing the issue of access to medicine in developing countries with the WTO, WHO, and WIPO (the top organizations) and did so, among other things, by crafting a licensing agency, the Medicines Patent Pool, to counter political resistance from competing professions and organizations. The Karlsrud and Mühlen-Schulte chapter similarly identifies a group of professionals within the UN system of humanitarian affairs (Chapter 13), so-called "mapsters," who brought in skills from IT and "big data" professionals (the lower professional groups) to advance a new mapping technology to identify humanitarian crises. Forming a cohesive network around the Standby Action Taskforce they challenged established professional boundaries of humanitarian work and succeeded in placing themselves between various UN agencies (the top organizations), changing how the issue of humanitarian crisis is identified and treated.

We suggest that decoupling, challenging, blocking, colonizing, mandating, and yoking are trajectories of change that not only appear in this volume but are more generalizable. All of these strategies speak to the two-level professional-organizational network presented in the Introduction. This conceptual device permits us to study relationships between professionals and organizations while isolating characteristics of both.

Matching Professional and Organizational Characteristics

An important claim in this volume is that professional characteristics matter for how networks are composed and articulated, and that these networks shape transnational governance. The various contributions to this volume discuss how often particular issue professionals are able to get action. Often, mixed career experience is important, permitting professional opportunities for "epistemic arbitrage" (Seabrooke 2014a) and to be recognized as those likely to have "good ideas" (Burt 2004). The chapters by Karlsrud and Mühlen-Schulte, Nilsson, and Thistlethwaite all contain such characteristics. Sometimes professionals create an organization to assist ulterior motives, as Wong, Levi, and Deutsch discuss in their case on the establishment of the Ford Foundation. Professionals also deliberately play off past experiences as a tactic to defend themselves against external pressures (as Sending demonstrates in his chapter) or to go on the offensive in legitimating their claims to issue control (as clearly seen in how Wigan and Baden's expert-activists operate, as well as in Eagleton-Pierce's "critical technicians"). Engaging in "identity switching" provides professionals with different repertoires of action from varied professional networks (Padgett and Ansell 1992; White 2008; Seabrooke 2014b). Having an ability to wear different hats, so to speak, allows issue professionals to weaken ties to well-established professional groups and to push their own views on issue control, as can be seen in cases where professionals break from or challenge existing groups. Baker's work on the macroprudential cognoscenti is one such example of professionals fighting their own. The chapters by Dezalay and Madsen and Faulconbridge and Muzio provide cases where professionals become more transnational and affirm their decoupling through identity construction and maintenance, a well-known trait of transnational communities (Djelic and Quack 2010).

And here we have an interesting aspect: the link between transnationality and assumed professional characteristics. Our contributions challenge the firmly established notion that the professionals operate at the behest of national professional associations and states. The long history of scholarship on the sociology of professions informs us that professions fight for jurisdictional control over how issues are treated, and who is permitted to treat them, which is supported by the state (Abbott 1988). This literature also tells us that professionalism provides a third logic compared to that of bureaucracy or the market (Freidson 2001). Our contributors suggest that when it comes to transnational governance we can relax both of these assumptions. Most of the attempts at issue control described in the volume do not rely on national professional associations, and indeed the examples of decoupling rely on professionals actively breaking away from them. Professional associations are also not a requirement for challenging, blocking, colonizing, or yoking. They may be involved in mandating where organizations seek to control professionals via associations, but the cases provided in this volume do not support that view.

A further assumption that needs to be relaxed is that the denomination of organizational types actually tells us something about behavior. We can assume that international organizations seek to fulfil the mandates given to them by states (Koremenos et al. 2001; Lall 2017), that NGOs operate through passionate transnational entrepreneurs and civil society networks (Keck and Sikkink 1998), and that firms aim to achieve profit and control (Fligstein 1990). The chapters in this volume show that matters are more complicated. All of these organizations are involved in processes of professionalization that are changing their work practices (Hopgood 2006; Barnett 2011). Organizational pressures may be encouraging a transnational way of organizing, where professionalism is conceived as a way of organizing rather than formally occupational training (Faulconbridge and Muzio 2008).

If there is a general trend toward transnational organizing, then we need theoretical tools to disaggregate what may appear to be an isomorphic process (Henriksen and Seabrooke 2016). We suggest that our two-level network is a useful conceptual device here. It helps us to isolate professional characteristics, as discussed above. It also assists us in specifying why organizational types should not necessarily follow through to particular forms of behavior, because the organizational network is responding to changes in the professional network, and vice versa. We suggest that organizational forms and logics can be differentiated by five characteristics that become increasingly important as competition within professional networks intensifies:

1. *Scope* – the scope of their mandate
2. *Autonomy* – the level of autonomy they have from their principals
3. *Resources* – how they acquire resources to fund their activities
4. *Staffing* – the openness of hiring of professionals
5. *Knowledge Centralization* – the degree of knowledge centralization within the organization on the issue they seek to control.

Scope, autonomy, resources, staffing, and knowledge centralization differ strongly within the conventional categories of IOs, NGOs, and firms. Common assumptions about interest formation as a linear process originating from organizational form have to be relaxed as a result. This volume suggests that reflecting on how professionals use networks to navigate organizational logics is much more a reflection of these characteristics rather than the formal designation of the organization, be it an IO, NGO, or firm. If patterns of professional competition lead to a widening of the overall scope of an issue, organizations must respond to such change.

Thinking through these organizational characteristics and the professional strategies and trajectories identified above can yield interesting findings about how institutions change and inform transnational governance. For example, Sending's chapter shows that UNHCR and OCHA do not have strong knowledge centralization on humanitarian issues and that staffing treatment (professionalization) is challenged. Here the call to "bearing witness" is a shared professional norm among humanitarian workers doing work for international organizations and also NGOs to block downward attempts at quantitative managerialism. It also affects what the organizations involved view as the scope of their mandate and how they relate to their principals. Our point here is that artificially separating the organizational types as IOs and NGOs that have assumed characteristics hinders our understanding of the case dynamics. Or to take another case, Thistlethwaite's chapter is a clear demonstration of how organizations blend assumed types to push forward their attempts at issue control. Thistlethwaite's discussion of accounting-led private governance notes how professionals used "epistemic arbitrage" to exploit differences between knowledge and staffing between firms and NGOs to push forward social, environmental, and financial reporting standards. The absence of knowledge centralization within organizational types permitted this arbitrage. Through initiatives such as the multistakeholder International Integrated Reporting Committee, the mandated issue treatment changes for NGOs and firms alike. In principle, the firms here should have a great deal of autonomy, in part because their resources are generated from the market rather than on a subscription basis. But Thistlethwaite finds that firms are encouraged to comply because they follow a logic of enhancing issue control rather than the logic of simply seeking profit (returning us to Fligstein 1990).

Our general point here is that matching professional and organizational characteristics permits us to disaggregate assumed organizational traits into smaller components that more feasibly engage with professionals who create action. Rather than reifying and idealizing organizational types as fixed properties, we argue that organizational characteristics provide opportunity structures that can be exploited by professionals.

Decomposing organizational traits is important for studies of issue control precisely because organizations and professionals treat different issues in different ways. Take, for example, an international organization known for its supposed military-like command structure, the International Monetary Fund (IMF). The IMF's treatment of capital controls as an issue is well known in the literature, with a range of scholars informing us about how IMF staff are hired and trained, how they attempted to centralize knowledge on the issue, and how they conform their mandates to please their principals on this politically sensitive issue (Chwieroth 2010; Nelson 2017). The same organization differs on the issue of how to conduct bilateral financial surveillance, where a lack of knowledge centralization leads to the hiring of external experts (which disturbed staffing), and where work has been criticized for not following its mandate (Seabrooke and Nilsson 2015). The IMF on the spread of Value-Added Taxation provides another contrast, whereby the scripts for policy reform were generated in-house and then diffused externally without much fuss (Kentikelenis and Seabrooke 2017). The general point is that organizations can behave very differently on issues, and that this variation is largely explained by how the issue is treated by the professional-organizational network.

The Future Research Agenda

Our general advice to students of transnational governance is to be wary about assuming the location and form of organizational action when investigating who or what controls issues. Our analytical move has links to problematizations of organizational nominalism that have been voiced as part of the "relational turn" in sociology (Emirbayer 1997). The methodological toolbox we have put forward helps us address the analytical challenge of locating at one and the same time organizational and professional action. Social network analysis allows us to trace the structure of social ties among actors involved in changing or maintaining

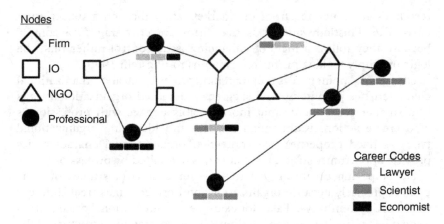

Figure 18.2 Transnational Governance as Hybrid Network

issue control and sequence analysis helps us to identify the skills and experience of professionals involved in transnational governance. While these methods clearly have a potential for mapping the microfoundations of professional and organizational power, including the formation of niches in professional communities (Seabrooke and Young 2017), this requires us to refine our strategies if we are not to simply reproduce classical organizational categories. For sequence analysis this forces us to develop coding techniques to not reduce work states to organizational domains but instead quantify careers as transitions in work roles or as linked to particular tasks.

The future research agenda can build upon the frames and methods discussed in Part I of this volume. Often these approaches talk across each other. One way is through the combination of methods to trace professional and organizational networks. We presented a demonstration of this in Chapter 4, but for those who skipped, or who are keen for more, Figure 18.2 provides an abstract example of a simple hybrid network on a transnational governance issue that applies a mixed methods approach by combining network analysis with sequence analysis.

Let's say that the object of study in Figure 18.2 is a transnational hybrid network to govern standards on household chemicals. The legend in the top left of the figure provides the symbols for the nodes in the network, showing different organizational types (IOs, NGOs, firms) and professionals.

One can see from Figure 18.2 that some organizations are connected to each other and that professionals serve an important role in connecting some organizations that would otherwise not be connected. The professional in the center of the figure is the most important in having significant ties to a firm, an NGO, and an IO, while these three organizations are not otherwise connected. Other brokers can be seen at the top of the figure between a firm and an IO and, separately, between a firm and an NGO. Still, the broker in the middle is most important in controlling flows of knowledge within this network. The legend at the bottom right of the figure provides shades for career codes according to roles during a career as a lawyer, scientist, or economist. There are only three stages here for simplicity and could be more refined in specifying different work roles and types of career experience rather than nominated by formal training (for an example see Henriksen and Seabrooke 2016). From our abstract example it can be seen that our central broker has a mixed career history and was a scientist, then a lawyer, then an economist. The two brokers at the top also have mixed careers, with a lawyer who became an economist, and a scientist who became a lawyer. They provide a contrast to those with steady careers as economists (on the left) or scientists (on the right) who are networked within their own professional community and organizational types, but not across types. From this hypothetical example we can speculate on who controls knowledge in this network and the drivers of transnational standard setting. We can note that mixed career histories may be important for "intrepid brokers" in having resources to make connections to different types of organizations on an issue (Burt 2010), as well as assessing how organizational characteristics matter in assisting or inhibiting such entrepreneurship (such as those listed in the previous section).

We may also wonder about the professional at the bottom of the figure who has ties to other professionals but no formal ties to an organization, and if this person has power in this network. To find this out we would have to delve further using different methods, such as ethnographic interviews (see Harrington, Chapter 3). We may also want to differentiate career roles and network locations from actual positions toward home chemical use, such as cost and efficiency questions, the legality of patents and use, and the risks and dangers of use on the inhabitants. This would require determining what is at stake for the different professionals and experts involved, as investigated using Bourdieusian "field" methods (Dezalay and Madsen, Chapter 2). A combination of ethnographic research and field methods could also establish positions on a subject as well as means of influence within the "advice networks" formed by those involved (Lazega 2001). Using a mix of methods we can distinguish not only professional and organizational characteristics but also different types of activities. As discussed in this volume it is important to separate work content, how issue treatment is practiced, from formal titles or assuming professional behavior based on organizational type.

The above methods could be used to further clarify the distinction between what we call "issue professionals" and "issue entrepreneurs" and how they operate in two-level networks (Carpenter 2011; Seabrooke and Tsingou 2014: 402). We already have a range of clues to draw upon. Consider the composition and mandates of "Expert Committees" or "Taskforces." Organizations commonly use expert committees to provide external validation for internal reform. For example, the IMF was formally advised by the amusingly named "Committee of Eminent Persons" – led by the late Andrew Crockett, former director general of the Bank for International Settlements and president of JPMorgan Chase International – to reform its fundamental business model (Seabrooke and Nilsson 2015: 243). Such committees explicitly rely on what we call "issue professionals" – people with long-term interest in maintaining control over an issue and who strategize to maintain their networks in doing so, relying on career prestige and professional recognition as sources of legitimacy and authority.

Independent taskforces are more likely to be comprised of issue entrepreneurs who wish to push forward a cause independent of organizational mandates, and where experience can be drawn upon as a source of authority (Eyal 2013; Seabrooke and Tsingou 2015). The issue entrepreneur versus issue professional distinction also helps us distinguish how experts engage power. While the stress in the literature has been on how professionals, notably economists, are used by politicians (Lindvall 2009; Hirschman and Berman 2014), the influence of experts is not only a function of how they are politically manipulated but also what they are willing to do. Using the methods outlined above we can distinguish different types of professionals in transnational governance, including whether they rely on occupational or organizational professional competencies (Faulconbridge and Muzio 2008; Postma et al. 2015). We can further distinguish organizational behavior that provides professionals with mandates and how professionals use different forms of organizing.

Our volume explores a range of cases where professionals interact with organizations over transnational governance issues. There is a diverse selection to choose from, including cases on environmental governance, climate change, health, humanitarian work, human rights, financial reform, internet regulation, taxation, professional service firms, and the new role of consultants. This mix is only a sample of what could be studied with the analytical and methodological tools offered in this volume. We can think through other cases where our professional-organizational nexus could be applied and where professional networks play an important yet understudied role. Among these are global corporate governance and elite networks (Apeldoorn van and de Graaff 2015), the politics of data creation for development policy (Jerven 2013), the rise of private security contractors (Abrahamsen and Williams 2010), and the privatization of migration management (Gammeltoft-Hansen and Sørensen 2013). All of these studies, excellent in their own right, could be recast through the lens of professional networks competing for issue control, as well as two-level professional-organizational networks. In short, the range of cases to be explored is far from exhausted and there is much work to be done.

Finally, this volume provides a unique take on transnational governance that blends conceptual and methodological insights from International Relations, International Political Economy, Organizational Sociology, Economic Sociology, Management Studies, and social sciences more broadly. We have demonstrated how interdisciplinary research calls us to think about how research problems can be addressed in a variety of ways, and how our assumptions about professions, organizations, and professional behavior should be questioned to delve deeper into who is doing the work of transnational governance.

References

Abbott, A. (1988) *The System of Professions: An Essay on the Division of Expert Labor* (Chicago: University of Chicago Press).

Abbott, A. (1991) "The Future of Professions: Occupation and Expertise in the Age of Organization," in P. S. Tolbert and S. R. Barley (eds.) *Research in the Sociology of Organizations* (Greenwich, CT: JAI Press), 17–42.

Abbott, A. (2001) *Time Matters* (Chicago: University of Chicago Press).

Abbott, A. (2005) "Linked Ecologies: States and Universities as Environments for Professions," *Sociological Theory* 23, 245–274.

Abbott, A. and A. Hrycak (1990) "Measuring Resemblance in Sequence Data: An Optimal Matching Analysis of Musicians' Careers," *American Journal of Sociology* 96(1), 144–185.

Abbott, A. and A. Tsay (2000) "Sequence Analysis and Optimal Matching Methods in Sociology," *Sociological Methods and Research* 29(1), 3–33.

Abbott, K. W. (2012) "Engaging the Public and the Private in Global Sustainability Governance," *International Affairs* 88(3), 543–564.

Abbott, K. W. and D. Snidal (2009a) "Strengthening International Regulation through Transnational New Governance: Overcoming the Orchestration Deficit," *Vanderbilt Journal of Transnational Law* 42(2), 501–578.

Abbott, K. W. and D. Snidal (2009b) "The Governance Triangle: Regulatory Standards Institutions and the Shadow of the State," in W. Mattli and N. Woods (eds.) *The Politics of Global Regulation* (Princeton, NJ: Princeton University Press), 44–88.

Abbott, K. W. and D. Snidal (2010) "International Regulation without International Government: Improving IO Performance through Orchestration," *Review of International Organizations* 5(3), 315–344.

Abbott, K. W., P. Genschel, D. Snidal, and B. Zangl (eds.) (2015) *International Organizations as Orchestrators* (Cambridge: Cambridge University Press).

Abbott, K. W., J. F. Green, and R. O. Keohane (2016) "Organizational Ecology and Institutional Change in Global Governance," *International Organization* 70(2), 247–277.

Abel, R. L. (1988) *The Legal Profession in England and Wales* (Oxford: Basil Blackwell).

Abrahamsen, R. and M. Williams (2010) *Security Beyond the State: Private Security in International Politics* (Cambridge: Cambridge University Press).

ACCA (2013) *The Draft Framework for Integrated Reporting* (London: Association of Chartered Certified Accountants), Available at: www.theiirc.org/wp-content/uploads/2013/08/184_ACCA.pdf.

Accenture (2012) *Delivering Public Service for the Future: Navigating the Shifts.* Available at: www.accenture.com/SiteCollectionDocuments/PDF/Accenture-Delivering-Public-Service-for-the-Future_112712.pdf, accessed 15 July 2014.

AccountAbility (2013) "Comments to Draft International IR Framework." Available at: www.theiirc.org/wp-content/uploads/2013/08/197_AccountAbility.pdf, accessed 15 July 2014.

Adler, E. and V. Pouliot (eds.) (2011) *International Practices* (Cambridge: Cambridge University Press).

Aharoni, Y. (1996) "The Organization of Global Service MNEs," *International Studies of Management and Organization* 26(2), 6–23.

Aharoni, Y. (2000) "The Role of Reputation in Global Professional Business Services," in *Globalization of Services: Some Implications for Theory and Practice*, 125–141.

Aikman, D., A. G. Haldane, and B. D. Nelson (2013) "Operationalising a Macroprudential Regime: Goals, Tools and Open Issues," *Estabilidad Financiera (Banco De España)*, 24. Available at: www.bde.es/f/webbde/GAP/Secciones/Publicaciones/InformesBoletinesRevistas/RevistaEstabilidadFinanciera/13/Mayo/Fic/ref2013241.pdf.

Aikman, D. H. and B. Nelson (2011) "Curbing the Credit Cycle," *Vox.* Available at: http://voxeu.org/index.php?q=node/6231, accessed 12 May 2011.

Ambos, T. C. and B. B. Schlegelmilch (2009) "Managing Knowledge in International Consulting Firms," *Journal of Knowledge Management* 13(6), 491–508.

Amin, S. (1976) *L'impérialisme et le développement inégal* (Paris: Les Éditions de Minuit).

Anderson, B. (1991) *Imagined Communities: Reflections on the Origins and Spread of Nationalism* (London: Verso).

Anderson-Gough, F., C. Grey, and K. Robson (1998) *Making Up Accountants: The Professional and Organizational Socialization of Trainee Chartered Accountants* (Aldershot: Ashgate/ICAEW).

Andonova, L. B., M. M. Betsill, and H. Bulkeley (2009) "Transnational Climate Governance," *Global Environmental Politics* 9(2), 52–73.

Andrew, J. and C. Cortese (2013) "Free Market Environmentalism and the Neoliberal Project: The Case of the Climate Disclosure Standards Board," *Critical Perspectives on Accounting* 24, 397–409.

Apeldoorn van, B. and N. de Graaff (2015) *American Grand Strategy and Corporate Elite Networks* (London: Routledge).

Arendt, H. (1953) "Understanding and Politics," *Partisan Review* 20(4), 377–392.

Arendt, H. (1958) *The Human Condition* (Chicago: University of Chicago).

Argyris, C. (2000) "The Relevance of Actionable Knowledge for Breaking the Code," in M. Beer and N. Nohria (eds.) *Breaking the Code of Change* (Boston, MA: Harvard Business School).

Armbrüster, T. (2004) "Rationality and Its Symbols: Signaling Effects and Subjectification in Management Consulting," *Journal of Management Studies* 41(8), 1247–1269.

Arnold, P. (2005) "Disciplining Domestic Regulation: The World Trade Organization and the Market for Professional Services," *Accounting, Organizations and Society* 30, 299–330.

Atkinson, P. and D. Silverman (1997) "Kundera's Immortality: The Information Society and the Invention of the Self," *Qualitative Inquiry* 3, 304–325.

Avant, D. D., M. Finnemore, and S. Sell (eds.) (2010) *Who Governs the Globe?* (Cambridge: Cambridge University Press).

Bach, J. and D. Stark (2002) "Innovative Ambiguities: NGOs' Use of Interactive Technology in Eastern Europe," *Studies in Comparative International Development*, 37(2), 3–23.

Backlund, J. and A. Werr (2004) "The Construction of Global Management Consulting – A Study of Consultancies' Web Presentations," in A. F. Buono (ed.) *Creative Consulting: Innovative Perspectives on Management Consulting* (Greenwich, CT: Information Age Publishing).

Bagchi-Sen, S. and J. Sen (1997) "The Current State of Knowledge in International Business in Producer Services," *Environment and Planning A* 29, 1153–1174.

Baker, A. (2013a) "The New Political Economy of the Macroprudential Ideational Shift," *New Political Economy* 18(1), 112–139.

Baker, A. (2013b) "The Gradual Transformation? The Incremental Dynamics of Macroprudential Regulation," *Regulation & Governance* 7(4), 417–434.

Baker, A. (2015) "Varieties of Economic Crisis, Varieties of Ideational Change: How and Why Financial Regulation and Macroeconomic Policy Differ?" *New Political Economy* 20(3), 342–366.

Baker, A. and W. Widmaier (2014) "The Institutionalist Roots of Macroprudential Ideas: Veblen and Galbraith on Regulation, Policy Success and Overconfidence," *New Political Economy* 19(4), 487–506.

Baker, A. and D. Wigan (2017) "Narrating, Constructing and Contesting City of London Power: NGOs and the Emergence of Noisier Post-Crash Financial Politics," *Economy and Society*, forthcoming.

Balasubramanyam, V. N. and D. Greenaway (eds.) (1996) *Trade and Development: Essays in Honour of Jagdish Bhagwati* (Houndsmills: Palgrave Macmillan).

Balizil, B. and M. Schiessl (2009) "The Man Nobody Wanted to Hear: Global Banking Economist Warned of Coming Crisis," *Spiegel Online*. 07/08/13, Available at: www.spiegel.de/international/business/0,1518,635051,00.html.

Baltzell, E. D. (1964) *The Protestant Establishment: Aristocracy and Caste in America* (New Haven, CT: Yale University Press).

Ban, C. (2016) *Ruling Ideas: How Global Neoliberalism goes Local* (Oxford: Oxford University Press).

Ban, C., L. Seabrooke, and S. Freitas (2016) "Grey Matter in Shadow Banking: International Organizations and Expert Strategies in Global Financial Governance," *Review of International Political Economy* 23(6), 1000–1033.

Bank of England (2011) "Instruments of Macroprudential Policy: A Discussion Paper."

Barnett, M. (1997) "The UN Security Council, Indifference, and Genocide in Rwanda," *Cultural Anthropology* 12(4), 551–578.

Barnett, M. (2005) "Humanitarianism Transformed," *Perspectives on Politics* 3(4), 723–740.

Barnett, M. (2011) *Empire of Humanity: A History of Humanitarianism* (Ithaca, NY: Cornell University Press).

Barnett, M. and M. Finnemore (2004) *Rules for the World: International Organizations in Global Politics* (Ithaca, NY: Cornell University Press).

Barnett, M. and R. Duvall (2005) *Power in Global Governance* (New York: Cambridge University Press).

Barnett, M. and T. G. Weiss (2008) *Humanitarianism in Question: Politics, Power, Ethics* (Ithaca, NY: Cornell University Press).

Barrett, M., D. Cooper, and K. Jamal (2005) "Globalization and the Coordinating of Work in Multinational Audits," *Accounting, Organizations and Society* 30, 1–24.

Bearman, P. (1993) *Relations into Rhetorics: Local Elite Social Structure in Norfolk, England, 1540-1640* (New Brunswick, NJ: Rutgers University Press).

Beaverstock, J. (2004) "Managing across Borders: Knowledge Management and Expatriation in Professional Service Legal Firms," *Journal of Economic Geography* 4, 157–179.

Beaverstock, J. V., J. R. Faulconbridge, and S. J. E. Hall (2010) "Professionalization, Legitimization and the Creation of Executive Search Markets in Europe," *Journal of Economic Geography* 10, 825–843.

Beaverstock, J., P. Hubbard, and J. Short (2004) "Getting Away with It? Exposing the Geographies of the Super-Rich," *Geoforum* 35, 401–407.

Beaverstock, J. V., R. Smith, and P. J. Taylor (1999) *The Long Arm of the Law: London's Law Firms in a Globalising World Economy. Environment and Planning A* 13: 1857–1876.

Beckert, J. (2007) *Inherited Wealth* (Princeton, NJ: Princeton University Press).

Beckert, J. and W. Streeck (2008) "Economic Sociology and Political Economy: A Programmatic Perspective," *Working Paper 08/4* (Cologne, Germany: Max Planck Institute for the Study of Societies).

Bell, S. (2011) "Do We Need a New 'Constructivist Institutionalism' to Explain Institutional Change?" *British Journal of Political Science* 41, 883–906.

Bell, T. B., F. O. Marrs, I. Solomon, and I. Thomas (1997) *Auditing Organizations through a Strategic Systems Lens* (Montvale, NJ: KPMG LLP).

Bendix, R. (1984) *Force, Fate, and Freedom* (Berkeley: University of California Press).

Berlinerblau, J. (2001) "Toward a Sociology of Heresy, Orthodoxy, and Doxa," *History of Religions* 40(4), 327–351.

Berman, H. J. (1983) *Law and Revolution: The Formation of the Western Legal Tradition* (Cambridge, MA: Harvard University Press).

Bernstein, S., M. Betsill, M. Hoffmann, and M. Paterson (2010) "A Tale of Two Copenhagens: Carbon Markets and Climate Governance," *Millenium: Journal of International Studies* 39(1), 161–173.

Best, J. (2012) "Bureaucratic Ambiguity," *Economy and Society* 4(1), 84–106.

Bhagwati, J. (2004) *In Defense of Globalization* (Oxford: Oxford University Press).

Bigo, D. (2011) "Pierre Bourdieu and International Relations: Power of Practices, Practices of Power," *International Political Sociology* 5(3), 225–258.

Bigo, D. and M. R. Madsen (2011) "Introduction to Symposium: A Different Reading of the International: Pierre Bourdieu and International Studies," *International Political Sociology* 5, 219–224.

BIS (2006) *76th Annual Report* (Basel, June).

Blanchard, P. (2011) "Sequence Analysis for Political Science," *Political Methodology Committee on Concepts and Methods, Working Paper Series 32*, October.

Blomgren, M. and C. Waks (2015) "Coping with Contradictions: Hybrid Professionals Managing Institutional Complexity," *Journal of Professions and Organization* 2(1), 78–102.

Blustein, B. (2009) *Misadventures of the Most Favored Nations: Clashing Egos, Inflated Ambitions, and the Great Shambles of the World Trade System* (New York: Public Affairs).

Blyth, M. (2002) *Great Transformations: Economic Ideas and Institutional Change in the Twenty First Century* (Cambridge: Cambridge University Press).

Bob, C. (2005) *The Marketing of Rebellion: Insurgents, Media, and International Activism* (New York: Cambridge University Press).

Bockman, J. and G. Eyal (2002) "Eastern Europe as a Laboratory for Economic Knowledge: The Transnational Roots of Neoliberalism," *American Journal of Sociology* 108(3), 310–352.

Boltanski, L. (1999) *Distant Suffering: Morality, Media and Politics* (New York: Cambridge Univeristy Press).

Boltanski, L. and E. Chiapello (2007) *The New Spirit of Capitalism* (London: Verso).

Borgatti, S. P., M. G. Everett, and L. C. Freeman (2014) "Ucinet," in R. Alhajj and J. Rokne (eds,) *Encyclopedia of Social Network Analysis and Mining* (New York: Springer), 2261–2267.

Borgatti, S. P. & D. S., Halgin, (2011) "On Network Theory," *Organization Science* 22(5), 1168–1181.

Borio, C. (2009) "Implementing the Macroprudential Approach to Financial Regulation and Supervision," *Financial Stability Review* 13 (Banque de France).

Borio, C. (2011a) "Implementing a Macroprudential Framework: Blending Boldness and Realism," *Capitalism and Society* 6(1), 1–23.

Borio, C. (2011b) "Rediscovering the Macroeconomic Roots of Financial Stability Policy: Journey, Challenges and a Way Forward," *BIS Working paper*. Available at: http://194.61.178.65/publications/Documents/events/ccbs_cew2011/paper_borio.pdf.

Borio, C., C. Furfine, and P. Lowe (2001) "Procyclicality of the Financial System and Financial Stability Issues and Policy Options," BIS Papers, 1 March, 1–57.

Borio, C. and W. White (2004) "Whiter Monetary and Financial Stability: The Implications for Evolving Policy Regimes," BIS Working Paper *147* (Basel: Bank for International Settlements).

Bornstein, E. and P. Redfield (2007) "Genealogies of Suffering and the Gift of Care," Working Paper (New York: Social Science Research Council).

Boswell, T. and C. Chase-Dunn (2000) *The Spiral of Capitalism and Socialism: Toward Global Democracy* (Boulder, CO: Lynne Rienner).

Bothner, M., E. B. Smith, and H. C. White (2010) "A Model of Robust Positions in Social Networks," *American Journal of Sociology* 116(3), 943–992.

Bott, M. and G. Young (2012) "The Role of Crowdsourcing for Better Governance in International Development," *PRAXIS* 27, 56–59.

Botzem, S. (2008) "Transnational Expert-Driven Standardisation: Accountancy Governance from a Professional Point of View," in Jean-Christophe Graz and Andreas Nölke (eds.) *Transnational Private Governance and its Limits* (London and New York: Routledge), 44–57.

Botzem, S. (2013) "Continuity of Expert Rule: Global Accountancy Regulation after the Crisis," in M. Moschella and E. Tsingou (eds.) *Great Expectations, Slow Transformations. Incremental Change in Financial Governance*. ECPR-Studies in European Political Science (Colchester: ECPR Press), 149–171.

Botzem, S. and S. Quack (2006) "Contested Rules and Shifting Boundaries: International Standard Setting in Accounting," in M.-L. Djelic and K. Sahlin-Andersson (eds.) *Transnational Regulation in the Making* (Cambridge: Cambridge University Press), 266–286.

Boulding, C. (2012) "Dilemmas of Information and Accountability: Foreign Aid Donors and Local Development NGOs," in P. A. Gourevitch, D. A. Lake, and J. G. Stein (eds.) *The Credibility of Transnational NGOs: When Virtue is Not Enough* (Cambridge: Cambridge University Press).

Boulet, P. and G. Velasquez (1997) *Globalization and Access to Drugs: Implications of the WTO/TRIPS Agreement* (WHO).

Bourdieu, P. (1975) "The Specificity of the Scientific Field and the Social Conditions of the Progress of Reason," *Social Science Information* 14(6), 19–47.

Bourdieu, P. (1977) *Outline of a Theory of Practice* (Cambridge: Cambridge University Press).

Bourdieu, P. (1983) "The Field of Cultural Production, or: The Economic World Reversed," *Poetics* 12(4–5), 311–356.

Bourdieu, P. (1987) "The Force of Law: Toward a Sociology of the Juridical Field," *Hastings Law Journal* 38, 805–853.

Bourdieu, P. (1991) *Language and Symbolic Power* (Cambridge, UK: Polity Press).

Bourdieu, P. (1992) *Les Règles de l'Art: Genèse et Structure du Champ Littéraire* (Paris: Seuil).

Bourdieu, P. (1993a) *Sociology in Question* (London: Sage).

Bourdieu, P. (1993b) *The Field of Cultural Production: Essays on Art and Literature* (Cambridge, UK: Polity Press).

Bourdieu, P. (1994) *Raisons pratiques. Sur la théorie de l'action* (Paris: Seuil).

Bourdieu, P. (2003) *Firing Back: Against the Tyranny of the Market 2* (London: Verso).

Bourdieu, P. (2004a) "From the King's House to the Reason of State: A Model of the Genesis of the Bureaucratic Field," *Constellations* 11(1), 16–36.

Bourdieu, P. (2004b) *Science of Science and Reflexivity* (Cambridge, UK: Polity Press).

Bourdieu, P. (2012) *Sur L'État: Cours Au Collège De France* (Paris: Seuil).

Bourdieu, P. and L. Wacquant (1992) *An Invitation to Reflexive Sociology* (Chicago: University of Chicago Press).

Bourdieu, P., J.-C. Chamboredon, and J.-C. Passeron (1991) *The Craft of Sociology. Epistemological Preliminaries* (Berlin: Walter de Gruyter).

Boussebaa, M. (2009) "Struggling to Organize across National Borders: The Case of Global Resource Management in Professional Service Firms," *Human Relations* (62), 829–850.

Boussebaa, M. (2015a). "Control in the Multinational Enterprise: The Polycentric Case of Global Professional Service Firms," *Journal of World Business* 50, 696–703.

Boussebaa, M. (2015b). "Professional Service Firms, Globalization and the New Imperialism," *Accounting, Auditing & Accountability Journal* 28(8), 1217–1233.

Boussebaa, M. and A. D. Brown (2016) "Englishization, Identity Regulation and Imperialism," *Organization Studies*. In print.

Boussebaa, M. and J. Faulconbridge (2016) "The Work of Global Professional Service Firms," in A. Wilkinson, D. Hislop, and C. Coupland (eds.) *Perspectives on Contemporary Professional Work: Challenges and Experiences* (Cheltenham: Edward Elgar).

Boussebaa, M. and G. Morgan (2014) "Pushing the Frontiers of Critical International Business Studies: The Multinational as a Neo-Imperial Space," *Critical Perspectives on International Business* 10(1/2), 96–106.

Boussebaa, M. and G. Morgan (2015) "Internationalization of Professional Service Firms: Drivers, Forms and Outcomes," in L. Empson, D. Muzio, J. Broschak and B. Hinings (eds.) *Oxford Handbook of Professional Service Firms* (Oxford: Oxford University Press).

Boussebaa, M., G. Morgan, and A. Sturdy (2012) "Constructing Global Firms? National, Transnational and Neocolonial Effects in International Management Consultancies," *Organization Studies* 33(4), 465–486.

Boussebaa, M., S. Sinha, and Y. Gabriel (2014) "Englishization in Offshore Call Centres: A Postcolonial Perspective," *Journal of International Business Studies* 45, 1152–1169.

Boussebaa, M., A. Sturdy, and G. Morgan (2014) "Learning from the World? Horizontal Knowledge Flows and Geopolitics in International Consulting Firms," *International Journal of Human Resource Management* 25(9), 1227–1242.

Bower, M. (1979) *Perspective on McKinsey* (McKinsey & Company (unpublished publication for internal use)).

Bradt, D. A. (2009) "Evidence-based Decision-making in Humanitarian Assistance," *Humanitarian Practice Network Paper* 67.

Breiger, R. L. (1974) "The Duality of Persons and Groups," *Social Forces* 53(2), 181–190.

Brennan, G. and P. Pettit (2004) *The Economy of Esteem: An Essay on Civil and Political Liberty* (Oxford: Oxford University Press).

Broome, A., A. Homolar, and M. Kranke (2018) 'Bad Science: International Organizations and the Indirect Power of Global Benchmarking'. *European Journal of International Relations* 24, forthcoming.

Broome, A. and J. Quirk (2015) "Governing the World at a Distance: The Practice of Global Benchmarking," *Review of International Studies* 41(5), 819–841.

Broome, A. and L. Seabrooke (2015) "Shaping Policy Curves: Cognitive Authority in Transnational Capacity Building," *Public Administration* 93(4), 956–972.

Brown, H. S., M. de Jong and T. Lessidrenska (2009) "The Rise of the Global Reporting Initiative: A Case of Institutional Entrepreneurship," *Environmental Politics* 18(2), 182–200.

Brown, W. (2001) "Human Rights Watch: An Overview in NGOs and Human Rights: Promise and Performance," in C. E. Welch (ed.) (Philadelphia: University of Pennsylvania Press).

Brundage, J. A. (2008) *The Medieval Origins of the Legal Profession: Canonists, Civilians, and Courts* (Chicago: University of Chicago Press).

Brunnemier, M., A. Crockett, C. Goodhart, A. Persaud, and H. Shin (2009) "The Fundamental Principles of Financial Regulation," in *Geneva Report on the World Economy* 11 (Geneva: International Centre for Monetary and Banking Studies, London: Centre for Economic Policy Research).

Buchanan-Smith, M. (2003) "How the Sphere Project Came into Being: A Case Study of Policy-Making in the Humanitarian Sector and the Relative Influence of Researchm," ODI Working Paper *215* (London: ODI).

Budría, Santiago, Javier Díaz-Giménez, José-Victor Ríos-Rull, and Vincenzo Quadrini (2002) "Updated Facts on the US Distributions of Earnings, Income, and Wealth," *Federal Reserve Bank of Minneapolis Quarterly Review* 26, 2–35.

Bulkeley, H. and A. Jordan (2012) "Transnational Environmental Governance: New Findings and Emerging Research Agendas," *Environment and Planning C: Government and Policy* 30, 556–570.

Burrage, M., K. Jarausch, and H. Sigrist (1990) "An Actor-Based Framework for the Study of the Professions," in M. Burrageand and R. Torstendahl (eds.) *Professions in Theory and History* (London: Sage), 203–225.

Burt, R. S. (1992) *Structural Holes* (Cambridge, MA: Harvard University Press).

Burt, R. S. (2004) "Structural Holes and Good Ideas," *American Journal of Sociology* 110(2), 349–399.

Burt, R. S. (2005) *Brokerage and Closure: An Introduction to Social Capital* (Oxford: Oxford University Press).

Burt, R. S. (2010) *Neighbor Networks: Competitive Advantage Local and Personal* (Oxford: Oxford University Press).

BusinessEurope (2013) *Re: Consultation Draft of the International Integrating Reporting Framework*, 1 August. Available at: www.theiirc.org/wp-content/uploads/2013/08/353_BUSINESSEUROPE.pdf.

Büthe, T. and W. Mattli (2011) *The New Global Rulers: The Privatization of Regulation in the World Economy* (Princeton, NJ: Princeton University Press).

Butler, D. (2013) *World Health Agency Gets a Grip on its Budget* (Scientific American), Available at: http://scientificamerican.com.

Cap Gemini (2011) *World Wealth Report.* Available at: www.capgemini.com/ser vices-and-solutions/by-industry/financial-services/solutions/wealth/ worldwealthreport/

Capelo, L., N. Chang, and A. Verity (2013) "Guidance for Collaborating with Volunteer & Technical Communities," *Digital Humanitarian Network.* Available at: http://digitalhumanitarians.com/collaboration-guidance, accessed 13 January 2014.

Caramanis, C. (2002) "The Interplay between Professional Groups, the State and Supranational Agents: Pax Americana in the Age of 'Globalisation,' " *Accounting, Organizations and Society* 27(4/5), 379–408.

Carmichael, W. D. (2001) "The Role of the Ford Foundation in NGOs and Human Rights: Promise and Performance," in C. E. Welch (ed.) (Philadelphia: University of Pennsylvania Press).

Carney, M. (2008) "From Hindsight to Foresight," *Address to Women in Capital Markets* (Toronto, Ontario, 17 December). Available at: www.bis.org/review/ r081218c.pdf.

Carpenter, R. C. (2007) "Setting the Advocacy Agenda: Theorizing Issue Emergence and Nonemergence in Transnational Advocacy Networks," *International Studies Quarterly* 51(1), 99–120.

Carpenter, R. C. (2010) *Forgetting Children Born of War: Setting the Human Rights Agenda in Bosnia and Beyond* (New York: Columbia University Press).

Carpenter, R. C. (2011) "Vetting the Advocacy Agenda: Networks, Centrality and the Paradox of Weapons Norms," *International Organization* 65(1), 69–102.

Carruthers, B. and T. Halliday (2006) "Negotiating Globalization: Global Scripts and Intermediation in the Construction of Asian Insolvency Regimes," *Law & Social Inquiry* 31, 521–584.

CDP (2010) "Carbon Disclosure Project 2010: Global 500 and S&P 500 Report Highlights," *CDP.* Available at: www.cdproject.net/CDPResults/2010-G500-SP500-report-highlights.pdf.

CDP (2013) *CDP S&P 500 Climate Change Report 2013* (London, UK: Carbon Disclosure Project). Available at: www.cdp.net/CDPResults/CDP-SP500-climate-report-2013.pdf.

CDSB (2010a) "Technical Working Group," *Climate Disclosure Standards Board.* Available at: www.cdsb-global.org/technical-working-group/.

CDSB (2010b) "The Board," *Climate Disclosure Standards Board.* Available at: www.cdsb-global.org/index.php?page=the-board.

CDSB (2010c) "Report on Consultation About CDSB's Reporting Framework," *CDSB.*

CDSB (2012) *Climate Change Reporting Framework – Edition 1.1* (London, UK: Climate Disclosure Standards Board). Available at: www.cdsb.net/sites/cdsbn et/files/cdsbframework_v1-1.pdf.

CDSB (2013a) "CDSB: History and Mission," *CDSB.* Available at: www.cdsb .net/about-cdsb/history-and-mission.

CDSB (2013b) "CDSB Investor Engagement Program," *CDSB*. Available at: www.cdsb.net/get-involved/cdsb-investor-engagement-program.

Ceres (2013) *Global Investor Survey on Climate Change: 3rd Annual Report on Actions and Progress* (Boston, MA). Available at: www.ceres.org/resources/reports/global-investor-survey-on-climate-change-2013/view.

Champagne, P., R. Lenoir, D. Merllié, and L. Pinto (1999) *Initiation Á La Pratique Sociologique* (Paris: Dunod).

Chang, H. (2003) *Kicking Away the Ladder: Development Strategy in Historical Perspective* (London: Anthem).

Chase-Dunn, C. (1998) *Global Formation: Structures of the World-Economy* (updated edition) (Oxford: Rowman & Littlefield Publishers).

Christensen, M., S. Newberry, and B. N. Potter (2010) "The Role of Global Epistemic Communities in Enabling Accounting Change: Creating a 'More Business-like' Public Sector," *6th Accounting History International Conference* (Wellington, New Zealand).

Christensen, M. and P. Skærbæk (2010) "Consultancy Outputs and the Purification of Accounting Technologies," *Accounting, Organizations and Society* 35(5), 524–545.

Christian Aid (2010) "Shifting Sands: Tax, Transparency and Multinational Companies," in *Accounting for Change* 1 (London: Christian Aid).

Chwieroth, J. M. (2010) *Capital Ideas: The Rise of the IMF and Financial Liberalization* (Princeton, NJ: Princeton University Press).

CIPIH (2006) *Commission on Intellectual Property Rights, Innovation and Public Health* (WHO).

Clapp, J. and J. Thistlethwaite (2012) "Private Voluntary Programs in Environmental Governance: Climate Change and the Financial Sector," in K. Ronit (ed.) *Business and Climate Policy: Potentials and Pitfalls of Voluntary Programs* (UN University Press), 43–76.

Clapp, J. and P. Utting (2009) *Corporate Accountability and Sustainable Development* (Oxford: Oxford University Press).

Clark, P. (2014) "Norway Spurs Rethink on Fossil Fuel Companies," *Financial Times*,. Available at: www.ft.com/cms/s/0/4b1c89dc-a313-11e3-ba21-00144fe ab7de.html#axzz2yDHtVeoM, accessed 4 March 2014.

Clement, P. (2010) "The Term 'Macroprudential': Origins and Evolution," *BIS Quarterly Review* (March), 59–67.

Clignet, R. (2009) *Death, Deeds and Descendants* (2nd edn.) (New Brunswick, NJ: Transaction Press).

Coffee, J. C. (2006) *Gatekeepers: Professions and Corporate Governance* (New York: Oxford University Press).

Cohen, A. (2013) "The Genesis of Europe: Competing Elites and the Emergence of a European Field of Power," in N. Kauppi and M. R. Madsen (eds.) *Transnational Power Elites: The New Professionals of Governance, Law and Security* (London: Routledge).

Cohen, A. and M. R. Madsen (2007) "Cold War Law: Legal Entrepreneurs and the Emergence of a European Legal Field (1945–1965)," in V. Gessner and D. Nelken (eds.) *European Ways of Law: Towards a European Sociology of Law* (Oxford: Hart Publishing), 175–202.

Cole, R. J. and M. J. Valdebenito (in press) "The Importation of Building Environmental Certification Systems: International Usages of BREEAM and LEED," *Building Research & Information*. Available at: www.tandfon line.com/doi/abs/10.1080/09613218.2013.802115#.UePlMaxdDR8.

Consoli, D. and R. Ramlogan (2008) "Out of Sight: Problem Sequences and Epistemic Boundaries of Medical Know-How on Glaucoma," *Journal of Evolutionary Economics* 18, 31–56.

Consoli, D. and R. Ramlogan (2012) "Patterns of Organisation in the Development of Medical Know-How: The Case of Glaucoma Research," *Industrial and Corporate Change* 21(2), 315–343.

Conti, J. and M. O.'Neil (2007) "Studying Power: Qualitative Methods and the Global Elite," *Qualitative Research* 7, 63–82.

Cooley, A. and J. Ron (2002) "The NGO Scramble: Organizational Insecurity and the Political Economy of Transnational Action," *International Security* 27(1), 5–39.

Cooper, D. J., R. Greenwood, B. Hinings, and J. Brown (1998) "Globalization and Nationalism in a Multinational Accounting Firm: The Case of Opening New Markets in Eastern Europe," *Accounting, Organizations and Society* 23, 531–548.

Cooper, D. J. and K. Robson (2006) "Accounting, Professions and Regulation: Locating the Sites of Professionalization," *Accounting, Organizations and Society* 31, 415–444.

Correa, C. (1997) "The Uruguay Round and Drugs. WHO Task Force in Health Economics" (WHO).

Covaleski, M. A., M. W. Dirsmith, J. B. Heian, and S. Samuel (1998) "The Calculated and the Avowed: Techniques of Discipline and Struggles over Identity in Big Six Public Accounting," *Administrative Science Quarterly* 43, 293–327.

Covaleski, M. A., M. W. Dirsmith, and L. Rittenberg (2003) "Jurisdictional Disputes over Professional Work: The Institutionalization of the Global Knowledge Expert," *Accounting, Organizations and Society* 28, 323–355.

Coviello, N. E. and K. A. M. Martin (1999) "Internationalization of Service SMEs: An Integrated Perspective from the Engineering Consulting Sector," *Journal of International Marketing* 7(4), 42–66.

Currion, P. and B. Willitts -King (2012) *ACAPs Mid -Term Review*.

Czarniawska-Joerges, B. (1990) "Merchants of Meaning: Management Consulting in the Swedish Public Sector," *Organizational Symbolism*, 139–150.

Damro, C. and P. L. Méndez (2003) "Emissions trading at Kyoto: from EU resistance."

Darcy et al. (2013) *The Use of Evidence in Humanitarian Decision Making. ACAPS Operational Learning Paper* (Feinstein International Centre).

Darcy, J. and C.-A. Hofmann (2003) "According to Needs: Needs Assessments and Humanitarian Decision Making," in *HPG Report* (London: ODI).

Davies, J., S. Sandström, A. Shorrocks, and E. Wolff (2008) "The World Distribution of Household Wealth," *Discussion Paper* (World Institute for Development Economics Research 2008/03. Helsinki: UNI-WIDER).

Davies, P. (2001) "Spies as Informants: Triangulation and the Interpretation of Elite Interview Data in the Study of the Intelligence and Security Services," *Politics* 21, 73–80.

De Laroisiere Group (2009) "Report of the High Level Group on Financial Supervision in the EU" (Brussels).

Deere, C. (2009) "The Implementation Game. The TRIPS Agreement and the Global Politics of Intellectual Property Reform in Developing Countries" (Oxford: Oxford University Press).

DeLaet, D. (2009) "Framing Male Circumcision as a Human Rights Issue? Contributions to the Debate over the Universality of Human Rights," *Journal of Human Rights* 8(4), 405–426.

Deloitte (2013) "Consultation Draft of the International Integrated Reporting Framework," 15 July. Available at: www.theiirc.org/wp-content/uploads/2013/08/311_Deloitte-Touche-Tohmatsu-Limited.pdf.

Deschamps, B. (2010) "Victims of Violence – A Review of the Protection of Civilians Concept and its Relevance to UNHCR's Mandate" (UNHCR Policy Development and Evaluation Service).

Descheneau, P. and M. Paterson (2011) "Between Desire and Routine: Assembling Environment and Finance in Carbon Markets," *Antipode* 43(4), 662–681.

DeWaal, A. (1997) *Famine Crimes: Politics and the Disaster Relief Industry in Africa* (Bloomington: Indiana University Press).

Dezalay, Y. (2004) "Les Courtiers De L'international: Héritiers Cosmopolites, Mercenaires De L'impérialisme Et Missionnaires De L'universel," *Actes de la Recherche en Sciences Sociales* 151–152, 5–34.

Dezalay, Y. (2007) "From a Symbolic Boom to a Marketing Bust: Genesis and Reconstruction of a Field of Legal and Political Expertise at the Crossroads of a Europe Opening to the Atlantic," *Law & Social Inquiry* 32, 161–181.

Dezalay, Y. and B. G. Garth (1996) *Dealing in Virtue. International Commercial Arbitration and the Construction of a Transnational Legal Order* (Chicago: University of Chicago Press).

Dezalay, Y. and B. G. Garth (2002a) "Legitimating the New Legal Orthodoxy," in Y. Dezaly and B. G. Garth (eds.) *Global Prescriptions: The Production, Exportation, and Importation of a New Legal Orthodoxy* (Ann Arbor: University of Michigan Press), 306–334.

Dezalay, Y. and B. G. Garth (2002b) *The Internalization of Palace Wars: Lawyers, Economists, and the Contest to Transform Latin American States* (Chicago: University of Chicago Press).

Dezalay, Y. and B. G. Garth (2006) "From the Cold War to Kosovo: The Rise and Renewal of the Field of International Human Rights," *Annual Review of Law and Social Science* 2, 231–255.

Dezalay, Y. and B. G. Garth (2010a) "Marketing and Selling Transnational 'Judges' and Global 'Experts': Building the Credibility of (Quasi) Judicial Regulation," *Socio-Economic Review* 8, 113–130.

Dezalay, Y. and B. G. Garth (2010b) *Asian Legal Rivals: Lawyers in the Shadow of Empire* (Chicago: University of Chicago Press).

Dezalay, Y. and B. G. Garth (2016) "'Lords of the Dance' as Double Agents: Elite Actors in and Around the Legal Field," *Journal of Professions and Organization* 3(2), 188–206.

Dezalay, Y. and M. R. Madsen (2006) "Henimod Entreprenant Miljøpraksis-En Præliminær Analyse Af Dansk Miljøekspertise Som Socialt Felt," *Dansk Sociologi* 11, 41–56.

Dezalay, Y. and M. R. Madsen (2009) "Espaces De Pouvoir Nationaux, Espaces De Pouvoir Internationaux," in A. Cohen, B. Lacroix and P. Riutort (eds.) *Nouveau Manuel De Science Politique* (Paris: La Découverte), 681–693.

Dezalay, Y. and M. R. Madsen (2012) "The Force of Law and Lawyers: Pierre Bourdieu and the Reflexive Sociology of Law," *Annual Review of Law and Social Science* 8, 433–452.

Dicken, P. (2010) *Global Shift* (6th edn.) (London: Sage).

Dikjzeul, D., D. Hilhorst, and P. Walker (2013) "Introduction: Evidence-based Action in Humanitarian Crises," *Disasters* 37(1), 1–19.

DiMaggio, P. J. and W. W. Powell (1983) "The Iron Cage Revisited: Institutional Isomorphism and Collective Rationality in Organizational Fields," *American Sociological Review* 48, 147–160.

Djelic, M. L. and S. Quack (2003) "Theoretical Building Blocks for a Research Agenda Linking Globalization and Institutions," in M. L. Djelic and S. Quack (eds.) *Globalization and Institutions: Redefining the Rules of the Economic Game* (Cheltenham: Edward Elgar).

Djelic, M. L. and S. Quack (2010) "Transnational Communities and Governance," in M. L. Djelic and S. Quack (eds.) *Transnational Communities. Shaping Economic Governance* (Cambridge: Cambridge University Press), 3–36.

Djelic, M.-L. and K. Sahlin-Andersson (eds.) (2006) *Transnational Governance: Institutional Dynamics of Regulation* (Cambridge: Cambridge University Press).

Dobbin, F., B. Simmons, and G. Garrett (2007) "The Global Diffusion of Public Policies: Social Construction, Coercion, Competition, or Learning?," *Annual Review of Sociology* 33, 449–472.

Dollar, D. and A. Kraay (2004) "Trade, Growth, and Poverty," *The Economic Journal* 114, F22–F49.

Donnelly, J. (2002) *Universal Human Rights in Theory and Practice* (Ithaca, NY: Cornell University Press).

Doremus, P., W. W. Keller, L. W. Pauly, and S. Reich (1999) *The Myth of the Global Corporation* (Princeton, NJ: Princeton University Press).

Dowie, M. (2001) *American Foundations: An Investigative History* (Cambridge, MA: MIT Press).

Doz, Y., J. Santos, and P. Williamson (2001) *From Global to Metanational: How Companies Win in the Knowledge Economy* (Boston, MA: Harvard Business School).

Drahos, P. and J. Braithwaite (2002) *Information Feudalism. Who Owns the Knowledge Economy?* (London: Earthscan Publications).

Drawbaugh, K. (2007) "Buffett Backs Estate Tax, Decries Wealth Gap," *Reuters News Service* (November 14).

Drori, G. S. (2008) "Institutionalism and Globalisation Studies," in R. Greenwood et al. (eds.) *The Sage Handbook of Organizational Institutionalism* (London: Sage).

DuBois, M. (2008) "Civilian Protection and Humanitarian Advocacy: Strategies and (False?) Dilemmas," *Humanitarian Exchange Magazine* 39, 12–15.

Dufour, C., de G. Veronique, H. Maury, and F. Grunewald (2004) "Rights, Standards and Quality in a Complex Humanitarian Space: Is Sphere the Right Tool," *Disasters* 28(2), 124–141.

Eagleton-Pierce, M. (2013) *Symbolic Power in the World Trade Organization* (Oxford: Oxford University Press).

Eagleton-Pierce, M., "All the Trader's Men: Expertise and Power in World Trade" (forthcoming manuscript).

EC (2010) *Public Consultation on Country-By-Country Reporting by Multinational Companies* (Brussels: European Commission).

EC (2011) "Impact Assessment for Financial Disclosures on a Country by Country Basis— Part II," Commission Staff Working Paper (Brussels: European Commission).

EC (2013) "Commissioner Barnier Welcomes European Parliament Vote on the Accounting and Transparency Directives (including country by country reporting)," *12 June Memo/13/546* (Brussels: European Commission).

Eccles, R. G. and M. P. Krzus (2010) *One Report: Integrated Reporting for a Sustainable Strategy* (New Jersey: Wiley & Sons).

Eccleston, R. (2012) *The Dynamics of Global Economic Governance: The Financial Crisis, the OECD and the Politics of International Tax Cooperation* (Cheltenham: Edward Elgar).

Egeland, J. (2009) *A Billion Lives: An Eyewitness Report from the Frontlines of Humanity* (New York: Simon & Schuster).

Emirbayer, M. (1997) "Manifesto for a Relational Sociology," *American Journal of Sociology* 103(2), 281–317.

Engelen, E., I. Ertürk, J. Froud, S. Johal, A. Moran, A. Nilsson, and K. Williams (2011) *After the Great Complacence: Financial Crisis and the Politics of Reform* (Oxford: Oxford University Press).

Epstein, C. (2008) *The Power of Words: Birth of an Anti-Whaling Discourse* (Cambridge, MA: MIT Press).

Eriksson, J., et al. (1996) *The International Response to Conflict and Genocide: Lessons from the Rwanda Experience: Synthesis report* (Joint Evaluation of Emergency Assistance to Rwanda).

Ernst & Young (2013) "Consultation Draft of the International Framework," 15 July. Available at: www.theiirc.org/wp-content/uploads/2013/08/252_Ernst-Young-Global-Limited.pdf.

Erturk, I., J. Froud, A. Leaver, M. Moran, and K. Williams (2011) "Haldane's Gambit: Political Arithmetic and/ or a New Metaphor," CRESC Working Paper 97. Available at: www.cresc.ac.uk/sites/default/files/wp%2097.pdf.

European Coalition for Corporate Justice (2013) "Comments on Draft International IR Framework," 15 July. Available at: www.theiirc.org/wp-content/uploads/2013/08/218_European-Coalition-for-Corporate-Justice.pdf.

European Commission (2002) "*Rigged Rules And Double Standards: Trade, Globalisation and The Fight Against Poverty*; Comments from the Commission,"

Available at: http://trade.ec.europa.eu/doclib/docs/2004/april/tradoc_111249 .pdf, accessed 17 April 2002

European Parliament (2011) *Report on an Effective Raw Materials Strategy for Europe* (2011/2056(INI) Committee on Industry, Research and Energy, Brussels: European Parliament).

Evetts, J. (1998) "Professionalism Beyond the Nation-State: International Systems of Professional Regulation" *Europe International Journal of Sociology and Social Policy* 18, 47–64.

Evetts, J. (2011) "A New Professionalism? Challenges and Opportunities," *Current Sociology* 59, 406–422.

Evetts, J. (2013) "Professionalism: Value and Ideology," *Current Sociology*, 61(5/6), 778–96.

Eyal, G. (2013) "The Origins of the Autism Epidemic," *American Journal of Sociology* 118(4), 863–907.

Eyal, Gil (2011) "Spaces between Fields," in P. Gorski (ed.) *Pierre Bourdieu and Historical Analysis* (Durham: Duke University Press), 159–182.

Falkner, R. (2003) "Private Environmental Governance and International Relations: Exploring the Links," *Global Environmental Politics* 3(2), 72–87.

Fathalla, M. F. and T. Varagunam (1988) "Highlights of the Biennium," in P. D. Griffin and J. Khanna (eds.) *Research in Human Reproduction. Biennial Report* (Geneva: WHO).

Faulconbridge, J. R. (2010) "Global Architects: Learning and Innovation through Communities and Constellations of Practice," *Environment and Planning A* 42, 2842–2858.

Faulconbridge, J. R. (2013) "Mobile 'Green' Design Knowledge: Institutions, Bricolage and the Relational Production of Embedded Sustainable Building Designs," *Transactions of the Institute of British Geographers* 38, 339–353.

Faulconbridge, J. R., S. Hall, and J. V. Beaverstock (2008) "New Insights into the Internationalization of Producer Services: Organizational Strategies and Spatial Economies for Global Headhunting Firms," *Environment and Planning A* 40, 210–234.

Faulconbridge, J. R. and D. Muzio (2007) "Reinserting the Professional into the Study of Professional Service Firms: The Case of Law," *Global Networks* 7, 249–270.

Faulconbridge, J. R. and D. Muzio (2008) "Organizational Professionalism in Global Law Firms," *Work, Employment and Society* 22(1), 7–25.

Faulconbridge, J. R. and D. Muzio (2012) "The Rescaling of the Professions: Towards a Transnational Sociology of the Professions," *International Sociology* 27, 109–125.

Faulconbridge, J. R. and D. Muzio (2016) "Global Professional Service Firms and the Challenge of Institutional Complexity: 'Field Relocation' as a Response Strategy," *Journal of Management Studies* 53(1), 89–124.

Faulconbridge, J. R., D. Muzio, and A. Cook (2012) "Institutional Legacies in TNCs and their Management through Training Academies: The Case of Transnational Law Firms in Italy," *Global Networks* 12, 48–70.

Faulconbridge, J.R. and S. Yalciner (2015) "Local Variants of Mobile Sustainable Building Assessment Models: The Marketization and Constrained Mutation of BREEAM ES," *Global Networks* 15, 360–378.

FEACO (2009) "Survey of the European Management Consultancy Market, 2007/2008" (Brussels: FEACO).

Feenstra, R. C., G. M. Grossman and D. A. Irwin (eds.) (1996) *The Political Economy of Trade Policy: Papers in Honor of Jagdish Bhagwati* (Cambridge, MA: MIT Press).

Feldman, I. (2007) "Difficult Distinctions: Refugee Law, Humanitarian Practice, and Political Identification in Gaza," *Cultural Anthropology* 22(1), 129–169.

Ferguson, J. (1990) *The Anti-Politics Machine* (Minneapolis: University of Minnesota Press).

Ferguson, K. (2013) *Top Down: The Ford Foundation, Black Power, and the Reinvention of Racial Liberalism* (Philadelphia: University of Pennsylvania Press).

Fillieule, O. and P. Blanchard (2013) "Fighting Together: Assessing Continuity and Change in Social Movement Organisations through a Study of Constitutencies' Heterogeneity," in N. Kauppi (ed.) *A Political Sociology of Transnational Europe* (London: Routledge), 79–108.

Fincham, R. (1999) "The Consultant–Client Relationship: Critical Perspectives on the Management of Organizational Change," *Journal of Management Studies* 36(3), 335–351.

Fine, B. and D. Milonakis (2009) *From Political Economy to Economics: Method, the Social and the Historical in the Evolution of Economic Theory* (Abingdon: Routledge).

Finnemore, M. and K. Sikkink (1998) "International Norm Dynamics and Political Change," *International Organization* 52(4), 887–917.

Finnemore, M. (1996) *National Interests in International Society* (Ithaca, NY: Cornell University Press).

Fleishman, J. L. (2007) *The Foundation: A Great American Secret* (New York: Public Affairs).

Fligstein, N. (1990) *The Transformation of Corporate Control* (Cambridge, MA: Harvard University Press).

Forsythe, D. P. (2012) *Human Rights in International Relations* (3rd edn.) (New York: Cambridge University Press).

Fortune Magazine (2014) "A New Perspective on the Corporate World," *CNN Money, Fortune Magazine*, retrieved online 19 May 2014.

Foucault, M. (1977) *Discipline and Punish: The Birth of the Prison* (New York: Pantheon).

Fourcade-Gourinchas, M. (2006) "The Construction of a Global Profession: The Transnationalization of Economics," *American Journal of Sociology* 112, 145–195.

Fourcade, M. (2009) *Economists and Societies: Discipline and Profession in the United States, Britain, and France, 1890s to 1990s* (Princeton, NJ: Princeton University Press).

Fourcade, M., E. Ollion, and Y. Algan (2015) "The Superiority of Economists," *Journal of Economic Perspectives* 29(1), 89–114.

Frenkel, M. (2008) "The Multinational Corporation as a Third Space: Rethinking International Management Discourse on Knowledge Transfer through Homi Bhabha," *Academy of Management Review* 33(4), 924–942.

Frenkel, M. and Y. Shenhav (2003) "From Americanization to Colonization: The Diffusion of Productivity Models Revisited," *Organization Studies* 24, 1537–1561.

Frenkel, M. and Y. Shenhav (2012) "Management Consulting in Developing and Emerging Economies: Towards a Postcolonial Perspective," in Matthias Kipping and Timothy Clark (eds.) *The Oxford Handbook of Management Consulting* (Oxford: Oxford University Press).

Frobel, F., J. Heinrichs and O. Kreye (1980) *The New International Division of Labour* (Cambridge: Cambridge University Press).

FSA (2009) *The Turner Review* (London: FSA).

FSF (2009) "Report on Addressing Procyclicality in the Financial System" (Basel: FSF, April). Available at: www.financialstabilityboard.org/publica tions/r_0904a.pdf.

Füglister, K. (2012) "Where does Learning take Place? The Role of Intergovernmental Cooperation in Policy Diffusion," *European Journal of Political Research* 51(3), 316–349.

G30 (2009) "Group of Thirty Financial Reform: A Framework for Financial Stability" (Washington, DC).

G30 (2010) "Group of Thirty Enhancing Financial Stability and Resilience: Macroprudential Policy, Tools and Systems for the Future" (Washington, DC).

G8 (2011) "Deauville G8 Declaration: Renewed Commitment for Freedom and Democracy" (Deauville, France).

G8 (2013) "Lough Erne G8 Leaders' Communiqué" (London, UK).

Gabadinho, A. et al. (2011) "Analyzing and Visualizing State Sequences in R with TraMineR," *Journal of Statistical Software* 40(4), 1–37.

Gaither, H. Jr. Rowan (1949) "The Report of the Study for the Ford Foundation on Policy and Program" (Rep. Detroit: Ford Foundation), accessed online on 20 November 2013.

Galaskiewicz (1985) "Professional networks and the institutionalization of a single mind set" *American Sociological Review* 50(5), 639–658.

Galati, G. and R. Moessner (2011) "Macroprudential Policy: A Literature Review," BIS Working Paper *337*.

Gallagher, K. P. (ed.) (2005) *Putting Development First: The Importance of Policy Space in the WTO and IFIs* (London: Zed Books).

Gallagher, K. P. (2014) *Ruling Capital: Emerging Markets and the Reregulation of Cross-Border Finance* (Ithaca, NY: Cornell University Press).

Gallemore, C. and D. K. Munroe (2013) "Centralization in the Global Avoided Deforestation Collaboration Network," *Global Environmental Change* 23(5), 1199–1210.

Galperin, E. and M. Marqis-Boire (2012) "Electronic Frontier Foundation (blog),". Available at: www.eff.org/deeplinks/2012/07/new-blackshades-mal ware, accessed 12 July 2012.

Gammeltoft-Hansen, T. and N. N. Sørensen (eds.) (2013) *The Migration Industry and the Commercialization of International Migration* (New York: Routledge).

Gauthier, J.-A., E. D. Widmer, P. Bucher, and C. Notredame (2009) "How Much Does It Cost? Optimization of Costs in Sequence Analysis of Social Science Data," *Sociological Methods & Research* 38(1), 197–231.

Geertz, Clifford (1973) *The Interpretation of Cultures: Selected Essays* (New York: Basic Books).

Ghoshal, S. and C. Bartlett (1997) *The Individualized Corporation* (HarperBusiness).

Gilding, M. (2010) "Motives of the Rich and Powerful in Doing Interviews with Social Scientists," *International Sociology* 25, 755–777.

Givoni, M. (2011) "Humanitarian Governance and Ethical Cultivation: Médecins sans Frontières and the Advent of the Expert-Witness," *Millennium – Journal of International Studies* 40(1), 43–63.

Global Witness (2005) "Extracting Transparency: The Need for an International Financial Reporting Standard for the Extractives Industries" (Global Witness Ltd.).

Glucker, J. and T. Armbruster (2003) "Bridging Uncertainty in Management Consulting: The Mechanisms of Trust and Networked Reputation," *Organization Studies* 24(2), 269–297.

Glynn, S. and A. Booth (1979) "The Public Records Office and Recent British Economic Historiography," *The Economic History Review* 32, 303–315.

Goddard, S. E. (2009) "Brokering Change: Networks and Entrepreneurs in International Politics," *International Theory* 1(2), 249–281.

Gold, R., T. Piper, J.-F. Morin, K. Durell, J. Carbone, and E. Henry (2007) "Preliminary Legal Review of Proposed Medicines Patent Pool" (The Innovation Partnership).

Goodale, M. and S. E. Merry (eds.) (2007) *The Practice of Human Rights: Tracking Law Between the Global and the Local* (New York: Cambridge University Press).

Goodhart, C. and M. A. Segoviano (2004) "Basel and Procyclicality: A Comparison of the Standardised and IRB Approaches to an Improved Credit Risk Method," *Discussion paper* 524 (London, UK: Financial Markets Group, London School of Economics and Political Science).

Goodman, L. (2014) "Inside the World's Top Offshore Tax Shelter," *Newsweek*, 16 January. Available at: www.newsweek.com/2014/01/17/inside-worlds-top-off shore-tax-shelter-245078.html, accessed 9 September 2015.

Gordon, A. (1997) *Ghostly Matters: Haunting and the Sociological Imagination* (Minneapolis: University of Minnesota Press).

Gould, R. V., and R. M. Fernandez (1989) "Structures of Mediation: A Formal Approach to Brokerage in Transaction Networks," *Sociological Methodology* 19, 89–126.

Gramsci, A. (1992) *Prison Notebooks* (New York: Columbia University Press).

Granovetter, M. S. (1973) "The Strength of Weak Ties," *American Journal of Sociology* 78(6), 1360–1380.

Granovetter, M. S. (1985) "Economic Action and Social Structure: The Problem of Embeddedness," *American Journal of Sociology* 91(3), 481–510.

Green, D. (2012) "Creating Killer Facts and Graphics," in *Oxfam Research Guidelines* (Oxford: Oxfam International).

Green, J. (2014) *Rethinking Private Authority: Agents and Entrepreneurs in Global Environmental Governance* (Princeton, NJ: Princeton University Press).

Greenwood, R., T. Morris, S. Fairclough, and M. Boussebaa (2010) "The Organizational Design of Transnational Professional Service Firms," *Organizational Dynamics* 39, 173–183.

Greenwood, R., R. Suddaby, and C. R. Hinings (2002) "Theorizing Change: The Role of Professional Associations in the Transformation of Institutionalized Fields," *The Academy of Management Journal* 45, 58–80.

Greenwood, R., R. Suddaby, and M. McDougald (2006) "Introduction," in R. Greenwood and R. Suddaby (eds.) *Research in the Sociology of Organizations*, 24 (Oxford: Professional Service Firms, JAI Press), 1–16.

Grey, C. (1998) "On Being a Professional in a 'Big Six' Firm," *Accounting, Organizations and Society* 23, 569–587.

Griffith, J. S. and J. Ocampo (2006) "A Countercyclical Framework for a Development Friendly International Financial Architecture," Working Paper (Institute of Development Studies).

Gross, A. C. and J. Poor (2008) "The Global Management Consulting Sector," *Business Economics* 43, 59–68.

Group, C. E. W. (2012) *Research and Development to Meet Health Needs in Developing Countries: Strengthening Global Financing and Coordination* (WHO: WHO).

Group, E. W. (2010) *Research and Development: Coordination and Finance* (WHO: WHO).

Grubb, M. (1989) *The Greenhouse Effect: Negotiating Targets* (London: Royal Institute of International Affairs).

Gupta, A. (2008) "Transparency Under Scrutiny: Information Disclosure in Global Environmental Governance," *Global Environmental Politics* 8(2), 1–7.

Haas, P. M. (1992). "Introduction: Epistemic Communities and International Policy Coordination", *International Organizations* 46(1), 1–35.

Hagan, J. and R. Levi (2007) "Justiciability as Field Effect: When Sociology Meets Human Rights," *Sociological Forum* 22(3), 372–380.

Haldane, A. (2012a) "A Leaf Being Turned," *Bank of England Discussion Paper*. Available at: www.bankofengland.co.uk/publications/Documents/speeches/2012/speech616.pdf.

Haldane, A. (2012b) "What Have the Economists Ever Done for Us?" Available at: www.voxeu.org/article/what-have-economists-ever-done-us.

Haldane, A. (2013a) "Macroprudential Policies: When and How to Use Them," Presentation at Rethinking Macro Policies II, Hosted by the International Monetary Fund (Washington, DC, 16–17 April). Available at: www.imf.org/external/np/seminars/eng/2013/macro2/pdf/ah.pdf.

Haldane, A. (2013b) "Why Institutions Matter More than Ever," Centre for Research on Socio-Cultural Change (CRESC) Annual Conference, School of Oriental and African Studies.

Haldane, A. and R. May (2011) "Systemic Risk in Banking Ecosystems," *Nature* 469, 351–355.

Halliday, T. C. and B. G. Carruthers (2009) *Bankrupt: Global Lawmaking and Systemic Financial Crisis* (Stanford, CA: Stanford University Press).

Halvorsen, T. (1995) "Sektorinteresser eller profesjonssystem," Skriftserie nr. 10 (TMV – Senter for Teknologi og Menneskelige Verdier: University of Oslo).

Hammack, D. C. and H. K. Anheier (2010) "American Foundations: Their Roles and Contributions to Society," in H. K. Anheier and D. C. Hammack (eds.) *American Foundations: Roles and Contributions* (Washington, DC: Brookings Institution).

Hammersley, M. and P. Atkinson (1995) *Ethnography: Principles in Practice* (2nd edn.) (London: Routledge).

Hannah, E. (2014) "The Quest for Inclusive and Accountable Governance: Embedded NGOs and Demand Driven Advocacy in the International Trade Regime," *Journal of World Trade* 48(3).

Hansen, M., N. Nohria, and T. Tierney (1999). "What's Your Strategy for Managing Knowledge?," *Harvard Business Review* March–April, 106–116.

Harrington, B. (2002) "Obtrusiveness As Strategy in Ethnographic Research," *Qualitative Sociology* 25, 49–61.

Harrington, B. (2003) "The Social Psychology of Access in Ethnographic Research," *Journal of Contemporary Ethnography* 32, 592–625.

Harrington, B. (2008) *Pop Finance: Investment Clubs and the New Investor Populism* (Princeton, NJ: Princeton University Press).

Harrington, B. (2012a) "Trust and Estate Planning: The Emergence of a Profession and Its Contribution to Socio-Economic Inequality," *Sociological Forum* 27, 825–846.

Harrington, B. (2012b) "From Trustees to Wealth Managers," in G. Erreygers and J. Cunliffe (eds.) *Inherited Wealth, Justice and Equality* (Abingdon: Routledge), 190–209.

Harrington, B. (2015) "Going Global: Professionals and the Micro-Foundations of Institutional Change," *Journal of Professions and Organizations* 2(2), 103–121.

Harrington, B. (2016) *Capital without Borders: Wealth Management and the One Percent* (Cambridge, MA: Harvard University Press).

Harrington, B. (2017a) "Trusts and Financialization," *Socio-Economic Review* 15(1), 31–63.

Harrington, B. (2017b) "Habitus and the Labor of Representation Among Elite Professionals," *Journal of Professions and Organizations* 4, forthcoming.

Harvard Humanitarian Initiative. Disaster Relief 2.0 (2011) *The Future of Information Sharing in Humanitarian Emergencies* (Washington, DC and Berkshire, UK: UN Foundation & Vodafone Foundation Technology Partnership).

Harvey, D. (2003) *The New Imperialism* (Oxford: Oxford University Press).

Harvey, P. et al. (2010) *The State of the Humanitarian System: Assessing Performance and Progress: A Pilot Study* (London: ALNAP).

Harvey, W. (2011) "Strategies for Conducting Elite Interviews," *Qualitative Research* 11, 431–441.

Haufler, V. (2010) "Disclosure as Governance: The Extractive Industries Transparency Initiative and Resource Management in the Developing World," *Global Environmental Politics* 10(3), 53–73.

Health Action International (1997) *Power, Patents and Pills: An Examination of GATT/WTO Policies and Essential Drug Policies* (Amsterdam: HAI-Europe).

Helfer, L. and E. Voeten (2013) "International Courts as Agents of Legal Change: Evidence from LGBT Rights in Europe," *International Organization* 67.

Helgadóttir, O. (2016) "The Bocconi Boys Go to Brussels: Italian Economic Ideas, Professional Networks and European Austerity," *Journal of European Public Policy* 23(3), 392–409.

Hellwig, M. (1995) "Systemic Aspects of Risk Management in Banking and Finance," *Swiss Journal of Economics and Statistics* 131, 723–737.

Henriksen, L. F. (2013) "Performativity and the Politics of Equipping for Calculation: Constructing a Global Market for Microfinance," *International Political Sociology* 7(4), 406–425.

Henriksen, L. F. (2015) "The Global Network of Biofuel Sustainability Standards-Setters," *Environmental Politics* 24(1), 115–137.

Henriksen, L. F. and S. Ponte (2017). "Public Orchestration, Social Networks and Transnational Environmental Governance: Lessons from the Aviation Industry", Forthcoming in *Regulation & Governance*.

Henriksen, L. F. and L. Seabrooke (2016) "Transnational Organizing: Issue Professionals in Environmental Sustainability Networks," *Organization* 23(5), 722–741.

Hermanowicz, J. (2002) "The Great Interview: 25 Strategies for Interviewing People in Bed," *Qualitative Sociology* 25, 479–499.

Heydemann, S. with R. Kinsey (2010) "The State and International Philanthropy: The Contribution of American Foundations, 1919–1991," in H. K. Anheier and D. C. Hammack (eds.) *American Foundations: Roles and Contributions* (Washington, DC: Brookings Institution).

Hirschman, D. and E. P. Berman (2014) "Do Economists Make Policies? On the Political Effects of Economics," *Socio-Economic Review* 12(4), 779–811.

't Hoen, E. (2002) "TRIPS, Pharmaceutical Patents and Access to Essential Medicines: Seattle, Doha and Beyond," *Chicago Journal of International Law* 3(1), 27–46.

Hodgson, D. (2007) "The New Professionals; Professionalisation and the Struggle for Occupational Control in the Field of Project Management," in D. Muzio, S. Ackroyd and J. F. Chanlat (eds.) *Redirections in the Study of Expert Labour: Medicine, Law and Management Consultancy* (Basingstoke: Palgrave Macmillan).

Hofri-Winogradow, A. (2013) "Professionals' Contribution to the Legislative Process: Between Self, Client, and the Public," *Law & Social Inquiry* 39(1), 96–126.

Hollister, M., (2009) "Is Optimal Matching Suboptimal?," *Sociological Methods & Research* 38(2), 235–264.

Hopewell, K. (2015) "Multilateral Trade Governance as Social Field: Global Civil Society and the WTO," *Review of International Political Economy* 22(6), 1128–1158.

Hopgood, S. (2006) *Keepers of the Flame: Understanding Amnesty International* (Ithaca, NY: Cornell University Press).

Hopgood, S. (2009) "Moral Authority, Modernity and the Politics of the Sacred," *European Journal of International Relations* 15(2), 229–255.

Hounshell, D. (1997) "The Cold War, RAND, and the Generation of Knowledge, 1946–1962," *Historical Studies in the Physical and Biological Studies* 27(2), 237–267.

Howe, J. (2008) *Crowdsourcing: Why the Power of the Crowd is Driving the Future of Business* (New York: CrownBusiness).

Howse, R. (1999) "Tribute: The House that Jackson Built: Restructuring the GATT System," *Michigan Journal of International Law* 20, 107–119.

Howse, R. (2002) "From Politics to Technocracy – and Back Again: The Fate of the Multilateral Trading Regime," *The American Journal of International Law* 96 (1), 94–117.

Huang, Y., L. Yadong, Y. Liu and Q. Yang (2013) "An Investigation of Interpersonal Ties in Interorganizational Exchanges in Emerging Markets," *Journal of Management* 42(6), 1557–1587.

Hussain, A. A. and M. J. Ventresca (2010) "Formal Organizing and Transnational Communities: Evidence from Global Finance Governance Associations, 1879–2006," in M. L. Djelic and S. Quack (eds.) *Transnational Communities: Shaping Global Economic Governance* (Cambridge: Cambridge University Press), 153–173.

Hutchins, E. (1995) *Cognition in the Wild* (Cambridge, MA: MIT Press).

IAASB (2002) Audit Risk: Proposed International Standards on Auditing and Proposed Amendment to ISA 200. Objective and Principles Governing an Audit of Financial Statements. Request for Comments and Explanatory Memorandum to Exposure Drafts (New York: IAASB).

IAASB (2003) *International Standard on Auditing 200. Objective and Principles Governing an Audit of Financial Statements* (New York: IAASB).

IASB (2013) "A Review of the Conceptual Framework for Financial Reporting," Discussion Paper (London, UK: International Accounting Standards Board), Available at: www.ifrs.org/Current-Projects/IASB-Projects/Conceptual-Framew ork/Discussion-Paper-July-2013/Documents/Discussion-Paper-Conceptual-Fra mework-July-2013.pdf.

IASB (2013) "Discussion Forum – Financial Reporting Disclosure: Feedback Statement" (International Accounting Standards Boards, London: IFRS Foundation, May).

IASB Staff (2009) "IAS 37 Redeliberation: Distinguishing Between a Liability and a Business Risk (Agenda Paper 3b)," *IASB*. Available at: www.iasb.org/ NR/rdonlyres/0D962775-6DFA-4D79-9438-3EABC67AD57C/0/Agendapa per3AIAS37redeliberationsCovernote.pdf.

ICRC (2009) *Professional Standards for Protection Work* (Geneva: International Committee of the Red Cross).

IETA (2013) *The IETA Membership Advantage: Climate Challenges, Market Solutions* (Geneva: International Emissions Trading Association), Available at: www.ieta.org/assets/SecretariatDocs/ieta_whatisietabrochure_2013-web21 july.pdf, accessed 5 November 2013.

IFRC (2013) *World Disasters Report: Focus on Technology and the Future of Humanitarian Intervention* (Geneva: International Federation of Red Cross and Red Crescent Societies).

IGCC (2010) "Investor Group on Climate Change Australia/New Zealand (IGCC)," *Investor Group on Climate Change*, September. Available at: www.ig cc.org.au/.

IIF (2011) *Macroprudential Oversight: An Industry Perspective* (Submission to the International Authorities). Available at: www.iif.com/regulatory/article+971.php.

IIGCC (2005) *A Climate for Change: A Trustee's Guide for Understanding and Addressing Climate Change Risk* (Institutional Investor Group on Climate Change). Available at: www.iigcc.org/__data/assets/pdf_file/0010/262/A_clim ate_for_change.pdf.

IIRC (2013a) "Key Milestones for International Integrated Reporting Committee." Available at: www.theiirc.org/about/the-work-plan/.

IIRC (2013b) "Working Group," *International Integrated Reporting Committee.* Available at: www.theiirc.org/the-iirc/structure-of-the-iirc/iirc-working-group/.

IIRC (2013c) *Board.* Available at: www.theiirc.org/the-iirc/structure-of-the-iirc/the-iirc-board/.

IIRC (2013d) *IIRC Pilot Programme Yearbook 2013* (London, UK: International Integrated Reporting Committee). Available at: www.theiirc.org/wp-content/uploads/2013/12/IIRC-PP-Yearbook-2013_PDF4_PAGES.pdf.

IIRC (2013e) "The International Framework" (London, UK: International Integrated Reporting Committee). Available at: www.theiirc.org/wp-content/uploads/2013/12/13-12-08-THE-INTERNATIONAL-IR-FRAMEWORK-2-1.pdf.

Ilcan, S. and A. Lacey (2006) "Governing Through Empowerment: Oxfam's Global Reform and Trade Campaigns," *Globalizations* 3(2), 207–225.

INCR (2013) "Investor Network on Climate Risk" (Investor Network on Climate Risk). Available at: www.ceres.org/investor-network/incr.

International Financial Services (2005) "Management Consultancy" (London: City Business Series).

Irwin, D. (1996) *Against the Tide: An Intellectual History of Free Trade* (Princeton, NJ: Princeton University Press).

ITU (2013) "Key ICT Indicators for Developed and Developing Countries and the World (Totals and Penetration Rates)" (ITU), Available at: www.itu.int/en/ITU-D/Statistics/Pages/stat/default.aspx, accessed 7 January 2014.

Jackson, J. H. (1990) *Restructuring the GATT* (London: Chatham House Papers).

Jackson, J. H. (1997) *The World Trading System: Law and Policy of International Economic Relations* (Cambridge, MA: MIT Press).

Jenson, J. and R. Levi (2013) "Narratives and Regimes of Social and Human Rights: The Jackpines of the Neoliberal Era," in P. Hall and M. Lamont (eds.) *Social Resilience in the Neoliberal Era* (New York: Cambridge University Press), 69–98.

Jerven, M. (2013) *Poor Numbers: How We Are Misled by African Development Statistics and What to Do About It* (Ithaca, NY: Cornell University Press).

Jick, T. (1979) "Mixing Qualitative and Quantitative Methods: Triangulation in Action," *Administrative Science Quarterly* 24, 602–611.

Joachim, J. (2003) "Framing Issues and Seizing Opportunities: The UN, NGOs, and Women's Rights," *International Studies Quarterly* 47(2), 247–274.

Johnson, J. (2016) *Priests of Prosperity: How Central Bankers Transformed the Postcommunist World* (Ithaca: Cornell University Press).

Jones, A. (2003) *Management Consultancy and Banking in an Era of Globalization* (Basingstoke: Palgrave Macmillan).

Kadushin, C. (1995) "Friendship among the French Financial Elite," *American Sociological Review* 60, 202–221.

Kahl, A., C. McConnell and W. Tsuma (2012) "Crowdsourcing as a Tool in Conflict Prevention," *Conflict Trends* 1, 27–34.

Kahler, M. (ed.) (2009) *Networked Politics: Agents, Power, and Governance* (Ithaca, NY: Cornell University Press).

Kaiser, K. (1971) "Transnational Relations as a Threat to the Democratic Process," *International Organization* 25(3), 706–720.

Kantorowicz, E. H. (1997) *The King's Two Bodies: A Study in Mediaeval Political Theology* (Princeton, NJ: Princeton University Press).

Kapczynski, A. (2008) "The Access to Knowledge Mobilization and the New Politics of Intellectual Property," *Yale Law Journal* 117, 804–885.

Karlsrud, J. (2016) *Norm Change in International Relations: Linked Ecologies in UN Peacekeeping Operations* (London: Routledge).

Kauppi, N. and M. R. Madsen (2013) "Transnational Power Elites: The New Professionals of Governance, Law and Security," in N. Kauppi and M. R. Madsen (eds.) *Transnational Power Elites: The New Professionals of Governance, Law and Security* (Abingdon: Routledge), 1–16.

Keck, M. E. and K. Sikking (1998) *Activists Beyond Borders: Advocacy Networks in International Politics* (Ithaca, NY: Cornell University Press).

Kellogg, K. C. (2014) "Brokerage Professions and Implementing Reform in the Age of Experts," *American Sociological Review* 79(5), 912–941.

Kennedy, D. (1995) "The International Style in Postwar Law and Policy: John Jackson and the Field of International Economic Law," *American University International Law Review* 10(2), 671–716.

Kennedy, Denis (2008) *Humanitarian NGOs and the Norm of Neutrality: A Community Approach* (Minnesota: University of Minnesota Press).

Kennickell, Arthur (2009) "Ponds and Streams: Wealth and Income in the US, 1989 to 2007," in *Federal Reserve Board Finance and Economics Discussion Series* (Washington, DC: Federal Reserve Board), Available at: www.federalreserve.gov/pubs/feds/2009/200913/200913pap.pdf, accessed 12 April 2012.

Kentikelenis, A. and L. Seabrooke (2017) "The Politics of World Polity: Script-Writing in International Organizations," *American Sociological Review* 82, forthcoming.

Keohane, R. O. (1984) *After Hegemony: Cooperation and Discord in the World Political Economy* (Princeton: Princeton University Press).

Keohane, R. O. and J. S. Nye (1977). *Power and Interdependence: World Politics in Tansition* (Boston: Little, Brown).

Khurana, Rakesh, Kenneth Kimura, and Marion Fourcade (2011) "How Foundations Think: The Ford Foundation as a Dominating Institution in the Field of American Business Schools," *Working Paper 11–070* (Boston, MA: Harvard Business School).

Kim, H. J. and J. C. Sharman (2014) "Accounts and Accountability: Corruption, Human Rights, and Individual Accountability Norms," *International Organization* 68(2), 417–448.

Kinnon, C. (1995) *WTO: What's in for the WHO?* (WHO).

Kipping, M. (2002) "Trapped in Their Wave: The Evolution of Management Consultancies," in T. Clark and R. Fincham (eds.) *Critical Consulting: New Perspectives on the Management Advice Industry* (Oxford: Blackwell), 28–49.

Kipping, M. and C. Wright (2012) "Consultants in Context: Global Dominance, Societal Effect and the Capitalist System," in M. Kipping and T. Clark (eds.) *The Oxford Handbook of Management Consulting* (Oxford: Oxford University Press), 165–185.

Klimkeit, D. and M. Reihlen (2016) "Local Responses to Global Integration in a Transnational Professional Service Firm," *Journal of Professions and Organization* 3, 39–61.

Knorr-Cetina, K. (1999) *Epistemic Cultures: How the Sciences Make Knowledge* (Cambridge, MA: Harvard University Press).

Knorr Cetina, K. and U. Bruegger (2002) "Global Microstructures: The Virtual Societies of Financial Markets," *American Journal of Sociology* 105(4), 905–950.

Knox-Hayes, J. (2009) "The Developing Carbon Financial Service Industry: Expertise, Adaptation and Complementarity in London and New York," *Journal of Economic Geography* 9(6), 749–777.

Koekkoek, A. and L. B. M. Mennes (eds.) (1991) *International Trade and Global Development: Essays in Honour of Jagdish Bhagwati* (London: Routledge).

Kogan, M. (1994) "Researching the Powerful in Education and Elsewhere," in G. Walford (ed.) *Researching the Powerful in Education* (London: UCL Press), 67–80.

Kolk, A., D. Levy, and J. Pinkse (2008) "Corporate Responses in an Emerging Climate Regime: The Institutionalization and Commensuration of Carbon Disclosure," *European Accounting Review* 17(4), 719–745.

Konings, M. (2016). Governing the system: Risk, finance, and neoliberal reason. *European Journal of International Relations*, 22(2), 268–288.

Koremenos, Barbara, Charles Lipson and Duncan Snidal (2001) "The Rational Design of International Institutions," *International Organization* 55(4), 761–799.

Korey, W. (1998) *NGOs and the Universal Declaration of Human Rights: "A Curious Grapevine"* (New York: St. Martin's Press).

Korey, W. (2007) *Taking on the World's Repressive Regimes: The Ford Foundation's International Human Rights Policies and Practices* (New York: Palgrave Macmillan).

Kossoy, A. and P. Guigon (2012) *State and Trends of the Carbon Market 2012* (Washington, DC: World Bank).

Krause, M. (2014) *The Good Project: Humanitarian Relief NGOs and the Fragmentation of Reason* (Chicago: University of Chicago Press).

Kroeger, F. (2011) "Trusting Organizations: The Institutionalization of Trust in Interorganizational Relationships," *Organization* 19(6), 743–763.

Krueger, A. O. (1998) "Why Trade Liberalisation is Good for Growth," *The Economic Journal* 108, 1513–1522.

Kuttner, R. (2007) "The Squandering of America," *New York Times*, 16 December.

Laber, J. (2002) *The Courage of Strangers: Coming of Age with the Human Rights Movement* (New York: Public Affairs).

Lall, R. (2017) "Beyond Institutional Design: Explaining the Performance of International Organizations," *International Organization*, forthcoming.

Lampel, J. and A. D. Meyer (2008) "Field-Configuring Events as Structuring Mechanisms: How Conferences, Ceremonies, and Trade Shows Constitute New Technologies, Industries, and Markets," *Journal of Management Studies* 45(6), 1025–1035.

Lang, A. (2011) *World Trade Law after Neoliberalism: Re-imagining the Global Economic Order* (Oxford: Oxford University Press).

Lapsley, I. and R. Oldfield (2001) "Transforming the Public Sector: Management Consultants as Agents of Change," *The European Accounting Review* 10(3), 523–543.

Latour, B. (1987) *Science in Action: How to Follow Scientists and Engineers through Society* (Cambridge, MA: Harvard University Press).

Laughlin, R. and J. Pallot (1998) "Trends, Patterns and Influencing Factors: Some Reflections," *Global Warning: Debating International Developments in New Public Financial Management* 376–399.

Lawrence, T. B., R. Suddaby, and B. Leca (eds.) (2009) *Actors and Agency in Institutional Studies of Organizations* (Cambridge: Cambridge University Press).

Lazega, E. (2001) *Micropolitics of Knowledge: Communication and Indirect Control in Workgroups* (New York, NY: Aldine de Gruyter).

Lazega, E., M. T. Jourda, L. Mounier and R. Stofer (2008) "Catching up with the Big Fish in the Big Pond? Multi-level Network Analysis through Linked Design," *Social Networks* 30(2), 159–176.

Lazega, E., E. Quintane, and S. Casenaz (2017) "Collegial Oligarchy and Networks of Normative Alignments in Transnational Institution Building," *Social Networks* 48, 10–22.

Lesage, D. and Y. Kaçar (2013) "Tax Justice through Country-by-Country Reporting: An Analysis of the Idea's Political Journey," in J. Leaman and A. Waris (eds.) *Tax Justice and the Political Economy of Global Capitalism, 1945 to the Present* (New York and Oxford: Berghahn Books).

Le Roux, B. and H. Rouanet (2010) *Multiple Correspondence Analysis* (London: Sage).

Lesnard, L. (2010) "Setting Cost in Optimal Matching to Uncover Contemporaneous Socio-Temporal Patterns," *Sociological Methods & Research* 38(3), 389–419.

Letouzé, E., P. Meier, and P. Vinck (2012) *Big Data for Development: Challenges and Opportunities* (New York: UN Global Pulse).

Levi Faur, D. and S. M. Starobin (2014) "Transnational Politics and Policy: From Two-Way to Three-Way Interactions," Jerusalem Papers in Regulation & Governance, Working Paper *no.* 62, February.

Levi, R. and J. Hagan (2008) "Penser les 'Crimes de Guerre'," *Actes de la Recherche en Sciences Sociales* 173, 6–21.

Levy, D. (2005) "Offshoring in the New Global Political Economy," *Journal of Management Studies* 42(3), 685–693.

Levy, D. L. and P. J. Newell (2002) "Business Strategy and International Environmental Governance," *Global Environmental Politics* 2(4), 84–100.

Lindquist, E. A. (2009) "There's More to Policy than Alignment," in *CPRN Research Report* (Ottawa: Canadian Policy Research Networks, May).

Lindvall, J. (2009) "The Real but Limited Influence of Expert Ideas," *World Politics* 61(4), 703–730.

Living Economies Forum (2013) "Feedback to the International Integrated Reporting Council (IIRC) on the Integrated Reporting Prototype Framework Working Document," July. Available at: www.theiirc.org/wp-con tent/uploads/2013/08/096_Living-Economies-Forum.pdf.

Loewenstein, J. (2014) "Take my Word for it: How Professional Vocabularies Foster Organizing," *Journal of Professions and Organization* 1(1), 65–83.

Longford, S. (1999) "OCHA One Year On: Is Humanitarian Coordination any Better," *Humanitarian Exchange Magazine* 13.

Lorrain, F. and H. C. White (1971) "Structural Equivalence of Individuals in Social Networks," *Journal of Mathematical Sociology* 1(1), 49–80.

Lovell, H. and D. MacKenzie (2011) "Accounting for Carbon: The Role of Accounting Professional Organisations in Governing Climate Change," *Antipode* 43(3), 704–731.

Løwendahl, B. (2000) *Strategic Management in Professional Service Firms* (Copenhagen: Copenhagen Business School Press).

MacDonald, K. M. (1995) *The Sociology of the Professions* (London: Sage).

MacLeod, M. (2010) "Private Governance and Climate Change: Institutional Investors and Emerging Investor-Driven Governance Mechanisms," *St Antony's International Review* 5(2), 46–65.

Macleod, M. and J. Park (2011) "Financial Activism and Global Climate Change: The Rise of Investor-Driven Governance Networks," *Global Environmental Politics* 11(2), 54–74.

Madsen, M. R. (2010) *La Genèse De L'europe Des Droits De L'homme: Enjeux Juridiques Et Stratégies D'etat (France, Grande-Bretagne Et Pays Scandinaves, 1945–1970)* (Strasbourg: Presses Universitaires de Strasbourg).

Madsen, M. R. (2011a) "Reflexivity and the Construction of the International Object: The Case of Human Rights," *International Political Sociology* 5, 259–275.

Madsen, M. R. (2011b) "The Protracted Institutionalisation of the Strasbourg Court: From Legal Diplomacy to Integrationist Jurisprudence," in M. R. Madsen and J. Christoffersen (eds.) *The European Court of Human Rights between Law and Politics* (Oxford: Oxford University Press), 43–60.

Madsen, M. R. (2016) "La Guerre Froide et la fabrication des droits de l'homme contemporains: Une théorie transnationale de l'évolution des droits de l'homme," *European Journal of Human Rights* 2, 197–220.

Mahoney, J. and K. Thelen (2010) "A Theory of Gradual Institutional Change," in J. Mahoney and K. Thelen (eds.) *Explaining Institutional Change: Ambiguity, Agency and Power in Historical Institutionalism* (Cambridge: Cambridge University Press), 1–37.

Malhotra, N. and T. Morris (2009) "Heterogeneity in Professional Service Firms," *Journal of Management Studies* 46, 895–922.

Malinowski, Bronislaw (2003) [1922] *Argonauts of the Western Pacific* (New York: Routledge).

Malkki, L. H. (1996) "Speechless Emissaries: Refugees, Humanitarianism, and Dehistoricization," *Cultural Anthropology* 11(3), 377–404.

Malsch, B. (2013) "Politicizing the Expertise of the Accounting Industry in the Realm of Corporate Social Responsibility," *Accounting, Organizations and Society* 38, 149–168.

Mancini, F. (ed.) (2013) *New Technology and the Prevention of Violence and Conflict* (New York: International Peace Institute).

Mangold, K. (2012) " 'Struggling to Do the Right Thing': Challenges during International Volunteering," *Third World Quarterly* 33(8), 1493–1509.

Marcus, G. (1983) "The Fiduciary Role in American Family Dynasties and Their Institutional Legacy," in G. Marcus (ed.) *Elites: Ethnographic Issues* (Albuquerque: University of New Mexico Press), 221–256.

Marcus, G. and P. D. Hall (1992) *Lives in Trust: The Fortunes of Dynastic Families in Late Twentieth-Century America* (Boulder: Westview Press).

Marcus, George (1995) "Ethnography in/of the World System: The Emergence of Multi-Sited Ethnography," *Annual Review of Anthropology* 24, 95–117.

Marcussen, M. (2006) "The Fifth Age of Central Banking in the Global Economy," paper presented at the conference "Frontiers of Regulation," University of Bath, 7–8 September 2006.

Martin, J. F. (1998) *Reorienting a Nation: Consultants and Australian Public Policy* (Aldershot: Ashgate).

Martines, L. (1968) *Lawyers and Statecraft in Renaissance Florence* (Princeton, NJ: Princeton University Press).

Massoud, M. F. (2011) "Do Victims of War Need International Law? Human Rights Education Programs in Authoritarian Sudan," *Law and Society Review* 45(1), 1–32.

Matthews, D. (2002) *Globalising Intellectual Property Rights: The TRIPs Agreement* (London: Routledge).

May, C. (2000) *A Global Political Economy of Intellectual Property Rights: The New Enclosures?* (London and New York: Routledge).

May, C. (2007) "The World Intellectual Property Organisation and the Development Agenda," *Global Governance* 13, 161–170.

McCallum, J. K. (2013) *Global Unions, Local Power: The New Spirit of Transnational Labor Organizing* (Ithaca, NY: Cornell University Press).

McCarthy, K. D. (1997) "From Government to Grassroots Reform: The Ford Foundation's Population Programs in South Asia, 1959–1981," in S. Hewa (ed.) *Philanthropy and Cultural Context: Western Philanthropy in South, East, and Southeast Asia in the 20th Century* (Lanham, MD: University of America).

McDowell, L. (1998) "Elites in the City of London: Some Methodological Considerations," *Environment and Planning* 30, 2133–2146.

McKenna, C. D. (2006) *The World's Newest Profession. Management Consulting in the Twentieth Century* (Cambridge: Cambridge University Press).

McNamee, S. and R. Miller (1989) "Estate Inheritance: A Sociological Lacuna," *Sociological Inquiry* 38, 7–29.

McTavish, D.-G. and E.-B. Pirro (1990) "Contextual Content Analysis," *Quality and Quantity* 24, 245–265.

Mears, Ashley (2013) "Ethnography as Precarious Work," *The Sociological Quarterly* 54, 20–34.

Medvedtz, T. (2012) *Think Tanks in America* (Chicago: University of Chicago Press).

Meier, P. (2015) *Digital Humanitarians: How Big Data Is Changing the Face of Humanitarian Response* (Boca Raton: CRC Press).

Meyer, J., J. Boli, G. Thomas and F. Ramirez (1997) "World Society and the Nation-State," *American Journal of Sociology* 103, 144–181.

Meyer, J. W. and R. L. Jepperson (2000) "The 'Actors' of Modern Society: The Cultural Construction of Social Agency," *Sociological Theory* 18(1), 100–120.

Mikecz, R. (2012) "Interviewing Elites: Addressing Methodological Issues," *Qualitative Inquiry* 18, 482–493.

Milner, M. E. and A. Verity (2013) "Collaborative Innovation in Humanitarian Affairs: Organization and Governance in the Era of Digital Humanitarianism," *Digital Humanitarian Network*. Available at: https://app.box.com/s/oq2gd cy466j6bpdvzyxt, accessed 13 January 2014.

Mir, R. and A. Mir (2009) "From the Corporation to the Colony: Studying Knowledge Transfer across International Boundaries," *Group and Organization Management* 34(1), 90–113.

Mitchell, S. M. and E. J. Powell (2011) *Domestic Law Goes Global: Legal Traditions and International Courts* (Cambridge: Cambridge University Press).

Montoya, C. (2013) *From Global to Grassroots: The European Union, Transnational Advocacy, and Combating Violence against Women* (Oxford: Oxford University Press).

Moore, K. and J. Birkinshaw (1998) "Managing Knowledge in Global Service Firms: Centers of Excellence," *Academy of Management Executive* 12, 81–92.

Morgan, G. (2006) "Transnational Actors, Transnational Institutions, Transnational Spaces: The Role of Law Firms in the Internationalization of Competition Regulation," in M.-L. Djelic and K. Sahlin-Andersson (eds.) *Transnational Governance. Institutional Dynamics of Regulation* (Cambridge: Cambridge University Press), 139–160.

Morgan, G. (2014) "Financialization and the Multinational Corporation," *Transfer: European Review of Labour and Research* 20(2), 183–197.

Morgan, G. and S. Quack (2006) "The Internationalization of Professional Service Firms: Global Convergence, National Path-dependency or Cross-border Hybridization?" in R. Greenwood and R. Suddaby (eds.) *Research in the Sociology of Organizations*, 24 (Oxford: Professional Service Firms, JAI Press), 403–431.

Morgan, G., A. Sturdy and S. Quack (2006) "The Globalization of Management Consultancy Firms: Constraints and Limitations," CSGR Working Paper no. *168/05*.

Morin, J.-F. (2014) "Paradigm Shift in the Global IP Regime: The Agency of Academics," *Review of International Political Economy* 21(2), 275–309.

Moyn, S. (2010) *The Last Utopia: Human Rights in History* (Cambridge, MA: Belknap Press).

Murdie, A. and D. R. Davis (2012) "Shaming and Blaming: Using Events Data to Assess the Impact of Human Rights INGOs," *International Studies Quarterly* 56(1), 1–16.

Murphy, H. (2010) *The Making of International Trade Policy: NGOs, Agenda-Setting and the WTO* (Cheltenham: Edward Elgar).

Murphy, R. (2003) "A Proposed Accounting Standard: Reporting Turnover and Tax by Location" (The Association for Accountancy and Business Affairs Ltd.).

Murphy, R. (2010) "Country by Country Reporting: Shining Light onto Financial Statements" (Tax Justice Network International).

Murphy, R. (2012) "Country-by-Country Reporting: Accounting for globalization locally, Edition 1.2" (Richard Murphy and the Tax Justice Network).

Murphy, R. and S.N. Stausholm (2017) 'The Big Four: A Study in Opacity. A Report for GUE/NGL (London:Tax Research LLP/CITYPERC).

Muzaka, V. (2011) "Linkages, Contests and Overlaps in the Global Intellectual Property Rights Regime," *European Journal of International Relations* 17(4), 755–776.

Muzio, D. and J. R. Faulconbridge (2013) "The Global Professional Service Firm: 'One Firm' Models versus (Italian) Distant Institutionalised Practices," *Organization Studies* 34, 897–925.

Muzio, D., D. Hodgson, J. Faulconbridge, J. Beaverstock, and S. Hall (2011) "Towards Corporate Professionalization: The Case of Project Management, Management Consultancy and Executive Search," *Current Sociology* 59, 443–464.

Nader, L. (1972) "Up the Anthropologist: Perspectives Gained from Studying Up," in D. Hynes (ed.) *Reinventing Anthropology* (New York: Pantheon), 284–311.

Neier, A. (2012) *The International Human Rights Movement: A History* (Princeton, NJ: Princeton University Press).

Nelson, S. C. (2014) "Playing Favorites: How Shared Beliefs Shape the IMF's Lending Decisions," *International Organization* 68(2), 297–328.

Nelson, S. C. (2017) *The Currency of Confidence: How Economic Beliefs Shape the IMF's Relationship with its Borrowers* (Ithaca: Cornell University Press).

Neumann, I. B. (2012) *At Home with the Diplomats. Inside a European Foreign Ministry* (Ithaca, NY: Cornell University Press).

Neumann, I. B. and O. J. Sending (2010) *Governing the Global Polity: Practice, Mentality, Rationality* (Michigan: University of Michigan Press).

Newman, A. (2012) "Building Transnational Civil Liberties: Transgovernmental Entrepreneurs and the European Data Privacy Directive," *International Organization* 62(1), 103–130.

Nilsson, A. (2017) "Making Norms to Tackle Global Challenges: The Role of Intergovernmental Organisations," *Research Policy*, 46(1), 171–181.

Nohria, N. and S. Ghoshal (1997) *The Differentiated Network* (San Francisco: Jossey-Bass Publications).

Noji, E. K. and M. J. Toole (1997) "The Historical Development of Public Health Responses to Disasters," *Disasters* 21(4), 366–376.

Nolke, A. and J. Perry (2007) "The Power of Transnational Private Governance: Financialization and the IASB," *Business & Politics* 9(3), 1–34.

Noordegraaf, M. and M. Schinkel (2011) "Professional Capital Contested: A Bourdieusian Analysis of Conflicts between Professionals and Managers," *Comparative Sociology* 10, 97–125.

Nunn, A., E. D. Fonseca and S. Gruskin (2009) "Changing Global Essential Medicines Norms to Improve Access to AIDS Treatment: Lessons from Brazil," *Global Public Health* 4(2), 131–149.

O'Dwyer, B., D. Owen, and J. Unerman (2011) "Seeking Legitimacy for New Assurance Forms: The Case of Assurance on Sustainability Reporting," *Accounting, Organizations and Society* 36, 31–52.

O'Shea, J. and C. Madigan (1997) *Dangerous Company: The Consulting Powerhouses and the Businesses They Save and Ruin* (New York: Time Business).

OCHA (2006) "OCHA's Role in Supporting Protection: International and Field Level Responsibilities," in *Policy Instruction* (New York: UN OCHA).

OCHA (2009) "Mapping of Key Emergency Needs Assessment and Analysis Initiatives," in *Assessment and Classification of Emergencies Project* (New York: United Nations Office for the Coordination of Humanitarian Affairs).

OCHA (2013) *Humanitarianism in the Network Age* (New York: UN OCHA).

Odendahl, T. and A. Shaw (2002) "Interviewing Elites," in J. Gubrium and J. Holstein (eds.) *Handbook of Interview Research: Context and Method* (Thousand Oaks, CA: Sage), 299–236.

OECD (2012) *Fragile States 2013: Resource Flows and Trends in a Shifting World* (Paris: OECD).

OECD (2013a) "Addressing Base Erosion and Profit Shifting" (Organization for Economic Cooperation and Development, Paris: OECD).

OECD (2013b) "Action Plan on Base Erosion and Profit Shifting" (Organization for Economic Cooperation and Development, Paris: OECD).

OECD (2014) "Discussion Draft on Transfer Pricing and CbC Reporting" (Organization for Economic Cooperation and Development, Paris: OECD).

OECD/G20 (2015) "BEPS 2015 Final Reports" (Paris: OECD), Available at: www.oecd.org/tax/beps-2015-final-reports.htm, accessed 24 march 2016.

Okediji, R. L. (2008) "WIPO-WTO Relations and the Future of Global Intellectual Property Norms," *Netherlands Yearbook of International Law* 39, 69–125.

Olesen, T. (2009) "The Transnational Zapatista Solidarity Network: An Infrastructure Analysis," *Global Networks* 4(1), 89–107.

O'Mahoney, J. and A. Sturdy (2015) "Power and the Diffusion of Management Ideas: The Case of McKinsey & Co.," *Management Learning* 47(3), 247–265.

Orbinski, J. (1998) "On the Meaning of SPHERE Standards to States and other Humanitarian Actors," Paper read at SPHERE closing ceremony 3 December 1998, London.

Ostrander, S. (1993) "Surely You're Not In This Just To Be Helpful: Access, Rapport and Interviews in Three Studies of Elites," *Journal of Contemporary Ethnography* 22, 7–27.

Ostrower, F. (1995) *Why the Wealthy Give: The Culture of Elite Philanthropy* (Princeton, NJ: Princeton University Press).

Ovodenko, A. and R. O. Keohane (2012) "Institutional Diffusion in International Environmental Affairs," *International Affairs* 88(3), 523–541.

Ovsiovitch, J. S. (1998) "Feeding the Watchdogs: Philanthropic Support for Human Rights NGOs," *Buffalo Human Rights Law Review* 4, 341–363.

Oxfam International (2002a) "Cultivating Poverty: The Impact of US Cotton Subsidies on Africa," Oxfam Briefing Paper *30* (Oxford: Oxfam International, September).

Oxford International (2002b) *Rigged Rules and Double Standards: Trade, Globalisation and the Fight against Poverty* (Oxford: Oxfam International).

Pache, A. C. and F. Santos (2010) "When Worlds Collide: The Internal Dynamics of Organizational Responses to Conflicting Institutional Demands," *Academy of Management Review* 35, 455–476.

Padgett, J. F. and C. K. Ansell (1992) "Robust Action and the Rise of the Medici 1400–1434" *American Journal of Sociology* 98(6), 1259, 1319.

Padgett, J. F. and P. D. McLean (2006) "Organizational Invention and Elite Transformation: The Birth of Partnership Systems in Renaissance Florence," *American Journal of Sociology* 111(5), 1463–1568.

Padgett, J. F. and W. W. Powell (2012) The Emergence of Organizations and Markets (Princeton: Princeton University Press).

Paik, Y. and D. Y. Choi (2005) "The Shortcomings of a Standardized Global Knowledge Management System: The Case Study of Accenture," *The Academy of Management Executive* 19(2), 81–84.

Palan, R. and D. Wigan (2014) "Herding Cats and Taming Tax Havens: The US Strategy of 'Not In My Backyard' Global Policy," 5(3), 334–343.

Palmisano, S. J. (2006) "The Globally Integrated Enterprise," *Foreign Affairs* 85(3), 127–136.

Parmar, I. (2012a) *Foundations of the American Century: The Ford, Carnegie, and Rockefeller Foundations in the Rise of American Power* (New York: Columbia University Press).

Parmar, I. (2012b) "Foundation Networks and American Hegemony," *European Journal of American Studies* 1, 2–25.

Parry, B. (1998) "Hunting the Gene-hunters: The Role of Hybrid Networks, Status, and Chance in Conceptualising and Accessing 'Corporate Elites'," *Environment and Planning A* 30, 2147–2162.

Partnership for Market Readiness (2013) "Partnership for Market Readiness: Pricing Carbon and Shaping the Next Generation of Carbon Markets," in *PMR Brochure* (Washington, DC: World Bank, May), Available at: www.thepmr.org/system/files/documents/PMR_brochure_web.pdf, accessed 5 November 2013.

Patent Pool Initiative (2009) *Patent Pool Implementation Plan* (UNITAID).

Paterson, M., M. Hoffmann, M. Betsill and S. Bernstein (2014) "The Micro foundations of Policy Diffusion towards Complex Global Governance: An Analysis of the Transnational Carbon Emission Trading Network," *Comparative Political Studies* 47, 3–4.

Paton, S., D. Hodgson and D. Muzio (2013) "The Price of Corporate Professionalisation: Analysing the Corporate Capture of Professions in the UK and Consequences for Expert Labour," *New Technology Work and Employment* 28(3), 227–240.

Pattberg, P. (2007) *Private Institutions and Global Governance: The New Politics of Environmental Stability* (Cheltenham: Edward Elgar).

Pattberg, P. and J. Stripple (2008) "Beyond the Public and Private Divide: Remapping Transnational Climate Governance in the 21st Century," *International Environmental Agreements* 8, 367–388.

Perry, J. and A. Nölke (2006) "The Political Economy of International Accounting Standards," *Review of International Political Economy* 13(4), 559–586.

Persaud, A. (2000) "Sending the Herd off the Cliff Edge: The Disturbing Interaction between Herding and Market-Sensitive Risk Management Systems," *World Economics* 1(4), 15–26.

Persaud, A. (2009) "Macroprudential Regulation: Fixing Fundamental Market and Regulatory Failures," *Crisis Response* (Note number 6) (The World Bank Group, Financial and Private Sector Development, July).

Peters-Stanley, M. and D. Yin (2013) *Maneuvering the Mosaic: State of the Voluntary Carbon Markets 2013. A Report by Forest Trends' Ecosystem Marketplace and Bloomberg New Energy Finance* (Washington, DC: Forest Trends' Ecosystem Marketplace), Available at: www.forest-trends.org/docu ments/files/doc_3898.pdf, accessed 5 November 2013.

Petitet, V. (2006) *Les Nettoyeurs* (Paris: Jean-Claude Lattès).

Phillips, N., T. B. Lawrence, and C. Hardy (2004) "Discourse and Institutions," *Academy of Management Review* 29, 635–652.

Picciotto, S. (1992) *International Business Taxation: A Study in the Internationalization of Business Regulation* (Cambridge: Cambridge University Press).

Picciotto, S. (2011) *Regulating Global Corporate Capitalism* (Cambridge: Cambridge University Press).

Porter, T. (2005) "Private Authority, Technical Authority, and the Globalization of Accounting Standards," *Business and Politics* 7(3).

Postma, J., L. Oldenhof, and K. Putters (2015) "Organized Professionalism in Healthcare: Articulation Work by Neighbourhood Nurses," *Journal of Professions and Organization* 2(1), 61–77.

Poulantzas, N. (2000) *State, Power, Socialism* (London: Verso).

Powell, W. W. (1990) "Neither Market nor Hierarchy: Network Forms of Organization," *Research in Organizational Behavior* 12, 295–336.

Powers, S. (2008) *Chasing the Flame: One Man's Fight to Save the World* (Westminister: Penguin Ltd.).

PriceWaterhouse Coopers (2013d) *Improving Public Sector Productivity through Prioritization, Measurement, and Alignment.* Available at: www.pwc.com/en_ GX/gx/psrc/pdf/pwc-improving-public-sector-productivity-through-prioritisa tion-measurement-and-alignment.pdf.

Project 88 (1988) *Project 88: Harnessing Market Forces To Protect The Environment. A Public Policy Study sponsored by Senator Timothy E. Wirth, Colorado, and Senator John Heinz, Pennsylvania* (Washington, DC December).

Projet Qualite (2002) "Proceedings of the Launching Seminar for the Quality Project," *Paper read at Quality Project,* Paris.

Provan, K., A. Fish, and J. Sydow (2007) "Interorganizational Networks at the Network Level: A Review of the Empirical Literature on Whole Networks," *Journal of Management* 33(3), 479.

Putnam, R. D. (1988) "Diplomacy and Domestic Politics: The Logic of Two-Level Games," *International Organization* 42, 427–460.

PWYP (2010) "Response to the European Commission's Public Consultation on Country-By-Country Reporting by Multinational Companies – Document 2" (Publish What You Pay).

Quack, S. (2007) "Legal Professionals and Transnational Law-Making: A Case of Distributed Agency," *Organization* 14(5), 643–666.

Quack, S. (2010) "Law, Expertise and Legitimacy in Transnational Economic Governance," *Socio-Economic Review* 8, 3–16.

Quick, Jonathan D. et al. (2002) "Twenty-Five Years of Essential Medicines," *Bulletin of the World Health Organization* 80(11), 913–914.

Ramalingam, B. and J. Mitchell (2008) *ALNAP's 8th Review of Humanitarian Action: Counting What Counts: Performance and Effectiveness in the Humanitarian Sector* (London: ALNAP).

Raucher, A. R. (1985) *Paul G. Hoffman: Architect of Foreign Aid* (Lexington, KY: University of Kentucky).

Rawls, J. (1999) *A Theory of Justice* (revised edn.) (Cambridge, MA: Harvard University Press).

Redfield, P. (2006) "A Less Modest Witness," *American Ethnologist* 33(1), 3–26.

Redfield, P. (2012) "The Unbearable Lightness of Ex-Pats: Double Binds of Humanitarian Mobility," *Cultural Anthropology* 27(2), 358–382.

Richards, D. (1996) "Elite Interviews: Approaches and Pitfalls," *Politics* 16, 199–204.

Richardson, B. J. (2002) *Environmental Regulation through Financial Organisations* (London: Kluwer Law International).

Ricoeur, P. (1965) *Fallible Man* (Chicago: Henry Regency).

Risse, T., S. C. Ropp, and K. Sikkink (eds.) (1999) *The Power of Human Rights: International Norms and Domestic Change* (Cambridge: Cambridge University Press).

Robson, K., C. Humphrey, R. Kalifa, and J. Jones (2007) "Transforming Auditing Technologies: Business Risk Audit Methodologies and the Audit Field," *Accounting, Organization and Society* 32, 409–432.

Rodríguez, F. and D. Rodrik (2000) "Trade Policy and Economic Growth: A Skeptic's Guide to the Cross-National Evidence," *NBER Macroeconomics Annual* 15, 261–325.

Rodrik, D. (2006) "Goodbye Washington Consensus, Hello Washington Confusion? A Review of the World Bank's Economic Growth in the 1990s: Learning from a Decade of Reform," *Journal of Economic Literature* 44(4), 973–987.

Roethlisberger, Fritz and William Dickson (1939) *Management and the Worker* (Cambridge, MA: Harvard University Press).

Romanin, E. A. (2012) "De la Resistencia a la Integración. Las Transformaciones de la Asociación Madres de la 'Era Kirchner,'" *Estudios Politicos* 41, 36–56.

Rose, T. and B. Hinings (1999) "Global Clients' Demands Driving Change in Global Business Advisory Firms," in D. Brock et al. (eds.) *Restructuring the Professional Organization: Accounting, Health Care and Law* (London: Routledge), 41–67.

Roth, K. (2004) "Defending Economic, Social and Cultural Rights: Practical Issues Faced by an International Human Rights Organization," *Human Rights Quarterly* 26(1), 63–73.

Ryen, A. (2004) "Ethical Issues in Qualitative Research," in C. Seale et al. (eds.) *Qualitative Research Practice* (Thousand Oaks, CA: Sage), 230–247.

Sachs, J. D. and A. M. Warner (1995) "Economic Reform and the Process of Global Integration," *Brookings Papers on Economic Activity* 1, 1–118.

Sacriste, G. and A. Vauchez (2007) "The Force of International Law: Lawyers' Diplomacy on the International Scene in the 1920s," *Law & Social Inquiry* 32, 83–107.

Sadler, D. and S. Lloyd (2009) "Neo-liberalising Corporate Social Responsibility: a Political Economy of Corporate Citizenship," *Geoforum* 40(4), 613–622.

Sahlin-Andersson, K. and L. Engwall (eds.) (2002) *The Expansion of Management Knowledge: Carriers, Flows, and Sources* (Stanford, CA: Stanford University Press).

Saks, M. (2016) "A Review of Theories of Professions, Organizations and Society: The case for neo-Weberianism, neo-institutionalism and eclecticism" *Journal of Professions and Organizations* 1, 1–18.

Salamon, Lester and William Burckart (2014) "Foundations as 'Philanthropic Banks'," in Lester Salamon (ed.) *New Frontiers of Philanthropy: A Guide to the New Tools and New Actors Reshaping Global Philanthropy and Social Investing* (New York: Oxford University Press), 165–208.

Sanday, Patricia (1979) "The Ethnographic Paradigm(s)," *Administrative Science Quarterly* 24, 527–538.

Sandvik, K. B., M. G. Jumbert, J. Karlsrud and M. Kaufman (2014) "Humanitarian Technology: A Critical Research Agenda," International Review of the Red Cross, 96(893), 219–242.

SASB (2013a) "Vision and Mission," *Sustainability Accounting Standards Board.* Available at: www.sasb.org/sasb/vision-mission/.

SASB (2013b) "Standards Council," *Sustainability Accounting Standards Board.* Available at: www.sasb.org/sasb/standards-council/.

SASB (2013c) "Determining Materiality," *Sustainability Accounting Standards Board.* Available at: www.sasb.org/materiality/determining-materiality/.

SASB (2013d) "The SASB Corporate Roundtable," *Sustainability Accounting Standards Board.* Available at: www.sasb.org/our-process/pilot-program/.

SASB (2013e) "Standards Outcome Review: Health Care," *Sustainability Accounting Standards Board.* Available at: www.sasb.org/wp-content/uploads/2013/07/SASB-Outcome-Review-Report-Healthcare.pdf.

SASB (2013f) "Conceptual Framework," *Sustainability Accounting Standards Board.* Available at: www.sasb.org/wp-content/uploads/2013/10/SASB-Conceptual-Framework-Final-Formatted-10-22-13.pdf.

Schemeil, Y. (2013) "Bringing International Organization In: Global Institutions as Adaptive Hybrids," *Organization Studies* 34(2), 219–252.

Schmidheiny, S. and F. Zorraquin (1996) *Financing Change: The Financial Community, Eco-efficiency, and Sustainable Development* (Cambridge, MA: MIT Press).

Schneider, H. (2002) "On the Fault-line: the Politics of AIDS Policy in Contemporary South Africa," *African Studies* 61(1).

Schwartz, T. P. (1993) "Testamentary Behavior: Issues and Evidence about Individuality, Altruism and Social Influence," *Sociological Quarterly* 34, 337–355.

Scott, W. R. (2008) "Lords of the Dance: Professionals as Institutional Agents," *Organization Studies* 29, 219–238.

Scott-Railton, J. (2013) *Revolutionary Risks: Cyber Technology and Threats in the 2011 Libyan Revolution* (Newport, Rhode Island: United States Naval War College).

Seabrooke, L. (2014a) "Epistemic Arbitrage: Transnational Professional Knowledge in Action," *Journal of Professions and Organizations* 1(1), 49–64.

Seabrooke, L. (2014b) "Identity Switching and Transnational Professionals," *International Political Sociology* 8(3), 335–337.

Seabrooke, L. and E. Nilsson (2015) "Professional Skills in International Financial Surveillance: Assessing Change in IMF Policy Teams," *Governance: An International Journal of Policy, Administration and Institutions* 28(2), 237–254.

Seabrooke, L. and E. Tsingou (2009) "Revolving Doors and Linked Ecologies in the World Economy: Policy Locations and the Practice of International Financial Reform," *Working Papers Centre for the Study of Globalisation and Regionalisation* (University of Warwick).

Seabrooke, L. and E. Tsingou (2014) "Distinctions, Affiliations, and Professional Knowledge in Financial Reform Expert Groups," *Journal of European Public Policy* 21(3), 389–407.

Seabrooke, L. and E. Tsingou (2015) "Professional Emergence on Transnational Issues: Linked Ecologies on Demographic Change," *Journal of Professions and Organization* 2(1), 1–18.

Seabrooke, L. and E. Tsingou (2016) "Bodies of Knowledge in Reproduction: Epistemic Boundaries in the Political Economy of Fertility," *New Political Economy* 21(1), 69–89.

Seabrooke, L. and D. Wigan (2014) "Global Wealth Chains in the International Political Economy," *Review of International Political Economy* 21(1), 257–263.

Seabrooke, L. and D. Wigan (2015) "How Activists Use Benchmarks: Reformist and Revolutionary Benchmarks for Global Economic Justice," *Review of International Studies* 41(5), 887–904.

Seabrooke, L. and D. Wigan (2016) "Powering Ideas through Expertise: Professionals in Global Tax Battles," *Journal of European Public Policy* 23(3), 357–374.

Seabrooke, L. and D. Wigan (2017) "The Governance of Global Wealth Chains," *Review of International Political Economy* 24(1), 1–29.

Seabrooke, L. and K. L. Young (2017) "The Networks and Niches of International Political Economy," *Review of International Political Economy* 24(2), 288–331.

Security Council (2007) "Report 29 May, Briefings by the High Commissioner for Human Rights to the Security Council and the Peacebuilding Commission," in *Update Report* (New York).

Security Council Report (2005) "Protection of Civilians in Armed Conflict," in *Monthly Forecast* (New York).

Security Council Report (2010) *Protection of Civilians in Armed Conflicts* (New York).

Security Council Report (2011) "Protection of Civilian/Children/Women in Situations of Armed Conflict," in *Cross-Cutting Report* (New York).

Sell, S. K. (2003) *Private Power, Public Law: The Globalization of Intellectual Property Rights* (New York: Cambridge University Press).

Sell, S. K. (2013) "Revenge of the Nerds: Collective Action against Intellectual Property Maximalism in the Global Information Age," *International Studies Review* 15(1), 67–85.

Sell, S. K. and A. Prakash (2004) "Using Ideas Strategically: The Contest Between Business and NGO Networks in Intellectual Property Rights," *International Studies Quarterly* 48(1), 143–175.

Sending, O. J. (2009) "Why Peacebuilders Fail to Secure Ownership and be Sensitive to Context," NUPI Working Paper 755 (Oslo).

Sending, O. J. (2015a) *The Politics of Expertise. Competing for Authority in Global Governance* (Michigan: University of Michigan Press).

Sending, O. J. (2015b) "Diplomats and Humanitarians in Crisis Governance," in Ole Jacob Sending, Vincent Pouliot, and Iver B. Neumann (eds.) *Diplomacy and the Making of World Politics* (Cambridge University Press).

Sending, O. J. (2017) "Recognition and Liquid Authority," *International Theory*, forthcoming.

Sending, O. J. and I. B. Neumann (2011) "Banking on Power. How Some Practices Anchors Others in International Organizations," in A. Adler and V. Pouliot (eds.) *International Practices* (Cambridge: Cambridge University Press).

Sending, O. J. and A. Ø. Stensland (2011) "Unpacking the 'Culture of Protection': A Political Economy Analysis of OCHA and the Protection of Civilians," in *Security in Practice* (Oslo: Nupi).

Shapiro, I. (2005) *The Flight from Reality in the Human Sciences* (Princeton, NJ: Princeton University Press).

Sikka, P. (2005) "Accountants: A Threat to Democracy: The Tax Avoidance Industry Has a Veto on What Services the Government Can Provide," *Guardian*, 5 September. Available at: www.guardian.co.uk/politics/2005/sep/05/publicservices.economy, accessed 8 April 2012.

Sims, R. (2009) "Towards a Better Understanding of Organizational Efforts to Rebuild Reputation following an Ethical Scandal," *Journal of Business Ethics* 90(4), 453–472.

Simmons, B. A. (2009) *Mobilizing for Human Rights: International Law in Domestic Politics* (Cambridge: Cambridge University Press).

Skocpol, T. (1979) *States and Social Revolutions: A Comparative Analysis of France, Russia, and China* (Cambridge: Cambridge University Press).

Slim, H. (2003a) "Humanitarianism with Borders? NGOs, Belligerent Military Forces and Humanitarian Action," in *ICVA Conference on NGOs in a Changing World Order: Dilemmas and Challenges* (Geneva: ICVA, 14–15 February).

Slim, H. (2003b) "Marketing Humanitarian Space: Argument and Method in Humanitarian Persuasion," in *Humanitarian Negotiators Network* (Talloires: Centre for Humanitarian Dialogue, May 12–14).

Slim, H. (2005) "Idealism and Realism in Humanitarian Action," Paper read at *ACFID Humanitarian Forum* (Canberra, 5 October).

Smart, D. and J. Higley (1977) "Why Not Ask Them? Interviewing Australian Elites about National Power Structure," *Australian and New Zealand Journal of Sociology* 13, 248–253.

Smets, M., T. Morris and R. Greenwood (2012) "From Practice to Field: A Multilevel Model of Practice-Driven Institutional Change," *Academy of Management Journal* 55, 877–904.

Smets, Michael and Paula Jarzabkowski (2013) "Reconstructing Institutional Complexity in Practice: A Relational Model of Institutional Work and Complexity," *Human Relations* 66, 1279–1309.

Smith, A. (1982) *The Theory of Moral Sentiments* (Indianapolis: Liberty Classics).

Smith, J. (2002) "Bridging Global Divides? Strategic Framing and Solidarity in Transnational Social Movement Organizations," *International Sociology* 17, 505–528.

Smith, J., A. M. Morreale and M. E. Mariani (2008) "Climate Change Disclosure: Moving Towards a Brave New World," *Capital Markets Law Journal* 3(4), 469–485.

Sneyd, A. (2011) *Governing Cotton: Globalization and Poverty in Africa* (Houndmills: Palgrave Macmillan).

Sommer, A., and W. H. Mosley (1972) "East Bengal Cyclone of November, 1970: Epidemiological Approach to Disaster Assessment," *The Lancet* 7759, 299, 1030–1036.

Spar, D. (1997) "Lawyers Abroad: The Internationalization of Legal Practice," *California Management Review* 39(3), 8–28.

Spence, C., C. Dambrin, C. Carter, J. Husillos, and P. Archel (2015) "Global Ends, Local Means: Cross-national Homogeneity in Professional Service Firms," *Human Relations* 68(5), 765–788.

SPHERE (2000) "Humanitarian Charter and Minimum Standards for Disaster Response," in *SPHERE Handbook* (Geneva: The SPHERE Project).

Stahl, Jason (2016) *Right Moves: The Conservative Think Tank in American Political Culture Since 1945* (Chapel Hill: University of North Carolina Press).

Starbuck, W. H. (1992) "Learning By Knowledge Intensive Firms," *Journal of Management Studies* 29(6), 713–740.

Steinmetz, G. (2008) "The Colonial State as a Social Field: Ethnographic Capital and Native Policy in the German Overseas Empire before 1914," *American Sociological Review* 73(4), 589–612.

Stephens, N. (2007) "Collecting Data from Elites and Ultra-Elites: Telephone and Face-to-Face Interviews with Macroeconomists," *Qualitative Research* 7, 203–216.

Stoianova, V. (2010) *Donor Funding in Haiti: Assessing Humanitarian Needs after the Earthquake* (Wells: Global Humanitarian Assistance).

Stone, D. (2013a) " 'Shades of Grey': The World Bank, Knowledge Networks and Linked Ecologies of Academic Engagement," *Global Networks* 13, 241–260.

Stone, D. (2013b) *Knowledge Actors and Transnational Governance: The Public-Private Policy Nexus in the Global Agora* (Basingstoke: Palgrave Macmillan).

Stone, Diane (1996) *Capturing the Political Imagination: Think Tanks and the Policy Process* (London: Frank Cass).

Stone, Diane (2001) "Think Tanks, Global Lesson-drawing and Networking Social Policy Ideas," *Global Social Policy* 1, 338–360.

Stone, Diane (2010) "Private Philanthropy or Policy Transfer? The Transnational Norms of the Open Society Institute," *Policy & Politics* 38, 269–287.

Stottlemyre, S. and S. Stottlemyre (2012) "Crisis Mapping Intelligence Information During the Libyan Civil War: An Exploratory Case Study," *Policy & Internet* 4, 24–39.

Stovel, K., M. Savage, and P. Bearman (1996) "Ascription into Achievement: Models of Career Systems at Lloyds Bank, 1890-1970," *American Journal of Sociology* 102(2), 358–399.

Strange, S. (1996) *The Retreat of the State: The Diffusion of Power in the World Economy* (Cambridge: Cambridge University Press).

Strathern, M. (2000) *Audit Cultures: Anthropological Studies in Accountability, Ethics and the Academy* (Edited by Jon P. Mitchel, European Association of Social Anthropologists, New York: Routledge).

Stroup, S. S. and W. H. Wong (2017) *The Authority Trap: Strategic Choices of International NGOs* (Ithaca: Cornell University Press).

Sturdy, A. (2011) "Consultancy's Consequences? A Critical Assessment of Management Consultancy's Impact on Management," *British Journal of Management* 22, 517–530.

Suddaby, R., D. J. Cooper, and R. Greenwood (2007) "Transnational Regulation of Professional Services: Governance Dynamics of Field Level Organizational Change," *Accounting, Organizations and Society* 32: 333–362.

Suddaby, R. and T. Viale (2011) "Professionals and Field-Level Change: Institutional Work and the Professional Project," *Current Sociology* 59, 423–442.

Svensson, P. (2010) "Doing Value: Exclusion and Inclusion in Management Consultant-Client Interactions," *Lund Institute of Economic Research Working Paper Series 2010/3.*

Swidler, A. (1986) "Culture in Action: Symbols and Strategies," *American Sociological Review* 51(2), 273–286.

Team, R. C. (2014) *R: A Language and Environment for Statistical Computing. Vienna, R Foundation for Statistical Computing.* Available at: www.R-project.org/.

Thérien, J.-P. (2007) "The Politics of International Development: Approaching a New Grand Compromise?" in S. Bernstein and L. W. Pauly (eds.) *Global Liberalism and Political Order: Towards a Grand New Compromise* (Albany, NY: SUNY Press).

Thirkell-White, B. (2009) "Dealing with the Banks: Populism and the Public Interest in the Global Financial Crisis," *International Affairs* 85(4), 689–711.

Thistlethwaite, J. (2015) "The Politics of Sustainability Accounting (CDSB)," *Environmental Politics* 24(6), 970–991.

Thistlethwaite, J. and M. Paterson (2015) "Private Governance and Accounting for Sustainability Networks," *Environment and Planning C: Government and Policy* 34(7), 1197–1221.

Thomas, R. (1993) "Interviewing Important People at Big Companies," *Journal of Contemporary Ethnography* 22, 80–96.

Tsingou, E. (2015) "Club Governance and the Making of Global Financial Rules," *Review of International Political Economy* 22(2), 225–256.

Tsingou, E., A. Baker, and L. Seabrooke (2017) "Ideational Ecologies in Central Banking," mimeo, Department of Business and Politics, Copenhagen Business School.

Turner, A. (2011) "Reforming Finance: Are We Being Radical Enough?" in *Clare Distinguished Lecture in Economics and Public Policy* (Cambridge, 18 February).

Tussie, D. (2009) "Process Drivers in Trade Negotiations: the Role of Research in the Path to Grounding and Contextualizing," *Global Governance* 15(3), 335–342.

United Nations Conference on Trade and Development (2002) *Trade and Development Report* (Geneva: UNCTAD).

US PSI (2013) "Exhibit 1A Subcommittee Memo on Offshore Profit shifting and Apple" (United States Permanent Subcommittee on Investigations, Committee on Homeland Security and Governmental Affairs: The United States).

Useem, M. (1984) *The Inner Circle: Large Corporations and the Rise of Business Political Activity in the U.S. and U.K.* (New York: Oxford University Press).

Uzzi, Brian, Satyam Mukherjee, Michael Stringer and Ben Jones (2013) "Atypical Combinations and Scientific Impact," *Science* 342, 468–472.

Vaara, E., J. Tienari, R. Piekkari and R. Säntti (2005) "Language and the Circuits of Power in a Merging Multinational Corporation," *Journal of Management Studies* 42(3), 595–623.

van Helden, G. J., Å. Johnsen, and J. Vakkuri (2012) "The Life-Cycle Approach to Performance Management: Implications for Public Management and Evaluation," *Evaluation* 18(2), 159–175.

van Maanen, J. (1975) "Police Socialization: A Longitudinal Examination of Job Attitudes in an Urban Police Department," *Administrative Science Quarterly* 20, 207–228.

VanGrasstek, C. (2013) *The History and Future of the World Trade Organization* (Geneva: WTO Secretariat).

Vauchez, A. (2010) "The Transnational Politics of Judicialization. Van Gend En Loos and the Making of EU Polity," *European Law Journal* 16, 1–28.

Veblen, T. (1905) *The Theory of the Leisure Class* (New York: Augustus Kelly).

Vedres, B. and Stark, D. (2010) "Structural Folds: Generative Disruption in Overlapping Groups," *American Journal of Sociology* 115(4), 1150–1190.

Velásquez, G. (2011) *The Right to Health and Medicines: The Case of Recent Negotiations on the Global Strategy on Public Health, Innovation and Intellectual Property* (The South Centre).

Vogel, A. (2006) "Who's Making Global Civil Society: Philanthropy and US Empire in World Society," *The British Journal of Sociology* 57(4), 635–655.

Von Nordenflycht, A. (2010) "What Is a Professional Service Firm? Toward a Theory and Taxonomy of Knowledge-Intensive Firms," *Academy of Management Review* 35, 155–174.

von Nordenflycht, A. (2014) "Does the Emergence of Publicly Traded Professional Service Firms Undermine the Theory of the Professional Partnership? A Cross-Industry Historical Analysis," *Journal of Professions and Organization* 1(2), 137–160.

Wacquant, Loïc (2004) *Body and Soul: Notebooks of an Apprentice Boxer* (Oxford: Oxford University Press).

Wade, R. (2003) "What Strategies are Viable for Developing Countries Today? The World Trade Organization and the Shrinking of 'Development Space'," *Review of International Political Economy* 10(4), 621–644.

Waldmann, A. P., A. Verity, and S. Roberts (2013) "Guidance for Collaborating with Formal Humanitarian Organizations," *Digital Humanitarian Network*. Available at: http://digitalhumanitarians.com/collaboration-with-orgs, accessed 13 January 2014.

Walker, P. and S. Purdin (2004) "Birthing Sphere," *Disasters* 28(2), 100–111.

Wallerstein, I. (1979) *The Capitalist World Economy* (Cambridge: Cambridge University Press).

Wallerstein, I. (2000) "Globalization or Age of Transition? A Long-term View of the Trajectory of the World-system," *International Sociology* 15(2), 249–265.

Wapner, P. (1997) "Governance in Global Civil Society," in O. Young (ed.) *Global Governance: Drawing Insights from Environmental Experience* (Cambridge, MA: MIT Press), 65–84.

Watkins, S. C., A. Swidler, and T. Hannan (2012) "Outsourcing Social Transformation: Development NGOs as Organizations," *Annual Review of Sociology* 38(1), 285–315.

Watts, D. J. (1999) *Small Worlds* (Princeton, NJ: Princeton University Press).

Weaver, C. (2008) *Hypocrisy Trap: The World Bank and the Poverty of Reform* (Princeton: Princeton University Press).

Weber, Max (1968) [1925] *Economy and Society*, 1 (New York: Bedminster Press).

Weber, R. P. (1990) *Basic Content Analysis* (Beverly Hills, CA: Sage).

Weiler, J. (2001) "The Rule of Lawyers and the Ethos of Diplomats: Reflection on the Internal and External Legitimacy of Dispute Settlement," in R. B. Porter, P. Sauvé, A. Subramanian, and A. B. Zampetti (eds.) *Efficiency, Equity, and Legitimacy: The Multilateral Trading System at the Millennium* (Washington, DC: Brookings Institution).

Weiss, Thomas G. and C. Collins (2000) *Humanitarian Challenges and Intervention: World Politics and the Dilemmas of Help* (Boulder: Westview Press).

Welch, C. E. (ed.) (2001) *NGOs and Human Rights: Promise and Performance* (Philadelphia: University of Pennsylvania Press).

Whaley, J. (2012) *Germany and the Holy Roman Empire 1493–1806*, 2 Vols. (Oxford: Oxford University Press).

White, H. C. (1981) "Where Do Markets Come From," *American Journal of Sociology* 87(3), 517–547.

White, H. C. (2008) *Identity & Control: How Social Formations Emerge* (Second edn.) (Princeton, NJ: Princeton University Press).

White, W. (2004) "Making Macroprudential Concerns Operational," *Financial Stability Symposium* (organised by the Netherlands Bank and held in Amsterdam on 25–26 October 2004), Available at: http://williamwhite.ca/sites/default/files/~1004_Amsterdam_presentation_25-26Oct2004_speech%20versionDecember04_0.pdf.

White, W. (2006) "Procyclicality in the Financial System: Do We Need a New Macrofinancial Stabilisation Framework?" BIS Working Paper no. 193, January.

Whittle, A., O. Suhomlinova, and F. Mueller (2011) "Dialogue and Distributed Agency in Institutional Transmission," *Journal of Management & Organization* 17(4), 548–569.

Widmaier, W., M. Blyth, and L. Seabrooke (2007) "Exogenous Shocks or Endogenous Constructions? The Meanings of Wars and Crises," *International Studies Quarterly* 51, 747–759.

Wilkinson, M. D. (1996) "Lobbying for Fair Trade: Northern NGDOs, the European Community and the GATT Uruguay Round," *Third World Quarterly* 17(2), 251–267.

Williams, H. (2001) "Business Risk," *Accountancy* 127, 140.

Winston, M. E. (2001) "Assessing the Effectiveness of International Human Rights NGOs: Amnesty International," in C. E. Welch (ed.) *NGOs and Human Rights: Promise and Performance* (Philadelphia: University of Pennsylvania Press).

Winters, A. (2004) "Trade Liberalisation and Economic Performance: An Overview," *The Economic Journal* 114, F4–F21.

Wong, W. H. (2012a) *Internal Affairs: How the Structure of NGOs Transforms Human Rights* (Ithaca, NY: Cornell University Press).

Wong, W. H. (2012b) "Becoming a Household Name: How Human Rights NGOs Establish Credibility through Organizational Structure," in P. A. Gourevitch, D. A. Lake and J. G. Stein (eds.) *The Credibility of Transnational NGOs: When Virtue is Not Enough* (Cambridge: Cambridge University Press).

World Bank (2011) *Volunteer Technology Communities: Open Development* (Washington, DC: Global Facility for Disaster Reduction and Recover, The World Bank).

Ziemke, J. (2012) "Crisis Mapping: The Construction of a New Interdisciplinary Field?" *Journal of Map & Geography Libraries: Advances in Geospatial Information, Collections & Archives* 8(2), 103.

Zuckerman, H. (1996) *Scientific Elite* (New Brunswick, NJ: Transaction Press).

Index